L. LLEWELLYN –
SCHWARZBURG

D1528208

Springer Series: FOCUS ON WOMEN

Violet Franks, Ph.D., Series Editor
Confronting the major psychological, medical, and social issues of today and tomorrow. Focus on Women provides a wide range of books on the changing concerns of women.

Ramona Thieme Mercer, R.N., Ph.D., F.A.A.N., has studied early parenting in low- and high-risk situations, and transition to the maternal role for the past 30 years. She retired as Professor Emeritus from the Department of Family Health Care Nursing, the University of California, San Francisco, where she taught from 1973 to 1988. Her career has included positions as head nurse in pediatrics and staff nurse in intrapartum, postpartum, and newborn nursery units. Her current activities include lecturer, consultant, writer, and visiting professor. She was selected as the 1990 recipient of the American Nurses Foundation's Distinguished Contribution to Nursing Science Award.

Becoming A Mother

Research On Maternal Identity
From Rubin To The Present

Ramona T. Mercer
RN, PhD, FAAN

SPRINGER PUBLISHING COMPANY

Springer Publishing Company, Inc.
536 Broadway
New York, NY 10012-3955

Cover design by Tom Yabut
Production Editor: Pam Lankas

95 96 97 98 99 / 5 4 3 2 1

Library of Congress Cataloging-in-Publication Data

Mercer, Ramona Thieme.
    Becoming a mother : research on maternal role identity from Rubin to the present
    Ramona T. Mercer.
        p. cm. — Springer Series Focus on Women :
    Includes bibliographical references and index.
    ISBN 0-8261-8970-9
        1. Pregnancy—Psychological aspects.   2. Puerperium—Psychological
   aspects.   3. Motherhood—Psychological aspects.   I. Title.
    II. Series: Springer series, focus on women : v. 18.
    618.2'4'019—dc20   95-2601
                                                              CIP

Printed in the United States of America

Contents

Preface

Women becoming mothers face increasingly complex situations with fewer role models. The period of transition into the new identity, from pregnancy and over the first year, is a time of much uncertainty that motivates the woman to seek out information and help. The kind of help or care she receives can have long-term effects for her and for her child. For that help or care to be relevant, the caregiver must understand the woman's experience in this process.

The overall goal for writing this book was to reexamine the major theories proposed by Reva Rubin within the context of recent published research related to the transition to the mothering role and the acquisition of a maternal identity. Three decades ago, Rubin first described the process of maternal behavior in achieving a maternal role identity, beginning during pregnancy and extending through the puerperium (Rubin, 1961a, 1961b, 1967a, 1967b). Her research provided the core knowledge base from which researchers and clinicians have worked since that time. As the first researcher to describe early maternal behavior and the process of maternal role attainment, Dr. Rubin elevated maternity nursing from a mechanistic level of routine to a creative, professional level of care focused on helping the childbearing woman achieve her mothering goals.

The format of the book was selected to derive hypotheses from theoretical concepts (conceptual statements) largely from Dr. Rubin's latest book, *Maternal Identity and the Maternal Experience* (1984). Dr. Rubin emphasized that these conceptual statements were her observations and that she did not see them at the level of theory. However, her concepts have been the building blocks for what has been incorporated in all maternity nursing texts since then. Importantly, research reported by scientists from nursing and other disciplines has supported the majority of her concepts. Therefore, her concepts are presented as the seminal contributions to knowledge gained since her work was published.

Throughout this book, Rubin's conceptual statements are presented as the basic premise. Hypotheses were derived from her conceptual statements; the reader will think of many more hypotheses to develop from the premises. The hypotheses are followed by reported research findings. Although, in most instances the research was not formulated to address the specific hypotheses, the findings relate to the underlying concepts and tangentially reflect support or lack of support for the posed hypotheses. No attempt was made to critique the individual research reports. Summaries throughout the text compare findings with Rubin's concepts and raise questions for further research.

Dr. Rubin's ideas are based on data gathered from around 1940 to 1975. Her research focused largely on pregnancy and the first month after birth. Much research since this time, including my own, has identified the process or facets of the process of maternal role attainment as continuing over the first year. In bridging the continuation of maternal work at maternal role achievement after the puerperium, I have developed concepts and definitions that drew from Rubin's theoretical constructs, role theory, ecological theory (from Urie Bronfenbrenner [1989], who built on Kurt Lewin's [1951] concepts), and data that I gathered from 1965 to 1990. The directions I have taken are different from those Rubin would have taken. For example, role theory that was helpful in her landmark "Attainment of the Maternal Role" (1967a, 1967b) articles was not used in interpreting maternal role identity in her 1984 book. Role transition theories have continued to be useful to me in describing the woman's process of achieving satisfaction, harmony, and confidence in her maternal identity and growing attachment to her infant. Recent qualitative analysis of women's descriptions of their experiences during the first year of motherhood discovered role concepts in the themes that emerged (Zabielski,

1994). Rubin's concepts and theories are clearly differentiated from those of others throughout the text.

Selecting an organizational scheme is perhaps the most difficult part of the task of presenting such a large volume of published research. Although the majority of the research reports address maternal behavior and/or role identity achievement during pregnancy and the first 4–6 weeks after birth, much has focused on maternal role behavior over the period of infancy. After careful thought, I selected my theoretical model of maternal role identity achievement to organize the data; the model continued to evolve as the writing of this book evolved.

A second difficult challenge in such an undertaking is delimiting content that interacts with or has impact on the woman making the transition to the maternal role. There is no maternal role without the role partner, her infant. Yet space limited elaboration about the infant's development, characteristics, and behaviors that influence the mother's response. Reviewed research is limited to interactions of maternal perceptions of the infant, infant temperament, and infant characteristics and/or health status with maternal behavior in work toward achieving confidence in the mothering role. The extant research on the cultural variations in mothering behavior is too extensive to synthesize in a book of this length; thus, the reported variations reflect only a fraction of examples. Much research has focused on very good intervention programs that could not be included. Research focused on infant feeding is presented only as it relates to the mother's developing synchronous responses to and responding sensitively to her infant.

An attempt was made to include all published research that related to transition to and achievement of the maternal role identity. The selected research included the mother's experience and behavior as opposed to research focused on infant outcome only. In an undertaking such as this, there will be omissions; I apologize in advance for this. Electronic and hand searches were made of nursing research and maternal–child, developmental, family, sociology, and psychology journals from 1980 through the first quarter of 1994. Some of the earlier research is included to reflect a historical perspective and to illustrate the evolution of attitudes about transition to the mother role and early mothering. The changing social and cultural context in the United States over the past three decades has led to changing directives or blueprints for women's roles in general and for the maternal role in particular.

In chapter 1, Reva Rubin's theories of clinical nursing and clinical research, Her definitions of maternal identity and its development, and the framework used to organize later chapters are presented. The non-nurse reader may prefer to skip the sections on clinical nursing and clinical nursing research. This first chapter is important in presenting Rubin's philosophical beliefs and the context in which Rubin's research occurred.

Following this, there are four parts: "Anticipating Motherhood" (chapters 2–4), "Achieving the Maternal Identity" (chapters 5–10), "The Mother in Social Context" (chapters 11–12), and "Conclusions" (chapter 13). In chapter 2, a brief discussion of the development of the feminine identity and feminine behavior as it directs maternal behavior is presented. Rubin's terms are defined and provide a background for moving to the cognitive work toward maternal identity during pregnancy presented in chapter 3. The maternal tasks of pregnancy as defined by Rubin and other researchers are discussed in chapter 4.

Chapter 5 discusses the mother's physical and psychological state in which she begins her first mothering acts. Chapter 6 addresses the mother's acquaintance/attachment process during the neomaternal stage as defined by Rubin, or the formal stage of maternal role identity as defined by role theorists. In chapter 7 the mother's work toward competence during the formal/informal stages of maternal role identity includes discussion of synchronizing her behavior with her infant's. Chapter 8 focuses on the personal-identity stage of maternal role identity and the mother's achieved competence and gratification in the role and attachment to her infant.

Interruptions in the process of maternal role attainment caused by the preterm birth are discussed in chapter 9. The transition to the maternal role following the birth of an infant with anomalies or chronic illness is addressed in chapter 10. In chapter 11, contrasts in the mother's life space and ecological environment are illustrated in maternal role attainment among teenagers, women aged 30 and older, and single women. In chapter 12, interactions of the woman's employment and maternal roles and their effects on maternal behavior are discussed. Conclusions, in chapter 13, address Rubin's major contributions and limitations, major gaps in the current knowledge base, and priorities for future research.

The book is written for upper-level and graduate courses and for use by health professionals providing care for the woman during the process of achieving a maternal role identity. It should be of value for courses in maternity nursing, women's studies, community psychology, social psychology, and social work.

The cultural values in the United States have changed from ostracizing the unwed mother to outward appearances of accepting single parenthood. However, social attitudes about women continue to devalue the role of motherhood, as reflected in societal and health policy support provided for mothers and their infants. The synthesis of the research to date on the transition to the maternal role identity has implications for both health care policy and future research.

Acknowledgments

This book is dedicated to Reva Rubin, whose work as teacher, clinician, and scientist made it possible. Her vision and wisdom paved the way and opened vistas for those following her. Her reports of the woman's experience in becoming a mother have informed researchers and clinicians, contributing to more sensitive care for mothers and increased research on the transition to motherhood. Her death on May 13, 1995, at the age of 76 was a loss to all.

Permission from both Reva Rubin and Springer Publishing Company to quote extensive excerpts from her book, *Maternal Identity and the Maternal Experience,* is gratefully acknowledged. Reva graciously shared time to discuss her concepts during the writing of the book.

Lorraine Walker urged me to write the book and encouraged me when I was bogged down. Special thanks go to Brooke Randell for her critique and support during the entire writing process. She identified confusing paragraphs, asked for further clarification, and told me when something didn't fit. This was integral to the revisions. Her generous help was invaluable throughout the early drafts. Ruth Chasek and Pam Lankas at Springer Publishing Company provided very helpful editing suggestions.

To my husband, Lewis, goes special appreciation for his loving support, and for keeping me functional with the word processor. His backing has made all of my work possible. To my daughter, Camille, thank you for showing me the joys of motherhood.

Ramona Thieme Mercer

■ 1
Introduction: Rubin's Theories and Philosophy

The philosophy of a period is
always an attempt to interpret
its most secure knowledge.
(Mead, 1934, p. ix)

Mothering is the maternal behavior learned in interaction with a particular child, beginning in the process of achieving a maternal role identity and continuing to evolve throughout the child's development. Maternal behaviors include the blend of nurturing, caring, teaching, guiding, protecting, and loving that enhances the infant's physical, emotional, social, and cognitive development to adulthood. Mothering, a science and an art, is derived from the mother's resources and extensive knowledge of each individual child that enable her to meet the child's needs in unlimited situations and conditions from a very expert and creative base. "The art of mothering is to teach the art of living to her children" (Heffner, 1978, p. 35). The self-centered newborn infant must learn to give and take, resolve conflict, and consider the social welfare of others. A

1

mother or mothering person, as part of a particular culture, is influenced by and influences that culture's values, customs, and rules of conduct as she socializes her child.

Maternal behavior was of interest only for its effects on the developing child during the first half of the 20th century; research and advice were from a patriarchal perspective based largely on psychoanalytic theory. Advice offered to mothers by early experts had little research as a basis; fads and prejudices were presented as expert opinion, along with the scant knowledge available about physical growth and childhood diseases (Sears, Maccoby, & Levin, 1957). Early editions of *Infant Care*, published by the U.S. Children's Bureau, reflected these prejudices (Wolfenstein, 1953). Thumb sucking and masturbation were treated very severely during the early 1900s; masturbation was considered particularly harmful so much so that it could wreck a child's life.

Benedek (1956, 1959) and Deutsch (1945) were among the first to describe women's psychological experiences and developmental changes during the transition to motherhood. Around this same time, researchers began to use observation and interview to identify mothering patterns in the feeding situation (Brody, 1956) and to focus on mothers' feelings about motherhood, their families, and their child-rearing practices (Sears et al., 1957). During this era, Rubin (1961a, 1961b, 1963a, 1967a, 1967b) used participant observation methodology to describe early maternal behavior and the mother's intense cognitive work in structuring a maternal identity during pregnancy and the first month after birth. She was the first to present the process of maternal role attainment in such detail and from women's subjective experiences. As a pioneer in research on maternal behavior and the maternal identity, she provided major theoretical concepts that have been used and quoted extensively across disciplines.

In 1970, Klaus, Kennell, Plumb, and Zuehlke cited Rubin's work in their research on initial human maternal behavior. By the mid-1970s, nursing and medical research increasingly focused on the psychosocial processes of normal maternal attachment behavior and the maternal–infant interactions that Rubin had described a decade earlier (Gay, Edgil, & Douglas, 1988). The increased awareness of these psychosocial processes by health care professionals and consumers' demands for greater participation in their birth experiences have led to important, humane changes in maternity care. "In essence, Rubin should be given a major share of the credit for providing the information that served as the initial stimulus for subsequent studies on maternal–infant behaviors and relationships" (Gay et al., 1988, p. 397).

L. O. Walker (1992; Walker, Crain, Thomson, 1986a) observed that the theoretical and operational properties of Rubin's concepts needed further clarification for maximization of their scientific utility. The goal of this book is to discuss major concepts from Rubin's works and synthesize related research in order to begin this clarification. Empirical evidence from research on various facets of the mother's achievement of a maternal identity was elicited, along with work toward developing instrumentation in measuring the process, to reflect the state of knowledge and highlight directions for future research.

The selected format for the book was to begin with Rubin's theoretical concepts in the form of selected conceptual statements (CS) that include both theoretical concepts and constructs. Theoretical concepts are located on a continuum from directly observable, to indirectly observable, to inferred from multiple direct and indirect observations, to relatively abstract (Chinn & Jacobs, 1983). Theoretical constructs are the more global and abstract concepts at the upper end of the continuum, whose reality base is inferred (Chinn & Jacobs, 1983). Some constructs have little meaning outside the context of a theoretical statement; however, even the most abstract concepts have some linkage to reality and in a sense are empirical (Chinn & Jacobs, 1983). Rubin's conceptual statements (CS) are presented as the basic premise and are followed by hypotheses (H). In many cases the hypotheses are at a more propositional level, and many hypotheses may be developed from the premises other than those posed. The hypotheses are followed by scientific evidence reported in the literature since Rubin's work, to indicate the current state of knowledge. For some hypotheses no research was found, and in some areas questions are raised for exploration. Reviewing Rubin's total context from which selected CS statements are taken is recommended; each person's interpretation is biased by her or his discipline, theoretical background, and experience with women during the transition to the maternal role.

Rubin's work is especially critical to nursing: "You may agree or disagree with Reva Rubin's theories, but you cannot be an expert in obstetrical nursing unless you know her work" (Bishop, 1992, p. 231). Her classical publications reporting her observations and research have provided a rich base for reviewing the knowledge gained to date about the woman's transition to the maternal role.

Rubin's theories and beliefs about maternal identity and maternal behavior were derived from her practice as midwife, clinician, teacher, researcher, and student at Yale University and the University of Chicago. In a 1988 interview about her theory of maternal identity, Rubin's reverence and awe for the maternal woman were evident as she cautioned, "We haven't begun to find out what is going on in the creative, experiential process of being a part of making a baby, making a mother" (Fuld Theorists Video Project, 1988).

Rubin's beliefs about clinical nursing and nursing research are examined to place her work within the context of the discipline of nursing and of maternity nursing as a clinical specialty. This is followed by her definition of maternal identity. Mercer's working model of maternal role identity attainment (Mercer, 1981; Bee, Legge, & Oetting, 1994), used as an organizing framework for the book, concludes the chapter.

RUBIN'S THEORY OF CLINICAL NURSING

Rubin's philosophical approaches to the person, health, environment, and nursing, the units that later became identified as the special phenomena of the metaparadigm of nursing (Fawcett, 1978), are evident throughout her work. Rubin's definitions of health problems and patients were articulated during the 1960s and reflect her philosophy and the state of the art at that time. Her definition of the creative nurse was years ahead of the discipline.

Person

The maternal person was described by Rubin (1984) as operating from an intellectual system that is continually renewed through her perceptive experience and feedback from her child. Rubin's definition of self is central to understanding her work. She defined self as a system of selves in communication and transaction with each of the other selves (Rubin, 1984). Self as person has two dimensions: as subject, "I," and as object, "me," "myself," in ongoing dialogue with the evolving self. The view of the "I" as searching out elements in the "accessible social ecosystem that are relevant to the ideal self" (Rubin, 1984, p. 13) reflects concepts from Mead's (1934) description of the "I" as the person's spontaneous and unique response to others' attitudes and the "me" as the assumed social attitudes of others. The "I," or the ego, not the "me," is what takes the step into the future (Mead, 1934, p. 177). The "I" is never entirely predictable and both seeks out the "me" and responds to it.

Taken together they [the "I" and the "me"] constitute a personality as it appears in social experience. The self is essentially a social process going on with these two distinguishable phases. If it did not have these two phases there could not be conscious responsibility, and there would be nothing novel in experience. (Mead, 1934, p. 178)

Rubin (1984) articulated three spheres of the self that influence any change in the person's identity: *ideal self, the known or actual self,* and *the body self;* these spheres are also referred to as ideal image, self-image, and body image. Unlike the reflexive dialogue between self as subject (I) and self as object (me, myself) that requires language, the three spheres of self are conceptual images not requiring language. "Images are reflections in the mind's eye, an encapsulatory summary of a felt experience of the self in action or interaction" (p. 13). Images tend to be fragmentary and as transitory as the situation in which they are generated.

The *ideal self* is the person's creation of desired attributes that are incorporated into the cognitive structure as a guide for behavior. When elements of the ideal self are achieved, there is pleasure and gratification, but once the desired quality is part of the self- or body image, it is no longer in the sphere of the ideal (Rubin, 1984). A person continues to update, restock, and advance goals for the ideal self. Societal customs and values and the mother's age stage and situation all influence selections for the ideal self. The gap between a person's ideal self and actual self is a void that has potential to cause depression and despair (Rubin, 1968a). The ideal image appears analogous to Freud's (1949) *ego ideal,* a subsystem of the superego, described as an internalized picture a person holds of what she would like herself to be.

The *self-image,* the known or actual self, arises from action in and interaction with the physical and social world and out of the spheres of the ideal and body selves (Rubin, 1984). The self-image is a mirror and an evaluator of self; as a severe critic, the self-image can lead to frustration. The strong drive of the self-image to learn and to understand the reality of the physical and social world leads to identification of attributes for the ideal image. Being knowledgeable—learning new facts, abilities, and interpersonal skills—leads to positive self-evaluation. The self-image's capacity for self-evaluation and correction makes this sphere a regulator of the self system, analogous to a governor or homeostat. The mother feels a satisfying equilibrium and extension with the world when she knows what to do and others recognize her abilities. The self-image construct has characteristics of Freud's ego, the developed ability to organize behavior and to delay behavioral response.

Body image plays a central role in the structure and function of the self-image, delineating and orienting the self as part of the environment (Rubin, 1984; Schilder, 1950). A body boundary defines self and separates self from the environment; there are reflexive, autonomic responses to threatening or unwanted intrusions into the body boundary. Informational feedback of any change or disruption in bodily sensations, postural tonus, mass, or movement demands awareness. Self-awareness of body imagery provides a warning signal for self-preservation. The long axis of the body orients self in physical space; up/down, right/left, anterior/posterior identify a location on the body and project this location into physical space (Schilder, 1950; Wapner & Werner, 1965).

The capacity to project one's body image in action in physical space makes it possible to try on conditions of another person in imagery with projections of body tonus and affect, resulting in empathy for that person (Schilder, 1950). The capacity for empathy is an important component of the maternal persona.

The person, or self, enlarges in scope and complexity in assuming a maternal identity (Rubin, 1984; 1994). The self-image, ideal image, and body image are interacting throughout the process of maternal identity formation.

Person and Environment

Experience is mediated by the self (system of selves) in communication and transaction with persons and events in the environment. Lewin's (1951) concept of life space, referring to all of the facets that determine a person's behavior at a particular time, is reflected throughout Rubin's conceptual statements. Lewin (1951) specifically stated:

> ... behavior and development depend upon the state of a person and his environment, B = F (P, E). In this equation the person (P) and his environment (E) have to be viewed as variables which are mutually dependent

upon each other.... to understand or to predict behavior, the person and his environment have to be considered as one constellation of interdependent factors ... called the life space (LSp) .... The life space ... includes both the person and his psychological environment. The task of explaining behavior then becomes identical with (1) finding a scientific representation of the life space (LSp) and (2) determining the function (F) which links the behavior to the life space. (pp. 239–240).

Rubin (1984) stressed the uniqueness of each maternal–child relationship, noting that each pregnancy and each childbearing experience is distinctively different, as is the individuality of each different child. The woman is different in age, historical experience, and life situation at each pregnancy.

A woman is quintessentially social and the transaction modality is in mutual and reciprocal giving and receiving.... A woman moves closer to family, and to society, during the intense experience of childbearing and childrearing.... There is a volitional act of lending oneself, one's life space and life course, for the very significant giving to another. (Rubin, 1984, p. 8).

Rubin stressed the importance of the environment, or the person's situation, in relation to specific roles. For example, the creative work of attaching to a child is "framed between the child and the mother's own significant social world" and "there is a claiming of her infant in a social context" (Rubin, 1977, pp. 67, 68). She stated that the infant's psychosocial thriving is "more directly dependent on the context of the feeding relationship than on the particular food" (Rubin, 1967c, p. 197). She argued that it was not the particular food that was important but "the setting of a shared, protected yet productive and gratifying experience in a social group .... In later years, memories are attached to and identified with certain foods as representative of the associations of this primary group, the family" (Rubin, 1967c, p. 199).

Person and Health

Patients were defined as "persons undergoing subjectively involved experiences of varying degrees of tension or stress in a health problem situation"

(Rubin, 1968b, p. 210). The implied definition of health is a continuum from a person's ability to attend to usual activities and goals in a relatively problem-free state to situations with increasing degrees of problems that require nursing (and/or other) intervention for optimal functioning.

Nursing

Rubin (1968b) emphasized that the definition of the situation distinguishes one profession from another. A primary goal of nursing is to help the patient adjust to, endure, and integrate the health problem situation and its ramifications. Her contextual model of nursing illustrated nursing care as specified by a fraction or ratio term with the patient placed over the situation. The symbol of infinity was used to represent the relationship between nursing care and the patient/environment ratio as an ever-changing interaction process. Rubin used the expression of the patient and situation in a ratio term to illustrate the fluidity of nursing, in which the effects of one situation may be minor or have no effect, whereas effects of another situation may be overwhelming. The phenomenon of situational fluidity characterizes and distinguishes nursing by time, definition (diagnostic sets), and actions.

Rubin's model placed nursing care in a one-to-one relationship, operating within the immediate present and within a dependency relationship; for example, nursing care is dependent on the best estimate of the patient's situation. Identification of the patient's emotional behavior and its intent provide the working diagnosis for reciprocal behavior in nursing care (Rubin, 1964). Nursing diagnoses are based on the patient's capacities and limitations in relation to the situation, obtained from two sets of relevant data, primary and secondary (Rubin, 1968b). The patient is the primary source of data; age, sex, marital status, race, occupation, and medical diagnoses are secondary information. Thus, nursing judgments depend on the nurse's understanding of the patient's subjective experience of a situation at a given time (Rubin, 1984, vii).

A primary goal of nursing is ego maintenance and support during the patient's stressful situation (Rubin, 1968a, 1968b). This includes helping the patient achieve control of function appropriately in time and space; the *nursing process* of enabling another to achieve or to maintain control is "lending ego" or "graciousness" (Rubin, 1968a). Nursing definitions of behavior specific to a person's control of function were proposed: *Frustra-*

tion results when a person wishes or intends some action but is unable to coordinate that action with the factors of time and place so that the action cannot be accomplished. When repeated attempts at such actions fail, *humiliation* or *anger* results; if the person anticipates an experience with concern about his adequacy, he *worries*; and if the same experience is in the immediate present and the person is deeply concerned about his adequacy, he is *frightened.* Rubin noted that if these behavioral definitions represent behavior correctly, then it is possible to identify which components may be altered by nursing intervention and which may not.

Rubin (1961b) described obstetrical nursing as a creative process when it is based on an understanding of the mother's physical and psychological tasks. *Creative nursing* protects the mother from unnecessary demands, appreciates the significance of what she is trying to do, and fosters her development to the fullest extent of her capacities.

Schafer (1987, 1990) analyzed Rubin's publications and concluded that Rubin's (1968b) theory of clinical nursing was a paradigm for nursing, "a transition model of nursing, undergirded by the major conceptualizations and methodologies of field, psychoanalytic, and social behaviorist traditions, but implicitly coalescing the art with the science of nursing" (1990, pp. 175–176). Importantly, Rubin developed theories within a paradigm of maternal identity, and these are the focus of this book.

RUBIN'S THEORY OF CLINICAL RESEARCH

In order to build the science of clinical nursing, research should focus on the patient (Rubin, 1968b). Rubin's preferred methodology and the one she used was participant observation. In participant observation, the nurse researcher's involvement as part of the health care setting is a matter of degree. The advantages of this method are that nursing spheres and nursing problems are clearly identified, and an artificial laboratory situation is avoided; however, the method is in itself therapeutic, making it a serious disadvantage (Rubin, 1968b). Also, in some situations, generalizability of findings is limited by sample biases such as parents' and professionals' values (e.g., belief in extraordinary intervention and geographic locations with hospitals equipped to provide highly technical care [Thomas,1987]).

Rubin and Erickson (1977, 1978) described their participation observation methodology as field research, with the overall orienting clinical research question "How does the patient feel about himself at this time and in this situation?" (1977, p. 152). The *independent variable* is the specific situation or condition that makes a person a patient and is a constant that is a matter of population sampling. A series of events or stages as subsets may serve to organize the framework of data and analysis. The question that is addressed or the subject under study is the *dependent variable* and includes subjective experiences such as concerns, attitudes, responses, awareness, feelings or sensations, and concepts in a given situation or condition (Rubin & Erickson, 1977). Rigorous analysis of the dependent variable for classification, structural relationships, and interpretation is required. *Intervening variables* include population characteristics such as age, gender, race, parity, educational level, and socioeconomic status (SES). After the findings of the dependent variables are derived, they are examined to see whether there are differences in behavioral outcome for any of the intervening variables (Rubin & Erickson, 1977). Because it is often difficult to obtain cases of the independent variables, it is costly to set too many restrictions on the intervening variables.

An illustration of this methodology is Rubin's (1967a, 1967b) study of maternal role attainment. The independent variable was a population of primiparous and multiparous pregnant women; the dependent variable was maternal role attainment. Three dimensions of maternal role attainment were identified through content analysis of women's descriptions of their experiences: the self system, cognitive maternal role-taking operations as process, and models or referents. The self system as determinant of what would be taken in during the role-taking process by selective perceptions was analyzed by ideal-image, self-image, and body-image responses and by parity and timeframe (pregnancy and postpartum). Maternal role-taking operations of mimicry, role play, fantasy, introjection-projection-rejection, identity, and grief work as process were analyzed by parity and occurrence during pregnancy and postpartum and frequency over 14 days postpartum. Referents or models were analyzed by previous child, baby, self, mother, peers, and generalized others by parity over time. To control for maternal response to interviewer in the longitudinal study, a cross-sectional group was obtained from the same population for one or two interviews and compared by parity and time.

From this landmark research Rubin's thinking and theory continued to evolve. Her book *Maternal Identity and the Maternal Experience* (1984), from which most of the CS in this book were selected, represents her later theory.

MATERNAL IDENTITY DEFINED BY RUBI

The maternal identity is incorporated "into the self idealized image of self as mother of this child" (Ru major theoretical assumption made by Rubin (1984) behavior and maternal identity is

> All behavior, manifest or latent, originates in the mind, in the cognitive processing of subjective experience. The most striking characteristic of maternal behavior is the openness to new and additional learnings, the silent organization in thought, and the high value placed on knowing. (p. 3)

Rubin (1984) described cognitive work as the creative process in interaction with the social environment that enables the unique mother–child relationship to develop. She stressed that maternal behavior is neither instinctive nor learned, like child play with dolls; rather, maternal behavior is a dynamic process derived from an extensive knowledge base of each child, which continues to evolve through experience with and feedback from the child.

Rubin (1967a) first defined *maternal identity* as the end point or goal in maternal role attainment, when mothers "had a sense of being in their roles, a sense of comfort about where they had been and where they were going" (p. 243). Two factors designated role achievement: the mother was clearly "I," without reference to a role model or to a reflection of self; and the tense was clearly the present (e.g., "I am...," "I do..."). Dedifferentiation from models (Rubin, 1984) directly precedes achievement of the maternal identity. Rubin's deletion of reference to "maternal role attainment" in her 1984 book reflected her changed perspective (personal communication, January 7, 1994); she prefers to describe the maternal identity as an enlargement or new part of self, an achieved identity that is greater than a social role. At each phase of pregnancy the woman works on her identity as a pregnant woman in replication behaviors that move to selection of behaviors that fit her style and values for that phase (Rubin, personal communication, January 7, 1994). Rubin's 1967a definition of the endpoint of maternal identity is used here with her later definitions.

The maternal identity develops interdependently with affiliative binding-in (translated from the German *Einbindung* and viewed as more

tive of the formative stages of the maternal–child relationship as cess than either attachment or bonding) to the child (Rubin, 1977; 1984). Maternal identity and binding-in are coordinates of the same process (Rubin, 1977; 1984). During pregnancy there is the binding-in to the child with a fusion of self and child, making it difficult for the woman to separate self from baby; what happens to one happens to the other.

There is ongoing reformulation of the maternal "I" in relation to the "you" (child) during pregnancy through the four interdependent tasks of ensuring safe passage and ensuring social acceptance for self and child, binding-in to the child, and exploring the meaning of giving of self. The woman addresses the maternal tasks according to her situation and resources. At birth, the separation of "I" from "you" as two discrete individuals begins with identification and claiming of the unique child, and progresses to polarization (Rubin, 1961a, 1963a, 1972, 1977, 1983, 1984). In polarization, the mother distances herself from the child in time, space, and objectives to achieve an object constancy and a continuing relationship of two individuals that is different from, but based on, the "unity of mother–child as one" during pregnancy (1972, 1984). The union established during pregnancy continues in the form of maternal empathy with the child.

The maternal identity develops gradually and systematically through the cognitive operations of replication, fantasy, and dedifferentiation (Rubin, 1984). Grief work, a process in letting go of former life-style or roles that are incompatible with motherhood occurs during fantasy and dedifferentiation. The progress of these cognitive operations parallels the development of the pregnancy and the infant.

Partridge (1988) used Rubin's (1967a) research on maternal role attainment in her theoretical exploration of the parental self-concept, noting that just as a child develops a sense of self, a personal identity, or a self-concept, a parent develops "a sense of self-as-parent." Partridge defined the parental self-concept "as a synthesis of self and object representations that surround a relationship between a particular child and a person who identifies himself or herself as that child's parent" (p. 281).

MERCER'S THEORETICAL FRAMEWORK

Rubin's research focused largely on pregnancy and the first postpartal month and provided the base for my work that has extended her concepts over the first year after birth. Based on Rubin's definition of maternal role attainment as women "having a sense of comfort about where they had been and where they were going" and her theory that maternal identity and binding-in to the child are interdependent coordinates of the same process, the process was defined:

> The maternal role may be considered to have been attained when the mother feels internal harmony with the role and its expectations. Her behavioral responses to the role's expectations are reflexive and are seen in her concern for and competency in caring for her infant, in her love and affection for and pleasure in her infant, and in her acceptance of the responsibilities posed by the role. (Mercer, 1979a, p. 374)
>
> Attachment is a process in which an affectional and emotional commitment or bonding to an individual is formed, and is facilitated by positive feedback to each partner through a mutually satisfying interactive experience. (Mercer, 1977a, p. 16)

In later research on maternal role attainment over the first year of motherhood the following components of the process were identified: "Major components of the mothering role include attachment to the infant through identifying, claiming, and interacting with the infant, gaining competence in mothering behaviors, and expressing gratification in the mother–infant interactions" (Mercer, 1986a, p. 6).

In my research focused on the process of maternal role attainment over the first year and later research on mothers' and fathers' parental competence and attachment and effects of stress on family functioning, abstract concepts such as maternal role competence and maternal attachment were operationalized to a more concrete level for empirical testing, resulting in both gains and losses. Although relationships, trajectories, and stages within the maternal role transition were identified, a highly complex process was oversimplified. Despite the study of numerous variables impacting on the process, the transition to the maternal role identity continues to be elusive in its complexity.

Concepts and definitions from role and transition theorists were used as a more universal language to describe the woman's developmental process in making the transition from nonmother or mother of one child to mother or mother of two or more children (Mercer, 1981c; 1985b). Concepts from transition theory that are applicable include pregnancy as a marker event upsetting the woman's status quo, requiring that the woman move from one reality to another, leading to vulnerability and uncertainty in defining the new role, and requiring a new role identity. In response, the woman has to recognize the permanency of the required change, seek out information, seek out models in the role, and test herself for competency and mastery.

Role theorists' (Thornton & Nardi, 1975) stages in the process of role identity achievement were adapted to the maternal role: anticipatory, formal, informal, and personal or identity stages (Mercer, 1979a; 1981c; 1985b; 1986a; 1990). The *anticipatory stage,* prior to role incumbency (pregnancy), is a time of initial social and psychological adjustment, when expectations of the role are learned by seeking information from those in the role and visualizing self in the role. This behavior is congruent with Rubin's cognitive operations of replication and fantasy. The *formal/role-taking* stage begins with actual movement into the role (birth of child); early role-taking behaviors are guided largely by directives from professionals and others in the mother's social system. The behaviors of this stage are largely replicative as described by Rubin. In the *informal/role-making* stage the woman structures the maternal role to fit herself according to her past experiences and future goals. Much cognitive restructuring occurs as she learns her infant's cues and begins to develop her unique style of dealing with the role during this creative role making. Thornton and Nardi's (1975) description of behaviors of this stage reflect dedifferentiation behaviors described by Rubin as immediately preceding achievement of the maternal identity. The *personal role/identity* stage is reached when the mother has integrated the role into her self system with a congruence of self and other roles; she is secure in her identity as mother, is emotionally committed to her infant, and feels a sense of harmony, satisfaction, and competence in the role. A role identity has internal and external components: the identity is the internalized view of self (the recognized maternal identity), and role is the external, behavioral component (Burke & Tully, 1977).

Although some women achieve the maternal role identity the first month, others work hard at achieving the identity well into the second and third quarters following birth (Mercer, 1985b; 1986a). The formal and informal stages of maternal role identity are not discrete. Informal-stage behaviors are evidenced from birth and extend into the personal identity stage as new repertoires of maternal behavior are created for the developing child.

The stages of maternal role identity are reflected by *a, b, c,* and *d* in Figure 1.1. To help illustrate the complexity of the process, the mother and child are placed within the family context. The father's (or mother's intimate partner's) interactions with both mother and infant help diffuse tension developing within the mother–infant dyad (Donley, 1993). The mother–infant attachment develops within the emotional field of the mother's and father's emotional functioning (Donley, 1993). This concept was added to the model since publication of an earlier model (Bee, Legge, & Oetting, 1994). In the interaction between mother and child, each affects the other as the maternal identity enlarges through the stages of maternal role identity development and the child reaches new developmental stages.

Characteristics of both mother and child interact to affect each other, achievement of the maternal role identity, and the child's outcome. Both are interacting with the father (or mother's intimate partner); the father's identity will also enlarge in taking on the father role, although the enlargement is not illustrated in the model. Mother–father relationships, family functioning, social support, and stress have direct and indirect effects on the mother and child and maternal identity.

To place the developing maternal identity and the mother–child relationship in the context of family and the woman's social world, Bronfenbrenner's (1977, 1986, 1989), ecological theory of development was selected. Bronfenbrenner (1989) built on Kurt Lewin's (1951) work and described relationships between the developing person and the environment somewhat less abstractly than Lewin did.

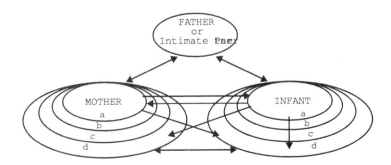

FIGURE 1.1 A microsystem within the evolving model of maternal role attainment. (This microsystem is embedded within the mesosystem, which is embedded within the macrosystem.)

The ecological developmental approach involves consideration of the progressive mutual accommodation between the developing person and the changing properties of the immediate settings in which the person lives, the relationships between these settings, and the larger contexts in which the settings are embedded. The ecological environment may be viewed as a nested arrangement of systems, each contained within the next (Bronfenbrenner, 1977). The *microsystem* includes the family context within which the maternal role identity develops. Visualize Figure 1.1 as the family system nested within larger systems. The family microsystem is nested within the *mesosystem*, which includes many microsystems that the mother may be interacting with and affected by. The *exosystem* refers to the interrelationships of two or more settings in which the mother participates, for example, relationships among home, work, or school and neighborhood peer group. The *macrosystem* encompasses all other systems and represents the transmitted cultural consistencies for other systems, along with beliefs or ideology underlying the consistencies.

SUMMARY

The brief overview of Rubin's theories of clinical nursing, clinical research, and maternal identity provide the background for considering Rubin's theories and concepts in relation to extant scientific evidence. The influence of Rubin's work on Mercer's work was shown, and the framework used as organization for the book was presented.

The centrality of the feminine identity to maternal identity is discussed in chapter 2. The feminine identity influences the evolution and development of a maternal role identity.

one
ANTICIPATING MOTHERHOOD

■ 2
Feminine Identity and Maternal Behavior

A person's role identities become organized over time into a hierarchy of identities with the most influential, salient, central, pervasive, and encompassing identities at the top. More salient role identities include gender, race, and age; these have an impact on most social interaction and contribute to the organization of a person's other role identities (Burke & Tully, 1977; Stryker, 1968). The status of mothers in any society is intimately tied to the status of women and the female role. This chapter focuses briefly on the development of the female identity, the mother–daughter relationship as a major influence on female identity, maternal behaviors learned through the development of the female identity and the childbearing experience, and situations that affect female identity and, in turn, the maternal identity.

DEVELOPMENT OF FEMALE IDENTITY

Female identity refers to the internalized, culturally proscribed qualities and role behaviors for women in a particular culture and the unique physical and physiological characteristics that are learned from infancy. Female identity continues to evolve in direct relationship to biological, cognitive, social, and environmental changes over the life course (Rubin, 1984).

As a more salient identity, the female identity is a principal organizer of other identities a woman holds. The basic determinants of a woman's capacity as a mother are her ego strength, self-confidence, and nurturant qualities (Shereshefsky, Liebenberg, & Lockman, 1973). The development of these qualities and the female identity are closely linked with the woman's psychological environment from childhood. Psychological development over the life span occurs through "progressive internalizations of aspects of relationships with significant others" (Behrends & Blatt, 1985, p. 12). Internalization is a process in which persons recover either real or fantasied regulatory, gratifying interactions with others by transforming significant facets of the interactions into enduring parts of themselves, their functions, and their characteristics (Behrends & Blatt, 1985). The sense of "femaleness" is fixed in the first few years of life and is so firm a part of identity that almost nothing can destroy it (Breen, 1975).

The girl's initial and primary role model for femaleness is her own mother. By early school age, her mother is becoming less the ideal role model but continues as a model of being knowledgeable (Rubin, 1984). How her mother feels about herself is critical at this time. Positive relationships between maternal self-acceptance and child acceptance were observed at this age (Medinnus & Curtis, 1963). Mothers' self-concepts were related to their kindergarten and first-grade children's self-concepts (Tocco & Bridges, 1973), and to their early adolescent daughters' self-concepts (Curtis, 1991).

Girls from school age through puberty play out the importance of knowing as they share secrets with their peers (Rubin, 1984). As secrets are replaced with excitement about mysteries, the capacity for using information is increased, and the suspense of mysteries necessitates the ability to delay gratification and to tolerate ambiguity. Although the school-age girl's body image is diffuse, sports, music, or crafts are used to impart a feeling of competence. Girls are more person-centered and perceive moral problems very differently from boys, focusing on relationships and connectedness for answers, as opposed to mathematical logic (Gilligan, 1982).

During adolescence, active exploration and organization of the maturing female identity occurs (Rubin, 1984). From the onset of puberty until around age 15, body-image changes are the major focus; the onset of menses heralds the unique female capacity to become a mother. From ages 15 to 17, the body image and self-image become reconciled. From ages 17 to 25, an alignment of self and the world occurs, with the young woman demonstrating the capacities and behaviors of an adult (Rubin, 1984). This age period involves more transitional roles than any other period in a woman's life span and is characterized by increasing autonomy and individuation (Mercer, Nichols, & Doyle, 1988, 1989). By early adulthood, women tended to see moral dilemmas in terms of conflicting responsibilities, reinterpreting conflict between selfishness and responsibility (Gilligan, 1982). Initial concern for survival moves to a focus on goodness, then to a reflective understanding of care as the appropriate guide for resolving conflicts in relationships.

Because girls do not have to break away from their original gender identity model, as boys do, less differentiation of self occurs among girls, leading to more diffuse boundaries between mother and daughter than between mother and son. Females continue to formulate their identity more in connection with others and through relationships, affiliation, and community, distancing themselves less from their families than males do (Josselson, 1987).

Freshman and sophomore college students' high identification with their mothers was associated with high ego identity (Dignan, 1965). Dignan proposed that the daughter's internalization of the maternal image helps safeguard the daughter's sense of self-continuity during life transitions.

However, daughters may face difficulty in delineating clear self and mother identities and may, against the best of their intentions, pattern their mothering behavior after their mothers. Three facets of mother–daughter identification resulting from the lack of separation or psychological distance within the mother–daughter dyad may occur: (1) the potential for high levels of attachment and connection; (2) periodic conflict over the daughter's individuation and separation struggles; and (3) the intensity and mutuality of their identification, which permits a merging of self-concept into a dyadic identity (Boyd, 1990).

Increased differentiation of self as a developmental process increases with life experience and maturation. Daughters' (aged 29 to 46) identity contributed more than their mothers' identity to a dyadic identity construct (Boyd, 1990). The daughters' conflict in the separation struggle was explained in part (36%) by the daughter's attachment to the mother, dyadic identity, and the mother's conflict. Daughters aged 25 to 48 were significantly less differentiated than their mothers were, but mothers and daughters were similar in their attachment, with mothers more strongly attached to daughters than daughters to mothers (Davis & Jones, 1992). Attachment and differentiation were independent of each other.

Lebe (1982) maintained that women complete their separation–individuation from their mothers between the ages of 30 and 40 years. During this decade a woman is able to identify with her mother positively and detach from her to become a completely autonomous woman. However, in a comparative study of mothers and nonmothers aged 60 to 95 years, women talked more about their mothers than about their experiences as mothers (Mercer et al., 1989). Both groups talked about conflictual relationships with their mothers. Unresolved mother–daughter conflict was associated with the daughter's low self-esteem, difficulty with intimate relationships, and conflict with her daughters. The psychological mother continued to thwart some women long after the mother's death. The process of a woman's individuation from her mother in some cases seems to be lifelong. Benedek (1970) noted that psychobiological motherhood ends only with the mother's death.

Interdependence between university student daughters and their mothers was unrelated to the role positions of either or to combinations of the roles of the two (Walker, Thompson, & Morgan, 1987). Less interdependence was observed among married daughters and their mothers than among single daughters and their mothers. A daughter's marriage and motherhood led to both symbolic and interactional reevaluation and reordering of the mother–daughter relationship (Fischer, 1981; Josselson, 1987; Mercer et al., 1989).

According to Chodorow (1978), the contemporary reproduction of mothering occurs through socially structured, induced psychological processes; both the capacity and desire to mother grow out of the mother–daughter relationship. As a psychologically based role, mothering requires relational capacities embedded in the personality and a sense of self-in-relationship.

Scientific evidence supports the importance of the mother in the daughter's evolving female identity. The mother's impact endures throughout the daughter's adulthood.

FEMALE BEHAVIOR AND MATERNAL BEHAVIOR

Female behaviors learned during the course of development, pregnancy, and the childbearing experience are a part of maternal behavior and include empathy, feminine or moral masochism (giving for the benefit of others), and the capacity to experience guilt, to delay gratification, to tolerate ambiguity and complexity, and to control body movement and expression (Rubin, 1984). Examination of the acceptance of a female body and biology and of specific female states (e.g., pregnancy and childbearing) should foster understanding of the female identity (Breen, 1975). (Conceptual statement = CS.)

> *CS:* The feminine identity is essential for orientation and definition of the self and of the outside world. The underlying stability and consistency of the feminine identity promotes accommodation and adaptation in an enlarging and changing interpersonal and physical space during the lifetime. (Rubin, 1984, p. 25)

H: There is a positive relationship between female identity and maternal behavior/identity (as reflecting accommodation to the new role).

Gladieux (1978) reported that comfort with the female identity and with a primary heterosexual relationship provided the foundation for an enjoyable pregnancy. Women who were more accepting of female and maternal roles during pregnancy were better adjusted during the first 6 weeks following birth (Klatskin & Eron, 1970). Sexual attitudes and acceptance of the female role were associated with overall adjustment to pregnancy (Heinstein, 1967).

Breen (1975) was surprised to find that well-adjusted women showed a decrease in femininity scores (measured by the Franck Completion Test, Franck & Rosen, 1948), and ill-adjusted women showed an increase from early pregnancy to 10 weeks postpartum. Well-adjusted women had a sense they were in control as the active partner, were creative, and were givers rather than passive receivers. Breen concluded that the Franck test, which claimed to tap latent aspects of masculinity and femininity and aspects of body image, measured an active creative element that is culturally defined as masculine but obviously was important to mothering.

Sense of femaleness, however, does not affect women's choice of

(handwritten margin notes: "Breastfeeding?" "Breastfeeding = so much self-esteem?")

infant feeding. No differences were observed in perceived levels of femaleness, mean masculinity or mean femininity scores (measured by Bem Sex Role Inventory [Bem, 1981]) between women who elected to breast- or bottle-feed (Barnes, Legget, & Durham, 1993). Those without a clear sense of identity more often bottle-fed.

Empathy

Empathy is "the ability to perceive and share the feelings of another through insightful awareness of that person's feelings and emotions and what they mean" (Duncan, 1989, p. 237). Deutscher (1970) suggested that women's tuning in to special rhythms and activity levels of fetal movements and active fantasies of interaction with the child were "a precursor to the sensual and empathic sensing that is characteristic of the communication of early mothering" (p. 27). Others observed that the increased dependency needs of pregnancy provided women with an opportunity to reexperience the infant's helplessness (Hees-Stauthamer, 1985; Leifer, 1977).

Rubin (1984) used experiences from pregnancy and childbirth experience to illustrate the woman's increasing ability to empathize with her child:

CS: Unable to move away quickly from onrushing forces, careless drivers, or impulsive actions of children, a [pregnant] woman rapidly develops an acute awareness of hazards in the ordinary environment.... This special awareness ... serves her as an invaluable maternal skill in the protection of the young child from the hazards to him in an ordinary environment. (p. 57)

A woman's capacity to observe absence or loss, such as amenorrhea or absence of well-being, like the scientist attentive to the empty cell, enables her to make valid inferences of presence when there is absence, ... This capacity serves ... well in child care as an early warning system promoting the preservation of the child. (p. 63)

Empathy, not instinct ... makes a mother respond to a child in pain. It is her own experience in receiving relief that makes her effective in providing relief from layered pain. (p. 75)

Through her own experience, a woman learns what is comforting or consoling when there are no answers, no solutions, and no escape.

She will use these learnings to comfort and to console her child through his difficult situations. (p. 90)

Each of these relief measures received by a woman in labor is given by her to her child after delivery when the child needs relief or comfort. (p. 93)

In the exhaustion from unending now-time or from its effect in the fear of losing her mind, a healthy woman protests and seeks relief.... when the growing child is bored or depressed in the loneliness and endlessness of now-time, a mother knows from experiential insight that relief lies in companionship and in activity that is novel. (p. 103)

There is nothing comparable to the entrapment within the limits and boundaries of one's own body to produce depression, hostility, and disorientation.... The intimate knowledge of this experience serves a woman as mother in infant care and childbearing. (p. 113)

The inability to cope with a strange or forbidding place, person, action, or experience is a characteristic and prevalent experience of childhood.... Maternal awareness and response is immediate and takes the form of lending ego to the child. There is a repertoire of helpful measures in supplementing the child's capacities to cope.... These skills in helping another are learned in direct experience, particularly in stress situations such as labor, by receiving skillful help. (p. 132)

H: Maternal empathy increases over pregnancy and the first year following birth. (No research.)

H: The greater the pain experienced during childbirth, the higher the woman's empathy with her child postpartum.(No research.)

H: There is a positive correlation between empathy and mothering behavior.

A significant inverse relationship between maternal empathy and child abuse was found (Disbrow & Doerr, 1982). A revised 12-item Empathy Scale published in Stotland et al. (Stotland, Mathews, Sherman, Hansson, & Richardon, 1978) was used to measure empathy (Caulfield, Disbrow, & Smith, 1977; Disbrow, Doerr, & Caulfield, 1977).

However, the relationship between empathy (measured by the revised 12-item scale reported above) and observed mothering behavior was not significant among 238 first-time mothers at 4 months after birth (Mercer, 1986a). Empathy explained 4% of the variance in gratification in the maternal role and 3% of the variance in maternal infant attachment. At 8 months, empathy explained only 2% of the variance in gratification in mothering and failed to enter regressions for other maternal behaviors. At 1 year, empathy failed to enter the regression for the maternal role index (factor of maternal competence, attachment, gratification, and infant growth), but the correlation between the two was significant (r = .30).

L. O. Walker (1991, October) studied maternal empathy as a partial explanation of mothers' provision of growth-enhancing environments for children. Maternal empathy measured at 4 to 6 weeks postpartum explained 20% of the child's social competence at age 5 years.

Quinn (1991) used LaMonica's (1981) Empathy Construct Rating Scale (ECRS) to study the relationship between empathy and maternal attachment (measured by Foley and Hobin's [1981], Attachment-Separation-Individuation Scale) among mothers with infants with Down syndrome. A low (r = .204) but significant correlation was found; however, there was little variability in the attachment and empathy scores. Quinn noted that although the ECRS measures empathy as a multidimensional phenomenon, it may not measure the empathic process between mother and infant. Comparisons of the ECRS with three empathy instruments found significant relationships between the ECRS and two of the instruments (Layton & Wykle, 1990).

Scientific evidence supports the relationship between empathy and maternal behavior in most tests, but results may reflect the difficulty in measurement of such a situation-specific, abstract construct. Less empathy was related to child abuse and neglect by Disbrow and associates (1977), and L. O. Walker's (1991) research indicated that maternal empathy contributed to the preschool-age child's social competence. Williams's (1990) multidimensional model of empathy illustrates its complexity and thus its problems inherent in measurement.

Female/Moral Masochism

Historical viewpoints toward female masochism and motherhood were reviewed by M. J. Flaherty (1973) and Litchfield (1981). Freud viewed masochism as a female trait imposed by society and by women's constitution. Moral masochism as an essential quality of femaleness and maternal behavior was introduced by H. Deutsch (1945), who identified components of masochism manifest in the mother's readiness for self-sacrifice without any demand on the part of the child; her willingness to undergo pregnancy, childbirth, and pain for the sake of her child; and her readiness to give the child his independence when the time comes. Moral masochism, as opposed to neurotic masochism, is normal and is defined as the behavior of suffering for the welfare of others (Rubin, 1964). Ultimate pleasure becomes more meaningful than immediate gratification. The capacity to endure suffering and deprivation for a purpose is admired among maternal women, much as physical prowess is among men; women tend to show rivalry by telling of their long, painful labors, of giving birth to the largest child, and of having the most children (Rubin, 1964).

Moral masochism is highly abstract and needs further explication to be operationalized for more extensive research. Rubin's (1992) "Reflections on the Gift of Birth" article summarizes many concepts about giving and receiving; however, there is no explication on the extent of giving.

Research questions to explore moral masochism could help clarify the construct:

Do women define areas in which they will sacrifice immediate gratification for later pleasure during pregnancy and early mothering?

Is the willingness to give at a woman's conscious level? Or is it a behavior learned as a child being given to and nurtured?

Is there a relationship between the ability to sacrifice or give of self and adaptation to the maternal role?

Breen (1975) observed that selfishness (which could be considered the opposite of the capacity to give or forgo self-interests for another) was a preoccupation for ill-adjusted women during pregnancy and the postpartum. Breen attributed the stereotyped image of the all-sacrificing perfect mother to society's narrow definition of the mother role. "She must be sacrificing at the expense of her own needs, and enjoy this—i.e., be masochistic" (p. 29).

Guilt

Guilt is the subjective feeling of having committed an error, offense, or sin; unpleasant feelings of self-criticism result from acts, impulses, or thoughts contrary to one's conscience (Laughlin, 1967). The amount of guilt a person feels may not be congruent with the actual injury or inconvenience caused when judged by an objective observer. H. Deutsch (1945) described the sense of guilt as one of the characteristics of motherliness and as "cruel, merciless, and appeasable only by absolute readiness for sacrifice" (p. 50).

Rubin (1984) viewed maternal guilt as derived from selfishness the mother feels, such as when she has enjoyed an outing away from the baby for the first time. The greater her enjoyment on her outing, the greater her guilt on return to the baby. Rubin proposed that out of this guilt there is a surge of energy to make up for the behavior, and the woman is more spontaneous and generous. Guilt, according to Rubin, does not usually appear before the end of the first postpartum month.

> *CS:* The capacity for guilt is a component of the maternal identity.... It originates in the intimately personal experience of having been delivered, of having been given life and a life.... Acts of commission contrary to this sense of personal entrustment produce guilt and the consequent corrective behaviors. (p. 126)

H: The greater the woman's guilt, the greater her positive responses to her child following behavior evoking maternal guilt. (No research.)

H: The greater the woman's anxiety and/or guilt at separation from her child, the greater her efforts toward mothering (overcompensation).

Maternal guilt in relation to separation from her child has been related to both maternal employment and maternal attachment. Separation from a loved person leads to distress, fear, anxiety, and anger (Bowlby, 1973). Klaus and associates (1972) measured a mother's attachment to her infant at 1 month with items that included how the mother felt if she had left the child to go out, with more favorable scoring given to the mother's worrying about the infant while out and not wanting to leave the infant.

Hock and Schirtzinger (1992) defined maternal separation anxiety as a construct that describes a mother's experience of worry, sadness, or guilt during short-term separations from her child. Employed mothers perceived less infant distress at separation, were less anxious about separation, and were less apprehensive about other caregivers than were nonemployed mothers; they did not differ on maternal attitudes of appropriate closeness (Hock, 1978). Women who preferred employment but who stayed home reported higher levels of depression when infants were 12 months old than did women who were employed (Hock & DeMeis, 1990). Thus, women appear to put together a set of attitudes to enable them to see employment as compatible with and/or fostering the care provided for a child without undue guilt (Hock, Gnezda, & McBride, 1984). Gardner (1970) proposed that guilt is used as a defense mechanism in handling anxiety and as a method of achieving control over the uncontrollable.

Mothers expressed less guilt and anxiety about separation from second-born children than they had from firstborn children at a similar age (Pitzer & Hock, 1989). First-time mothers of daughters decreased in separation anxiety from 3 to 9 months, whereas mothers of sons increased in separation anxiety over that time (McBride & Belsky, 1988). No gender differences were observed using the Maternal Separation Anxiety Scale, but differences were observed using an interview-based scale; mothers of second-born sons were more anxious than mothers of second-born daughters (Pitzer & Hock, 1992).

Schroeder-Zwelling and Hock (1986) compared separation anxiety between diabetic and nondiabetic women at 6 weeks postpartum and found no differences between anxiety and guilt about being separated from their infants. Women who were diabetic prior to pregnancy tended to score lower on anxiety and guilt than women who had gestational diabetes ($p < .09$).

H: Feelings (anger, hostility) that are unappreciative of the gift of a child lead to guilt.

Guilt was very early associated with angry feelings and hostile impulses toward the child (Zilboorg, 1929). Maternal guilt is expressed following the birth of preterm infants and infants with anomalies concerning maternal acts of omission or commission to ensure the safety of the unborn infant (Mercer, 1977a, 1990; Van Riper, Pridham, & Ryff, 1992; Van Riper & Selder, 1989). Guilt follows parental expressions of anger at having had a child with a defect and often in wishing that the child would die.

Guilt was also associated with postpartal depression and with mothers of girls more often losing their tempers or feeling shame (Breen, 1975). Leifer (1980) reported that two-thirds of mothers were depressed and so preoccupied with their infants that they felt alone and detached from other people. Some experienced fleeting regrets at having had a baby, then immediately felt guilty. Several reported feeling self-absorbed and indifferent to their babies initially; they expressed guilt at not feeling immediate and intense love for their babies. The infant's crying also evoked feelings of guilt and anxiety.

McBride (1973) described the anger–depression–guilt go-round experienced by mothers as anger and depression leading to feelings of guilt. McBride suggested that all mothers get angry at their children and feel depressed; therefore, it is important to learn how to deal with anger and to relieve tension and stress.

Further examination of the role of guilt is warranted. How does it affect mothering behavior? Is the mother's ability to feel guilt related to her socialization of her child in the development of a conscience?

SITUATIONS AFFECTING FEMALE IDENTITY AND MATERNAL BEHAVIOR

The self- and body image evolve from reflected appraisals of others in interaction with the person's ability to learn, to know, and to function (Mead, 1934; Rubin, 1984). The deep narcissistic involvement of self with the body is the basis for the fear of mutilation (Schilder, 1950). Anxiety impairs the experience of the body image, and self-esteem is threatened when the body fails to work under conscious control or motility is hampered.

> *CS:* There are times of instability or diffusion of the sense of identity as a woman. Massive physical and physiological change, such as at puberty, childbirth, and the menopause, or following a mastectomy or hysterectomy, destabilizes the identity as feminine, the orientation to self, and the value or worth of self. (Rubin, 1984, p. 25)

Many hypotheses may be derived from this statement related to each of the developmental stages and situations in the CS. However, the focus of the posed H are limited to events of pregnancy and mothering.

H: Feminine identity and self-concept scores will be lower following childbirth than during pregnancy or prepregnancy.

H: Feminine identity and self-concept scores will be lower during the first month after childbirth than at later periods.

S. H. Brouse (1985) studied gender role identity (measured by the Bem [1981] Sex Inventory) and self-concept scores during the third trimester of pregnancy, 7 to 10 days postpartum, and 4 to 6 weeks postpartum. A destabilization of self and identity following birth was observed. Having had a previous child was not associated with a greater increase of female attributes. Primiparous women had higher self-concept scores than did multiparous women at all three test periods. The masculine-undifferentiated group experienced a greater increase in feminine and self-concept scores than did the androgynous-feminine group. Significant correlations were found between femininity and self-concept during pregnancy and at 5 to 6 weeks postpartum; no correlation existed at 7 to 10 days postpartum. The less feminine (masculine-undifferentiated) group had higher femininity scores in the early postpartum period, which decreased slightly by 4 to 6 weeks, but self-concept scores decreased at early postpartum and increased at 4 to 6 weeks.

Significant decreases in mothers' (aged 20 to 42) self-concepts (measured by the Tennessee Self Concept Scale [Fitts, 1965]) occurred from early postpartum to 8 months after birth (Mercer, 1986a). However, women hospitalized for a pregnancy risk condition and women experiencing a normal pregnancy reported significantly lower self-esteem (measured by Rosenberg's [1965] Self-Esteem scale) during the 24th to 34th weeks of pregnancy than at birth or at 1 month postpartum (Mercer, Ferketich, May, DeJoseph, & Sollid, 1987). At 4 and 8 months, both groups' self-esteem was higher than at 1 month, providing support for Rubin's theory.

H: Health problems that alter/deter the childbearing experience pose increased threats to the female identity.

Leeman (1970) observed that pregnant diabetic women thought of themselves as defective. Their feelings of defectiveness were associated with guilt and punishment and with alienation from nondiabetic persons, who did not understand them. All expressed extreme dependence on their physicians. Their fear of injury and conflicts about self-control were exaggerated by the stresses of pregnancy. The diabetic women seemed to be making childbearing a test issue in an attempt to prove their femaleness and worth. In the late 1960s, when this research was conducted, management and care of diabetic women was less sophisticated, with a much poorer outcome than currently.

A relationship between maternal risk status and maternal sensitivity in maternal–infant interaction was observed (Crittenden & Bonvillian, 1984). Middle-class nonrisk mothers demonstrated the greatest sensitivity to infant cues, and deaf mothers were the second most sensitive, above socioeconomically stressed, mentally retarded, and abusive and neglectful mothers.

Corbin (1987) found that women with chronic illnesses actively used protective governing through assessing, balancing, and controlling events during their pregnancies. All women expressed attachment to their infants following birth; some mentioned feeling especially close to their infants after their experiences during pregnancy.

No significant differences were found between diabetic and nondiabetic women's anxiety levels or sensitive maternal behavior during the last month of pregnancy, during postpartal hospitalization, and at 6 weeks postpartum (Schroeder-Zwelling & Hock, 1986). In both groups, lower SES mothers were more sensitive to their infants than higher SES mothers.

MATERNAL IDENTITY FOLLOWING THREATS TO BODY COMPETENCE

When unique female functions such as conceiving do not occur as expected, women tend to view their bodies as incompetent. Some then feel their competencies in other areas are threatened.

> *CS:* Infertility, miscarriages, a stillborn or a defective child produce traumatic misgivings about the competence of self as a woman and as a person of worth. (Rubin, 1984, p. 25)

H: Women experiencing infertility will have lower maternal identity scores, and lower self-confidence than women who have not experienced infertility.

Dunnington and Glazer (1991) tested whether the identity of self as previously infertile (associated with feelings of defectiveness and stigmatization) would be reflected in mothering behavior. Previously infertile (n = 6) and never infertile women (n = 5) were tested during the 36th to 40th weeks of pregnancy and at 4 to 6 weeks postpartum. Due to the small number, the 64.2 maternal identity mean of never infertile women was not significantly higher than the 59.0 mean of previously infertile women. However, at 4 to 6 weeks postpartum, never infertile women scored significantly higher in maternal identity and ratings of their babies, and women who had been infertile reported a decrease in maternal identity.

Previously infertile women differed in three ways from never infertile women. They used denial as emotional protection in the event a problem arose and expressed a lack of self-confidence in all mothering tasks. They tended to be more invested in their career identity and experienced feelings of loss over any potential change in this identity.

Although previously infertile mothers did not differ significantly from never infertile mothers in mothering behaviors or organization of the home environment, their reported behaviors were different. One-half of the previously infertile women did not set up the infant's room until after the birth.

The large number of women undergoing fertility treatment and conceiving warrants further study in this area. Qualitative research would identify more clearly how they move through the stages of maternal role identity.

H: Women having had a previous miscarriage will have lower self-concepts and lower maternal identity scores than will women who have not had a miscarriage.

H: Women having had a previous stillborn will have lower self-concepts and lower maternal identity scores than will women who have not had a stillbirth.

H: Women having had an infant with a birth defect will have lower self-concepts and lower maternal identity scores than will women with normal infants.

No research related to these specific hypotheses was found; however, the literature search was not focused on miscarriages, stillbirths, and infants with a birth defect. The development of maternal role behavior following the birth of an infant with a birth defect is discussed in chapter 10.

SUMMARY

The importance of the female identity to the maternal identity is reflected in the research to date. The abstractness of the concepts related to female and maternal behavior may be a factor in the paucity of research in this area. Some of the female characteristics have psychoanalytic roots (e. g., moral masochism and guilt). Possible conflict with contemporary feminist perspectives may in part account for the lack of research on these theoretical constructs' relationship to maternal behavior.

Measures of femaleness reflect biased and outdated views of gender behavior. If female identity behaviors are to be measured, instruments have to be revised or new ones constructed. How is the female identity defined in the United States at this point in history? How do the mixed sociocultural signals seen within subcultures in the larger culture affect women's evolving female identity?

The centrality of female identity to women's other identities speaks to the importance of female behaviors. As such, female characteristics identified as maternal characteristics cannot be ignored if the science is to advance.

The mother's effect on the daughter's evolving female identity is well documented. Unique female characteristics observed by Gilligan (1982) and Josselson (1987) may be attributed to socialization and to daughters' slower differentiation from their mothers. This socialization affects maternal behavior. How may dysfunctional cycles of behavior from mother to daughter be broken if daughters continue to mother as they were mothered? For example, daughter's memories of their childhood experiences of being mothered enabled 80% and 85% correct classification of their infant's attachment responses to them; these responses occurred in dyadic interactions (Main, 1990).

Problems such as child abuse and neglect, and violence in general, may be related to maternal female behaviors transmitted early in life and to the social values placed on this important identity. Are empathy and the ability to sacrifice one's pleasures for another or for later gratification learned as a young child receiving these gifts from the mother? Is the maternal capacity to experience guilt related to the child's learned ability to experience guilt for unacceptable or destructive behavior? The prominent role of maternal self-sacrifice or giving of self in the achievement of the maternal identity is discussed in chapter 4 as one of the important tasks of pregnancy.

■ 3
Cognitive Work During Pregnancy

"Pregnancy is a period of gestation of a child and of the maternal persona" (Rubin, 1992, p. 315). Others have described pregnancy as a period of "psychological reorientation" (Hees-Stauthamer, 1985, p. 144), a "transition between two lifestyles—two states of being: the woman-without-child and the woman-and-child" (Lederman, 1984b, p.12), and "an important biosocial event ... accompanied ... by a reappraisal of her image of herself and her relation to important people in her life" (Breen, 1975, p. 191). The woman's life experiences, values, attitudes, self-concept, and other personality traits define her life space, from which she begins the cognitive restructuring to take on the maternal role.

The process of self-socialization in constructing a new identity occurs through constant self-examination and modification as relevant information is sought and testing of self in the context of the approaching life change (Ruble, 1987). There is also the "work of worrying" (Janis, 1958), as relationships with her partner and family members are reconstructed in preparation for the demands of the new role (Breen, 1975). This psychological work facilitates a more realistic image of self as mother, a sense of relatedness to the baby, and family preparation for incorporation of the expected baby (Leifer, 1980). Both the expectant mother and the family

35

system experience vulnerability as the potential for both problems and growth emerges (Phillips, 1992). The characteristics of cognitive activity during pregnancy and cognitive operations oriented toward learning behaviors for the new maternal role identity are addressed in this chapter. The change in cognitive work during pregnancy and the cognitive work dealing with change in the mother's ideal self, known self, and body self reflect her concerns and her developmental progress toward the maternal identity.

CHANGE IN COGNITIVE ACTIVITY DURING PREGNANCY

As the woman deals with the reality of pregnancy and the impending new role as mother, she feels uncertainty and vulnerability with the disruption of her sense of stability and continuity of self. Cognitive activity during pregnancy appears to differ from other stable periods in a woman's life. The change in cognitive style has historically been associated in part with physiological and hormonal changes as well as with active preparation for a new role identity.

> *CS:* A woman who is pregnant ... is different in what she perceives, in how she interprets situations that are present or pending, and in how she responds in established interpersonal relationships.... There is a change in her cognitive style that makes her seem less predictable to those who know her well, and sometimes to herself. (Rubin, 1970, p. 502)

H: Change in cognitive style and/or activity is associated with change in self in transition to the maternal role.

Early psychoanalysts described cognitive changes in pregnancy as an increase in introversion and withdrawal from usual activities, an emergence of unconscious urges and wishes into consciousness, usually through fantasy, without the accompanying anxiety present in nonpregnant states (Benedek, 1949; Caplan, 1959; Deutsch, 1945; Winnicott, 1958). The pregnant woman is well aware that her fantasies are fantasies. Fantasies that represent unresolved problems from childhood provide an opportunity for new solutions fostering psychological development at a higher level; they may merge with the developing mother–child relationship (Benedek, 1959; Caplan, 1959). Although the emotional state during pregnancy may appear regressive, it represents a growth of the integrative span of the personality that in general improves (Benedek, 1949, 1959).

Winnicott (1958) called the temporary mental state of pregnancy, "primary maternal preoccupation" and observed that women had difficulty recalling the state once recovered from it. Primary maternal preoccupation develops gradually to a state of heightened sensitivity toward the end of pregnancy and continues for a few weeks postpartum. During this period of heightened sensitivity the woman is preoccupied with her infant to the exclusion of all other interests.

Colman and Colman (1973–1974) used the term "altered state of consciousness" to describe the woman's experience of her conscious world during pregnancy. The different patterning of mental functioning and different way of experiencing the conscious world fostered a growth experience.

Empirical evidence indicates both change and an increase in cognitive functioning during pregnancy. Condon (1987) reported a shift toward primary process thinking during pregnancy, with diminishing logical and critical thought processes. An increase in the intuitive, less rational mode, and primitive fantasies was observed.

Pregnant and postpartum women had difficulty concentrating and planning ahead; women reported insomnia, mood lability, anxiety, and increased tendency to worry (Jarrahi-Zadeh, Kane, Van de Castle, Lachenbruch, & Ewing, 1969). Multiparous women were more depressed, had more fogginess and mood change, and performed less efficiently on a cognitive function test (tracing a maze path from the center to the exit).

Women took longer to complete a cognitive test measuring field dependence during the first 5 postpartum days (mean, 113.1 seconds to search for an embedded figure), compared to 50.4 to 84.2 seconds in standardized studies (Blumberg, 1980). Anxiety was higher among field-dependent mothers; field independence is correlated with ability to tolerate ambiguity. Another study found deficits in cognitive function, particularly memory, on the first postpartal day only; mothers were compared with nonpregnant women (Eidelman, Hoffman, & Kaitz, 1993).

In contrast, Lips (1982) found that pregnant women of 2 to 5 months gestation reported significantly less performance decrement than did nonpregnant women; 57% of the sample had no previous children. Performance decrement was weighted by difficulty concentrating, decreased efficiency, lowered school or work performance, and lowered motor coordination.

Retrospectively self-reported change in cognitive functioning during the third trimester of pregnancy was compared with nonpregnant functioning among 236 women in areas of concentrating on daily activities, difficulty in remembering things, and absent-mindedness (Parsons & Redman, 1991). Only 21% reported no problems with cognition; 19% reported one problem, 24% reported two problems, and 37% reported experiencing all three problems. An increase in cognition problems was associated with older age, married or partnered status, a higher level of education, having private insurance, and having a private obstetrician. Eighty-six percent attributed changes in cognition to their changing physiology. Multiparous women reported that such symptoms subsided within 4 weeks postpartum, agreeing with Winnicott's (1958) observed end of primary maternal preoccupation.

An in-depth study of one primigravida's experiences during pregnancy illustrated her cognitive work as leading to a more integrated self-concept and closer links with her close social network (Smith, J. A., 1990). The woman's self-rating for control of responsibility and indecision fell at 6 and 9 months; seeing ambiguities fell steadily over pregnancy. O'Connell (1983) reported a significant relationship between primiparas' expectancies and belief in control by powerful others and chance events.

Problems in comparing scientific evidence include the differences in time frames for measuring cognitive performance and often the failure to include comparative groups. Lips's (1982) comparative study indicated that pregnant women's cognitive functioning was at a higher level than nonpregnant women's. Rubin described cognitive functioning during pregnancy as different, not impaired. It makes intuitive sense that cognitive activity is increased during an identity change in self. How does the extraordinary commitment required to produce, bear, and support a child to adulthood affect the pregnant woman's cognitive functioning at different stages during the transition to the maternal role? With greater choice available in making the decision to become pregnant, does the cognitive restructuring for motherhood begin prior to pregnancy?

COGNITIVE WORK IN DEALING WITH CHANGE IN BODY IMAGE

Cognitive restructuring to take on the maternal identity requires that the pregnant woman also deal with a constantly changing body image. As described in chapter 1, the spheres of self-, ideal, and body images are interacting in the evolving self. The evolving body image plays a central role in the evolving structure and function of the self-image and is heavily invested with both emotion and action (Rubin, 1984; Schilder, 1950). Perceptions of others' responses and actions directed toward self constantly alter how the self is perceived. The deep narcissistic involvement of self with the body contributes to a fear of mutilation (Schilder, 1950). A person's self-esteem is threatened when the body does not work under conscious control or when motility is threatened. Thus, much of the pregnant woman's cognitive work is directed toward threats to her body self, in efforts to reduce uncertainty and gain some sense of how she will manage as her body experiences change, with symptoms and discomforts that are foreign to her.

Reducing Uncertainty About Pregnancy Diagnosis

The suspicion of pregnancy leads to cognitive activity to confirm the diagnosis as the woman assesses what is required of her in producing a baby. Fear of body mutilation and permanent change and of surviving childbirth with dignity and intactness must be dealt with.

CS: The two questions, "Now?" and "Who, me?" persist throughout pregnancy. (Rubin, 1970, p. 502)

H: The possibility of pregnancy leads to intense cognitive work to resolve the uncertainty.

A cognitive style of inconclusive questioning and uncertainty begins with early pregnancy (Rubin, 1970). Technology that enables a self-diagnosis with a urine sample within 24 hours after the first missed period and seeing the fetus by sonography has not reduced that uncertainty. A sense of unreality persists (Randell, 1993). Many women do several home tests before seeing a physician; even then, the sense of unreality continues: "I definitely see that my stomach is getting bigger and I've seen the fetus but there are times when it's just not real at all" (Randell, 1993, p. 521).

Patterson, Freese, and Goldenberg (1986) observed a diagnostic process begun by women to reduce uncertainty about the possibility of pregnancy. All were engaged in a process to answer the question "Am I pregnant?" before seeing a physician. The urgency of the diagnostic process differed according to whether the woman intended to make a decision about continuing a pregnancy, had a poor obstetric history, or just wanted to validate suspicions. The self-diagnosis began with a focus on a salient indicator of pregnancy such as a missed or changed menstrual period or morning sickness. Once the salient indicator was focused on, a working interpretation was formed, and the woman searched for evidence to support or refute her working interpretation. After the evidence and her social network confirmed the pregnancy, she sought professional confirmation. The absence of an indicator did not weigh against a working interpretation of pregnancy if the indicator was not experienced in a previous pregnancy. However, the absence of previously experienced indicators led to a state of cognitive dissonance.

Couples who had experienced infertility resolved conceptional ambiguity through three patterns: reconstruction of a pregnant/not pregnant dichotomy, construction of new pregnancy dichotomies (no baby but sac and symptoms or a baby), and reconstruction of pregnancy as a continuum (Sandelowski, Harris, & Holditch-Davis, 1990). The process of achieving an identity of self as pregnant was difficult because of biomedical therapies to induce conception and therapy-related pregnancy symptoms.

Cognitive Work to Maintain Control of Body Function

Seeking information and identifying resources help the pregnant woman proceed with her work of pregnancy. In the woman's formulation of an image of the mother she aspires to be, her ability to function is critical.

> *CS:* There is a drive to reduce uncertainty by acquiring information, insights, and confirmed probabilities.... The felt presence of the child within accentuates the drive to reduce uncertainty and to increase security. (Rubin, 1984, p. 129)

To lose or be threatened with the loss of a complex, coordinated, and controlled functional activity which has been achieved and integrated into the personal system is to lose or be threatened with the loss of self. (Rubin, 1968a, p. 22)

H: Cognitive work during pregnancy includes gaining and maintaining control of one's self and body functioning.

Pregnancy represents some loss of control over one's body, not only of an enlarging, more awkward body form but also symptoms of pregnancy, obstetrical examinations and tests, and childbirth. During the first trimester, before the body is visibly enlarging, nausea and vomiting affect about 70% of women; these symptoms imposed substantial life-style limitations in family, social, and occupational functioning (O'Brien & Naber, 1992). The role change from a healthy support person for her family and friends to a person in need of support was disturbing. Many had to stop work for a time. Although the term "morning sickness" is frequently referred to, this is misleading; more episodes of nausea were reported between 3 p.m. and 6 p.m. (DiIorio, Van Lier, & Manteuffel, 1992). Fatigue among women of less than 20 weeks gestation was significantly related to nausea; this fatigue hampered performance of usual activities (Reeves, Potempa, & Gallo, 1991).

Subsiding first-trimester symptoms meant regaining control over one's body (Gara & Tilden, 1984). Women with positive perceptions of their pregnancies had rationalized or reasoned to achieve "adjusted control" by accepting and coming to terms with their pregnancies (Gara & Tilden, 1984). Adjusted control seemed to be part of the process of the women's psychological reorganization to master the required tasks.

During the third trimester, fear of loss of self-esteem and of control during labor was precipitated by women's doubts about their bodily endurance and emotional stability (Lederman, 1984b). Fear of loss of control during labor was eased by the woman's self-confidence, trust in others, and anticipation of the reward of her infant. Women with low self-esteem avoided confrontation and expressing their fears; they were more passive and experienced depressive symptoms when others could not anticipate and address their unstated concerns.

Women who have greater experience with the health care system may be more assertive in maintaining control over their care. Women with chronic health problems managed their obstetric risk factors through a process of protective governing, utilizing strategies of assessing, balancing, and controlling (Corbin, 1987). They assessed the regimens for their potential benefit or harm, then balanced or modified what they would actually do.

> *CS:* There is a boundary defining self, containing and demarcating self as an entity separate from the surroundings. (Rubin, 1984, p. 17)
>
> Permitting intrusion into the body boundary takes work, concentration, and tension. There is fatigue from the body efforts and the self-controls to be passive, to endure, and to permit the breaking of body boundaries. (p. 19)
>
> Adequate functioning is the predominant qualification of the inner contents of the body mass. The substantive body-self is defined in functional terms. (p. 21)
>
> Sleep patterns are not good in the last trimester, and when the dreams fill with the dreaded fantasies of this child or of the subjective meaning of delivery, sleep is disrupted and shortened. The sleep deprivation decreases control so that her feelings are expressed more and in ways not too endearing to herself or to others. (p. 58)
>
> There is no change in the body boundary during the first trimester and only a slight but pleasurable change in the contained size ... the second trimester. There is a remarkable change in the third. (pp. 72-73)

H: As pregnancy advances, women have more negative perceptions of their body image.

Women feel more negatively about their body image during pregnancy than during the postpartum period (McConnell & Daston, 1961; Strang & Sullivan, 1985). Moore (1978) observed that women's body images became more negative as pregnancy progressed; they saw themselves as less attractive. Their bodies were more annoying than pleasing and more dirty than clean. She used Osgood's Semantic Differential comparing "The Body of the Ideal American Woman" with "My Body." Moore suggested that the dirty–clean set could be considered in terms of the increased vaginal secretions during pregnancy and the increase in weight and decrease in heat tolerance, probably leading to more perspiration, agreeing with Rubin's (1984) theory about the repugnance toward bodily secretions.

In contrast, primiparous adolescents in their third trimester of pregnancy reported higher self-esteem, a more positive body image, a surer self-identity, and feeling more productive as a family member (measured on the Tennessee Self-Concept Scale) than never-pregnant peers matched by age, race, SES, and pubertal development (Matsuhasi & Felice, 1991). However, pregnant adolescents were limited in their capacity for self-criticism.

H: As pregnancy advances, body boundaries become more diffuse and feelings of vulnerability increase.

The more definite a person's perceived body boundaries, the greater the perceptually intensified impression of external stimuli (Fisher, 1968). Pregnant women tend to overestimate their physical proportions, both as they are and relative to nonpregnant women (Slade, 1977). Greater body distortion was observed during pregnancy than during the postpartum (Karmel, 1975). Women's attitudes toward pregnancy were associated with their evaluation of their bodies and the extent of invulnerability of body-image boundaries (McConnell & Daston, 1961).

Previously infertile women experienced body boundary ambiguity during the first trimester (Sandelowski et al., 1990). Their expanded conceptual system included strangers such as inseminating clinicians, egg-harvesting technicians, and sperm donors; the researchers raised the question whether this may raise questions about the integrity and ownership of both body and baby.

Pregnant women reported an increase in body space over pregnancy (Drake, Verhulst, Fawcett, & Barger, 1988; Fawcett, 1977; Fawcett, Bliss-Holtz, Haas, Leventhal, & Rubin, 1986). In some situations, the husband shared the body experience during pregnancy in both symptoms and increase in body space (Burritt & Fawcett, 1980). No research was found linking enlarging body boundaries with increased vulnerability. However, body boundary diffuseness occurred during the first trimester in the different situation of infertility.

H: Physical change during pregnancy affecting function is associated with increased stress, anxiety, and depression.

Physical changes of pregnancy were the most frequent stressors identified by pregnant women (Affonso & Mayberry, 1990). Disruptions in body image, emotional functioning, and relationship with the baby's father were triggered by normal physical changes of pregnancy.

Somatic symptoms at the second, fifth, and eighth months of pregnancy were not significantly related to depressive mood, but significant relationships were observed between somatic symptoms and anxiety (Lubin, Gardener, & Roth, 1975). No differences were found in psychological variables or psychiatric disease between a group of women with hyperemesis gravidarum and a control group to link those symptoms to hyperemesis (Majerus, Guze, DeLong, & Robins, 1960).

The number of pregnancy concerns were related to extent of anxiety ($r = .57$); 91% of women were concerned about how they looked; 80%, about their health; 70%, about gaining too much weight; 65%, about being depressed (Glazer, 1980).

Women in the second trimester of pregnancy did not differ significantly from nonpregnant women on Beck Depression Inventory scores, but pregnant women scored higher on two symptom checklist factors, "feeling ill" and "feeling overweight" (Lips, 1982). Although pregnant women's depression scores increased from the middle of pregnancy to the ninth month, the scores never approached the level of moderate depression (Lips, 1985). Pregnant women at 6 to 8 months gestation were distinguished from nonpregnant women and expectant and nonexpectant fathers by "feeling overweight" and at 9 months by "feeling overweight/physical stress."

Most women report changes in sleep during pregnancy (Mauri, 1990): women reported difficulty initiating and maintaining sleep; the major reason for midsleep awakenings was urinary frequency; sleep interruptions from a frightening dream or nightmare were reported by 72% (Lee & DeJoseph, 1992). No research was found relating sleep disruptions to mood state over pregnancy.

Earlier research on maternal anxiety's influence on the course and outcome of pregnancy was reviewed by Lederman (1984a) and Reading (1983); Kaplan (1986) reviewed depression during pregnancy. The effects of stress and anxiety on birth outcomes were reviewed by Istvan (1986) and Lederman (1986).

Summary

Physical and physiological changes contribute to women's loss of control of body function and to body-image change during pregnancy. These changes are associated with an anxious and/or depressed mood state and require much cognitive work to reconcile conflict about them. Tulman and associates (1991) developed an Inventory of Functional Status for the Antepartum Period for clinical and research use. The inventory measures functional status in household, social and community, child-care, personal-care, and occupational activities. What are the relationships between number of sleep interruptions, mood states, pregnancy symptoms, fatigue, and functional status over the course of pregnancy? What is the relationship between functional status during pregnancy and identification with a maternal role?

CHANGE IN COGNITIVE THEMES OVER PREGNANCY

Cognitive restructuring toward a maternal identity appears to have themes that continue over the pregnancy. Other themes, however, have precedence at specific gestational periods.

> *CS:* Fetal movement … ushers in a new set of attitudes and behaviors characterizing the middle stage of pregnancy … distinctly different from the preceding and subsequent stages of pregnancy … uncertainty about her status has been removed. (Rubin, 1970, p. 505)
>
> She has to loosen existing relationships, untie some commitments. (p. 506)
>
> As she enters the third trimester, aware of the child within her, time and identity take on new significance for her in a new sense of alienation and uncertainty for what is real and what is unreal… Time begins to be increasingly burdensome…. Particularly in the seventh month … she feels highly vulnerable to loss or rejection, to damage or insult…. In her sense of vulnerability to loss or intrusion, she feels unsafe, unprotected, alone. (p. 508)

H: As pregnancy progresses, the focus of women's cognitive work changes.

Cognitive themes were identified by trimester to formulate a model for clinicians delivering care (Affonso, Mayberry, et al., 1992). First-trimester themes included the following: am I really pregnant, what does it mean to be pregnant, what's happening to me and my baby, having status as a pregnant woman. Second-trimester themes included staying healthy through self-care; is my baby okay? Third-trimester themes included preparing for labor and birth, expectations for baby and self, and lady-in-waiting. Themes of questioning and uncertainty in the third trimester also included uncertainty about the effects of pregnancy on relationships with the baby's father and whether pregnancy fit into the women's lives (Affonso & Sheptak, 1989).

Richardson (1990) concluded from her study of body change over pregnancy that vulnerable periods during pregnancy needed to be redefined. She observed four distinct body-change phases: reduction from time of awareness of pregnancy to quickening; expansion occurring after fetal movement between the 21st and 26th weeks; tension between the 27th and 32nd weeks characterized by increased concern for adequacy and integrity of the maternal body; and a stabilization phase from 33+ weeks. She identified the reduction and tension phases as the most critical for the woman as the woman dealt with body uncertainties.

Hees-Stauthamer (1985) suggested that the three trimesters do not reflect the emotional dividing lines for women's reckoning with their pregnancy experiences. The greatest change in psychological work fell into the first 4 months, characterized by a sense of separateness and removal from the outside world; the fifth through the seventh months, dominated by the beginning of fetal movement and accompanied by the women's distancing themselves from their husbands and from men in general between 21 and 24 weeks (a vulnerable period for marriages) during the intense preoccupation with the unborn infant; and the last 2 months of nesting and preparing for the birth accompanied by feelings of disorientation, poor coordination, and heightened vulnerability. Hees-Stauthamer's observations about the middle stage of pregnancy agree with Rubin that fetal movement ushers in a new set of attitudes and behaviors very different from early or late stages of pregnancy.

Gloger-Tippelt (1983) proposed a four-stage model of pregnancy as affected by biological and psychosocial processes: a disruption phase of radical change from conception to Week 12; an adaptation phase from 12 to 20 weeks, when active attempts are made to reduce the disruptive impact of pregnancy; a centering phase from 20 to 32 weeks, dominated by the task of production with a focus on the developing child; and the 32nd week to birth, future-oriented and preparing for the birth phase. Research findings indicate that adaptation work begins early and extends over pregnancy; otherwise, Gloger-Tippelt's centering and anticipation phases are congruent with others' findings.

The observed change in the cognitive work of pregnancy does not fit neatly into the long-used three-trimester (3 months each) category. Recognition of fetal movement is pivotal for the beginning of the second cognitive phase of pregnancy. Multiparous women tend to report fetal movement earlier than do primiparous women; the variation in when fetal movement is first felt should alert the clinician that the beginning of this phase is variable. Both Richardson (1990) and Hees-Stauthamer (1985) identified the 21st week as beginning a vulnerable period. There is agreement that the third cognitive phase occurs in the last 2 months, with future-oriented work of preparing for birth and the baby. These works underscore the inappropriateness of "routine care" by trimester of pregnancy. A closer look at the period of vulnerability beginning at 21 weeks is warranted.

RUBIN'S COGNITIVE OPERATIONS IN WORK TOWARD THE MATERNAL ROLE IDENTITY

Rubin (1967a) initially identified five progressive operations actively pursued by all women in the process of attaining the maternal role: mimicry, role play, fantasy, introjection-projection-rejection, and identity. Grief work was defined as an accompanying process of letting go of former identities that were incompatible with the maternal role. These cognitive behaviors occur over a 12- to 15-month period through pregnancy and 6 months after birth, culminating in a maternal role identity (Rubin, 1977). As Rubin's theory evolved, along with a wish to clarify language for the clinician (personal communication, January 7, 1994), she described the cognitive operations as *replication* (copying behaviors of role models and role play), *fantasy* (imagining what it will be like for herself, mentally placing herself in the role), and *dedifferentiation* (decision about how she will perform and what fits her style for maternal behavior) (Rubin, 1984). Each successive operation represents movement toward greater internalization of the maternal *identity*. "The accommodations made in the wish for replication, the felt experience in fantasy, and the preparatory relinquishment and reorganization of bonds to self and to others form the substantive core of a maternal identity" (p. 50). The woman's desire for a child and her binding-in to the child occurs interdependently with the progressive cognitive operations as the woman strives toward attaining ideal maternal behaviors (p. 51).

Replication

Women copy the practice and customs of other women or of experts at the beginning of pregnancy, early in labor, and in the early neomaternal stage (first month after birth) (Rubin, 1984). Copying a successful role model or expert provides a degree of certainty at a time of great uncertainty. Role play extends beyond replication and represents a test of ability with a role partner, such as offering to baby-sit (Rubin, 1967a; 1984). Multiparas tend to do less role play during pregnancy and use themselves as models.

> *CS:* A woman tends to be pragmatic in her search for expectations in the experience pattern of childbearing, focusing on the current and next stages of experience. In early and midpregnancy the overly anticipatory anecdotes or overzealous preparation for childbirth are received as noisy communication or as malevolent overdosage. In the second and third trimesters there is pleasure in seeing babies, but communications about bathing or feeding are screened out as irrelevant or shelved in memory as disjunctive imagery. But when labor is imminent or the baby is born, there is a rush of interest and a searching for models and patterns for expectation in childbirth and in child care. (Rubin, 1984, p. 41)

H: Replicative behaviors are associated with the woman's reduction of anxiety/uncertainty about her behavior and ability as mother.

Women's behavior in copying role models has not been systematically observed longitudinally except by Rubin. In defining the anticipatory stage of role achievement in general, Thornton and Nardi (1975) described both replicative and fantasy behaviors and a tendency of the role taker to idealize role expectations; they described replicative behaviors of modeling experts' behavior as continuing to predominate during the formal stage (after birth).

Gage and Christensen (1991) reported that 88% of 454 mothers reported role rehearsal activity such as baby-sitting; 51% reported observing role models. Three-fourths attended parenting classes. Mothers reported that watching friends and relatives, talking with spouses, talking with doctors, and taking parenting classes were helpful. Mothers' higher socialization (through classes and talking with other parents or professionals) scores were related to greater personal happiness, positive self-esteem, positive parental self-concept, satisfaction with role performance, and fewer perceived parenting worries.

Women who were more passive during pregnancy were ill-prepared for the activity required by childbearing and child rearing (Breen, 1975). Anticipatory self-definitions formulated through information seeking were related to maternal self-definition during pregnancy (Deutsch, F. M., Ruble, Fleming, Brooks-Gunn, & Stangor, 1988).

H: Replicative behaviors change by stage of pregnancy and at post-partum.

First-time parents' concurrent socialization for parenthood, such as parenting classes or talking with parents or professionals, was far more effective than anticipatory socialization such as role rehearsal activities of baby-sitting or caring for pets (Gage & Christensen, 1991). Information seeking played an important role in women's developing self-conceptions as first-time mothers (Deutsch et al., 1988). Although information was sought at the beginning of the transition period and through 3 months postpartum, the peak of information seeking occurred when the information was actually used. The greatest amount of information about pregnancy was gained during the first and second trimesters; the greatest amount of information about labor and delivery was gained during the third trimester. The greatest amount of information about motherhood was gained at 1 and 3 months postpartum.

Although pregnancy and mothering required different kinds of information and the timing of receiving the information followed different courses, the two types of information were not mutually exclusive. High correlations were observed between the amounts of information gained about pregnancy and mothering at prepregnant (r = .75), pregnant (r = .70), and postpartum (r = .44) phases (Deutsch et al., 1988). The basis for women's self-definition of the maternal role shifted from primarily indirect or outside information during pregnancy to primarily direct experience with child care at postpartum. Information gained about the mother role seemed to alter the self-concept with the cognitive restructuring of information about self, but during the actual transition at birth, the direct self-perception of performance in the mother role became a compelling mediator of self-concept change.

Information desired by women at their first antenatal visit varied by parity and by type of care, public or private (Freda, Andersen, Damus, & Merkatz, 1993). The majority were very interested in fetal development, nutrition, and vitamins as opposed to information about breast-feeding or childbirth.

There is evidence that replication behaviors change by stage of pregnancy and after birth. Rubin noted that the multipara used herself as role model. Are there additional factors that influence the extent of replicative behaviors engaged in?

CS: Replication serves as a guide through the course and sequence of situations in pregnancy, in childbirth, and in the puerperium. There is considerably more stress and turbulent confusion when a woman is isolated and deprived of cohort and expert models. (Rubin, 1984, p. 44)

H: The greater the woman's social isolation, the fewer the role models for replication behaviors and the greater her anxiety.

Lederman (1984b) observed that primiparas' progress in identifying with a motherhood role was inhibited by lack of a good role model, low self-esteem, excessive narcissism, and motherhood–career conflict. Women who had strong doubts had difficulty thinking about the new role and found it hard to "try on the new role" (p. 61). No research was found regarding the relationship between availability of suitable role models and women's anxiety and/or progress in the maternal role.

Summary

Role models provide guidelines about how maternal behavior is enacted. Women seek out professional and lay experts as they learn the formalized expectations for the maternal role. Women seek models for their current status, copying behavior for a pregnant woman, a woman in labor, and mother in face-to-face interaction with her child. How does a lack of available role models to choose from affect maternal role taking?

Fantasy: Mental Rehearsal for Motherhood

Fantasy, the cognitive exploration of future possibilities for the mother and her child, moves the role-taking operations to internalization, "the projection in imagery of mother and child into the future: 'how it will be'" (Rubin, 1984, p. 44). There are no third persons in fantasy, and fantasy is independent of time and place (Rubin, 1984). The woman develops a complex, highly diversified system of symbolic relationships with her unborn child, which serves to integrate both her real and imagined interactions with it (Hees-Stauthamer, 1985). In visualizing herself in the mother role, she also visualizes her infant, with unknown characteristics.

Lederman (1984b) identified the initial steps in identifying a motherhood role as envisioning self as mother, thinking about desired characteristics as a mother, and anticipating future life changes through fantasizing. As the woman imagines herself as mother, she visualizes the infant and works at discovering characteristics that a good mother should possess.

CS: Pleasurable fantasies generate hope. Unpleasant fantasies generate anxiety. (Rubin, 1984, p. 45)

H: There is a positive correlation between mood state or affect and pleasant or unpleasant fantasies during pregnancy.

Reported fantasies during the third trimester fell into two thematic categories; they were associated either with positive emotions, such as pleasure, joy, or peace, or with negative emotions, such as fear, guilt, and panic (Sherwen, 1981). Fantasies associated with negative emotions included having an abnormal infant, being attacked, being enclosed or drowning, forgetting or losing things, and being unprepared. Positive fantasies included multiple birth, sexuality with husband, restoration (linking the birth of coming child with a dead family member), and everyday fantasies such as characteristics of the infant. Fantasies were about equally divided between positive and negative (Sherwen, 1987).

CS: Fantasy is the cognitive exploration of possibilities in situation and experience of the self the child. (Rubin, 1984, pp. 44–45)

H: Mental rehearsals for the maternal role are associated with adaptation to the role.

Imagining future events increases the reality and expectations for the event (Carroll, 1978). Several have observed the association between women's imagining themselves as mothers and their later adjustment as mothers, their greater sense of attachment to the infant, and their positive relationships with family members (Ballou, 1978b; Hees-Stauthamer, 1985; Leifer, 1980). Fantasy and dreaming prepared women for their future experiences through a mental rehearsal for both labor and delivery and for mothering (Lederman, 1984b).

Primiparous women aged 30 and older used mental mechanisms of balancing and buffering to maintain their self-patterns during early pregnancy (Randell, 1993). The balancing behaviors, categorized as unreal, ambivalent, and labile, were an apparent attempt to persist in a harmonious self-view by bringing the long-held view of the self as not pregnant into harmony with the pregnant self. Buffering behaviors neutralized or lessened the impact of the impending change by viewing the self as mother, in opposition to the "real me" or valued self, and were categorized by polar opposites—self-centered/martyr, responsible/irresponsible—and the "real me." These repeated contrasts of self-images with maternal images reassured the women that the self could remain intact; to see self as mother in early pregnancy meant a destruction of the "real me." The women's persistence allowed them to maintain goal-directedness and represented growth while their striving to protect the "real me" maintained some stability. By the third trimester, the women came to view themselves as having the potential to be mothers, and their earlier conflict over their perceptions of self as pregnant had declined significantly (Randell, 1988).

The ability to conceptualize the maternal role during the third trimester differed by maternal maturity (Gottesman, 1992). Women aged 20 to 24 years less often reported thinking about themselves as mothers and were more vague and unenthusiastic in their responses. Women aged 25 to 29 years shared similar feelings with younger and older women, with some indicated fear of the mothering role. Women aged 30 and older reported a wider range of projected activities with their anticipated child; none described fear of the mothering role. The active cognitive work of balancing and buffering by mature women during the first trimester (Randell, 1993) may place them farther along on the maternal role identity continuum. Older women used more extensive resources; the youngest group read less and relied more on their mothers and sisters as guides for their experiences (Gottesman, 1992).

Lederman (1984b) described three themes of fantasies that comprised the steps of identifying a motherhood role gained from primigravidas during the third trimester of pregnancy: envisioning self as mother, thinking about characteristics wished for as mother, and anticipating necessary future life change. Women were also fantasizing about labor, with fear of loss of control and fear of loss of self-esteem.

A study of women's desire to learn infant care, including psychological and pragmatic components, at early (5–15 weeks), middle (16–25 weeks), and late (26–39 weeks) stages of pregnancy found that late-stage scores overall were higher than those of early and middle stages (Bliss-Holtz, 1988). The pragmatic component, infant care activities, were higher during the late stage of pregnancy than during the early or middle stages. However, the psychological component, focused on concerns about being a good provider and the emotional bond with the infant, did not change over the three stages of pregnancy.

McDonald (1965) did not find differences in women's fantasies when they experienced abnormalities during pregnancy or childbirth. Women who had normal perinatal experiences tended to rely on repression and denial as ego defenses, whereas women who had complications used intellectualization and obsessive rumination more.

Primiparous women who were well adjusted at 6 weeks postpartum gave a higher ratio of female to male percepts and greater acceptance of the maternal or female role during pregnancy on Rorschach and TAT protocols than did poorly adjusted women (Klatskin & Eron, 1970).

Expectant parents identified available external and internal supports during the third trimester in projecting their transition to parenthood (Imle, 1990). External resources that were identified and evaluated for future help and support included health care givers; occupational, financial, and community resources; and partner, relatives, and friends. Internal resources identified included their own strengths, such as maturity, attitudinal and philosophical approaches to childbearing and child rearing, and memories of their own parenting.

Evidence supports the value of mental rehearsals in identity reformulation to take on the maternal role. Fantasies, however, were not related to physical outcomes of the pregnancy.

Women's cognitive work of projecting self in the role of mother leads to resolving dissonance about the fit of current self with a mother self and to seeking social resources to aid with the maternal role. Thinking about the role also helped polarize initial attitudes about the role (Deutsch et al., 1988). Maternal concerns arise in mental rehearsal work. A Transition to Parenthood Concerns Scale was developed to measure concerns during the third trimester (Imle & Atwood, 1988).

> *CS:* One fantasy ... after the 28th–32nd week of pregnancy seemed to be universal ... that of intrusion from without, and that always appeared as ominous or dangerous. (Rubin, 1967a, p. 242)
>
> The fantasies of a woman in late pregnancy do not have the daydream quality usually associated with fantasy.... The woman at term is reality bound and distinguishes between real and fantasied experience.... There is fear, there is dread of delivery, but there is also hope and the wish for the child and for relief from the burdensome pregnancy. The fear and dread are for her baby as well as for herself. There would be no fear for the baby's welfare and wholeness if there were no affiliative bonds of physical and fantasied experience with the child. (Rubin, 1984, pp. 46–47)

H: Fantasy themes change over the course of the pregnancy.

During early pregnancy, fear of miscarriage was observed (Leifer, 1977). Fears about fetal abnormality predominated from the time of fetal movement to the last trimester, when anxieties about labor and delivery, including fear of death and fear of loss of husband, were commonly expressed (Leifer, 1977).

Sherwen (1987) reported that 38% of third-trimester fantasies from day and night dreams related to the baby; 21% were of being attacked or of intruders in the home. Giving birth to a defective infant made up 12% of fantasies; restoration or reparation, 11%; sexuality, 8%; being inside a tunnel or subway or drowning, 2.5%; and being unprepared, 2.5%.

H: A positive correlation exists between a pregnant woman's fear for the infant's outcome (anxiety) and maternal–fetal attachment.

Leifer (1977) observed that anxiety directed toward the unborn child appeared to reflect the developing maternal bond, and anxiety directed toward self had regressive overtones. Anxieties about the unborn child were high during all periods of pregnancy (Gloger-Tippelt, 1988). Anxiety did not differentiate whether the mother viewed the unborn child as undifferentiated, as an independent being, or as an individual.

No relationship was found between trait (proneness to) anxiety and maternal–fetal attachment (Cranley, 1981a; Gaffney, 1986) or state anxiety (response to situational stress) and maternal–fetal attachment among hospitalized high-risk women and women experiencing a normal pregnancy (Mercer, Ferketich, May, DeJoseph, & Sollid, 1988). Gaffney (1986), however, reported a significant inverse relationship between state anxiety and maternal–fetal attachment. Anxiety measures are problematic in not differentiating between maternal anxiety about self and about fetus.

CS: The pregnant woman ready to give birth has images of what she is about to produce from her body as amorphous, without shape or skin, dark, hairy, slippery, and malodorous. (Rubin, 1984, p. 23)

During pregnancy, the fantasies of the child begin with the image of an adolescent or teenager, move to school-age child, to preschool child, to a toddler, and finally to a baby.... By the end of pregnancy, the image of the child in appearance and behavior is that of a baby six months of age and weighing about fifteen pounds, the ideal baby. (Rubin, 1984, p. 120)

H: Women's images of their unborn infants change as pregnancy progresses.

Lumley (1980) found that first-time mothers grossly underestimated the size, development, and activities of their fetus during the first trimester. They described the fetus as formless, unattractive, or having animal-like features; only 30% viewed the fetus as a real person at this stage. By midpregnancy most women held accurate views of their unborn child's development, and this was maintained through the last month before birth (Lumley, 1982). Only 7% maintained at 36 weeks gestation that the fetus was not a real person. By 18 to 22 weeks, 63% were attached to their unborn child, and by 36 weeks, 92% were attached.

Women reported day and night dreams with more vague and imper-
sonal images of the baby during the first trimester; during the second trimester, women's fantasies about the fetus began to merge with what the
baby would be at birth (Leifer, 1980). Gloger-Tippelt (1988) reported a
sequential emerging of conceptions of the child. Early conceptions of the
child were undifferentiated and biological in content; after fetal movement, the child was described as an independent being with continued
elaboration as an individual person until birth. A wanted pregnancy was
negatively related to undifferentiated conceptions of the child; the more
complications of pregnancy, the greater the anxiety about the child.

Stainton (1990) observed four levels of cognitive and sensory awareness of the unborn infant during the third trimester: as an idea, its presence, specific infant behavior, and interactive ability. Parents described
their infant's appearance in relation to hair, eyes, and/or size (Stainton,
1985). The baby they night-dreamed about was always an older infant or
toddler.

Sweeney and Bradbard (1988) studied women who had ultrasonography and knew the baby's sex and women who did not know the sex, to
compare change in perceptions of the baby over pregnancy. After the
sonogram, parents who knew their infant's sex described girls as finer
(contrast to large); both boys and girls were rated as bigger after the sonogram and smaller after birth. No effects of known sex during pregnancy
were found on parental descriptions of the infants at birth.

Scientific evidence does not support the statement that women about
to give birth fantasize the infant as about the size of a 6-month-old or as
amorphous, without shape or skin, hairy, slippery, and malodorous. Evidence indicates that variability in perceptions occurs, but overall perceptions tend to indicate increasing congruence with a newborn baby by the
third trimester. Perceptions of the unborn baby are influenced by ongoing
visualization through ultrasonography.

> *CS:* Depending on the age-stage of the fantasied child during preg-
> nancy, there is a "giving" of food treats to the child ... [that she] received
> and enjoyed as a child.... clothing is also used.... Dressing a child in
> fantasy is a series of exploratory locations of the child in size, shape, and
> gender. (Rubin, 1984, p. 45)

H: Women eat special foods for the baby, depending on the age stage of the fantasied infant.

Eating special foods during pregnancy is closely related to cultural customs. Korean women adhering to custom avoid sour, spicy, and fatty foods during pregnancy (Pritham & Sammons, 1993). The Maasai women in Kenya practice dietary restriction to control weight gain of both themselves and their unborn infants (Mpoke & Johnson, 1993). Filipinos also restrict their diets so that their babies will be smaller for an easier delivery; they also avoid drinking milk as it is very expensive (Stern, Tilden, & Maxwell, 1980).

Lederman (1984b) reported that many women had dreams about food, picnics, or feasts. Food seemed to represent the fetus or nourishment for the baby in many dreams, but no age-stage differences were reported.

> *CS:* A woman who wishes very much to have a child, or a child of a particular gender, learns to avoid the capriciousness of luck and the consequences in disappointment by modifying her behavior.... she avoids buying or making any [baby clothes] until late in pregnancy, and the articles of clothing are few or of any pleasant color other than pink or blue (Rubin, 1984, p. 58)

H: Women make few wish statements regarding the coming child's specific characteristics.

Leifer (1980) observed that 74% of first-time mothers preferred a boy, 11% preferred a girl, and only 15% would give no preference. Many viewed the baby as a replication of the husband and regarded this first child as a gift to him.

M. K. Walker (1992) found that 49% of 88 women having an amniocentesis preferred a male, and 51% preferred a female infant; 68% of first-time mothers preferred a female, and women with children tended to prefer the sex they did not have. Sixty percent had a belief or intuition about the child's sex, with 26% believing the child was female and 74% believing the child was male. There was two-thirds agreement with women's belief about the baby's sex and the sex of the children they had.

M. K. Walker and Conner (1993) found that 81% of women declared a sex preference during second trimester. Thirty-nine percent preferred a son, and 42% preferred a daughter.

Night Dreams

The significance of anticipation and preparation for becoming a mother also leads to unconscious dream work. Emotional content of dreams was more vivid than that expressed in interviews (Lederman, 1984b).

> *CS:* Because anticipation and preparation for becoming a mother and having a child are so important, fantasies of how it will be occur in dream work as well as during the day. (Rubin, 1984, p. 45)

H: Concerns expressed in dreams foster resolution of conflicts about the mother role.

The dream content reported during third trimester seemed to parallel women's reported concerns and fell into the following categories: reliving childhood, school dreams, motherhood–career conflict, confidence in maternal skills, food dreams, and infant intactness (Lederman, 1984b). Through childhood dreams, one woman relived a conflict with her siblings, resolved it, and achieved a sense of readiness to help her child resolve a similar conflict. School dreams represented grief work in loss of a former life-style and the impossibility of retrieving it. Dreams about maternal skills reflected fears: of failure, of the child's ability to thrive, of ability to identify the infant's needs and provide adequate care, and of infant anomalies.

Sherwen (1987) also saw night dreams as a means of solving problems during pregnancy. Gillman (1968) reported that half of pregnant women's dreams were about the baby, and the other half focused on misfortune, harm, or environmental threat to either the mother or the baby. Dream content did not correlate with the degree of emotional disturbance.

Women who had more dreams of anxiety and threat during pregnancy had a shorter labor than did those who reported such dreams infrequently (Winget & Kapp, 1972), supporting the theory that dreams may function to master in fantasy an anticipated threat in waking life. However, the grouping of dreams (unconscious fantasy work) by masochistic and hostile elements were neither predictive of adjustment to the maternal role nor related to emotional disturbance (Gillman, 1968). Ego strength was associated with the absence of masochistic dreams.

Grief Work

Grief work is a process of relinquishing any role or identity that is incompatible with the forthcoming maternal role (Rubin, 1967a, 1984). Giving up current life-style also entails grief work.

> *CS:* There is also a loosening of facets of her own personality, her own identity in aspiration and in action in the life style and in the life space of her world.... Binding-in to the child in fantasies of how it will be to have a child and to be a mother of this child promotes the loosening and distancing from other roles, other commitments, aspirations, and involvements....
>
> There is also a preparatory releasing of former historical self-concepts. There is a review of a past stage of the life stream, a recognition that this aspect in life space is irreversibly finished, a possession of memory, not action, and a turn in fantasy toward the future....
>
> The review in memory of who and what she has been is a self initiated process of disengagement from the self and from ideal imagery which is no longer relevant or compatible with becoming a mother....
>
> There is a distancing of self, the present and the future self from the historical self, in time and space. Disappointments and frustrations of the past are reviewed and resolved as bygones. (Rubin, 1984, pp. 48–49)

H: Grief work indicates progress in cognitive restructuring for the maternal role identity.

Women were beginning grief work during the first trimester in relinquishing identities of their "real me" as self-centered, irresponsible, professional, and a nonmother, in their attempts to maintain a sense of continuity with self as mother in Randell's (1988, 1993) research described above. Prior to experiencing fetal movement, they were not ready to relinquish images of themselves as selfish, self-centered, or as professional women. The reports of third-trimester fantasies by Lederman (1984b) and Sherwen (1987) above included much grief work content that was indicative of cognitive restructuring for the maternal identity.

Other reports specifying a focus on grief work during pregnancy were not found. However, ambivalence, the simultaneous existence of conflicting feelings about a person or object, may reflect grief work in experiencing the cost of what is given up while looking forward to the rewards of motherhood. If loss of the former life-style was not offset by perceived satisfaction in the coming child, ambivalence increased and the transition was resisted (Lederman, 1984b). One-half of adult married women in stable family support systems were accepting of the pregnancy, identifying with the maternal role yet feeling moderate ambivalence toward impending motherhood during the third trimester (Winkles, 1987).

A study of 369 pregnant women and 345 expectant fathers in Sweden found that ambivalence was a normal process in the adaptation to pregnancy and parenthood (Wikman, Jacobsson, Joelsson, & von Schoultz, 1993). Children were viewed as restricting freedom and as providing existential satisfaction. The researchers urged that expectant parents be informed about the normality of ambivalence during prenatal counseling to decrease their anxiety and guilt about such feelings.

Dedifferentiation

With dedifferentiation the woman has tested behavior for a fit with her current values and self-image; she either accepts or rejects the behavior as congruent with her self-image in the maternal role. Although this occurs during pregnancy, it increases postpartally and directly precedes achievement of the maternal identity (Rubin, 1984). Dedifferentiation and identity achievement are discussed in chapter 9.

SUMMARY

Scientific evidence supports the idea that the cognitive and social restructuring engaged in by women during the anticipatory stage of maternal identity is pivotal to becoming a mother. Rubin's theoretical concepts about the woman's cognitive work during pregnancy are largely supported by later scientific evidence. Differences may in part be explained by the impact of technological advances and social change on the cultural milieu of childbearing women since the period of Rubin's major research.

The cognitive restructuring that is necessary to accommodate the changing self-, ideal, and body images within the mother–child and mother–father subsystems of the family is unique among identity transitions. The intimate gestation of the role partner, the irrevocability of the role, and the body-image changes add to the complexity of the process of maternal identity achievement as compared to other identities (e.g., wife or professor). This complexity adds to difficulty in researching the process. What are the interactions between the cognitive restructurings of the mother–father and mother–child subsystems and self-, ideal, and body images, and how do these interactions affect replicative, fantasy, grief work, and dedifferentiation behaviors?

Rubin's cognitive operations, replication, fantasy, and dedifferentiation have not been systematically studied since her work. Some replicative behaviors of copying and role play have been included in research; however, no delineation of how these behaviors are currently expressed and how they change over the course of pregnancy has been done. Although fantasy during pregnancy has been researched and several have reported that the woman's ability to visualize herself in the role was related to her later adaptation, the construct has not been described across the course of pregnancy. Maturity and innate intelligence bias mental operations, such as mental rehearsals for motherhood.

How do individual variations in ability to fantasize or project oneself into different situations influence achievement of the maternal role identity? Individuals' ideal images of mother vary considerably; how does the range of ideal-image behavior influence achievement of the maternal role identity? Role models are selected for a best fit with oneself and one's values; what difference does it make in maternal role identity which role models are selected and at which point in the process specific models are selected?

Grief work has not been researched in the context of transition to the maternal role identity. However, it emerged in the fantasy research in dealing with loss of the known self and life-style. With greater control over conception and the decision to continue a pregnancy, how much grief work is done prior to conception?

Has the terminology—replication, fantasy, grief work, and dedifferentiation—been a factor in the paucity of research viewing these cognitive movements? For example, has the term "fantasy" inhibited research in mental rehearsals because of the psychiatric definition of fantasy? Would a term such as "mental rehearsal" or "visualization of self in role" be more helpful? Qualitative research could help clarify these theoretical constructs, identify current language used by women to describe them, and note the change in their frequency and focus and over pregnancy.

Cognitive restructuring in the areas of Rubin's four maternal tasks are discussed in the next chapter.

■ 4
Maternal Tasks During Pregnancy

Progressive tasks of pregnancy were first identified by Bibring and associates (Bibring, Dwyer, Huntington, & Valentstein, 1961) as accepting the intrusion of the fetus and incorporating it as part of self, recognizing the fetus as the coming baby, perceiving the fetus as a separate individual, and preparing for delivery and anatomic separation. Bibring (1965) later expanded the maternal tasks that begin during pregnancy and extend into motherhood as follows: (1) the woman loves the child as an independent person while experiencing a deeper, permanent bond with the child; (2) she accepts and fulfills her changing role with her husband while assuming the position of mother of his child; and (3) she moves from the role of child to her mother's co-equal in function and stature.

Rubin (1975) also stressed that the maternal tasks worked through during pregnancy are elaborated and transformed after birth to form "the qualitative matrix of mothering, the context in which specific child-care activities are enacted" (p. 152). The pregnant woman realizes that unalterable changes will occur as she exchanges a known self in a known world for an unknown self in an unknown world in the reformulation of her identity (Rubin, 1984). Rubin (1984) noted that mental development was not a linear increment of steps over time, but was

... a spiraling, a widening in scope of capacities and experience at advancing points of the life stream for increased hierarchical forms in mentation and behavior. The spiral stages are effected by a confluence of novel biological and social developments. Elements of the previous stage are regrouped to accommodate the novel elements in experience: there is articulation, transformation, and consolidation into the personality structure and then progression to the next stage. (p. 4)

The development of a maternal identity is "actively woven in the themes of the maternal tasks" (p. 54) and is fostered by support from the woman's family and other significant persons and feedback from her infant. Maternal tasks identified by Rubin (1984) address the self system, the maternal–child subsystem, and the larger family system:

1. "To ensure safe passage for herself and the baby through pregnancy and childbirth" (p. 10).
2. "To ensure social acceptance for herself and her child (p. 10), by significant family members" (p. 54).
3. "To increase the affinal ties in the construction of the image and identity of the 'I' and the 'you'" (p. 10). " Commitment of self as mother... binding-in to this child" (p. 54).
4. "To explore in depth the meaning of the transitive act of giving/ receiving" (p. 10). "Exploration of the meaning ... of giving of self in behalf of another" (p. 54) .

RESEARCH ADDRESSING ALL MATERNAL TASKS

The maternal tasks are discussed first as a group because some researchers have addressed all of the tasks. Each task is then presented separately with relevant research.

CS: Each woman addresses these maternal tasks in relation to her existing situation and with the resources currently available to her so that there is a distinctively personal imprimatur in maternal behavior in relation to the tasks of childbearing. (p. 10)

Although all four task areas are advanced progressively during pregnancy, the blocking of either of the first two tasks arrests the pursuit and furtherance of the remaining self-assigned tasks. (p. 10)

H: Accomplishment of the maternal tasks of pregnancy is positively related to mothering behavior.

Josten (1981) reported the development of a prenatal assessment guide based on Rubin's (1975) tasks of pregnancy for identifying parents who might have problems with parenting. Women were scored on their achievement of the pregnancy tasks by public health nurses, and there was 87% accuracy in predicting their mothering. During infancy, 27 of 52 mothers were providing excellent care for their infants, and 25 were providing inadequate care (child's basic physical or psychosocial needs were not being met or there was child abuse or neglect) (Josten, 1982). Twenty of the excellent mothers and only one inadequate mother were prepared for pregnancy, labor and delivery, and the infant. Twenty-four of the excellent mothers and seven of the inadequate mothers scored positive on ensuring physical well-being during pregnancy.

Nicoll (1988) developed the Prefatory Maternal Response Measure (PMRM) to measure maternal progress during pregnancy toward maternal role attainment. The PMRM is based on Mercer's (1981c) conceptualized components of the maternal role, Budd's (1986) psychosocial health as an outcome of pregnancy (Budd used Cranley's [1981a] Maternal Fetal Attachment Scale and Josten's [1981] conceptualization of the maternal role during pregnancy), and Rubin's (1975) maternal tasks of pregnancy.

Malnory (1982) developed a Maternal-Paternal Developmental-Psychological Assessment Tool (MPDP) for four observation–interview periods: the first prenatal visit; the second trimester, 20–24 weeks; early third trimester, 30–34 weeks; and term. Rubin's and Bibring's tasks of pregnancy, other literature, and clinical observations provided the content that was designed to show progress over the four observation periods. Flagler and Nicoll (1990) used Rubin's theories of the self system and maternal tasks to explicate nursing diagnoses and nursing action relevant to maternal identity formulation during pregnancy.

Lederman (1984b) reported conflict during pregnancy and childbearing centered around the challenges of maternal role development that, if met successfully, led to adaptation. The challenges were (1) acceptance of and adaptation to pregnancy; (2) progressive development in formulating a parental role and relationship with the coming child; (3) the woman's relationship with her husband as it affects her pregnancy and vice versa;

(4) her relationship with her mother; (5) gaining knowledge about and preparing for labor; (6) anticipating how to cope with fears about loss of control in labor and labor pain; and (7) coping with loss of self-esteem in labor. Lederman and Lederman's (1981) Prenatal Self-Evaluation Questionnaire (PSEQ) is based on those seven challenges. Lederman's challenges 2 and 5–6 are subsumed under Rubin's tasks of binding-in to the infant and ensuring safe passage.

H: Work on maternal tasks varies by obstetrical situation and environment.

Hospitalized pregnant women scored significantly lower on acceptance of pregnancy but did not differ from women experiencing normal pregnancies on identification with a motherhood role or fetal attachment (Curry, 1987). The women described their feelings as being on a roller coaster.

Others also found that women hospitalized for a high-risk condition did not differ in fetal attachment from women experiencing a normal pregnancy (Kemp & Page, 1987; Mercer et al., 1988). In contrast, women's health problems were negatively related to fetal attachment among ambulatory high-risk women (Wiggins, 1983), but no relationship was found between fetal attachment and physical symptoms of pregnancy among women experiencing a normal pregnancy (Lerum & LoBiondo-Wood, 1989).

The greatest stress reported by hospitalized pregnant women, in order of reported stress, was in relation to separation from home and family, disturbing emotions, changes in family circumstances, health concerns, and changing self-image (White & Ritchie, 1984). The experience is one of loneliness, boredom, and powerlessness (Loos & Julius, 1989); in addition, physical discomforts, loss of control, medication side effects, and uncertainty are problematic (Waldron & Asayama, 1985). In these situations of increased vulnerability, the woman's commitment to the pregnancy, ensuring safe passage, and giving of self are intensified (Mac-Mullen, Dulski, & Pappalardo, 1992; Mercer, 1990).

Stainton, McNeil, and Harvey (1992) observed that high-risk women's increased uncertainty altered their work on maternal tasks. Ensuring safe passage dominated their pregnancies and early motherhood. Other persons were of more importance in the high-risk situation in which the mother was more dependent; the mother had no choice but to depend on health care providers, family members, and particularly her husband. During long hospitalizations, other patients also become a source of much support (Williams, M. L., 1986). A wide variation was observed in binding-in, depending on previous loss of a child and when the loss occurred; however, as pregnancy progressed and the fetus became viable, women expressed attachment to the unborn (Stainton et al., 1992). The giving of self was intensified as high-risk women saw it as their job to endure whatever was required in the situation. Some high-risk women saw the situation as a test of their marriage. Others observed no differences between high- and low-risk mothers' satisfaction with their partner relationships; however, high-risk women's partners were less satisfied with their partner relationship than were low-risk women's partners during pregnancy and through 8 months postpartum (Mercer, Ferketich, & DeJoseph, 1993).

Women on complete bedrest during pregnancy had greater gastrocnemius muscle dysfunction, weight loss, and dysphoria than did women on either partial or no bed rest, prolonging postpartum recovery (Maloni & Kasper, 1991; Maloni et al., 1993). These side effects may interact with the woman's feelings about self and inhibit her role-taking tasks.

H: Maternal tasks are universal, although the approaches to the tasks and expressions of the behavior will vary by culture or specific situation.

A comparison of single and partnered women during the second trimester of pregnancy found that all were engaged in Rubin's tasks of pregnancy (Tilden, 1983a). However, the single women had four additional areas of concern to work through: decision making following conception, disclosure following the decision to continue the pregnancy, seeking social support, and legal issues regarding their unwed status. Single women had greater life stress, less tangible support, and greater anxiety (Tilden, 1984).

Wismont and Reame (1989) proposed that the lesbian couple faces greater barriers than do heterosexual parents in achieving Rubin's developmental tasks of safe passage and others' acceptance of the pregnancy. The lesbian pregnancy experience is characterized by donor insemination, social discrimination, and dependence on a peer rather than family networks for social support. Fear and the unpleasantness of coming out lead to seeking prenatal care later (Zeidenstein, 1990). Lesbians who had midwives for delivery reported higher levels of support from their care provider (Harvey, Carr, & Bernheine, 1989).

H: When support from the husband or father of the baby and family members is absent or withheld, there is no binding-in to the baby nor exploration of the of giving of self. (No research.)

SEEKING SAFE PASSAGE

Seeking safe passage takes as many forms as there are cultural guides. It also overlaps with giving of self, for in ensuring safe passage some lifestyle practices may need to be relinquished. For many women there are several barriers to their seeking safe passage.

> *CS:* Seeking and ensuring safe passage through pregnancy and childbirth involves more than obstetrical and prenatal services, though these are of great importance to the pregnant woman. In the first trimester the concern for safety is more related to herself, not to the baby.... By the end of the second trimester ... she begins to be protective of her unseen child. It is in the second trimester that a woman seeks prenatal care in order to make a good baby and in order to protect the child from being marked or damaged. (Rubin, 1984, pp. 54–55) In the third trimester, the concern is for both self and baby. There is no separation: what endangers one endangers the other. (p. 55)

H: Pregnant women seek safe passage for themselves and their infants by enrolling in prenatal care during the second trimester.

After the reality of pregnancy had "sunk in" and a decision was made to continue the pregnancy, safe passage through pregnancy and childbirth was sought by all women (Patterson, Freese, & Goldenberg, 1990). The woman's estimate of her vulnerability and/or her baby's influenced her emotional affect in seeking safe passage. Safe passage was sought for both mother and infant in most situations, but in some cases the focus was more on the mother (as in hypertension) or the baby (a relative having a deformed baby). Seeking safe passage was for some a single approach: enrolling in prenatal care. Others followed complicated patterns, involving processes of waiting, searching, enrolling in care, consulting, and transferring. Self-care emerged as an important part of ensuring safe passage regardless of when prenatal care was sought. Multiparas who felt their pregnancies were going well tended to postpone prenatal care, with its long waits and negative experiences, until later in pregnancy, confident of their knowledge in ensuring safe passage.

Omar and Schiffman (1993) found evidence that some women seek prenatal care for the symbolic value of prenatal vitamins, seeing them as helping to assure safe passage. The vitamins seemed to offer comfort to the women.

Barriers to seeking prenatal care include poverty, lack of child care, and lack of transportation (Leatherman, Blackburn, & Davidhizar, 1990; Lia-Hoagberg et al., 1990). A study of low-income white, black, and Native American women identified consideration of abortion, an unplanned pregnancy, late confirmation of pregnancy (late periods were not unusual in their stressed lives), ambivalence about the pregnancy, personal or family problems, and the health belief of seeking care only when ill as reasons for late prenatal care (Lia-Hoagberg et al., 1990). Women who received adequate care (47%) were more often motivated by their belief that prenatal care would ensure a healthy baby than were women receiving inadequate care (27%). Eighty-six percent of 206 Maasai women attended antenatal clinic; reasons given for those who did not attend were that they lacked time, they did not want to, the distance to the clinic was too far, and the husband refused (Mpoke & Johnson, 1993).

Pregnant prison inmates are another group who have not demonstrated seeking safe passage (Fogel, 1993). Chemical dependency, poor nutritional status, and inadequate prenatal care were found among prison inmates, along with high levels of anxiety and depression.

Scientific evidence indicates that there is a range of time from first to third trimester (to no prenatal care) in which women seek prenatal care to assure safe passage. The time that a woman seeks safe passage via prenatal care varied by ambivalence about whether to carry the pregnancy to term, her culture, her support system, stressors in her life, and her SES; however, no longitudinal study was found on seeking safe passage. How do the woman's behaviors in seeking safe passage change over the course of pregnancy?

H: The expectant woman's male partner influences her seeking prenatal care.

White women (43%) reported significantly more often than did black (23%) or Native American women (35%) that a significant male encouraged them to seek prenatal care; white women also more often identified husbands or boyfriends as giving advice such as eating well, not smoking or drinking, and resting (Lia-Hoagberg et al., 1990). Black women more often received such advice from their mothers. Filipino women shared their pregnancy concerns with close women relatives more easily than with spouses, and Mexican-American women identified spouses as their major support (Lantican & Corona, 1992).

Abused women seek prenatal care late; 22% of teens and 16% of adults reported physical and/or sexual abuse during pregnancy (Parker, McFarlane, Soeken, Torres, & Campbell, 1993). Abusers try to isolate the victims, and this contributes to late or little prenatal care (McFarlane, 1993). Abused women are in great jeopardy healthwise because partner support, network support, and stress are associated with expectant mothers' health (Brown, 1986b). More sadly, their abusers are demonstrating nonacceptance of the baby. Does the father's rejection of the baby stop the mother's progression in ensuring safe passage, binding-in to the baby, and committing self to the pregnancy and baby?

H: There is a significant correlation between the number of antepartal visits (seeking safe passage) and maternal–fetal attachment and/or maternal behavior after birth.

A study of mothering behaviors of mothers with infants in the intensive care unit (ICU) found that women who had not received prenatal care (had not assured safe physical passage) were not as involved with their infants as were mothers who had (Giblin, Poland, Waller, & Ager, 1988). These mothers were more often single, without support from the baby's father, and lacked financial resources.

H: Women change behavior to assure safe passage for themselves and the infant.

Behavior to ensure safe passage is culturally defined and is sensitive to evolving knowledge and social change. For example, during the 1950s and 1960s physicians monitored women's weight gain during pregnancy, and women were urged to limit weight gain to 20 pounds; overweight women were encouraged to lose weight during pregnancy. This may have been a response to the knowledge that toxemia is associated with rapid weight gain. Rothman (1989) noted that the July 15, 1962, issue of the *American Journal of Obstetrics and Gynecology* had four full-page ads for drugs (phenobarbital and amphetamines) recommended to suppress the appetite during pregnancy. Currently in the United States, a total weight gain of 25 to 30 pounds is recommended for all pregnant women, regardless of whether they are overweight or not. As noted in chapter 3, both Maasai and Filipino cultures continue to restrict weight gain to assure a smaller infant for an easier birth.

The pregnant woman's family has a strong effect on her health behavior (Aaronson, 1989). Women smokers living with smokers received less support to abstain from smoking during pregnancy, and women living with others who drank alcohol and/or caffeinated beverages drank more of these beverages than did women who did not have anyone at home drinking these beverages.

Women who either quit drinking or reduced their alcohol consumption during pregnancy had a larger group of people who boosted their self-esteem and who were available to help with specific tasks (Coleman, Ryan, & Williamson, 1989). Two-thirds of the sample were unpartnered. Pregnancy-specific support, however, was negatively related to change.

The extent to which persons see events in their lives as a consequence of their actions or beyond their personal control may influence whether they change health behavior for safe passage. Cigarette and caffeine consumption during pregnancy were related to locus of control expectancy; women who had higher internal control scores did not smoke or drink coffee and planned to attend childbirth classes (a means of control over labor and delivery) (Labs & Wurtele, 1986).

Others found no relationships between fate locus of control and internal locus of control with health-promoting behaviors during pregnancy (Kruse, Zweig, & LeFevre, 1988). However, a powerful-others locus of control orientation (belief in power of health professionals and friends to help them keep well) was strongly related to pregnancy health behaviors. Women scoring high on the powerful-others subscale were most often of low income, had less education, had higher social support, more often smoked, less often drank alcohol, and were more likely to decrease their alcohol consumption. Cranley (1984) found that the higher the woman's education, the lower she rated medical support.

Almost one-fourth (24%) of a Mexican-American sample of women smoked during pregnancy, and their infants weighed 101 g less at birth than nonsmoking mothers' infants (Wolff, Portis, & Wolff, 1993). This is similar to the rate for non-Hispanic-American women; thus, despite widespread knowledge about the deleterious effects of smoking on the fetus, roughly one-fourth of American women do not choose to ensure safe passage by quitting during pregnancy. In contrast, a study of 86 adolescents' work toward seeking safe passage found that those who smoked or used alcohol gave up these behaviors for the duration of pregnancy, ate better, rested more, and led a more settled life (Salisbury, 1993).

Low-risk women used more health-promoting and protective behaviors during pregnancy than did high-risk women (Kemp & Hatmaker, 1993). Low-risk women also had significantly higher scores on self-actualization and health responsibility. It was unclear whether women who experienced a high-risk pregnancy concentrated more on their infant's welfare and less on their own health and development. High-risk women hospitalized during pregnancy viewed their health status as poorer than did low-risk women during pregnancy and 8 months following birth (Ferketich & Mercer, 1990). High-risk women reported greater stress from negative life events in addition to their greater pregnancy risk. Stress from negative life events had indirect effects on health status over time, through self-esteem, among both high- and low-risk women. No differences were found for self-esteem between the two groups (Mercer & Ferketich, 1988). Kemp and Page (1987), however, found that self-esteem was higher among low-risk women than among high-risk women.

Learning the infant's sex following amniocentesis increased work on the maternal tasks of pregnancy (Walker, M. K., 1992). Twice as many who were not having a child of the preferred sex made statements about safe passage. Most women felt others were accepting of the baby's sex.

Women's employment and work conditions have been related to adverse outcomes during pregnancy (Keith & Luke, 1991). However, the choice to quit work to ensure safe passage is sometimes not an option. Brown (1987a) reported that employed women reported somewhat better health during pregnancy than did homemakers. Women who planned employment the first year following birth and who had higher-status jobs had fewer somatic and psychological symptoms. Employed women were more satisfied with their social support and received a greater percentage of support from their social network.

Summary

The woman's seeking safe passage through prenatal care and practicing good health habits is affected by multiple variables. With access to prenatal care equal, is there a difference in time first care is sought and number of prenatal visits according to partnered status, family support, and SES or financial assets? With these variables controlled, is there a relationship between number of prenatal visits and maternal–infant attachment and maternal identity behaviors? These are questions for future research.

SEEKING SOCIAL ACCEPTANCE FOR SELF AND CHILD

The woman's gestation and delivery of a child as a gift for her husband and family requires that they accept the expected child, acknowledging the involved sacrifice and their willingness to make required changes. Other family members whose acceptance is critical are the woman's mother, and if the woman is a multigravida, her previously born child/children.

Husband/Partner Relationship

In the majority of situations, the father of the infant is central to the woman's support system. "If there is a disordered relationship between the husband and wife, especially around the end of pregnancy, you tend to get a disordered mother-child relationship" (Caplan, 1959, p. 55).

> *CS:* The family is made for the intimate care, protection, and supportive nurturance that is necessary for the baby and the growing child.... The woman's husband is the key contributor. The course of the pregnancy, the formation of a maternal identity, and the execution of the maternal tasks are profoundly influenced by the qualitative relationship of husband and wife. (Rubin, 1984, p. 59)
>
> A woman who is aware of her husband's appreciation, reordering of priorities, and efforts in husbanding readily forgoes the pursuit of the now trivial pleasures and objectives and binds in with greater love for her husband in the maternal tasks of pregnancy. (p. 61) There is resistance to loosening the amount of time for the exclusive relationship between husband and wife for the first child. (p. 62)

> *H:* As pregnancy progresses, important relationships are restructured.

whose tradition?

All important relationships were observed to change during pregnancy, those with husbands and children changing more than all others (Richardson, P., 1981). Richardson observed that relationships with husbands and parent figures became increasingly more satisfactory as pregnancy progressed (Richardson, P., 1983a, 1983b). Others reported that spousal relationships improved from second to third trimester (Rankin & Campbell, 1983). Cranley (1984) reported no difference in the marital relationship between couples studied during the first half of pregnancy and couples studied in the last half of pregnancy.

Women scored significantly more needy than their partners in the areas of affection and inclusion during pregnancy (Griffith, 1976); if partners do not recognize this, an imbalance could occur. Women who anticipated satisfaction with motherhood shared affective expression and traditionally oriented attitudes toward marriage and parenthood with their spouses, and their spouses reinforced their wives' viewpoints (Gladieux, 1978). Women with traditional gender-role beliefs had more relatives in their social network, and women with modern gender-role views had largely friends in their network. During the first trimester, networks that were more supportive and close-knit included more relatives. During the second trimester, social network variables were more strongly related to pregnancy satisfaction than to marital relationship variables. During the third trimester, social networks included friends and relatives who had experienced labor, delivery, and parenthood, supporting Rubin's (1984) theory that role models relevant to the specific phase of pregnancy are sought. Women with modern views and more distant family connections were more likely to experience dissatisfaction with their pregnancy experience (Gladieux, 1978).

H: Partner and significant other support are positively related to maternal health and pregnancy outcome.

Receiving adequate help from others enhances self-esteem and feelings of being in control (Belle, 1982). The need for social support during pregnancy was reported by all women (Brown, 1987b). Women in unstable social situations were less happy to be pregnant and more anxious, alienated, and emotionally maladjusted (Davids & Rosengren, 1962). Emotional and tangible support provided by the spouse during pregnancy was positively related to the expectant mother's mental well-being (Gjerdingen, Froberg, & Fontaine, 1991). Husband–wife and mother–daughter attachments were significantly related to primiparas' psychological well-being during pregnancy (Zachariah, 1994b). The husband–wife attachment was the strongest predictor of psychological well-being, with the woman's age, mother–daughter attachment, weeks of gestation, and loss of support explaining a total of 36% of the variance.

Social support was particularly critical among those with higher stress from life change; women with high stress and greater social support had one-third the pregnancy complications that women with high stress and low support had (Nuckolls, Cassel, & Kaplan, 1972). Interaction effects of social support with life events stress were found for emotional disequilibrium, gestational complications, and infant complications (Norbeck & Tilden, 1983). Decreased stress and increased social support were associated with decreased emotional disequilibrium during pregnancy (Tilden, 1983b).

Low-income Hispanic, black, and white women (N = 190) who reported high life stress and low partner support had the highest anxiety from mid- to late pregnancy (Norbeck & Anderson, 1989b). Life stress, partner support, and anxiety were consistent from mid- to late pregnancy.

High-risk pregnant women's higher norepinephrine levels were associated with less perceived support from the male partner (Kemp & Hatmaker, 1989); norepinephrine increases the blood pressure by constricting the blood vessels. Turmoil in marital relationships was associated with preterm labor, as was being tied to critical or controlling parental figures (Richardson, 1987). The absence of a partner is a stressor variable weighted for identifying women at risk for preterm labor (Gonik & Creasy, 1986). Stress is related to catecholamine (epinephrine, norepinephrine, dopamine) release and is thought to be mediated by social support; women in the lowest social class experience the greatest stress, have less social support, and have the highest rates of preterm birth (Berkowitz & Kasl, 1983; Bryce, Stanley, & Enkin, 1988).

The importance of support in predicting pregnancy outcomes varied by ethnic group (Norbeck & Anderson, 1989a). Social support from the black woman's partner or mother explained 33% of the variance in gestation complications and 14% of the variance in prolonged labor or cesarean birth complications. An unexpected finding among white women was that high, as opposed to low, social support was associated with poorer pregnancy outcome and substance use, indicating that their social network had a negative influence on them. As noted above, Aaronson (1989) found that pregnant women (91% white) were less likely to give up smoking and drinking coffee when their family members indulged. Among Hispanic women who had a very low complication rate, no relationship between complications and social support was found (Norbeck & Anderson, 1989a).

Among a sample of 74% white and 26% black pregnant women, significant relationships between both high state and high trait anxiety levels and lower levels of social support were found (Albrecht & Rankin, 1989). Life events stress was a major predictor of both anxiety and depressive symptoms during pregnancy among high- and low-risk women; social support did not predict high-risk women's anxiety or depression and explained less than 2% of low-risk women's anxiety and depression (Mercer & Ferketich, 1988).

Marital satisfaction during late pregnancy was positively related to health status; ill health was linked to a decline in and low final level of marital well-being (Snowden, Schott, Awalt, & Gillis-Knox, 1988). A link was observed between conflict in becoming pregnant and low marital satisfaction; uncertainty and conflict were associated with diminished marital satisfaction. Improved marital satisfaction was related to having a first child and religious involvement.

H: There is a positive relationship between expectant mother–expectant father relationships and maternal behaviors.

The better the reported marital adjustment, the greater the woman's acceptance of her pregnancy (Porter & Demeuth, 1979). Marital adjustment was also associated with a planned pregnancy.

Some women were highly satisfied with support from their partners (Brown, 1986a), but their satisfaction was not dependent on the partner's involvement in the pregnancy. D. Moore's (1983) hypothesis that the woman's marital satisfaction would be positively associated with the husband's greater involvement, as measured by his attending childbirth classes, was not supported. Schodt (1989) hypothesized that maternal–fetal attachment would be related to fathers' couvade symptoms (associated with high emotional involvement), but no relationship was found.

Prenatal ratings of marital competence were positively related to maternal warmth and sensitivity to the infant at 3 months (Lewis, Owen, & Cox, 1988). Mothers who were above average on adaptation–competence, capacity for relationships, and positive view of marriage during pregnancy were interacting positively with their infants at 6 and 12 months (Oates & Heinicke, 1985).

Summary

Scientific evidence supports the importance of social support from the partner for the pregnant woman's health and her adaptation to pregnancy. There is beginning to be physiological evidence to support qualitative data that the poor relationship between expectant mother and expectant father may contribute to preterm labor.

Mother–Daughter Relationship

The pregnant woman turns to her mother for information about childbearing and child rearing and validation of her ability to mother. During the daughter's pregnancy, mother–daughter relationships may be strengthened as the daughter assumes more of a peer relationship with her mother.

> *CS:* The woman's own mother is the strongest maternal role model by virtue of the self-evident expertise.... The loosened bonds between mother and daughter during adolescence are realigned and tightened on a new basis as the woman searches for models for becoming a mother. Contacts between mother and daughter are increased during pregnancy. ... The incidence of hyperemesis and toxemia is high in women who are deprived of even symbolic contact with their mothers during pregnancy. The effector of childhood happiness and character traits—such as honesty, despite relative or actual poverty—takes on greater significance as source and model for a woman wanting to become mother. (Rubin, 1984, pp. 41–42)

> *H:* Earlier mother–daughter conflicts are resolved during the daughter's pregnancy, leading to improved relationships.

Although not directly testing the hypothesis that mother–daughter relationships are strengthened during pregnancy, research to date has supported this hypothesis. Bibring and associates (1961) identified the daughter's resolution of mother–daughter conflicts and the establishment of a sense of autonomy and differentiation from her mother to permit a peer relationship to develop as a major task.

Ballou (1978a) observed that women who resolved dependency conflicts with their mothers during pregnancy could allow themselves to be dependent on their mothers during pregnancy and childbirth. They were then able to accept their infants' dependency. Husbands played a large role in women's reconciliative process with their mothers by providing the psychological context. Husbands functioned both as maternal figures who gave and approved and as paternal figures who appreciated their wives' sexuality while protecting them from their mothers.

Daughters' (aged 18 to 30) relationships with their mothers improved during their pregnancy (Martell, 1990a). Mothers and daughters reported a desire to see each other more often and made statements indicative of resolving old conflicts. Mothers viewed their daughters as more sharing. Emotional closeness was more strongly associated with perceptions of equitable exchange of support than with actual help given or received between mothers and daughters (Martell, 1990b). Psychological support was the most frequent type of help received. The relationship between emotional closeness and feelings of equitable relationship between mother and daughter increased significantly for mothers from early pregnancy to middle to late pregnancy but not for daughters (Martell, 1990b). Because resolution of conflicts tends to increase the daughter's dependence on her mother, it is understandable that the daughter would not perceive the relationship as equitable yet could feel emotionally close to her mother.

A significant decrease in mother–daughter conflict was observed from the first to third trimester of pregnancy (Randell, 1988). Mother–daughter conflict was a core issue, as opposed to family conflict, in the transition to the motherhood role.

Mercer (1985a) reported that the majority of women (88%) at 1 year after birth rated the quality of their relationships with their mothers as good or better than prior to birth. The reported relationships with their mother did not differ by maternal age.

H: There is a positive relationship between the mother–daughter relationship and adjustment to pregnancy and mothering.

Deutsch (1945) warned that a woman's refusal to identify with her mother could weaken her capacity for mothering. Conflict stemming from the rejection of their mothers as adequate role models was associated with women's conflict in assuming the mothering role (Melges, 1968;

Uddenberg & Nilsson, 1975). Women's rejection of their mothers was related to poor postpartal adaptation at 4 months (Uddenberg & Nilsson, 1975) and 6 months (Nilsson & Almgren, 1970).

The pregnant daughter's positive relationship with her mother was not associated with satisfaction with pregnancy until the third trimester (Gladieux, 1978). However, a positive relationship with her father was associated with a satisfying experience throughout pregnancy. *explanation*

Women who were unable to use their mothers as role models also had problems concerning femininity and emotional difficulties during pregnancy (Wenner et al., 1969). Mothers who reported better adaptation to parenting at 3 months after birth had mothers who did not intrude in their lives, good support from fathers as adolescents, and sensitive treatment from their fathers as children (Cox et al., 1985).

Important components of the pregnant woman's relationship to her mother contributing to her adaptation during the perinatal period included the mother's past and current availability, acceptance of the daughter's pregnancy and recognition of her as a mother, respect for the daughter's autonomy as a mature adult, and reminiscences about her own childbearing experiences (Lederman, 1984b). A positive relationship was found among multiparous mothers' relationships with their own mothers and identification of the motherhood role at 6 weeks postpartum (Lederman, Lederman, & Kutzner, 1982).

The woman's positive relationship with her mother during pregnancy was associated with her self-definition and self-confidence as a mother at 1 and 3 months postpartum (Deutsch et al., 1988). The strength of the impact of the woman's relationship with her mother was independent of her overall level of self-esteem, supporting the theory that maternal self-definition developed in part through identification with the woman's mother.

No relationship was observed between the quality of first-time mothers' relationships with their mothers and their maternal role behavior at 1 year (Mercer, 1985b). The relationship between mother and daughter appears more critical during the early transition to the maternal role than in later mothering.

H: Mothers view pregnant daughters as adult peers, more so than nonpregnant daughters or daughters without children. (No research.)

H: Women identify their own mothers as primary role models for mothering.

Pregnant women viewed themselves as more like their mothers than did a group of nonpregnant women (Breen, 1975). In qualities related to the maternal role, pregnant women saw themselves as more like their mothers than their fathers during the first trimester of pregnancy and at 10 weeks postpartum; nonpregnant women saw themselves as more like their fathers than their mothers.

Cohler and associates (Cohler, Grunebaum, Weiss, & Moran, 1971) studied the relationship between mothers and *their* mothers' child-care attitudes. A mother's self-reported ability to channel the child's expression of angry feelings, to respond to the infant's demand for a social relationship, and to interpret the infant's cues competently were related to her mother's attitudes on these issues. Attitudes unrelated to her mother's were self-sacrifice for the infant, separating her needs from the child's needs, and the expressing of ambivalent feelings about child care. These last two attitudes reflect individuality in the development of the maternal task of giving of oneself.

The majority of 242 first-time mothers (52%) listed their mothers as their major role models at 1 year after birth (Mercer, 1986a, 1985a). Yet the mothers tended to rate their child-rearing practices as dissimilar to their mothers'; 53% saw themselves as more liberal, 10% as more conservative. Only one-third of the mothers felt their child-care activities were similar. Almost one-half (49%) described their judgment in child care as on a par with their mothers', with 39% perceiving better judgment and 6% indicating that their judgment was poorer than their mothers'.

Rubin (1967b) reported that women began with their mothers as models for each phase of maternal role taking but soon replaced them with peers who were in advanced stages of role acquisition. Mothers were too competent, knowledgeable, and overwhelming as role models for sustained periods during initial role-taking in pregnancy. Mothers were seen as a source of comfort and help.

The woman's relationship to her mother was related to psychosocial conflicts in pregnancy and identification with the mothering role (Lederman, 1984b). Women who had adjusted to childbearing at 10 weeks postpartum were more differentiated and less enslaved by the experience; they did not see themselves as passive, had more open appraisals of themselves and others, did not strive to be the "perfect selfless mother" that their own mother might not have been but were able to project a good mother image with which they could identify (Breen, 1975).

H: The poorer the mother–daughter relationship, the poorer the pregnant daughter's health and the greater the perinatal complications.

As noted above, a significant relationship was found between 115 primiparas' mother–daughter attachment and their general well-being (*r* = 0.25) (Zachariah, 1994b). Among nonclinical daughters aged 28 to 45, the greater the frequency of mother–daughter contact and the fewer the number of children, the greater the daughter's attachment to her mother (Davis & Jones, 1992). Higher levels of attachment were seen among women who were mentally healthy and functioning effectively.

No differences were found in relationships with either the mother or mother-in-law between women with hyperemesis and a group of controls (Majerus et al., 1960). Greater anticipated life change by motherhood was related to increased nausea and vomiting among primiparas (Steinberg, 1984).

Daughters of reproductively maladjusted mothers had higher rates of toxemia, premature rupture of membranes, episiotomies, and total obstetrical pathology (Uddenberg & Fagerstrom, 1976). Although the mothers' conflicts about reproduction are not a measure of the mother–daughter relationship, the daughter probably heard negative reports about her own birth.

Prolonged labor due to inefficient uterine activity was associated with a poor relationship with the gravida's mother (Kapp, Hornstein, & Graham, 1963). The woman's relationship with the mother was positively related to physiological measures of progress in labor (Lederman, 1984b).

Women who experienced childbirth difficulties reported a greater dissimilarity of perception of self in relation to their mothers at 10 weeks postpartum (Breen, 1975). Women who had no difficulties reported a greater perception of self in relation to their mothers.

H: Women's childhood memories of being mothered are positively related to their maternal behaviors.

The mothers' childhood experience was found to be important in relationships with their infants (Frommer & O'Shea, 1973a, 1973b). Women who were separated from their mothers prior to their 11th birthday had more marital problems, more problems managing their infants, and a poorer quality of family life.

Evidence that the quality of early childhood experiences affect the quality of later adult attachment relationships was found among college students (Flaherty & Richman, 1986) and mothers (Main, 1990). As high as 85% of infants' attachment has been correctly predicted by their mothers' descriptions of their parenting during childhood; infant attachment is dependent on maternal sensitivity and responses to the infant (Main, 1990).

Crowell and Feldman (1991) referred to the mother's working model of attachment relationships as the unconscious use of relatively stable cognitive, affective constructs incorporated into her personality structure during childhood in interaction with her parents. Mothers' working models of attachment were classified as secure, dismissing, or preoccupied; their behaviors with their children pre- and postseparation and at reunion varied by their classification.

Maternal self-esteem and role satisfaction were associated with loving and accepting mothers who were less hostile and controlling (Sholomskas & Axelrod, 1986). Women's maternal role decisions were related to their mothers' messages to them as children rather than their mothers' careers or homemaker status.

Neither multiparous or primiparous mothers' relationships with their mothers as children predicted maternal competence during the first 8 months postpartum (Mercer & Ferketich, in press). However, at 8 months, a poorer relationship with their fathers as children was associated with multiparas greater maternal competence, explaining 4% of the variance. Relationships with their mothers was not associated with either high- or low-risk mothers' maternal competence over the first 8 months postpartum (Mercer & Ferketich, 1994b).

Maternal recall of parental acceptance, sense of self, and perceptions of the child were all related to each other and to mother–child interactions (Biringen, 1990). A significant negative relationship was found between parental acceptance and maternal covert anxiety. Classification of dyadic harmony by recall of parental acceptance was correct 84% of the time.

Summary

Just as the mother is a major role model for the female identity, she is a major model for the maternal identity. Scientific evidence supports the importance of the pregnant daughter–mother relationship to the pregnant daughter's general health status during the perinatal period, to her formulation of attitudes about mothering, and to her adaptation to the maternal role and ability to provide nurturing for her infant. All but one of the studies supported the hypothesis that poor mother–daughter relationships are associated with poorer health status and perinatal complications.

Although not researched as frequently, the woman's relationship with her father also contributes to her maternal role behaviors. The family context or microsystem provides the emotional milieu for formulation of affective and psychosocial responses.

Mother–Previous Child Relationships

The woman expecting a second or later child has a more complex family for her cognitive restructuring of relationships. In this area, her work in assuming a maternal identity for the new child is harder.

> *CS:* With the coming of the second child, there is more stress. The woman's resistance to loosening the bonds with her first child for the time, attentive interest, and caring for a second child is a felt experience, confusing and disarming. (Rubin, 1984, p. 62)

> *H:* Changed relationships with her earlier-born children are a major focus of the multipara's cognitive work.

The multipara begins pregnancy with different concerns from those of the first-time mother (Mercer, 1979b, 1991; Merilo, 1988). In addition to being concerned about her changing relationship with earlier-born children, she experiences less excitement when the pregnancy is confirmed and has specific fears about the impending birth. Multiparas are more fearful of miscarriage; preterm labor; technological care, such as sonograms and amniocentesis; and physical symptoms of pregnancy, such as fatigue, sleep disturbances, and physical restrictions (Affonso, Mayberry, & Sheptak, 1988).

Jenkins (1976) identified three basic conflict themes in a case study of a secundigravida's pregnancy: (1) her ability to physically care for two children at the same time; (2) her feelings of betrayal and guilt as she anticipates the first child's reaction to his or her sibling; and (3) her ability to love two children equally. In the midst of her concerns and conflicts the multipara is faced with less time (Sammons, 1990).

Multiparas perceive more worrisome than pleasant or satisfactory changes in their relationships with other children during pregnancy (Richardson, P., 1987). Overall, 63% of multiparas described worrisome changes in their relationships with their children. "Guilt" is the descriptor secundigravidas most commonly use to describe their feelings of doubt and betrayal (Sammons, 1990).

Becoming a Brother (Mendelson, 1990) is a detailed account of the preparation of a 4-year-old son for the birth of a sibling. Although the focus is the son, the parents' diligent preparation of their son for his new role and their carefully planned continuity for him in family relationships reflect the importance and time that parents devote to this task.

ATTACHING (BINDING-IN) TO THE UNBORN CHILD

Attaching/attachment is used as synonymous with Rubin's term "binding-in." The process, which begins during pregnancy, is a strong emotional component of the maternal role identity and provides both motivation to achieve competence and satisfaction in the role (Mercer, 1977a; 1990).

> *CS:* The maternal tasks volitionally undertaken in behalf of the unborn child are not conditional on the actual characteristics and behavior of the child. A maternal identity is developed in a sustained act of faith independent of the specific characteristics of this child. The unconditional love of a mother for her child originates in the binding-in process of pregnancy. (Rubin, 1984, p. 128)
>
> A woman binding-in, becoming a mother in the qualitative and affiliative context, actively recruits the functionally supportive behaviors of persons with whom there are strong affiliative bonds: husband and mother, family and friends. There is a direct relationship between the strength and function of the intrafamilial bonds of a woman and the quality and strength of her binding-in to the child. (p. 7)
>
> Within the context of the supportive relationship a new and enduring relationship with an unknown and unknowable individual is begun. There is an incorporation and elaboration of the idea of a child and of an idea of a self as mother of this child into the woman's self system and self-concept. The psychological incorporation is interdependent and

symmetrically parallel with the biological development of the fetus and the pregnancy. The incorporation is a progressive binding-in, a progressive investment of self in ideation and behavior, in active adaptation and accommodation, to both sides of the equation of having a child and of becoming a mother. (pp. 8–9)

When a woman loves, her attractiveness is increased, there are social rewards, and the love bond grows. This love for the child who enriches her comes on strong in the second trimester, goes into abeyance during the third and fourth trimesters, and then increases again as the child responds and thrives in her maternal care. (p. 65)

Cranley's (1981a) Maternal Fetal Attachment Scale (MFAS) has been the most extensively used measure of maternal–fetal attachment. The MFAS items were derived from pregnant women's statements and were based on theory from Bibring and Valenstein (1976), Deutsch (1945), Rubin's (1975) tasks of pregnancy, and Leifer's (1977) work. Subscales of the MFAS include differentiation of self from the fetus, interaction with the fetus, giving of self, and role taking; however, the lack of reliability of the subscales indicates the need to use the total MFAS (Cranley, 1992). Muller (1993) developed a Prenatal Attachment Inventory (PAI) in an effort to clarify the construct of fetal attachment; however, the PAI was strongly related to the MFAS ($r = .72$), indicating much overlap between the two scales.

H: There is a positive relationship between a woman's self-concept and attachment to her fetus.

Several studies have failed to find a significant relationship between fetal attachment and maternal self-esteem (Cranley, 1981b; Gaffney, 1986; Koniak-Griffin, 1988a; Mercer et al., 1988). Lindner (1984) observed a positive relationship between self-esteem and attachment to the fetus among adolescents; Koniak-Griffin's (1988a) sample in which no relationship was found was also adolescent.

H: There is a positive relationship between social support and fetal attachment.

Significant positive relationships between women's social support and maternal–fetal attachment were found by Cranley (1984) ($r = .51$) and Mercer et al. (1988) ($r = .23$). Significant relationships between support of health care professionals and fetal attachment (r = .74) were also observed (Cranley, 1984).

A comparison of black, Hispanic, and white pregnant adolescents found that black adolescents had lower emotional and tangible support than whites (Hispanics were closer to whites); blacks identified fewer persons in their social networks, but the proportion of family support was greatest for them (Koniak-Griffin, Lominska, & Brecht, 1993). No relationship was found between social support and prenatal attachment as measured by the MFAS.

H: There is a significant relationship between the woman's relationship with her mother and her attachment to her fetus.

Zachariah (1994a) failed to find a significant relationship between primigravidas' mother–daughter attachment and fetal attachment. Mother–daughter attachment was significantly related to the daughter's emotional support.

No relationship was found between either high- or low-risk women's relationships with their mothers as children, teenagers, or adults and their fetal attachment (Mercer et al., 1988). Adolescents' MFAS scores were significantly related to their perceived close relationships with their mothers, however (Wayland & Tate, 1993).

H: There is a significant relationship between the woman's relationship with her partner and her attachment to her fetus.

Cranley (1984) observed a positive relationship between the marital relationship and fetal attachment (r = .32). A small but significant relationship was observed between maternal–fetal attachment and the woman's relationship with her mate (r = .17) (Mercer et al., 1988). Others failed to find a significant relationship between the woman's relationship with her husband and attachment to her unborn child (Muller, 1993; Zachariah, 1994a).

Adolescents' relationship with the infant's father (.28), frequency of contact with the infant's father (.31), and marital status (.26) were all positively related to their MFAS scores at significant levels (Wayland & Tate, 1993). Mexican-American adolescents scored significantly lower than Caucasians, suggesting cultural differences in responding to the MFAS.

H: As pregnancy advances, the woman's attachment to her unborn child increases.

Women's total scores on the MFAS increased significantly as pregnancy progressed; all subscale scores also increased, except for the subscale Giving of Self (Grace, 1989). Muller (1993), however, reported a very low but significant relationship (.14) between the PAI and gestational age; the MFAS in the same sample had a correlation of .28 with gestational age. Wayland and Tate (1993) also reported a significant correlation of .28 between MFAS and gestational age among adolescents.

Fetal attachment scores showed a significant linear increase over pregnancy (Reading, Cox, Sledmere, & Campbell, 1984). However, no relationship was found between MFAS and ultrasound feedback.

H: Multiparous women report significantly lower fetal attachment than do primiparous women.

Parity was negatively related to maternal fetal attachment (Grace, 1989). Multiparous mothers scored significantly lower on fetal attachment than did primiparous mothers (Mercer & Ferketich, 1994a). Curry (1987) did not find differences in maternal–fetal attachment by parity.

H: Fear of fetal anomaly delays the development of maternal attachment.

Cranley (1981b) observed a negative relationship between stress and fetal attachment (-.41). The stress measure included anxiety and amount of stress caused by the woman's health, fetal health, and difficulties during the pregnancy.

A comparison of women using the diagnostic techniques of amniocentesis and chorionic villus sampling (CVS) found that women having an amniocentesis were more highly committed to the pregnancy and were anxious about the possibility of an abnormality and termination of the pregnancy (Burke & Kolker, 1993). Most women had experienced fetal movement and were wearing maternity clothes by the time the amniocentesis results were known. CVS provides earlier results and has a somewhat higher risk of miscarriage; women having this procedure were less bonded to the fetus and were less concerned about losing the pregnancy. This finding supports the progression of maternal attachment to the fetus from early to midpregnancy, despite what Rothman (1986) referred to as the "tentative" pregnancy, in which the freedom to choose testing and/or abortion is illusory.

Real-time ultrasonographic scanning led to a change in women's views of their fetus; for many a greater sense of attachment was felt, but a few felt a greater sense of vulnerability about the outcome of the pregnancy (Kohn, Nelson, & Weiner, 1980; Milne & Rich, 1981). Although women tended to feel anxious about the baby, 30% continued to be worried or anxious following the sonographic visualization (Milne & Rich, 1981). Women were worried about fuzzy images of parts that they did not see well. All women were excited after the procedure, and many expressed an increased sense of knowing their babies and used the information to relate to their babies.

Women who had amniocentesis to rule out fetal anomalies did not begin to think of a child until the result was known; during the first 4 months the pregnancy was likely to be discontinued, and a child did not come into the picture (Silvestre & Fresco, 1980). Although parents accepted the diagnosis of absence of anomalies from the tests, they joked about whether a mistake was made in identifying the infant's sex suggesting a distrust of the diagnosis of no anomaly.

Heidrich and Cranley (1989) found that women who had genetic amniocentesis had lower attachment scores prior to the procedure but 1 month afterward had higher scores than did other women. The earlier fetal movement was felt, the higher the women's maternal–fetal attachment and perception of fetal development scores; ultrasound scans had no effect on either.

Scientific evidence indicates that the mother who is considering whether to abort a defective fetus (diagnosed by testing) is more tenuous in her attachment until she has test results. However, the concern shown by mothers awaiting amniocentesis results (and after having experienced fetal movement) is greater than that of the earlier gestational CVS-tested mothers, suggesting that, despite possibilities of a congenital anomaly or of aborting, they have attached to their fetus.

H: Prenatal knowledge of fetal sex facilitates maternal–infant attachment.

Ninety-five percent of women who found they were having their preferred sex after amniocentesis expressed binding-in statements contrasted to 29% of those not having their preferred sex (Walker, M. K., 1992).

Mothers saw themselves as givers and their partners as receivers of the son or daughter and often named the child after the sex was known.

No differences were found in mother–infant interaction behaviors during the postpartum between women who had knowledge of the infant's sex during pregnancy and those who had not (Grace, 1984). Unexpectedly, women who knew their infant's sex during pregnancy used the baby's name less frequently than did women without this knowledge (Grace, 1984).

H: A strong positive relationship exists between attachment to the fetus and maternal acceptance of and adaptation to the pregnancy.

Rees (1980a, 1980b), although not focusing on the maternal tasks, developed three scales as prenatal measures of identification with the mothering role: feelings of motherliness (FOM), conception of the fetus as a person (CFP), and appropriateness of fantasies about the baby (AFB). Although Rees established good reliabilities and criterion validity for the Identification with the Mothering Role measure, it has not been used in research. A positive relationship between age and FOM and CFP was found. A positive correlation of .59 was also observed between FOM and CFP to support an interdependence between early binding-in to the fetus and development of a maternal identity.

Muller's (1993) PAI correlated with the Maternal Adjustment and Maternal Attitude (MAMA) scale (Kumar, Robson, & Smith, 1984) ($r = -.25$), indicating a positive relationship between fetal attachment and adjustment to the pregnancy. Low MAMA scores reflect increased adjustment.

Summary

Two reviews of maternal fetal attachment research have raised important questions for future research and for clinicians (Gaffney, 1988; Muller, 1992). The lack of control over circumstances of diagnostic tests and extraneous variables, such as settings and different circumstances of the tests, raise concern about research outcomes in those situations (Muller, 1992). Cranley (1992) cautioned that the MFAS has items that are not relevant during early pregnancy (e.g., quickening and fetal parts) and that the items are instructive, suggesting activities that women might not engage in—all of which could result in higher scores over time. Thus, although scientific evidence supports the hypothesis that maternal attachment to the fetus increases over pregnancy, Cranley's comments must be kept in mind.

An important question raised by Muller (1990) is, does the ability to influence the binding-in or attachment process mean that it should be influenced? (p. 300). Modern technology has opened many doors, but should it; and if so, how it should be used in the formation of intimate relationships has yet to be determined. The differences in levels of cognitive and sensory awareness about the fetus during the third trimester, described by Stainton (1990), suggest a wide range of behavior in developing attachment. Do these levels of awareness make a difference in the continuing relationship as long as there is warmth, nurturance, and positive, accepting feelings toward the unborn baby? Further qualitative research needs to be done in several cultural groups to describe binding-in or attaching from the mother's cognitive and sensory awareness. Perhaps from a larger pool of descriptive language, more useful items may emerge to aid in clinical and research assessment.

Sandelowski and Black (1994) discovered in a study of couples making the transition to parenthood that much of the work of expectant parenthood was oriented toward getting to know the fetus as distinct from attaching to the fetus. In attempts to identify what was real or knowable about the fetus, the couples moved back and forth during pregnancy and the immediate postpartum period, from the "child in the head to the child in the womb to the child on screen and to the child they anticipated in their arms (p. 610)." This finding indicates that there are several objects as fetus that the mother focuses on.

Findings concerning the relationships between social support and maternal fetal attachment are mixed. Evidence supports the positive relationship between the woman's partner and her attachment to her unborn baby; however, her relationship with her mother was not related to the MFAS. The multiparas' concerns about their earlier-born children's acceptance of a new baby may explain why they have scored lower on the MFAS than primiparas.

GIVING OF SELF

Whether the transition to the maternal role is viewed from a purely physical basis, in terms of gains and losses in a career or educational trajectory, or of social and psychological costs, the mother is unequivocally the parent who gives and sacrifices the most in creating, bearing, and rearing a child. The ability and willingness to postpone self-gratification for another's well-being was discussed in chapter 2 as a feminine characteristic, moral masochism.

> *CS:* The prospect of becoming the bearer and giver in pregnancy, in labor, and in delivery is a costly and hazardous prospect. This giving involves giving up or giving away of the physical, mental, and social self. (Rubin, 1984, p. 8)
>
> The supportive sharing by significant persons is not so much a matter of dependence but a necessary condition for the giving of self in the totality required for childbearing. (p. 8)
>
> The progressively consummatory demands and deprivations of pregnancy, particularly on the woman's body-self but also psychologically and socially, cannot be passively endured as self-sacrifice without purpose. The multigravidous woman is more aware of the prospective demands and deprivations and has more to lose in another pregnancy. (p. 66)
>
> It becomes apparent that in giving there is caring involvement and a self-deprivation of the giver in behalf of the receiver. (p. 68)
>
> It is this distillation of what is involved in the complete transaction of giving and receiving that becomes the hallmark of maternal behavior; the giving of one's time; of caring attention, interest, or concern; of companionship in stress and in pleasure; and of relief from degradation. (p. 69)

The giving of self continues to develop through mothering experiences with additional children to reach a higher state, moral masochism (Rubin, 1984, p. 69). Rubin described a yet higher state of giving of self, a state of grace, in which the mother appears unaware of her self-denials, hardships, or personal sacrifices, or of their influences on the child, in her profound pleasure in the child and his or her accomplishments.

H: There is a positive relationship between gifts received during pregnancy and the woman's self-esteem.

According to Rubin (1984), gifts enhance the pregnant woman's self-esteem through their symbolic expression of the giver's respect for and esteem for her. Time, interest, companionship, and relief are particularly valued (Rubin, 1992). No research was found that looked at gifts in relation to self-esteem. In social support research, many forms have been identified, such as tangible goods, emotional and physical help, appraisal, and information that are congruent with Rubin's definitions of gifts. Is one type of gift or social support more valuable than others at specific stages of pregnancy? How much does the giver of the gift affect the impact of the gift on the woman's self-esteem? What kind of gift—time, information, emotional support (e.g., demonstration of love)—is more strongly related to the woman's self-esteem? Does this vary by stage of pregnancy?

H: There is a positive correlation between the number of pleasurable behaviors and activities that the expectant woman gives up and her attachment to her fetus, as well as to her later mothering behavior.

Giving up recreational drugs may be viewed as ensuring safe passage and giving of oneself. The mother's drug use during pregnancy was negatively related to her mothering behavior in the ICU (Giblin et al., 1988). Mothering behavior included frequency of visits, bonding behaviors, and response to discharge teaching.

SUMMARY

Rubin's four maternal tasks as core areas to which the cognitive work of pregnancy is directed have provided much direction for both research and clinical application. Josten's (1981, 1982) work illustrated that public health nurses could translate these tasks into observable, quantifiable behaviors that predicted later ideal and dysfunctional mothering with 87% accuracy. However, the task of "giving of self" was called "perception of complexities of mothering"; behaviors to assess perceptions of complexities were congruent with Rubin's described giving-of-self behaviors. The change in labeling could reflect that "giving of self, moral masochism and the state of grace" may be too abstract for clinicians and/or objectionable because of psychoanalytic overtones and reluctance to equate sacrifices in mothering with masochism.

The breadth of the four tasks allows for inclusion of most of the cognitive work during pregnancy. The tasks appear to assume that the pregnancy has been accepted, an initial task described by Bibring (1961). The tasks are inhibited if the pregnancy remains unaccepted for a long period (e.g., 4+ months), however. Does lack of progress on maternal tasks indicate nonacceptance of the pregnancy and unborn infant? Nonacceptance goes beyond normal ambivalence and grief work, both of which occur normally with acceptance.

What are the effects of parity, partner status, family support, and SES on seeking safe passage in pregnancy? What are their indirect effects, through seeking safe passage, on attachment to the fetus and identification with the maternal role?

Sandelowski and Black's (1994) findings of womens' perceptions of their role partners as many objects (object in the head, womb, on the screen, and in future in the arms) that are juggled back and forth in an attempt to know the unknown fetus is an important discovery. All images are in the mind, except for those on the screen; the object embodied in the womb is experienced through fetal movement. Which fetus as object is being measured in attachment measures? Acquaintance, or coming to know the other, is part of the attachment/bonding process (Gay, 1981; Kennedy, 1973; Mercer, 1977a; 1983; 1990). Which of the fetal images offers greater acquaintance for attaching? Should measures of fetal attachment focus on those fetal images?

When testing the relationship of fetal attachment to another variable, it is important that the measure used reveal data about that variable specific to the fetus. For example, most anxiety measures tap general anxiety, and Levin's (1991) Pregnancy Anxiety Scale has only 2 items out of 10 that specifically refer to the baby.

The act of giving of self appears to be a learned behavior. To give to another emotionally, one must have something to give. The woman's partner and mother were identified as two persons who were important as givers. Once an emotionally deprived pregnant woman is identified, how does the health care system facilitate her learning to give? Who can serve best as surrogate givers to the woman who has no givers in her system? Given that the complexities of mothering and other tasks of pregnancy proceed through replication, fantasy, and dedifferentiation cognitive behaviors, how is this ability for abstract conceptualization enhanced if a woman has difficulty in visualizing herself as a mother?

■ two

ACHIEVING THE MATERNAL IDENTITY

■ 5
Physical and Psychological Recovery Postpartum

With the birth of her child, the mother moves to the formal stage of maternal role identity. Physically and socially, she has become a mother; however, psychologically, she has much more work to accomplish before she has integrated the mother role into her self-concept.

The formal stage of maternal role identity begins with the mother emerged in dealing with her feelings about childbirth and her recovery from the process; this work preempts much of her energy the first 4 to 6 weeks of motherhood. A period of reality shock occurs if the anticipatory work and expectations of pregnancy are incongruent with the demands of the neonate, disrupted routines and schedules, and interrupted sleep. Rubin (1967d) referred to the first month after birth as the neomaternal period, noting that "the physical and psychosocial adjustments of a new mother in the neomaternal period are comparable to the adjustments of a baby in the neonatal period" (p. 391).

The formal stage of maternal role identity may not extend over the entire puerperium; but for the majority of women, replicative behaviors predominate, especially during the first couple of weeks. Many tasks face the mother during this period of initial adaptation: resolving the gap between reality and her expectations for the birth, her infant, and her body; identifying and placing her infant within her family context; assuring acceptance of the infant by other family members; developing competence in caring for the infant; learning to care for the infant while meeting other role requirements (e.g., wife, employee, mother of older child); and redefining her roles in relation to her mate, her infant, her parents, her career, and other roles (Mercer, 1981a; Sheehan, 1981).

In this chapter, the woman's recovery and sequelae of the birth are addressed. The mother's resolution of pregnancy and birth events, taking-in and taking-hold phases, body-image concerns, fatigue, and depression all portray the physical and mental restructuring that influence her ability to engage in the acquaintance–attachment process and work toward maternal role competence. The progression of maternal attachment and competence during the formal stage of maternal role identity are discussed in the next two chapters.

EFFECTS OF THE CHILDBIRTH EXPERIENCE

The uniquely female function of giving birth tests the very core of female identity. Mothers experience bewilderment and confusion as they begin to work on their new reality and new identity as mother (Carlson, S. E., 1976). Dramatic body changes have occurred within a very short time, and the experiences of childbirth, such as pain and loss of control, influence mothers' perceptions postpartally.

> *CS:* Established body boundaries become diffuse in conditions of pain.. .. As long as the body boundaries are diffuse, there is reduction in self-control and in localization of the pain. In the diffusion of the boundaries of the body-self there is a recognition that one is not one's self at the time. Body boundary and ego boundary become identical. (Rubin, 1984, p. 20)
>
> Unrelieved pain is subjectively experienced as social rejection of the self. Being rejected as a person tends to produce rejection, an antipathy toward life, the child, and the self. (p. 95)
>
> The woman who has had scopolamine in labor or a general anesthetic for delivery has difficulty realizing that she has delivered, that she

is no longer in labor, no longer in pain. It can take quite a while before this woman marshals sufficient evidence to backfill for the end of labor and delivery events and the beginning of the neomaternal and neonatal events. (p. 130)

There is pleasure in function, whether enabled by the help of another or not. But there is no pleasure in the helplessly dependent state, only hostility, resentment, and death wishes. (p. 22)

Pain and Function

Pain, both during childbirth and afterward, may affect the mother's ability to care for her infant. Being able to function physically is central to mothering.

H: The greater the woman's unrelieved pain during childbirth, the greater her antipathy toward self, the experience, and the infant.

Women who received more medication during labor had a more painful birth experience; however, both analgesia and anesthesia had negative relationships with enjoyment of the birth experience and a positive relationship with pain perception (Norr, Block, Charles, Meyering, & Meyers, 1977). Women who had cesarean births reported more positive perceptions about the births when they had regional anesthesia rather than general anesthesia (Cranley, Hedahl, & Pegg, 1983; Fawcett, Pollio, & Tully, 1992; Marut & Mercer, 1979; Mercer, Hackley, & Bostrom, 1983).

Vaginally delivered women who received epidural anesthesia reported less positive feelings about the childbirth experience early postpartum (Fawcett et al., 1992; Slavazza, Mercer, Marut, & Shnider, 1985); however, their descriptions of their infants were more positive and they made more identifying remarks than did women who had locals or pudendal blocks for delivery (Slavazza et al., 1985).

A study of videotapes taken at the time of the newborn's presentation to the mother, with follow-up at 6 months, found that the extent of pain experienced during delivery was associated with postpartal illness and depression (Carek & Capelli, 1981). Postpartal illness was associated with infants failing to double their birthweight by 6 months. Mothers who were in pain at their first interaction with their infants and who looked preoccupied and anxious appeared to identify with their infants and project their own physical states onto the infants.

Women were disturbed about the unexpected emotional reaction of detachment from their babies and their own bodies following birth, with feelings of sadness or disappointment in their functioning in contrast to the expected joy (DiMatteo, Kahn, & Berry, 1993). Earlier research found that mothers who were greatly pleased by their initial reactions with their newborn had been more quiet, relaxed, and cooperative in labor, had better emotional relationships with attendants, and received more solicitous physical care than did women who were indifferent or disgusted (Newton & Newton, 1962).

Close to 40% of primiparas and 25% of multiparas described feelings of indifference when they held their infants for the first time (Robson & Kumar, 1980). Lack of maternal affection was associated with having had an amniotomy or a painful and unpleasant labor and receiving more than 125 mg of meperidine.

From pregnancy through 3 months postpartum, no significant differences were observed in personality characteristics, maternal psychological functioning, and attitudes toward the infant among women who had either spontaneous vaginal, forceps, or cesarean deliveries (Bradley, 1983). Women who had cesarean births were more dissatisfied with the method of delivery but were more satisfied with nurses' help (Bradley, Koss, & Warnyca, 1983). Cesarean births (and possibly greater discomfort) were not associated with maternal feelings toward the infant.

Research findings are mixed regarding the woman's feelings toward self and experiences following the pain of childbirth. Although scopolamine is no longer routinely administered during labor as it was during the 1960s and earlier, research indicates that maternal affect was dulled by medications. The relief found in nurses' help and more nurturing care appeared to offset mothers' negative reactions to infants. DiMatteo and associates' (1993) findings indicate that some women are not prepared for the let-down feeling that follows for some after the bodily demands of childbirth. The relationship of this feeling to pain relief needs further exploration.

H: Women experiencing profound pain and/or unexpected complications will have difficulty recalling passage of time and events postpartally.

From 86% to 89% of women reported an inability to remember periods during their labor and/or delivery 2 to 3 days postpartum (Affonso, 1977). Situations associated with the "missing pieces" phenomenon included a long labor (fatigue), a rapid labor (sensory overload), a high-risk condition, unfulfilled expectations, and medications. A decade later, only 17% of women interviewed 24 to 74 hours postpartum described confusing events or missing pieces (8.5%) during labor (Stolte, 1986). Ten of 47 multiparas in the 1986 study reported missing pieces with previous births; women who had experienced this phenomenon immediately recognized the term. Specific events related to missing pieces were equipment, directions from others, and the actual birth. Global events, such as losing track of time, or perplexity about labor, were associated with confusion. The decrease in numbers of women reporting missing pieces since Affonso's study may be related to less medication, having a support person in labor, and being awake at delivery.

Women's temporal experience differed by vaginal and cesarean births on the first postpartal day: cesarean-delivered mothers' subjective time estimates (verbal estimate of a 40-second interval) were the highest, the vaginally delivered mothers who were hospitalized 3 days were the next highest, and the early-discharge mothers the lowest (Beck, 1987). Subjective times decreased and the level of consciousness increased significantly each day closer to discharge among both cesarean- and 3-day-hospitalized vaginally delivered mothers.

H: The greater the woman's loss of function, such as in cesarean birth, the greater her depression and anxiety and the lower her self-esteem.

Women who had Lamaze preparation and were able to follow through with it during labor had higher self- and ideal concepts, both prenatally and postnatally, than did women who had preparation but were unable to follow through with it because of complications (Hott, 1980). In a case study a primigravida focused on body-image change with multiple boundary intrusions, painful sensations, inadequate function, and unattractiveness after cesarean birth (Berry, 1983). Others reported greater body-image distortion and feelings of inadequacy among women having cesarean births (Birdsong, 1981; Mercer & Marut, 1981). An unplanned cesarean birth was associated with altered body perceptions and death fears (Affonso & Stichler, 1978, 1980; Marut, 1978). Women who had cesarean births reported lower self-esteem scores than did women who delivered vaginally (Cox & Smith, 1982). Later research found that mothers having cesarean births did not differ from women delivering vaginally in physical appearance, depression, anxiety, or confidence in mothering (measured by Maternal Self-Report Inventory) during postpartal hospitalization (Padawer, Fagan, Janoff-Bulman, Strickland, & Chorowski, 1988).

A positive relationship was found between self-concept and perception of the birth experience among 192 first-time mothers aged 15 to 42 years (Mercer et al., 1983). Self-concept explained 3% of the variance in perception of the birth experience. A 29-item measure tapping perceptions of the labor and delivery experience (PLDE) developed by Marut and Mercer (1979) with items from Samko and Schoenfeld's (1975) measure was based on Marut's (1978) research.

Padawer and associates (1988) concluded that under optimal conditions there were no differences in psychological adjustment by type of delivery. Their findings may reflect a trend toward less anxiety and depression about having a cesarean birth as rates have increased.

Satisfaction with the Birth Experience

A mother's evaluation of her childbirth experience is multifaceted and affected by many factors. Chertok (1969) observed that views of the childbirth experience were related more to maintaining control than to the extent of pain experienced.

H: The greater the woman's loss of body function, such as ability to deliver vaginally, the less positively she perceives her experience.

Perinatal complications were negatively related to satisfaction with the childbirth experience (Kearney & Cronenwett, 1989). Cesarean births, longer hospitalizations of mother and infant, and lower 1-minute Apgar scores were associated with less satisfaction.

Women who delivered vaginally reported significantly more positive perceptions of their labor and delivery experience than did women who delivered by cesarean (Marut & Mercer, 1979; Mercer et al., 1983). However, type of delivery explained only 1% of the variance in perception of the birth experience. Others observed that medical factors had small effects on enjoyment of the birth experience (Norr et al., 1977). Some women welcomed a cesarean as relief from a long, nonproductive labor; many variables influenced its psychological impact (Tilden & Lipson, 1981). See Mutryn (1993) for a review of variables influencing the psychological impact of the cesarean birth.

Canadian women who had cesarean births also reported less positive perceptions of the labor and delivery experience (PLDE) than did women who delivered vaginally (Mercer & Stainton, 1984). Women having emergency cesarean births reported more negative perceptions than did women who had planned cesarean or vaginal births; the PLDE was modified for women having planned cesarean births (Cranley et al., 1983). Women having vaginal deliveries reported more positive perceptions than did women having emergency cesareans, but no differences were observed between planned and unplanned cesarean groups or planned cesarean and vaginal groups (Fawcett et al., 1992). Pain intensity and physical distress had negative relationships with PLDE. White Caucasian, Hispanic, and Asian women who had cesarean births did not differ in their responses to PLDE (Fawcett & Weiss, 1993). Women in all three cultures identified problems with early role function due to lack of ability to care for themselves and their infants early postpartum. Tcheng (1984) did not find differences in emotional responses between women having primary and repeat cesarean births.

Cesarean births were viewed as less difficult but also as less fulfilling and more distressing experiences than forceps or spontaneous births (Salmon & Drew, 1992). Childbirth was more distressing among women whose pregnancy was unplanned and who had had a previous pregnancy terminated but was less distressing for those who had attended antenatal classes.

Others have not observed negative responses to unplanned cesarean birth (Culp & Osofsky, 1989; Sargent & Stark, 1987). Sandelowski and Bustamante (1986) found that women of lower SES and outside the natural childbirth culture did not view cesareans negatively. This changing view in later studies may be a response to the high prevalence of cesarean births (25%) and the seemingly normalcy of such a birth (Shearer, 1989). A comparison of women's responses to planned and unplanned cesarean birth in three studies (data collected 1973–1990) found diminishing disappointment about cesarean births; the dominant responses to cesarean births were happiness and excitement about the birth of a healthy baby (Reichert, Baron, & Fawcett, 1993).

The trend toward viewing cesarean births more positively may be in part due to better preparation prenatally, especially in childbirth classes. However, no differences in PLDE means were observed between cesarean-delivered mothers who attended a standard preparation class and a group that received comprehensive cesarean birth information as part of their childbirth class (Fawcett et al., 1993).

H: The greater the woman's sense of control, the greater her satisfaction with her birth experience.

Humenick (1981) projected two models of childbirth satisfaction; one proposed pain management and a second proposed mastery as leading to satisfaction with childbirth, with potential to change self-esteem and locus of control. Mastery was a key in childbirth satisfaction, and satisfaction was associated with an increase in personal attributes (Humenick & Bugen, 1981). Perception of control explained 59% of the variance in satisfaction with the birth experience (Bramadat & Driedger, 1993).

A major theme among women in early postpartum was disturbed feelings about loss of personal control during the childbirth process (DiMatteo et al., 1993). Having one's glasses removed, immobilization by having one's arms strapped down, and being on the fetal monitor were instances of loss of autonomy and personal control. Women who viewed videotapes of themselves during the second stage of labor described the tapes as weird, gross, wild, embarrassing, exciting, strange, and intense; some had difficulty identifying with themselves on tape (McKay & Barrows, 1992).

Several instruments have been developed to measure control during childbirth that should facilitate future research in this area. Humenick and Bugen (1981) reported four measures: Prenatal Attitude Towards Childbirth Participation, Labor/Delivery Evaluation Scale, Labor Agency Scale, and Delivery Agency Scale. Prenatal expectations of childbirth participation were predictive of postpartum descriptions of childbirth experiences.

Schroeder (1985) developed a Labor Locus of Control Scale (SLLOC) for administration pre- and postlabor. Determining the congruence between expectations of and experience of control is important; Rubin (1984) maintained that the gap between expectations and reality led to depression.

Lowe (1993) developed the Childbirth Self-Efficacy Inventory (CBSEI) to measure outcome expectancies and expectancies for coping with approaching childbirth. The CBSEI is unidimensional and has high internal consistency reliability. Its validity was supported by significant positive correlations with criterion variables of generalized self-efficacy, self-esteem, and internal health locus of control. Multiparous women reported significantly higher self-efficacy scores than did primiparous women.

Effects of Birth Experience on Maternal Behavior

Threats to the mother's ideal, self-, and body-image make it difficult for her to see how she can manage to care for her infant.

> *CS:* The biological experience of childbearing serves to promote or to inhibit the incorporation of a maternal identity in relation to this child into a woman's self-system. (Rubin, 1984, p. 11)
>
> An overwhelmingly difficult labor or a debilitating illness following delivery temporarily arrests the progression in development of the maternal identity. (Rubin, 1984, p. 10)

H: The more difficult the labor and birth, the more negative the mother's response to her infant.

Negative views of labor as difficult were associated with negative coping and negative perceptions of the baby (Priel, Gonik, & Rabinowitz, 1993), supporting negative effects of anxiety on maternal perceptions of their infants. Others reported a positive relationship between the birth experience and later emotional responsiveness to the infant (Entwisle & Doering, 1981).

PLDE scores were significantly related to observed maternal behavior at 1, 4, and 12 months after birth among teenage mothers and 20- to 29-year-olds; at 8 months the relationship was significant for teenagers (Mercer, 1985b). The more positively the childbirth experience was viewed, the more competent the maternal behavior. No significant relationship between birth experience and later maternal behavior was observed among women aged 30 and older.

Mothers having an unanticipated cesarean birth have experienced obstetrical complications or prolonged labor. Initial responses of cesarean-delivered mothers upon seeing their infants for the first time were significantly less positive (Hwang, 1987; Mercer & Marut, 1981). Delay of mother–infant interaction with less energy available to begin mothering were found as expected (Hassan, 1990; Marut & Mercer, 1979; Tryphonopoulou & Doxiadis, 1972). Cesarean-delivered mothers described motherhood in more negative terms and directed more hostile, angry remarks toward their infants, smiled at them less often, and were ambivalent about caring for them (Marut & Mercer, 1979; Trowell, 1982, 1983).

Mothers who delivered by cesarean expressed greater concern for themselves and less concern for their infants (Hassan, 1990). Cesarean-delivered women handled their infants significantly less, probably a factor of fatigue and pain (Tulman, 1986). No differences were observed between cesarean- and vaginally delivered women's initiation of touch or sequence of handling their infant at the initial bedside visit. When a videotape focused on infant communication abilities was shown to a group of mothers on the third day after birth, attachment behaviors were higher on the fourth day than among a group not seeing the tape (Moore, 1987).

Using a construct of hardiness as indexed by commitment, control, and challenge, high hardiness scores related to women's evaluations of labor as easier and positive perceptions of their infants (Priel et al., 1993). Subscales of commitment and challenge and the interaction between challenge and control predicted outcomes independent of negative affectivity. An anxious cognitive style was observed among non-hardy women.

There is support for Rubin's hypothesis that a difficult labor temporarily impedes progress in maternal identity. However, difficulty in the labor and delivery experience also varies by women's characteristics, as noted by Priel and associates (1993), and other environmental factors, such as support.

Childbirth Classes and Early Maternal Behavior

Numerous childbirth education classes are available for expectant mothers. Persons are open to information during important transition periods, and a small amount of intervention has the potential for long-range beneficial effects. Women may attend classes as a means of enhancing their functioning and coping skills; both are important to mothering.

H: There is a positive relationship between attendance at childbirth classes and early mothering.

No differences were observed in self-esteem, feelings about the childbirth experience either at the time of delivery or at the time of the interview, and maternal perception of the newborn between those who attended childbirth classes and those who did not (Slavazza et al., 1985). Women completed two identical questionnaires, one asking for a rating of feelings about the childbirth experience at the time of delivery and the second asking for feelings at the time of the postpartal interview (5 to 48 hours postpartum). Mothers' feelings about the childbirth experience became more positive with time.

When both lower-class and middle-class couples attending childbirth classes were compared, effects of the classes were negative to neutral among lower-class women in regard to mothering (Entwisle & Doering, 1981). Preparation classes taught by middle-class instructors may not be geared to lower-class needs. Childbirth preparation was associated with positive childbirth experiences, and birth experiences affected emotional responsiveness to the infants. Preparation was not helpful in fostering maternal role integration; however, classes did not have parenting content.

Childbirth class attenders in Australia were no more confident than nonattenders in caring for their infants at home or less likely to be depressed 8 months following birth (Lumley & Brown, 1993). No differences were found between the two groups in birth events, satisfaction with care, or emotional well-being.

A meta-analysis of 27 studies from 1960 to 1981 reported beneficial effects of childbirth education on the parent–infant relationship, with the magnitude of effect greater for middle-income parents than for parents with low income (Jones, 1986). Out of 199 effect sizes, 80% were positive, but the more frequently the parent–infant relationship was measured, the smaller the effect size. Parents participating in childbirth education were more attentive and responsive to their infants and more satisfied with the infant's behavior; they reported fewer feeding problems, had more positive feelings toward their infants, and spent more time playing with and cuddling their infants.

Findings are mixed about the effects of childbirth classes on parenting behaviors. Classes seem to be less effective among lower-SES parents, for whom content and presentation may be irrelevant or unclear. Future studies need to consider potential biases in class attenders' characteristics, such as demographic variables, locus of control, and attitudes about childbearing.

COMING TO TERMS WITH BIRTH EVENTS AND THEIR SEQUELAE

In the early days following birth, the woman strives to validate her experiences with those who were present, to fill in gaps in her memory and to establish biological baselines for the future (Highley, 1967). There is a sense of immediacy and concern over the new present and the immediate past. The mother's ego or self, which constricted during labor (Rich, 1973; Rubin, 1961b, 1984), now begins to expand.

If the pregnancy and childbirth experience fell short of the mother's projected ideal self, she feels distress, shame, and frustration. Unexpected interventions or complications add to her dissonance.

> *CS:* Missing elements are backfilled for wholeness and then summed up for perspective: it was worth it; it was a good or a terrible pregnancy. The review and summary provide a debriefing for an intense experience.
>
> ... to finish them so that they become past experiences, put away in memory to free both mind and body for future experiences in a new life. (Rubin, 1984, p. 96)
>
> She needs to review what happened, to ferret out the missing details, to put the pieces together to make sense out of chaos, to comprehend, and to be able to move on to what is now real. (Rubin, 1961b, p. 754)

H: Review of the birth experience is related to moving on to maternal tasks.

Eight out of 10 women wanted to reconstruct their childbirth experience and to fill in "missing pieces" (Sullivan & Beeman, 1981). Women who had not integrated their labor and delivery experiences verbalized themes from the experience over and over, had dreams that disrupted their sleep, and were unable to focus on their present situation due to preoccupation with the experiences (Affonso, 1977).

During the third week postpartum, 81% of mothers continued to report frequent thoughts about labor and delivery (Affonso & Arizmendi, 1986). At 8 weeks, 66% reported frequent thoughts about labor and delivery.

Women reported greater stress about their labor and delivery several weeks after birth ($M = 70.53$) than they did during first ($M = 61.23$) or third trimesters of pregnancy (M = 57.74); two-thirds of the sample were multiparas (Arizmendi & Affonso, 1987). The researchers suggested that women may continue to review the process of labor and delivery as a means of understanding or integrating the experience.

Research supports the need for the woman to review her childbirth experience, to discuss stressful aspects of the experience, and to clarify events. Evidence indicates that distress about childbirth extends far beyond the puerperium. Further research is needed to determine whether opportunity for early maternal reviews prevents prolonged stress and anxiety about events around childbirth and facilitates movement toward postpartal tasks. Clarification by the mother is needed, whether reviewing childbirth as a means to gain control in anticipation of the next childbirth, as a way of evaluating her behavior at the time, or as a way of diffusing the anxiety accompanying such a traumatic event (Arizmendi & Affonso, 1987).

TAKING IN, TAKING HOLD

Rubin (1984) did not elaborate on the movement from the mother's taking-in to taking-hold behaviors in her later work. She emphasized the mother's shift in orientation at birth to the child and to herself as the mother of the child. The concept of taking-in was enlarged to emphasize the cognitive taking-in of the infant (discussed in the next chapter) and was closely linked to the woman's experience of time and space that changed as her body changed over pregnancy (when time was forever) and the postpartum "as a product of the developing maternal identity" (Rubin, 1984, p. 86). This altered experience of time and space enables the mother to have sympathy and tolerance for the infant who "lives in a world of forever-time and minuscule space" (p. 86). Rubin's 1984 CS related to taking-in are presented first, followed by those of the 1961 work.

> *CS:* And there is a transition in the identification of self as mother from the predominantly receptive mode of taking-in to taking-on and actively doing and being mother of this child. (Rubin, 1984, p. 100)
>
> In duration time, the centered taking-in phase postpartally is equivalent—three weeks—to the preparatory labor phase at the end of pregnancy.

The subjective experience of time during the first three weeks after delivery is related to her own activity.... She depends on the activities of others for orientation in time and for her own behavior: time for meals, time for the baby, time for visitors....

It is in this behavioral mode of receptivity, of taking-in, in the constricted action-space and time, that neomaternal behaviors are begun. There is a taking-in, cognitively, of the child. (1984, p. 96)

The first phase of the restorative period in the puerperium is a "taking-in," and it lasts for two to three days. Sleep is a part of this phase of taking-in, restoring, or recovery; food is another...

She is a receiver at this point.... She accepts what she is given, tries to do what she is told, awaits the actions of others, and initiates very little herself....

... the "taking-hold" phase ... she becomes the initiator, the producer.... Sometime during the third day she will arrive at the second phase. This phase requires new behaviors, and begins with her own body functions.... There is a strong element of anxiety here in this phase. If she cannot control her own body, how can she expect to assume responsibility for anyone or anything else?...

It is at this time, when she has successfully coped with the autonomy of her own body, that she begins to take hold of some of the tasks of mothering. (Rubin, 1961b, pp. 754–755)

H: A predominance of taking-in behavior occurs the first 2 days after birth, followed by a predominance of taking-hold behaviors on the third day.

An attempt was made to duplicate the setting and population from which Rubin's observations were made to test this hypothesis; however, changes in obstetrical management and society since 1961 and lack of a description of observed populations hindered replication (Martell & Mitchell, 1984). A questionnaire format was used to test 20 vaginally delivered women's taking-in and taking-hold behaviors during a 2-day hospitalization, with 14 women's behaviors observed on the third day of hospitalization. Both taking-in (M = 5.6) and taking-hold (M = 5.4) behaviors were observed on Day 1. On Day 2 a decrease in taking-in behaviors (M = 4.0) and an increase in taking-hold (M = 6.7) behaviors occurred. On Day 3, the mean of taking-in behaviors was 4.4 and the mean of taking-hold behaviors was 6.3. An examination of questionnaire items found that the only taking-in behavior that was significant (compliant) was significant on all 3 days. Women reported experiencing eight of the nine taking-hold behaviors on the second day and only two (wants visitors and concern for others) on the first day, which supports a movement to taking hold on the second day postpartum.

Wrasper (1987) used Martell and Mitchell's (1984) questionnaire to determine whether taking-in and taking-hold behaviors varied over the first 3 postpartal days and found that both taking-in and taking-hold behaviors occurred over all 3 days. However, a trend of increasing taking-hold behaviors and of decreasing taking-in behaviors was observed.

Ament (1990) modified Martell and Mitchell's (1984) questionnaire to study 50 vaginally delivered women's taking-in and taking-hold behaviors 1 hour after leaving the delivery room, 2 hours later, at 10:00 p.m. the same evening, and the next 2 mornings of hospitalization. Significant temporal patterns of a decrease in taking-in and an increase in taking-hold were found. The first 24 hours following birth was a strong taking-in phase. Women who were 28 years or younger had higher scores in both taking-in and taking-hold, but by the second morning the scores merged. Primiparas had higher taking-in scores than did multiparas, but taking-hold scores were similar by parity and maternal age.

Rubin (1961b) referred to concern about body functions (voiding and bowel movement) that were resolved by the third postpartum day; by the 1980s women ambulated immediately after birth, largely eliminating those functional concerns. The interdependence of taking-hold behaviors and functional ability indicates that taking hold would occur earlier, especially in the absence of hangovers from drugged labors. For example, mothers who had no sedation during labor and delivery were more adaptive mothers during the first 4 postpartal days (Funke-Furber, 1979).

No research has tested whether mothers defer to others for orientation in time and behavior during a 3-week taking-in period, as suggested by Rubin (1984); the cognitive disorganization or confusion and "primary maternal preoccupation" described in chapter 3 fits with deferring to others for orientation in time and behavior during this period.

The taking-hold behaviors described by the researchers are not incongruent with the taking-in as described by Rubin's evolving theory. With earlier hospital discharge, these studies cannot be replicated; observations in the home setting, with variables such as household help, would affect taking-hold maternal behavior. Ament's (1990) study raised the issue of the effects of age and parity. Although there is support for taking-in and taking-hold, the phases are not discrete. Many variables could affect these behaviors, such as type of birth and the mother's and infant's physical status.

The physical fatigue and physiological status of the newly delivered mother warrant nurturing care to meet her comfort, nutritional, and rest needs. A question that needs to be researched is whether women who have no opportunity for a taking-in period (discharged a few hours following delivery and with no help at home other than the husband's) have greater difficulty in their recuperation and in assuming the maternal role.

BODY IMAGE

Once the infant is born, women expect their bodies to quickly resume their prepregnant condition. In addition, they are concerned about possible mutilation from birth (Highley, 1967).

> CS: On taking the upright position after delivery, the discovery of the abdominal size and mass, like a 6-month pregnancy, is an appalling and disjunctive anachronism. Disparaging terms like useless, fat, or blubber are used to describe the abdomen and the figure. (Rubin, 1984, p. 122)

> H: Concern about the body image early postpartum adds to the woman's anxiety and stress.

Most (95%) new mothers reported concern about their bodies and a return to prepregnancy status; their flabby abdomens were a source of anxiety (Gruis, 1977). The return of normal figures and exercise were concerns of the majority of mothers (Lemmer, 1987). Not one of 20 women used any positive adjectives to describe themselves during the postpartal hospitalization (Flagler, 1990). Only one made a positive statement at 6 weeks postpartum.

This disparagement continues for weeks following birth. During the third postpartal week, 65% of 80 mothers reported feeling less attractive; and at 8 weeks, 53% reported feeling this way (Affonso & Arizmendi, 1986). The third greatest source of postpartal stress was losing weight and getting back to earlier shapes (Arizmendi & Affonso, 1987).

CS: There is, in addition, a nostalgia for the intimate and pleasant experiences with the child in utero. There is a sense of emptiness, of the body and of the self. The emptiness is relieved in the contact with and responsiveness from the infant. (Rubin, 1984, p. 123)

Holding a baby stabilizes the reality of the baby in real space rather than an image, a fantasy, or a dream that appears and disappears but never endures. The weight, smell, and the warmth of the baby in contact with the surface of her body also help to redefine her own body boundaries. (p. 78)

H: Mothers who are unable to hold their infants following birth have less well defined body boundaries and lower feelings of well-being than do mothers who hold their infants from birth on. (No research.)

H: Women place their infants on their abdomen following birth to relieve the sense of loss.

Stainton (1986a) observed that women automatically placed their infants against their abdomens during the first postpartal week. The mothers were unaware of this until asked about it; they confirmed that they knew their babies best there. Their bodies were accustomed to sensing the infant within the uterus, and some mothers described feelings of loss in these sensations.

CS: The body image and subjective experiences postpartally are symmetrically similar to the body image and experience antepartally. There is progression antepartally and retrogression postpartally.... Both the third and fourth trimesters follow an experience of heightened narcissistic gratification in making and having a baby. Both trimesters contain the experience of body-boundary diffusion, restrictions in time and space orientation, diminished mobility, hostility toward self and the baby, and the feeling of entrapment in an unlovable and poorly functioning body. (Rubin, 1984, p.124)

H: There are no differences in the body image the ninth month of pregnancy and first month postpartum.

As noted in chapter 3, women felt more negatively about body image during pregnancy than during the postpartum period (McConnell &

Daston, 1961; Strang & Sullivan, 1985). Fawcett (1977) reported that women's perceived body space increased during pregnancy and decreased markedly the first postpartal month as expected; a slight increase was reported the second postpartal month.

Negative statements about self were somewhat higher during pregnancy than at 1 month postpartum (Fleming, Ruble, Flett, & Van Wagner, 1990). Body-image scores were significantly higher at postpartum than during pregnancy (Ruble et al., 1990). Research to date does not support this hypothesis.

H: Body-boundary diffusion and negative body image continues over the first 3 months postpartum.

Grubb (1980) reported that a sample of multiparous women had not reached stabilization of body image and concepts of self at the end of the first month postpartum. At 12 months after birth, the mother's inability to see herself as separate from her infant was associated with less ability to deal with stress; without clear boundaries, there was inability to isolate stress to the event (Egeland, Breitenbucher, & Rosenberg, 1980). Ego boundary appeared to be a critical concept in understanding the mother's coping with stress and her relationships with others.

No research was found that focused on the length of time body-boundary diffusion continues after birth. What is the relationship of body-boundary diffusion to maternal attachment and competence?

H: There is a negative correlation between body image and feelings about the baby and maternal role behaviors during the postpartum.

The number of mothers' negative physical descriptors was strongly associated with less mother–infant mutuality (-.72) and anxiety about child rearing (-.47) at 4 to 6 weeks postpartum (Flagler, 1990). The women's negative emotional descriptors were related to their relationships with their husbands, general satisfaction with life, and support for the maternal role from family and friends.

Physical discomforts contributed to women's emotional distress postpartum by decreasing their endurance for coping with the demands of motherhood (Tulman, Fawcett, Groblewski, & Silverman, 1990). Failing to recognize negative or ambivalent feelings about the transition to motherhood means that the mother is not accepting and dealing with them (Niemela, 1980). Negative evaluations are incompatible with the woman's ideal image. Failing to deal with ambivalent feelings was associated with overprotectiveness and failure to create a secure base for the infant.

> *CS:* In the isolation of the nuclear household, the diffusion in body-self boundaries increases. Social contact and social interaction help define the parameters of the self. The interface in social contact provides a sense of controlled containment of the self, a good feeling. (Rubin, 1984, p. 123)

H: The early postpartal woman who is isolated has more diffuse body boundaries, poorer self-esteem, and poorer body image. (No research.)

> *CS:* Healing of incisions and restoration of the body boundary takes two to three weeks for an episiotomy, longer for a laceration or extension, and six to eight weeks for a Caesarean section. (Rubin, 1984, p. 75)

H: A woman's ability to attain prepregnancy function returns by the end of the 4-to-6-week postpartal period.

Just 72% of 30 women who had vaginal deliveries and 34% who had cesarean births reported that they had regained their usual level of physical energy by 6 weeks after birth (Tulman & Fawcett, 1988). Many reported that they had to resume activities before they were ready because of family obligations or financial constraints. Women who had cesarean births took longer to assume infant care responsibilities and some household tasks, socialize with friends, and participate in religious activities. Recovery of functional ability was affected by maternal and neonatal complications.

Women hospitalized for high-risk pregnancies reported significantly poorer health status than did women experiencing normal pregnancies during the third trimester, early postpartal hospitalization, and at 8 months following birth (Ferketich & Mercer, 1990). Negative life events stress had indirect effects on health status over time through either self-esteem, family functioning, mate relationships, or perceived support. High-risk women reported an increase in health status following birth that remained constant for 8 months, when a decrease occurred (Mercer et al., 1987). Low-risk women reported a nonsignificant higher health status during pregnancy than at any time over the first 8 months. Miller and Sollie (1980) also reported a higher sense of well-being soon after the baby was born than when the baby was 7 or 8 months old.

FATIGUE

Fatigue from lack of sleep is pervasive during the postpartum. There seems to be no relief for the weary mother.

> *CS:* Fatigue is a normal consequence of labor and delivery, of the protective tension to control both the hazards and the pain of labor....
>
> The prolonged fatigue of the postpartal phase makes this phase one of the most difficult in the childbearing experience. (Rubin, 1984, pp. 78–79)
>
> The fatigue in the postpartum period is superordinate.... dominates the three or more weeks following delivery. (p. 97)
>
> The fatigue of the puerperium is overlayed by sleep hunger, sleep deprivation, and sleep disruption. (p. 114)

> *H:* A major complaint during the first month postpartum is fatigue.

Eighty-three percent of women reported fatigue during the puerperium, and the problem was greater for multiparas than for primiparas (Gruis, 1977). The majority (55%) of first-time mothers complained of fatigue during the first month after birth (Mercer, 1986a). Many mothers reported that they never felt rested. Almost all women in other studies described some fatigue postpartum (Entwisle & Doering, 1981; Grossman et al., 1980).

Three-fourths of mothers reported feeling tired, exhausted, or fatigued at 4 to 6 weeks following birth (Flagler, 1990). During the third postpartal week, 85% of 80 mothers reported feeling fatigue, and at 8 weeks, 70% continued to report fatigue (Affonso & Arizmendi, 1986).

Because sleep interruption accounts for much fatigue, mothers may decline rooming in during hospitalization. Keefe (1988) found that mothers whose infants were returned to the nursery at night did not sleep better or longer (5.35 hours compared to 5.55 hours for rooming-in mothers). Both groups complained of lack of sleep due to roommates, physical discomfort, or environmental factors. Others observed that despite frequent interruptions in women's sleep during postpartal hospitalization, the majority reported sleeping soundly and feeling rested on awakening (Lentz & Killien, 1991).

Ball (1987) reported that mothers' self-image in feeding their infants was negatively affected by increased stress from lack of sleep and conflicting advice during the mothers' hospital stay. The mothers' emotional well-being was positively related to their satisfaction with motherhood.

Rich (1969) postulated that hospital routines may serve as rites of passage in developing maternal identity. However, sleep interruptions from hospital routine also interfere with maternal behavior.

H: The greater the postpartal fatigue, the greater the depression and anxiety.

An increase in sleep during the third trimester of pregnancy was reported, but significant sleep loss occurred during the intrapartal period (Mead-Bennett, 1990). However, the intrapartal sleep loss was not significantly related to moods of anxiety, hostility, and depression on the first postpartal day.

No relationship was observed between the extent of fatigue at 2 to 3 weeks postpartum and when postpartal depression occurred (Entwisle & Doering, 1981). The extent of fatigue was associated with the seriousness of postpartal depression.

H: Fatigue levels are higher the first month following childbirth than at any of the three trimesters prior to birth, making this the most difficult period.

The greatest number of physical complaints was observed during the 4 to 6 weeks following birth (Leifer, 1980; Mercer, 1986a). First-time mothers reported lack of time and the extreme pressure from this lack of time as the most difficult things about mothering at 1 month (Mercer, 1986a). Mothers had no time to read or take an outing; they felt tied down and isolated. Feelings of incompetence and inadequacy were the next most frequent difficulty, followed by sleep deprivation and the difficulty of the constant responsibility. LaRossa (1983) discussed social time, as opposed to physical time, as more critical, observing that parental reports of boredom and isolation suggest physical time.

The universality of fatigue during the postpartal period demands further research. Are sleep deficits, tension, anxiety, and worry major causes of fatigue? What is the relationship between social support and fatigue? Is the method of infant feeding associated with fatigue? How can causes of fatigue be dealt with by health professionals?

SELF-ESTEEM/SELF-CONCEPT (SELF SYSTEM)

Self-concept represents the global sense or picture of self (Fitts, 1965). The construct of self-esteem is the cognitive evaluation of self with accompanying feelings about the evaluation (Rosenberg, 1965). Maternal self-esteem is the value a woman places on her appraisals of self as mother (McGrath & Meyer, 1992). Positive maternal self-esteem enhances a woman's global self-concept. Self-esteem and self-confidence forecast the woman's capacity as a mother and affect her response to her infant (Bullock & Pridham, 1988; Mercer, 1986a; Shereshefsky et al., 1973; Walker, Crain, & Thompson, 1986a).

> *CS:* The depressed postural model of the body [experience in body position and movement in relation to the environment] pervades the concept of self.... Between aspiration and reality there is a void filled with a self-estimate resulting in depression, a despair of self, or in hostility, a self-hate....
>
> The self-image and the body image share the same postural model instrumentally and expressively. It is only the ideal image that is desynchronized for time and space in the postpartal healing and recovery period. (Rubin, 1984, p. 79)

H: Self-esteem or self-concept will be lower the first 4 to 6 weeks postpartum than in later months after birth.

First-time mothers aged 20 to 42 years reported self-concept Tennessee Self-Concept Scale (TSCS) (Fitts, 1965) scores that were significantly higher the first 3 days postpartum than at 8 months (Mercer, 1986c). Teenagers' scores showed a nonsignificant decrease over that period.

Women's self-esteem (measured by Rosenberg's scale [1965]) was significantly higher during postpartal hospitalization and at 1 month than during pregnancy or at 8 months postpartum. (See chapter 2 for other reports discussing self-esteem following childbirth.)

Despite the insult to the body during childbirth and self-disparagement about the body image, self-esteem and self-concept were higher during the early postpartum than at later months. Does the ability to function by giving birth to a healthy infant buoy self-esteem sufficiently to offset lesser body concerns?

DEPRESSION

Literature reviews of postpartum depression distinguish the early, transitory maternity blues from postpartal depression (Affonso & Domino, 1984; Hopkins, Marcus, & Campbell, 1984; Landy, Montgomery, & Walsh, 1989; True-Soderstrom, Buckwalter, & Kerfoot, 1983). However, in most research reports, depression is used synonymously with depressive symptoms or with women saying they were depressed. The self-report scales are not diagnostic but are very sensitive to depressive symptoms and help to identify potentially depressed patients with varying degrees of power exceeding chance (Depression Guideline Panel, 1993). Thus, studies using self-report scales are reporting depressive symptoms; depressive symptoms overlap with maternity blues symptoms.

As many as 80% of postpartum women experience the blues. Maternity blues symptoms occur early, are transitory, and include weeping (often alternating with elation), depression, anxiety, confusion, forgetfulness, depersonalization, irritability, headache, disturbances in sleep patterns, and fatigue (Beck, Reynolds, & Rutowski, 1992; Hansen, 1990). Postpartum blues were associated with acceptance of the role as mother, high trait anxiety (Ehlert, Patalla, Kirschbaum, Piedmont, & Hellhammer, 1990), and a sense of pessimism during late pregnancy (Condon, W. S., & Watson, 1987). A nighttime labor and a history of sleep disruption during late pregnancy were associated with postnatal blues, indicating a relationship with sleep deprivation (Wilkie & Shapiro, 1992).

Postpartum depression may occur during the postpartum or several weeks or months later and has serious effects on the mother, her infant, and her family. The depressive symptoms lead to the mother's feelings of guilt and inadequacy and increase her worry about her competence and adequacy as a parent (Kumar, 1990). Entwisle and Doering (1981) reported that 81% of the 120 mothers in their study reported being depressed during the first few weeks following birth.

Postpartum depression has been consistently linked with depression during pregnancy (Gordon, Gordon, Gordon-Hardy, Hursch, & Reed, 1986; Gotlib, Whiffen, Mount, Milne, & Cordy, 1989; O'Hara, Neunaber, & Zekoski, 1984; O'Hara, Rehm, & Campbell, 1982). Factors that place a woman at risk for experiencing postpartum depression were identified from a literature review (Landy et al., 1989): more than three children; poor SES; lack of support from spouse, family, or friends; stressful events; psychiatric history; excessive repressed anger, anxiety, and guilt during pregnancy; excessive narcissistic preoccupation with self; history of premenstrual stress; poor parenting experiences; poor relationship with mother; loss of parent during childhood or in the past 2 years; unwanted pregnancy or extreme ambivalence; extremely difficult infant; and extremely traumatic pregnancy or birth experience.

> *CS:* The social isolation that occurs ... for the postpartum woman in a nuclear household reduces contact with the real world. The contact socially helps to maintain self-boundaries and to maintain an openness of the self-system and the maternal-child system to a larger system. Without the social contact as interface between systems there is entropy: disorientation, depression, despair. (Rubin, 1984, p. 97)
>
> It is the disparity between the expected and the real, between the ideal image of self as woman, wife, and mother and the experience of self in body postpartally, that produces the self-disparagement. The self-deprecation results in depression and in hostility. The depression is a sense of hopelessness or despair that occurs in roller coaster fashion on the third, fifth, and seventh days postpartum. The depression becomes characteristic of the second and third weeks of confinement within her own lowered energy levels and continues in inverse relation to the feedback of competence and rising self-esteem. The hostility is a self-depreciation without despair or hopelessness, has a higher energy level than depression, and is directed primarily at self, and, by extension, to those belonging to her, such as her husband or child. Whereas depression is privately personal and apathetic, hostility disparages loved ones in a spread-effect. The spread of hostility is incompatible with self-control and self-esteem and therefore generates further self-depreciation. (p. 110)

H: There is an association between depressive symptoms and hostility postpartum.

State hostility (measured by Multiple Affect Adjective Checklist [Zuckerman, Lubin, Vogel, & Valerius, 1964]) at 1 month postpartum was predicted by the woman's prenatal depression state (27% of variance), internal locus of control regarding health (17%), belief in chance regarding health (4%), and health status (7%) (Laizner & Jeans, 1990). Stable traits of anxiety, depression, and hostility were influenced by in-hospital anxiety, depression, and hostility in the presence of external locus of control.

Postpartal depression (measured by the Zung [1965] depression scale), was associated with either overall hostility and extrapunitiveness or external locus of control and intrapunitiveness during pregnancy (Little et al., 1981). Women with high anxiety or hostility scores had a more pronounced heart response to the sound of a baby crying than to a noise of similar frequency and intensity during pregnancy; this more pronounced heart response was related to later postpartal depression.

H: Maternity blues (depressive symptoms) peak on the third, fifth, and seventh postpartal days and the second and third postpartal weeks.

There is no agreement in the reported research on which days maternity blues symptoms occurred most frequently or were the most severe during the first week to 10 days (Beck, 1991). A peak in blues symptoms has been observed on the third postpartal day (Levy, 1987; Pitt, 1973); around the fourth to sixth day (Stein, 1980), and on the fifth day after delivery (Kendell, McGuire, Connor, & Cox, 1981; Kennerley & Gath, 1989).

Affonso and associates (1992) identified dysphoric distress (depressive symptoms present in the absence of a full syndrome of clinical depression) at first and third trimesters of pregnancy, 1–2 weeks, and 14 weeks postpartum. The most frequent symptoms reported were anger, psychic anxiety, fatigue, and worry. From 1–2 weeks to 14 weeks postpartum, the increase in the percentage of women reporting anger was from 18% to 29%, almost reaching first and third trimester of pregnancy reports of 30% and 31%. The percentage reporting anxiety decreased from the third trimester of pregnancy (21%) to 13% during the first 2 weeks postpartum and 14% at 14 weeks. The same percentage (10%) reported worry in those three periods. The researchers raised the question of whether dysphoria may be an adaptive mechanism to ward off clinical depression or is related to the development of clinical depression.

Significant relationships were observed between maternity blues the first week (measured by Stein's [1980] Maternity Blues Scale) and depression, measured by the Beck Depression Inventory (BDI) (Beck, A., Ward, Mendelson, Mock, & Erbaugh, 1961), at 1 week (r =.85), 6 weeks (r =.43), and 12 weeks (r =.32) postpartum (Beck, C. T. et al., 1992). From the first to the fifth days, the percentage of primiparas reporting severe maternity blues increased. More women reported blues on the fourth day (65%), with the fewest reporting symptoms on the seventh day (50%). At 6 weeks postpartum, 15.4% of all first-time mothers had experienced mild to moderate depression. Based on A. Beck's (1978) guidelines, a score higher than 9 indicated postpartum depression; a score of 10 to 15 was considered mild depression; from 16 to 19, moderate depression; from 20 to 29, moderate to severe depression, and 30 to 63, severe depression. Primiparas who had more severe maternity blues were at increased risk for postpartal depression. At 12 weeks, 16.2% of all mothers experienced mild to moderate depression, consistent with the incidence reported at 3 months by O'Hara et al. (1982) but lower than the 20% reported by Cutrona and Troutman (1986).

Depression, defined as a depressed mood for a period of at least 2 weeks during the first 9 months after birth, was reported by 63% of first-time mothers and tended to have an early onset and lengthy duration (McIntosh, 1993). Others suggest that the correct name would be post-puerperium depression, as opposed to postpartum depression, because they observed the peak of depression at 10 weeks after birth (Pop, Essed, deGeus, van Son, & Komproe, 1993).

Rubin's informal observations of a roller-coaster occurrence of depression (depressive symptoms) seems accurate, although the days she identified for higher depression have not been documented. Observed variations may be explained by different definitions of blues symptoms and different population variables and social context.

H: There are negative relationships between support, marital relationship, family relationships, and postpartal depression.

Problematic marital relationships were associated with postpartal depression by several (review by Arizmendi & Affonso, 1984; Cox, Connor, & Kendell, 1982). Women who reported marital difficulties or ambivalence about the infant during pregnancy were more depressed and anxious and had more punitive child-rearing attitudes at 3 and 5 months postpartum (Field et al., 1985). Women who had a history of marital problems, poor relationships with immediate family, or disrupted family relationships had greater emotional disturbance following childbirth (Ballinger, Buckley, Naylor, & Stansfield, 1979). In addition to a history of psychiatric disorder, younger age, and early postpartum blues, a poor marital relationship and no social support were characteristic of postpartal depression at 6 weeks (Paykel, Emms, Fletcher, & Rassaby, 1980). Marital satisfaction, parental relationships during childhood, and early separation from mother explained 35.5% of the variance in maternal depression (Hock, Schritzinger, & Lutz, 1992). Depressed women viewed their mothers as less caring, scored one or both parents in the extreme of care dimension (affective coldness), and had significantly more dysfunctional marriages than did nondepressed women (Vega et al., 1993).

Intimacy with spouses was associated with less depression at the time of either term, preterm, or cesarean delivery but not 3 months later (Hobfoll & Leiberman, 1987). Women's benefits of intimacy with their spouses were dependent on situational demands and environmental constraints. Others reported that social support in the form of companions who used comfort measures, reassurance, and praise during labor was associated with significantly lower depression scores (Pitt Depression Inventory [Pitt, 1968]) at 6 weeks postpartum (Wolman, Chalmers, Hofmeyer, & Nikodem, 1993).

H: Disorientation and depression are associated with the mother's isolation.

Depressed women (measured by the BDI and meeting research diagnostic criteria) did not differ from women who were not depressed in the number of confidants reported (O'Hara, Rehm, & Campbell, 1983). Depressed women reported less instrumental and emotional support from their support network.

Women discharged from the hospital on the traditional third postpartal day did not differ significantly in reported depression from women having an early discharge on the first or second day (Beck, C. T. et al., 1992). Information about the extent of isolation or available help at home was not given.

Affonso and Arizmendi (1986) reported that 65% of mothers reported feeling isolated from adults at 3 weeks postpartum and 60% at 8 weeks. Feeling isolated was significantly related to both the BDI and Pitt's (1968) questionnaire scores. Significant relationships between both measures of depression and decreased time for fun activities and deceased opportunity for social activities were found at both 3 and 8 weeks postpartum.

At 1 month postpartum, women who listed themselves as housewives were more often depressed (measured by BDI) (Gotlib et al., 1989). One-third of the women who were depressed during pregnancy were also depressed postpartally. Yet McIntosh (1993) reported that the majority of depressed mothers did not seek help from any source; only 25% consulted a health professional, indicating a reluctance to admit their emotional difficulties.

In a qualitative study of the lived experience of postpartal depression, (diagnosed by psychiatrist for all but one) C. T. Beck (1992) found that the mothers were enfolded in loneliness. Their depression was a living nightmare filled with anxiety attacks, consuming guilt and obsessive thinking. In a second qualitative study, women with postpartal depression described a process of teetering on the edge, walking a fine line between sanity and insanity:

Stage 1. Encountering terror with enveloping fogginess, horrifying anxiety attacks, and relentless obsessive thinking.

Stage 2. Dying of self, with alarming unrealness, contemplating and attempting suicide, and isolating oneself.

Stage 3. Struggling to survive by battling the system, seeking comfort at support groups and praying for relief.

Stage 4. Regaining control with unpredictable transitioning, guarded recovery, and mourning the lost time (C. T. Beck, 1993).

The basic problem was the women's loss of control over emotions, thought processes, and actions. Whereas isolation may contribute to depression, depressed women also tend to isolate themselves, as they believe they are the only ones who experience such frightening symptoms.

H: The greater the gap between the mother's expectations and reality, the greater her depression.

In a theoretical paper, Driscoll (1990) illustrated subjective data related to maternal loss from Rubin's perspective, using real versus ideal events. Examples from the puerperium included feeling worse than during pregnancy; feeling inadequate, guilty, and ashamed; and relationship and life-style losses.

Several authors have reported a gap between women's anticipation about motherhood during pregnancy and the actual experience during the first postpartal month but did not relate the gap to depression (Glass, 1983; Humenick & Bugen, 1987; Pellegrom & Swartz, 1980). Mothers did not anticipate so little time for household tasks, with husbands, for themselves, and for recreational activities or that so much time would be spent in caring for their infants. The parental combination of very positive with very negative sentiments during pregnancy enhanced maternal perceptions of their infants at 1 month, leading Glass (1983) to conclude that "preparing for the worst" is helpful.

H: Maternal depression is associated with the perception of the infant's difficulty.

Depressed mothers perceive their infant's behavior more negatively than do objective observers (Field, Morrow, & Adlestein, 1993). Difficult infant temperament was associated with postpartal depression at the second month in a literature review (Mayberry & Affonso, 1993). Parents who were depressed and anxious viewed their infants as less soothable and more easily distressed (Ventura, 1982). Interactional effects of each on the other are evident, however.

H: Depression has negative effects on maternal behavior and role identity.

Mothers who are depressed have to give at a time when they are in need of nurturance (Gross, 1989). High correlations were found between depression and postpartal adaptation at 8 weeks using the BDI (.53) and the Pitt questionnaire (.64) (Affonso & Arizmendi, 1986). Smaller but significant correlations were observed for negative emotions while with baby (BDI, .24; Pitt, .43), and lack of comfort at being a mother (BDI, .30; Pitt, .20). During the third week, 65% reported negative emotions when with their baby; at 8 weeks, 45%.

Cognitive thoughts related to a sense of mastery and control were highly related to primiparas' depression symptoms at 14 weeks postpartum (Affonso et al., 1991). Negative thought patterns about abilities to handle the demands of pregnancy and parenthood were associated with the most severe depression symptoms during pregnancy and at 1–2, 8, and 14 weeks postpartum.

At 1 and 3 months postpartum, depressed mothers exhibited fewer affectionate contact behaviors toward their infants and less often vocalized in response to infant's vocalizations (Fleming, Ruble, Flett, & Shaul, 1988). Pregnancy and postpartum mood states had significant effects on maternal attitudes during the postpartum.

At 1 month postpartum, depression (depressive symptoms) explained 24% of the variance in maternal role competence among 93 women who had been hospitalized during pregnancy for a high-risk condition (Mercer & Ferketich, 1994b). Depression was measured by the Center for Epidemiologic Studies Depression Scale (CES-D) (Radloff, 1977), and maternal role competence was measured by Gibaud-Wallston and Wandersman's (1978) Parenting Sense of Competence Scale (PSOC). Depression explained 6.4% of the variance in PSOC of women who had experienced normal pregnancies at 1 month after birth. Depression did not predict multiparous mothers' competence on the PSOC during the first month after birth; however, among primiparous mothers, depression had negative effects on competence (Mercer & Ferketich, 1995).

CS: The disorientation and fear that one is losing one's mind postpartally is not all that different from the behavior at the end of pregnancy when extra locks were put on the doors and when every strange sound or strange person elicited apprehension....

Postpartally the hostility, anger, and the wish to separate out leads to impulses of infanticide, and this is indeed frightening. The fear of loss of self-control which existed in anticipation of and during labor is even more overwhelming, an insanity, postpartally (Rubin, 1984, p. 124).

Self-orientation to a new role requires human responses, relatedness, feedback. In some ways taking care of a newborn infant is like taking care of a comatose patient all day, everyday, without a day off. Unkind, selfish, even insane ideas cross one's mind.... As her morale and self-esteem lower, the low regard which she has for herself is extended to her baby.... An impulse to harm the baby is not uncommon. Some mothers with less ego strength act out the impulse; others are more fortunate and can verbalize their feelings and thereby control the impulses. (Rubin, 1967d, p. 390)

H: Postpartal feelings of anger at the child arouse fear in the mother.

H: Depressed mothers experience negative feelings toward their infants.

During the third postpartal week, 65% of mothers reported experiencing negative emotions when with their infants (Affonso & Arizmendi, 1986). By 8 weeks, 45% continued to report these feelings.

Mothers with postpartum depression considered harming both themselves and their infants (Beck, C. T., 1992). They were then consumed with guilt for having had such thoughts and terrified that at some point the thoughts might be carried out.

C. T. Beck's (1992, 1993) research has provided rich insight into the experience of postpartal depression (diagnosed by psychiatrists) and the negative effects on the mother and her mothering. The dying of total self with self-hatred, obsessive thoughts of being a bad mother, a burden of fear and guilt over thinking about harming the infant, and loss of control of emotions and feelings are incompatible with caring for a dependent infant.

Summary

C. T. Beck (1992) emphasized that only 3 of 11 themes she identified among her sample are found on the BDI, a frequently used measure of postpartal depression. A newer instrument, designed specifically to detect postpartum depression, the Edinburgh Postnatal Depression Scale (EPDS) (Cox, Holden, & Sagovsky, 1987), also fails to address most of the identified themes. Use of the EPDS and early intervention of emotional support has led to lower rates of postnatal depression (Holden, 1991).

Postpartal depression is extremely complex; however, the gravity and frequency of the condition merit research to develop a more valid and reliable instrument to identify symptoms. In a study that differentiated pregnancy and postpartum symptoms from perinatal clinical depression, women consistently reported a high frequency of dysphoric mood, worrying, somatic and psychic anxiety, insomnia, fatigue, anger, and irritability (Affonso, Lovett, Paul, & Sheptak, 1990). The findings indicated that perinatal depression may be underdiagnosed if complaints are attributed to time-limited conditions and overdiagnosed if only self-reported measures are used without interviews to separate symptoms of depression from perinatal symptoms, and responses to perinatal symptoms may be related to later development of depression.

SUMMARY

The events of childbirth threaten the woman's already vulnerable self-, body, and ideal images. Her major concerns are her ability to function within the norms established by others before her, to maintain control of her body and behavior and situations within her control, and to survive the experience intact. Whether the woman's inability to function in the childbirth process according to her projected ideal is viewed by her as a forecast of her functional capacity in the mothering role or indicates a loss of control and consequently loss of self, or both, remains unclear.

Some women viewed their birth process positively despite profound pain and a cesarean birth. Cognitive restructuring of threatening events is based on illusions that protect the person while constructive thought and action are pursued (Taylor, 1983). Adaptive efforts enable a return to or movement beyond a person's earlier level of psychological functioning through the search for meaning and finding a causal explanation, to gaining some control over the event. A young woman's remarks illustrate the cognitive restructuring of her childbirth: "I feel power in being able to reproduce. It put me in touch with some sort of basic values. I faced an extreme situation in labor and I survived it. Labor was very hard; it was like facing death—the pain was that bad" (Mercer, 1986a, p. 64).

It is also difficult to separate the concept of "missing pieces" of labor and delivery from levels of ego defenses in response to threatening situations. Detachments from reality, partial withdrawal or partial distortion of reality, and disorganized explosive outbursts of aggression with brief loss of ego control are ego defenses that reflect this concept. The constriction of the ego during labor and missing pieces following birth both seem to reflect the intense threat of the childbirth experience that called out to ego or self for such levels of defense to survive.

The newly delivered mother must begin her tasks of identifying and claiming her infant and learning to mesh her caretaking behavior with the infant's response in a handicapped physical and psychological state. Recognition of these handicaps is necessary to provide supportive care during this vulnerable period and in researching maternal role identity behaviors.

How is the woman's receptivity or taking-in behavior related to the disorientation in time and space and the change in cognitive functioning that was described in chapter 3? What is the relationship of a change in cognitive functioning to maternity blues symptoms such as confusion and anxiety? Are women allowed the opportunity to become immersed with their infants (primary maternal preoccupation)?

How can women be helped to achieve a more defined body boundary following birth? Does fostering increased interaction with the infant and assuring social interactions with experienced role models foster definition of body boundaries? Do women differentiate between physical time, which is short for accomplishing tasks, and social time, which, with isolation, leads to boredom, as time affects their efficiency?

Under what conditions, other than sleep deprivation, is fatigue greatest? What factors contribute to fatigue (e.g., anxiety and depressive symptoms)?

Evidence supports the theory that depressive symptoms interfere with the woman's ability to function and affect her infant and family. The maternity blues may be limited to the first week; in other situations depressive symptoms occur much later and over longer periods of time. Whiffin and Gotlib (1993) reported that a group of depressed postpartum women had less anxiety than a group of depressed nonpostpartum women had. Without psychiatric evaluation and diagnosis, true postpartal depression may be missed, or depressive symptoms may be falsely considered as clinical depression. Multiple measurement issues were raised, indicating the difficulty in appropriate diagnosis and subsequent treatment.

Boyd (1990) raised the question of whether the less severe, transitory maternity blues differed from responses during other transitional periods in life, such as bereavement. Affonso (1992) suggested three alternative hypotheses for future research directions: the potentially different nature of postpartal depression necessitates exploration of unique symptom constellations that dictate alternative care; the symptoms of postpartal depression may reflect a distress-coping/adaptation in a plea for help; and motherhood is a developmental process along an emotionally healthy to depressed continuum that changes over pregnancy–postpartum.

Romito (1990) reviewed literature on postpartum depression and the experience of motherhood and found that common experiences of mothers led to a reality of "maternal unhappiness." Romito concluded that it was illegitimate to maintain that postpartum depression is a special category of depression. The medical model of depression has not proved an inner origin of postpartum depression, while psychological and sociological studies have provided evidence linking social conditions and depression (Romito, 1990).

■ 6
The Process of Becoming Acquainted with and Attached to the Infant

Maternal role identity has a behavioral component, role competence, and an affective, motivational component, maternal attachment. In a role identity, role is the external component, and identity is the internal component in the cognitive structure of self (Burke & Tully, 1977). The emotional component of attachment is internalized with identity, but attachment behaviors are external. Maternal attachment is a developmental process beginning during pregnancy and continuing over the months following birth in which the mother forms an enduring affection for and commitment to the child. Following birth, pleasurable bidirectional interaction between mother and infant amplifies and escalates the process (Mercer, 1977a, 1990).

Maternal attachment is different from the commonly used term "bonding," the unidirectional mother-to-infant response shortly following birth (Campbell & Taylor, 1979). Bidirectional interactions occur from birth; the infant's abilities to alert to and track voices, to be quieted with caresses and voice tones, and to maintain eye contact all influence maternal responses.

R. H. Turner (1970) described two kinds of family bonds that develop through the attachment process, identity and crescive bonds. Identity bonds strengthen attaching partners' self-concept, linking bonded persons through shared or complementary qualities. The identification and claiming process discussed below is a beginning linking of family members as the infant is claimed as a part of the family. Crescive, or interaction, bonds develop more slowly in the formation of irreplaceable links between two family members; development of interaction bonds between mother and child form the basis for their continuing relationship after dependency is no longer involved (Turner, 1970). A reinforcement of the maternal identity occurs as mother and infant develop irreplaceable attachment links through both identity and interaction bonds (Mercer, 1983).

As discussed in chapter 4, maternal attachment to a specific child begins during pregnancy as the woman works at her acceptance, involvement, and commitment as a mother (Rubin, 1977, 1984). Cognitive work during the anticipatory stage of role development provides the structure for continuing postpartal maternal attachment. Favorable maternal characteristics for the development of attachment include emotional health (including ability to trust another person); a social support system of partner, friends, and family; a competent level of communication and caretaking skills; a history of being loved and nurtured as a child; proximity to the infant; and maternal–infant fit (e.g., temperament, interactive style, expectations) (Mercer, 1983). (See Cranley (1993) for a review of the origins of the mother–child relationship.)

The infant derives warmth and security from the developing bond (Bretherton, 1992). Interactional attachment behaviors are dynamic and evolve with the child's development.

SENSORY EXPERIENCES IN MATERNAL–INFANT ACQUAINTANCE

Relationships begin with an acquaintance process; information is sought in order to know the other person (Newcomb, 1961). Through acquaintance, the attachment process deepens to form the identification and interaction family bonds described by R. H. Turner (1970). Women work at getting to know the unborn child (Sandelowski & Black, 1994), but following birth they eagerly begin to take in their infants' characteristics visually, by touch, and by holding. Through this active exploration, mothers identify their infants' unique characteristics for future interactions and claim them as part of the family. Mothers sing, coo, and speak to their infants to elicit response.

Visual Contact

> *CS:* There is an eagerness to replace the indirect and inferential sources of information about the child, the various and transitory models and images of pregnancy, with direct observation. There is a visual and tactile hunger for primary observations. (Rubin, 1984, p. 134)

> *H:* Women take in their infants through gazing.

Robson (1967) maintained that eye contact was an innate releaser of maternal caretaking responses. The importance of mothers' gazing at their infants has been validated by the inclusion of the mother's visual contact in observer-rated measures of early maternal–infant interactions, usually with reference to the *en face* position (mother's eyes are on the same vertical plane as her infant's) (e.g., Avant, 1982; Cropley, Lester, & Pennington, 1976; Funke & Irby, 1978; Hayes, 1983; Lobar & Phillips, 1992; Price, 1983).

Three-fourths of observed mothers attempted to get their infants' eyes open; several stated that once their infant looked at them they felt closer to the infant (Klaus et al., 1970). Over one-half (57.63%) of mothers gazed *en face* at their infants during early observation–interaction periods, and 35% of mothers smiled at their infants as they gazed (Govaerts & Patino, 1981). Korean-American mothers spent much time looking at their infants during observation periods; they did not stimulate the infant but held the infant close (Choi, 1986).

All mothers looked at their infants *en face* during the first hour after birth, indicating that the infant's eyes and face are highly attractive to the mother during the first postpartal hour; the actual time was highly variable, with a mean of 23.78 minutes for 97 women (Trevathan, 1983). Women who spent more time in *en face* gazing during the first hour were more likely to speak English as a primary language and to have good relationships with their husbands, and they had positive attitudes.

CS: The woman traumatized by delivery, however, as with a caesarean section, a general anesthetic, or exhaustion from labor has little unbound energy for either fantasy imagery or direct visualization of the child. (p. 134)

H: Women experiencing complications or a cesarean birth do not begin identifying behaviors as early as do those with uncomplicated births.

A case study of a mother separated from her newborn for several days because her complications required intensive care on another unit highlighted the lack of energy available to deal with her infant in early days (Mercer, 1977b). The mother lamented on her first visit to the nursery that it was "hard to look at him and not hold him" (p. 1176); without tactile contact, her acquaintance process proceeded very slowly. A case study of a woman hospitalized for thrombophlebitis after her twins were discharged from the hospital revealed the woman's feelings of guilt and failure at not being able to care for her infants, as well as much concern about her own physical condition (Dickerson, 1981). When she left the hospital, she experienced a sense of powerlessness and lack of control, as others were already skillfully caring for the twins. During the fifth week, the mother was able to begin to identify the twins by specific behaviors and began to cuddle, talk to, and play with them.

A study of 10 mothers whose physical conditions led to separation from their infants for 24 hours or more found that 90% had attachment scores on Cropley and associates' (1976) Maternal Attachment Tool well below 18.5 (Boudreaux, 1981). Cropley and associates found that scores below 18.5 were associated with parenting disorders.

Women who had cesarean births more often had not named their infants (Marut & Mercer, 1979). Naming the infant is a part of identification in the acquaintance–attachment process (Rubin, 1984).

Others reported that parents whose mental representations of their infants' temperament changed dramatically from the third trimester of pregnancy to birth had experienced labor quite differently than they had expected (Zeanah, Keener, Stewart, & Anders, 1985). Their violated expectations with regard to the labor experience was related to the stability of views they held of their infants. A higher rate of child abuse was reported among mothers who had gestational illness and were separated from their infants during the early postpartum (ten Bensel & Paxton, 1977).

Maternal Touch

The tactile experience of touch conveys the infant's intactness, softness, smoothness, and contour. Rubin (1963a, 1984) defined a progression in maternal touch.

> *CS:* Neomaternal touch is hesitant, uncertain, tenuous, and lacks the secure possessiveness of later maternal touch. Neomaternal touch, mostly fingertip touch, is receptive, enquiring, a learning about self and about the other in progressive claiming and binding in to a "we-ness."
>
> Visualization precedes touching. Touch is inhibited if the neonate is wet with amniotic fluid, blood, spilled or expelled food, tears, urine or feces. (1984, p. 139)
>
> In the beginning maternal relationship … there is a definite progression and an orderly sequence in the nature and amount of contact a mother makes with her child. She moves from very small areas of contact to those more extensive. At first only her fingertips are involved, then her hands (including her palms) and then, much later, her whole arms as an extension of her body….
>
> The rate of progression from one predominating form of touch or contact to another is dependent on how she feels about herself in this particular function of her role, on how she perceives her partner's (the infant's) reciprocal response to her, and on the character of the relationship at any given time. All three factors operate in determining the extent to which she dares permit herself to become progressively and more intimately involved. (1963a, pp. 829–830)

H: Maternal touch progresses from finger tip to palmar to embracing with arms over a period of several days.

An orderly progression of maternal touch was observed among mothers of full-term nude infants, from fingertip touch on the infant's extremities that proceeded in 4 to 8 minutes to massaging, encompassing palm contact on the trunk (Klaus et al., 1970). No differences were observed by primiparous, multiparous, or marital status. Mothers of preterm infants who were permitted to touch their infants during the first 3 to 5 days followed the same sequence but at a much slower rate. Mother-to-infant eye contact was particularly important.

Gottlieb (1978) observed the same touch progression over the same time frame as Rubin (1963a) noted, with dressed infants. Cannon (1977) found that all mothers progressed to fingertip touch of the trunk more rapidly when infants were nude than when infants were dressed, but fewer mothers advanced to completely enfolding the infant with arms against the body when infants were nude. No differences in touch progression were observed between primiparas and multiparas. Undressed infants were more active.

This sequence of touch has not been observed in different cultures, including black teenagers (Bampton, Jones, & Mancini, 1981). No evidence of a pattern of touch progression was observed among Hispanic women immediately following birth (Trevathan, 1981). A more typical pattern was cradling or encompassing the infant for the first few minutes with palmar massaging for warmth and respiration; finger exploration of the face, hands, and extremities followed palmar contact when the mother was not distracted. Primiparas spent less time touching their infants than did multiparas but tended to exhibit exploratory behavior more so than multiparas. Women had a natural tendency to place their infants on the left side of their bodies during the first hour following birth (Trevathan, 1982).

Liberian women did not demonstrate an orderly progression of maternal touch during a 10-minute observation the first hour following birth (Olsen, 1982). No mother touched the infant's face or kissed the infant. The most frequent behavior was to look at the infant; however, one-third of the mothers breast-fed their infants without overtures of caressing or cuddling.

No differences in the frequency or type of maternal touching (fingertip or palmar) were observed among Egyptian mothers by 0–18 or 19–96 hours postpartum, regardless of parity, age above or below 28 years, and whether infants were alert or sleepy (Govaerts & Patino, 1981). Egyptian mothers largely used their fingertips to touch their infants, with very little palmar contact observed. The infant's head was the most frequently touched body part, and the hands were the only extremity touched. The researchers hypothesized that mothers might not have progressed in touch as reported by Klaus et al. (1970) because the hospital room was cool, and infants needed several layers of clothing for warmth.

Mothers of newborns did not follow the sequence of fingers, palms, arms, and trunk in handling their newborns, but student nurses did (Tulman, 1985). Initially, mothers tended to use their fingers and palms simultaneously, then their arms and trunk simultaneously in contact with the infant.

Tulman (1986) found that the initial sequence of maternal touch did not differ by type of birth, vaginal or cesarean. Both groups simultaneously used fingers and palms to handle the infant initially, followed by simultaneous use of arms and trunk; both groups touched the trunk, followed by the head, followed by the extremities. Vaginally delivered mothers handled their infants more.

A study of all tactile activities of the mother toward her newborn in feeding or holding situations the 9th or 10th day after birth found differences by the infant's state (awake vs. asleep), feeding versus not feeding, and maternal characteristics (Millot, Filiatre, & Montagner, 1988). Tactile behaviors included stroking the infant's skin, gently scratching the infant's skin, touching the infant's clothes, passing a hand over infant's hair, kissing the infant, and squeezing the infant's hand. Tactile behaviors reached 117 seconds for a 5-minute period when the newborn was asleep, 64.8 seconds when the infant was awake and not feeding, and 43.5 seconds when the infant was feeding. The mother seemed to attach more importance to tactile stimulation when the newborn was nonreceptive.

The duration of tactile behavior was negatively correlated to the newborn's birthweight in feeding observations; mothers may have felt a need to stimulate the smaller babies. During sleep observations, the duration of tactile behavior was negatively related to the number of days between the estimated birth date and actual birth date; mothers who went beyond their due dates used less tactile contact. Greater tactile behavior was demonstrated toward female infants in feeding situations. Mothers squeezed their babies' hands more often when the baby was asleep.

Although the progression of touch was suggested as a universal maternal behavior by Rubin (1963a, 1984) and by Klaus et al. (1970), research has not supported this. Touch may vary by infant's dress as well as culturally.

Maternal Holding

Rubin (1984) emphasized the importance of the mother's being able to hold her infant early following birth for mutually rewarding experiences leading to increasing affectional bonds. She did not suggest a critical period following birth for this to occur, however. The research that followed in relation to early contact dominated all other topics related to the maternal identity for over a decade.

CS: The act of giving birth is not completed for a woman until she can hold her baby. The child remains a phantom, unreal, until he is experienced again and again in the mutually responsive and rewarding holding/cuddling embrace. (p. 108)

The delightful surprises of the child's behavior and expressions contribute exponentially to maternal bonds of affection. (p. 135)

H: There is a positive relationship between holding and interacting with the infant following birth and maternal attachment behaviors.

Klaus and associates (1972) reported that early extended contact with the newborn was associated with maternal behaviors of 14 (13 black, 1 white) low-income teenagers at 1 month. Mothers who had extended contact were reluctant to leave their infants with someone else; they stood and watched during the infant's examination, exhibited more soothing behavior, and engaged in more eye-to-eye contact and fondling. At 1 year, mothers with extended contact did not differ from mothers who did not have this contact in play behavior, but those with extended contact were more responsive to the child's distress (Kennell et al., 1974). At 2 years, five of the extended-contact mothers talked more to their infants than did five of the control mothers (Ringler, Kennell, Jarvella, Navojosky, & Klaus, 1975).

Less separation following birth was associated with greater maternal attachment behaviors at 7 days and 1, 2, and 6 months after birth (Peterson & Mehl, 1978). Primiparas having skin-to-skin and suckling contact during the first hour after birth demonstrated more holding, encompassing, and *en face* behaviors at 36 hours postpartum and more kissing and looking *en face* at 3 months (deChateau, 1976). Primiparas who had extra contact resembled multiparas in their competence in routine care at 36 hours postpartum (deChateau & Wiberg, 1977a). At 3 months, extra contact was associated with breast-feeding among Swedish women (deChateau & Wiberg, 1977b), and Jamaican women who also gazed at and vocalized more with their infants (Ali & Lowry, 1981). However, no differences were observed in U.S. mothers' maternal attachment behaviors on the second postpartum day by whether they were breast-feeding or bottle-feeding (Martone & Nash, 1988).

No effects on maternal attachment behaviors at either 36 hours or 3 months were observed by whether the infant was naked or wrapped during early contact during the first hour following birth (Curry, 1979, 1982). Curry used deChateau's (1976) measure of maternal attachment. Mothers who had their infants rooming in demonstrated closer mother–child relationships as indicated by thoughts about and feelings toward their infants and demonstrated greater competence in caretaking activities during hospitalization (Schroeder, 1977). Infants of mothers who had extra contact with them in the recovery room following birth lost less weight and took more formula for the first 12 feedings (Brodish, 1982).

Kontos (1978) also reported more attachment behaviors among mothers who had extended contact following birth and rooming in. Rooming in was associated with early attachment behavior, measured by Avant's (1982) maternal attachment scale (AMAS), among medically indigent primiparas (Norr, Roberts, & Freese, 1989). Early discharge from the hospital was associated with higher AMAS scores and fewer maternal concerns among low-income mothers (Norr, Nacion, & Abramson, 1989).

Inadequate parenting as measured by reports to protective services for child mistreatment was associated with not rooming in among low-income mothers (O'Connor et al., 1980). Anisfeld and Lipper (1983) reported that extra contact was equally effective for multiparous and primiparous mothers but was particularly effective among women who had less social support.

Early and extended postpartum contact explained 2.4% of the variance in the mother's acceptance of the infant and 2.5% of the variance in consoling the crying infant at 4 months (Siegel, Bauman, Schaefer, Saunders, & Ingram, 1980). At 12 months, only 3.5% of the variance was explained by early contact for infants' positive versus negative behavior.

A carefully controlled study of the effects of extended skin-to-skin contact following birth did not find any significant differences in maternal behavior by contact (Svejda, Campos, & Emde, 1980). Others were unable to support effects of early contact on maternal behavior at 3 days or 1 month (Campbell & Taylor, 1979).

Maternal–infant contact the first 24 hours after birth was associated with maternal confidence during the first week but not at 4 to 6 weeks or 6 months after birth (Sostek, Scanlon, & Abramson, 1982). Mother–infant interaction patterns did not differ by early or later contact at 1 week, 4 to 6 weeks, and 1 year; newborn behavior at 2 days and 4 to 6 weeks and infant development at 1 year did not differ by postpartum contact.

First-time mothers who had interactional contact with their infants the first 2 hours following birth did not differ in their maternal role attainment at 1 year from mothers who did not have this contact (Mercer, Hackley, & Bostrom, 1982). Williams and associates (1987) found that early mother–infant contact in the hospital was unrelated to parenting attachment behaviors at 2 years after birth.

Patterns of progression and regression in maternal feelings and behavior were observed over the first year of motherhood, regardless of the time of first contact with their infants (Stainton, 1986a). At 4 weeks after birth, mothers scored the lowest on maternal–infant interactions than at any other time.

Later contact with infants following birth was associated with higher maternal attachment at 8 months following birth (Mercer & Ferketich, 1990b). Later contact within the current hospital environment usually occurs when the infant needs examination and/or treatment or the mother has general anesthesia for a cesarean birth or other complications. This finding suggests that there is a tendency to form a stronger tie when events around the birth increase the infant's vulnerability.

Summary

Rubin (1994) did not approach the concept of the mother's ability to hold and identify her infant following birth as having long-term effects but as fulfilling her need to get to know the unknown infant to amplify her maternal identity. However, after the Klaus et al. (1972) report suggesting that the early hours following birth were a sensitive period for the development of attachment, a proliferation of research on the long-term effects of the early contact occurred. Perhaps the greatest benefit of the research by Klaus and associates was its impact on removal of hospital restrictions on parental access to newborn infants both in delivery rooms and in nurseries, to allow parents and infants to become acquainted with each other.

Caldwell (1962) cautioned that individual differences made it dangerous to emphasize a critical period for the development of infant attachment; this statement is magnified when speaking of mother–infant attachment. Critical reviews of the research on the effects of early contact agreed that there is no critical period for maternal–infant bonding (Goldberg, 1983; Herbert, Sluckin, & Sluckin, 1982; Meyers, 1984). The wide range of developmental, cognitive, emotional, and coping capacities of the adult suggest an infinite range of abilities to form intimate relationships.

Rubin's observations that the infant's responses increase the mother's bonding exponentially were not formally measured; she described the mothers' obvious joy and pleasure in interacting with their infants. Attachment is a difficult construct to measure, and no one behavior can be taken as evidence of attachment (Campbell & Taylor, 1979; Mercer, 1983). The findings that women with low income and low social support seemed to benefit from extended contact with their infants raises the question of why, because many variables of concern to this group of women also affect their maternal behavior.

Twin Births

Mothers did not view an early separation from one or both twins as detrimental to their long-term relationship despite the emotional trauma around the uncertainty and concern for their babies (Abbink, Bank, Dorsel, Flores, Meyners, & Walker, 1982). Only 5 of 18 mothers described differences in early feelings toward their twins, and the differences were deference and protectiveness toward an ill twin.

Others hypothesized that twin births were associated with an increased incidence of child abuse and neglect (Robarge, Reynolds & Groothuis, 1982); 38 families with twins were matched with 97 single-birth families for maternal age, race, and socioeconomic status, with slightly over 50% on welfare. Seven documented cases of abuse and neglect occurred in the twin-birth families and only two in single-birth families; twin-birth mothers reported that their infants were more difficult to feed than did single-birth mothers. In four of the abusive twin-birth families, a sibling was abused, and in three cases, one twin was abused at 6 months; both twins were abused in two cases at 8 and 12 months. No mention was made of extent of early separation from infants.

Infant's Sex and Holding

Rubin observed that women seemed to respond differently with girls than with boys. Others observations concurred that tactile behaviors were more frequent with girls during feedings (Millot et al., 1988).

> *CS:* A woman is more comfortable, can empathize with and understand a little girl at all ages.... Whether it is maternal distancing or the little boy's angularity, a boy baby tends to be less cuddly after the neonatal period. (Rubin, 1984, p. 105)

H: Mothers cuddle and interact more with girl babies than with boy babies.

Mothers more often avoided touching their male infants for long periods of time than did mothers of female infants (Trevathan, 1981). Mothers of males were more active in exploring their infants.

Differences in mother–infant interaction by baby's sex were found in studies focused on effects of early contact. Mothers were more affectionate toward female infants regardless of whether or not there was early extended contact (Anisfeld & Lipper, 1983).

Extra contact early postpartum was associated with more pronounced behavior differences in boy–mother than in girl–mother pairs (deChateau & Wiberg, 1977b). Mothers who had extended contact looked *en face* at boys more often; mothers without extended contact cleaned their girl infants more often.

Mothers with early extra-contact talked more to female infants, whereas mothers receiving routine care touched female infants and looked *en face* at male infants more (Svejda et al., 1980).

Mixed feelings at birth about the infant's sex was associated with the infant's development of colic (Carek & Capelli, 1981). Mothers who were pleased with their infant's sex had names ready, expressed a sense of achievement, and appeared quite happy.

Verbal Interaction

Rubin did not address the mother's verbalizations to her infant as part of the process in achieving maternal identity. Tomlinson (1990) observed that mothers with highest nonverbal attachment behaviors also were higher in verbal behaviors. Mothers talked to others about their infants and talked to the neonates; as nonverbal attachment scores increased, so did verbal behavior.

Others suggested that use of pronouns in describing newborns was a linguistic component in parental role development (Cogan & Edmunds, 1980). One-fourth of 255 mothers used the neuter pronoun "it" to describe their new baby. Mothers who used "it" were more often multiparous and older and more likely to have attended childbirth classes than were mothers who identified the baby as "he" or "she." Only 4% of first-time mothers referred to their infants as "it" during postpartal hospitalization; 95% referred to "he" or "she," with 1% referring to the infant by name (Mercer, 1986a).

IDENTIFYING AND CLAIMING THE NEONATE

There is no maternal behavior or role without a child. The mother must become acquainted with her infant in order to know how to mother her child and gain competence in the mother role.

Identification Behavior

In the identification process, the mother carefully takes in every detail about the infant. She identifies not only features and characteristics but the infant's ability to function.

> CS: With the birth of the child there is a massive shift in orientation to the child and to herself as mother of this child. There is transition in location of the child from the innermost body space to the external, environmental space, from the child in fantasy to the known real child, from the futuristic "someday, a child" to the immediate present "now, this child of mine." ... The greatest part of the relocation and reorientation is achieved in the first month postpartally, but the binding-in process is not stabilized until the second or third month. (Rubin, 1984, p. 100)
>
> There is a taking-in, cognitively of the child. The whole child, the macroscopic appearance, characteristics, and behaviors, and the rules of conduct in the mother–child subsystem are absorbed through all sensory modalities. There is a cognitive imprinting, the formation of a cognitive map to know everything about this child. There is an eager, appetitive quality to this taking-in behavior....
>
> In duration time, the centered taking-in phase [cognitively of the child] postpartally is equivalent—three weeks—to the preparatory labor phase at the end of pregnancy. (p. 96)
>
> The biological mother experiences the child not only as an individual but as an extension of herself. In action and particularly in feelings there is a highly permeable border between the actions and feelings of the child and the self. (p. 143)

In establishing the identity of the child, the maternal identity in relation to this child is established. In knowing the child there is a knowing of self in relation to the child and a more active, more securely certain behavior with or in behalf of the child. (p. 142)

H: Identification and claiming of the newborn is ongoing over the first month.

Gottlieb (1978) described a discovery process in which women became acquainted with their infants at birth to transform the unknown "strangers" into their babies. The process began in the delivery room and extended through the third and fourth weeks postpartum and was a key to the development of maternal–infant attachment. Three forms of discovery were reported: identifying, relating, and interpreting behaviors. *Identifying* included the mother's pointing out physical characteristics and actions. In *relating*, the identifying behaviors were associated with pregnancy and other familiar events, persons, or objects. The meaning that mothers attributed to the baby's actions and needs was *interpreting* behavior. Identifying behaviors predominated through the first postpartal day, interspersed between long silent periods; relating statements at that time referred largely to the events of pregnancy and family members. By the fourth or fifth day, silent periods had decreased, as the mother talked more to her infant, and interpretative statements increased and became richer in detail. First-time mothers described their infants' appearance, unique responses, good responses, and health or feeding problems when asked to describe their infants during postpartal hospitalization (Mercer, 1986a).

Kennedy (1973) drew on Newcomb's (1961) acquaintance theory in describing the process between mother and newborn as having three components: gaining information about the infant and assessing the infant's response to her, with the infant responses either reinforcing or changing her orientation toward the infant. A positive acquaintance process occurred during the first 2 weeks, when the mother had adequate levels of basic trust, social skill, and emotional–physical strength; mothers with positive experiences also had a rewarding pregnancy, and the infant's responses were positive. The converse led to a negative experience among one-half of the mothers. Mothers who could not trust themselves did not trust their infants as evidenced by comments such as "I think he's a little schemer" (p. 553).

Chao (1979) identified three distinct but complementary cognitive operations used by American mothers in conceptualizing their infants during the first 3 days postpartum—orienting, evaluating, and delineating. Mothers' *orienting* behaviors were ascertaining tentative ideas, expectations, or hypotheses about the newborn. *Evaluating* behaviors were attempts at making value judgments after determining the accuracy or validity of their expectations for the infant. *Delineating* behaviors were the mothers' efforts at differentiating the actual newborn's image from the ideal image they held.

Chao (1983) then studied Chinese mothers to compare their behaviors to American mothers. Orienting behaviors made up 78%; evaluating, 16%; and delineating, 5% of Chinese mothers' cognitive behaviors. The infant's body functions (biological capacities, motor and sensory abilities) were the mothers' major concern, 66% of all of her cognitive efforts. The infant's appearance was the second area of concern for Chinese mothers, 25% of her cognitive behaviors. American mothers used evaluating and delineating behaviors significantly more often than did Chinese mothers. American mothers focused more on physical state and body function than did Chinese mothers.

Korean mothers viewed their infants as more passive and dependent than did American mothers at 2 to 3 days postpartum (Choi & Hamilton, 1986). Korean infants demonstrated a more rapid habituation on the Brazelton Neonatal Behavioral Assessment Scale (BNBAS) (Brazelton, 1973), and American infants demonstrated greater state regulation.

H: The adoptive mother's identification behaviors will differ from the biological mother's.

A comparison of adoptive and biological mothers' feelings and reactions to their infants was more similar than different except in one area (Koepke, Austin, Anglin, & Delesalle, 1991). Two-thirds of birth mothers and 58% of adoptive mothers reported that the first sight of their infants evoked very strong, positive feelings. Two-thirds of adoptive mothers and 54% of birth mothers first felt love for their infants at the initial contact; 8% of adoptive and 13% of birth mothers reported feeling love for their infants before seeing them. When asked what they liked best about their infants, birth mothers focused on the infants' physical features, but adoptive mothers focused more on the fact that the baby was theirs.

CS: Confirmation of the baby's good condition by others affords welcome objectivity and reality testing, but there continues to be an ongoing independent verification of the baby's condition by the mother herself. (Rubin, 1984, p. 133)

H: Mothers test their observations of their newborns with others' observations. (No research found for mothers of normal infants.)

Identification in Twin Births

A study of 10 mothers with twins over the first month reported that mothers developed early relationships with their twins by differentiating their physical characteristics and polarizing their personality characteristics (Anderson & Anderson, 1987). At 1 month, the twins' personalities were described as opposites, and differences in feeding, vocal behaviors, and awareness of the environment were emphasized, rather than similarities. Mothers wanted to give their infants the same amount of attention but treat them differently; they had conflict about their ability to treat them equally and fairly. Leonard (1981) reported that three mothers of identical twins were both fascinated and frustrated by the identical behaviors of their twins.

The identification process continued for mothers of twins over a period of a year through a process of differentiation, polarization, individuation, and maternal justice (Anderson & Anderson, 1990). Differences rather than similarities continued to be the focus; similarities were related to development and sleep and eating patterns. Physical and personality differences were polarized by 4 months. The conclusion was that differences had to be dealt with before similarities, as noted by Fraser (1977). At 4 months, mothers were able to adapt to individual differences and needs of the twins (called individuation by the authors); by 8 and 12 months maternal responses became increasingly individualized.

Claiming the Infant

As the mother identifies her infant, she and other family members attribute familial characteristics to the infant. This behavior indicates an acceptance of the child as a family member.

CS: Each element of appearance and behavior identified in the child is linked and bonded into the self and family systems at the time of discovery in a process of claiming….

Claiming moves the identification process beyond a simple inventory of parts and beyond simple judgments of attractiveness to awareness of the composite of attributes of those persons the woman loves. (Rubin, 1984, p. 135)

H: Women relate identified features of their infants to someone they love.

Robson and Moss (1970) observed that women began to deal with their infants' anonymity by creating a sense that their infants were unique individuals who belonged to them. They often personalized characteristics by relating them to family members (e.g., a temper like their husband's or placidity or hearty appetite like that of different family members). During the first 2 weeks, knowledge gained about the infant's characteristics and family resemblances was greatest on the first day (Maloni, 1994).

Summary

Research supports the woman's drive to become acquainted with and to know her neonate both in appearance and in function during the first week following birth. This drive may be viewed as genotypical or universal, although phenotypical cultural variations occur. Taking in the features of the infant continued over a year for mothers of twins, rather than ending after the neonatal period as suggested for mothers of singles (Rubin, 1984). Is the maternal claiming process facilitated by family members' claiming behaviors? The adoptive mother did not focus on physical characteristics; how do adoptive parents claim their infants as family members?

MATERNAL–INFANT ATTACHMENT

Following birth, the binding-in process of pregnancy continues interdependently with cognitive and behavioral work toward the maternal role identity. The attachment process is ongoing with the identification of the infant.

CS: There is the construction of a stable and constant image of the child as object in external space. And there is an extension, transformation, and elaboration of the maternal bonds and the maternal identity in the present relationship. (Rubin 1984, pp. 133–134)

The child is an experientially known being [after birth]. The complementary "I" in relation to "you" is a maternal identity. The joyously accepted child enhances both the child's and the self's worth, strengthening the bonds between the woman and her child. The responsibility for protecting and caring for the child as "my child," an especially valuable gift and possession, is given added surgence and significance. It is the possessive love that endures during the fourth, postpartum trimester when romantic love dissipates under the pressure of everyone's advocacy of the child and when the enhanced body-self image is replaced by the limited and confined puerperal body-self image. The baby's smile replaces the earlier fetal movement to signal the renewed and reinvigorated commitment in love. (Rubin, 1984, p. 65)

The serenity, induced and shared in the reciprocal relationship between mother and infant, is the substantive bond, the gift given and received each to the other, and the goal to be attained again and again in the maternal identity. (p. 108)

H: Maternal–infant attachment increases during the first month.

Maternal attachment, defined as the extent to which the mother felt her infant held an essential position in her life, developed slowly over 3 months following birth among 54 primiparas (Robson & Moss, 1970). Vague responses, a sense of unreality, and feelings of estrangement were evident in the 4 days of hospitalization, during which nurses did most of the caretaking at a distant room. At their first real contact with their infants, 59% reported positive feelings, 34% said the infant elicited no feelings at all, and 7% had negative feelings. The attachment process did not differ among the 24% who had rooming in. All mothers had difficulty describing their infants during the early days. During their first 3 to 4 weeks at home, mothers reported feeling tired and insecure, with their energies focused on mastering the tasks of infant care and meeting the unpredictable needs of their infants. Many reported fears of harming in handling their infants. The modal mothers began to have positive feelings for their infants during the third week of life, when the babies began to smile. Several noted that it had been easier to feel warmly toward their infants in the hospital than during the first weeks at home. From 4 to 6 weeks was a transitional period, as the women began to feel better physically and gained more confidence in their abilities, and infants' schedules were more predictable. During this period the infant was becoming a person to the mother.

No significant differences were found between high-risk and low-risk mothers' attachment from the first postpartal week to 1 month, although scores were slightly lower at 1 month (Mercer et al., 1987). Experienced and inexperienced mothers' maternal attachment means were significantly lower at 1 month than in the first week postpartal (Mercer & Ferketich, 1994a).

The mother's previous experience with infants and her prenatal expectations about her ability to interpret her infant's signals predicted her postpartal confidence in mothering and postpartal attachment (Williams et al., 1987). Stainton (1986a) concluded that the origins of attachment were in the embedded cultural meanings and embodied experiences. Multiparas' value on success and achievement led to a project-like, cognitive orientation toward pregnancy and child rearing, which was transformed during the first 8 weeks after birth by the transactional experiences with the baby that were pleasurable and satisfying. These feelings were motivational for giving time and energy.

Robson and Moss's (1970) report seems congruent with Rubin's observations, and appears to reflect a passivity related to medications during labor. Evidence does not support maternal attachment increases during the first month postpartum.

> *CS:* At the end of pregnancy there is a developed strong attachment to the unborn infant.... There is an inordinately high cost of investment and commitment to the child in labor and delivery. In the pleasure of the birth of a perfect child, she will assert that the high cost "was worth it." There will be many times, particularly in the first postpartal month, when she will reconsider and be dubious about the value of that investment. However, the bonds created by involvement, identification and commitment formed during pregnancy secure the fabric of the relationship. (Rubin, 1977, p. 69)

H: Attachment to the unborn child is predictive of maternal–infant attachment during the first postpartal month.

Cranley (1981a) found no relationship between maternal perceptions of the neonate as an indicator of maternal attachment and fetal attachment. Others found that that fetal attachment at 32 weeks gestation explained 13% of the variance in attachment to the infant 24 hours after birth, but no relationship was found at 3 months (Reading et al., 1984). Researcher-developed adjective checklists were used to measure maternal attachment.

Positive significant relationships between maternal–fetal attachment (according to the Cranley [1981a] MFAS) at 35 to 40 weeks gestation and maternal–infant interactive behaviors on the second and third postpartum days were observed (Fuller, 1990). Interactive behaviors were measured by the Nursing Child Assessment Feeding Scale (NCAFS) (Barnard, 1978) and the Funke-Furber (1978) Mother–Infant Interaction.

Fetal attachment explained 3.3% of maternal attachment, measured by Leifer's (1980) Feelings About My Baby (FAB) scale, among multiparous mothers and 10.6% among primiparous mothers at early postpartal hospitalization (Mercer & Ferketich, 1994a). At 1 month, fetal attachment explained 7% of the variance in primiparous mothers' attachment to their infants but was not a predictor for multiparous mothers.

Fetal attachment explained 6.8% of the variance in high-risk women's maternal infant attachment (FAB scale) at early postpartal hospitalization and 1.7% of the variance for low-risk women (Mercer & Ferketich, 1990b). At 1 month, fetal attachment was no longer explanatory for high-risk women but explained 2.4% of the variance for low-risk women (Mercer et al., 1987).

Attempts at promoting postpartal attachment through antenatal intervention have been mixed. Carter-Jessop (1981) demonstrated that increasing the mother's acquaintance with her infant during pregnancy, by pointing out body parts and fetal responses to maternal movement, was related to postpartal attachment. Carson and Virden (1984) did not find significant differences in postpartal attachment behaviors when replicating Carter-Jessop's intervention prenatally; however, they observed that Caucasian mothers talked more to the baby, touched the baby's trunk, and used their palms more than did black mothers. Others were unable to find significant differences replicating Carter-Jessop's intervention using Cranley's (1981a) MFAS and Avant's (1982) AMAS postpartally (Davis & Akridge, 1987).

> *CS:* The process [binding-in] is active, intermittent and accumulative, and occurs in progressive stages over a period of 12–15 months. The origin and end-point of the process are in the maternal identity itself.
>
> Maternal identity and binding-in to the child are two major developmental changes, each dependent on the other, in the three trimesters of pregnancy and the two trimesters following delivery of the child. (Rubin, 1977, p. 67)
>
> Binding-in in affiliative attachment to the child and the formation of a maternal identity are interdependent coordinates of the same process. (Rubin, 1984, p. 51)

H: There is a positive relationship between the maternal attachment and maternal competence components of maternal role identity.

On the first postpartal day there was no relationship of affectionate behaviors to caretaking behaviors, measured by Avant's Maternal Attachment Assessment Scale (Avant, 1981). On the third postpartal day, a significant negative relationship was observed ($r = -.449$).

Significant but modest correlations between observed maternal competence (measured by a revised M. Blank's [1964] scale) and attachment (measured by Leifer's [1980] FAB scale) were noted at 1 ($r = .28$), 8 ($r = .21$), and 12 months following birth ($r = .19$) (Mercer et al., 1982). Walker et al. (1986a) found an interdependence between primiparas' relationship with their infants and their self-confidence in the caregiving role at 6 weeks postpartum; however, the relationship was not observed among multiparas. Mercer and Ferketich (1994a) reported significant relationships between maternal competence, measured by Gibaud-Wallston and Wandersman's (1978) Parental Sense of Competence Scale (PSOC), and maternal attachment (measured by FAB) for both primiparas and multiparas at early postpartal hospitalization, 1, 4, and 8 months. Correlations for primiparas from the first week to 8 months were .55, .62, .46, and .39. Correlations for multiparas for the same test periods were .34, .38, .45, and .56.

The interdependence between maternal attachment (on the FAB scale) and maternal competence (on the PSOC) was also observed among women hospitalized for a high-risk pregnancy and women having a normal pregnancy (Mercer & Ferketich, 1994b). The correlations of the two variables for high-risk women at 1 week and 1, 4, and 8 months were .36, .49, .47, and .45. Among women having normal pregnancies, correlations for the same periods were .53, .54, .45, and .52.

By 1 month postpartum, maternal confidence, attachment, emotional state, and adaptation to the maternal role were strongly linked (Williams et al., 1987). Evidence at 2 years after birth supported the interrelationships of maternal confidence and the development of maternal attachment.

Summary

Coffman's (1992) review of parent–infant attachment from 1981 to 1990 identified four theoretical frameworks that were used: Ainsworth's (1973), Bowlby's (1969), Klaus and Kennell's (1982), and Rubin's (1975, 1977). Ainsworth and Bowlby focused on infant to mother attachment, and Klaus and Kennell's focus was the early affectionate attachment the mother forms to her infant. Rubin's framework is unique in addressing pregnancy as the time of beginning maternal attachment.

Research supports the interdependence of the emotional and behavioral components of maternal role identity as described by Rubin. The mother becomes acquainted with her infant following birth, identifies unique characteristics of her infant in order to identify her role in interaction with the infant, and claims the infant within her family context.

CHANGE IN MATERNAL PERCEPTIONS OF THE NEONATE

> *CS:* There are so many changes during the first week in the appearance and tonus of the newborn that it is difficult to establish what is a temporary and transient feature and what is a true, permanent feature.
>
> ... the irrationality of the neonate's behaviors can be overwhelming, producing rigid and inflexible maternal behaviors, or producing premature and antipathetic polarization between mother and infant. (Rubin, 1984, p. 105)

H: Maternal perceptions of the neonate change as the neonate changes.

The Neonatal Perception Inventories (NPI), administered at 1 to 2 days (NPI-I) and 4 weeks (NPI-II) following birth (Broussard & Hartner, 1971), have been used extensively to test maternal perceptions of the neonate. The assumption underlying the NPI was the American cultural emphasis on being better than average; thus, mothers who perceive their children as above average will respond accordingly, affecting the children's behavior by a more positive response. The mother rates her perception of an average baby on six items (e.g., crying, spitting up, or vomiting) and then rates her perception of her baby on the same items. Scores are summed, and her baby's score is subtracted from the average baby score; a score of 0 or a negative number is considered high-risk, and a score of +1 or greater is considered low-risk. Changes were observed in maternal perception of the firstborn during the first month of life; 40% of mothers did not view their infants positively at 1 month (Broussard & Hartner, 1971). Infants who were not viewed positively needed therapeutic intervention at age 4H years more often than did infants who were viewed positively. The NPI-I was not associated with subsequent child development at age 4H years.

Palisin (1980) was unable to replicate Broussard and Hartner's (1971) findings; she found that 33% of the children she followed to age 4H years had problems, but no relationship between the problems and earlier maternal perceptions was found. Broussard (1979) assumed that the NPI were projective measures because the items were ambiguous stimuli; although this may have been true in the early 1960s, when the instrument was first developed and mothers were allowed very limited contact with infants, it was not true in the late 1970s (Palisin, 1981).

No differences were observed between rooming-in and non-rooming-in mothers' perceptions of their infants for either the NPI-I or the NPI-II; both groups viewed their infants positively (Lotas & Willging, 1979). Mothers who had natural childbirth viewed their infants significantly more positively than mothers who did not, but no differences were observed by bottle- or breast-feeding.

Women who participated in Lamaze childbirth classes scored no differently on NPI-I 1 day postpartum from women who did not take the classes (Croft, 1982). At 1 month, women who did not take classes scored significantly higher on NPI-II than did women taking classes.

Women who rated their infants positively on both NPI-I and NPI-II scored significantly higher in gratification in the mothering role and maternal–infant attachment at 8 months after birth than did mothers whose infants were rated as average or below on both inventories (Mercer, 1986a). Women who rated their infants positively on NPI-I and NPI-II scored higher on observed maternal behavior than did those who changed from positive to negative or who rated infants as average or below on both inventories. At 1 year, no significant differences were observed by NPI-I and NPI-II and maternal behaviors.

Perry (1983) reported no relationship between NPI and infant behavior. Maternal perceptions increased among mothers having a structured interaction with their infants 1 week after the intervention; however, no differences were observed at 4 weeks after the structured intervention, indicating that all mothers became more sensitized to their infants through caretaking. Others reported short-term effects of mothers' increasing awareness of behavioral potential of both term and preterm infants; mothers of term infants receiving intervention reported significantly more infant behaviors 2 to 4 days after discharge, and mothers of preterm infants at 8 days after birth (Riesch & Munns, 1984).

Women's self-concept (TSCS) during pregnancy was not significantly related to NPI-I or NPI-II (Lee, 1982). However, all women who had negative scores on both self-concept and NPI also had negative scores on at least two subscales of the Michigan Screening Profile of Parenting Scale.

L. A. Hall (1980) provided information about infant behavior to an experimental group of women 2 to 4 days after their discharge from the postpartal unit. At 1 month, the group of women who received the infant information reported less favorable perceptions of normal infants and significantly more positive perceptions of their own infants on the NPI-II. The slight change among mothers in the control group toward more positive perceptions was not significant. The two groups of women did not differ on the NPI-I. Maternal perceptions of the neonate change during the first month and input from professionals can enhance this change.

CS: There is no experience of the neonate to provide even a familiarity with his appearance, size, functional behavior, and personality at birth. (Rubin, 1984, p. 105)

H: Fantasies about and experiences with the unborn baby have no relationship to maternal perceptions of their infants after birth.

Upper-middle-class parents had stable perceptions of their infants' temperament as measured by a modified Infant Temperament Questionnaire (Carey & McDevitt, 1978) from the third trimester of pregnancy until after birth of their infants (Zeanah et al., 1985). During pregnancy vivid abstract personality traits were attributed to their infants. When the study was replicated with teenage mothers, their perceptions of their unborn infants' temperament remained largely stable from 32 to 36 weeks gestation. Few changes were observed from pregnancy to 1 month postnatally (Zeanah, Keener, & Anders, 1986). Mothers rated their infants significantly more adaptable at 1 month.

Neither self-concept nor anxiety measured during pregnancy were related to adolescents' temperament ratings of their infants during pregnancy; prenatal anxiety was not related to infant behavior as measured on the BNBAS (Brazelton, 1973) or to mothers' ratings of infant temperament following birth at 1 month (Zeanah et al., 1986). More anxious mothers had infants who oriented better. Avant (1981) observed that mothers with higher anxiety scored lower on early postpartal attachment measured by her maternal attachment assessment scale (Avant, 1982).

Prenatal fantasies and maternal conflicts structured the postnatal relationship through effects on perception of the infant as an individual, the infant's psychological "usefulness" and narcissistic meaning for the mother as a woman, and the self-esteem of the mother (Ainslie, Solyom, & McManus, 1982). For a healthy relationship to evolve the mother had to either direct her prenatal feelings to fit with her infant or force her infant into prenatally determined perceptions.

CS: The neonate looks but does not see.... The gazing is nonperceptive—perception requires a framework of experience and cognition—but provides contented pleasure. (Rubin, 1984, p. 106).

The newborn is asocial. (p. 101)

Mahler, Pine, and Bergman (1975) described the neonatal period as a phase of primary narcissism "marked by the infant's lack of awareness of a mothering agent" (p. 42). Mahler et al. maintained that "although the autistic phase is characterized by relative absence of cathexis of external stimuli, this does not mean that there can be no responsiveness of external stimuli" (p. 43). During this sleepy stage, physiological rather than psychological processes are dominant.

The school of thought holding that the infant is asocial does not assume that the infant is either prosocial or antisocial but that infants' natures are determined by what they encounter and their reactions to encounters, rather than by predispositions to act in certain ways (Burr, Leigh, Day, & Constantine, 1979). As the focus of this book is not infant competencies, only brief counterarguments to these concepts are presented. It is important that mothers be informed about infant competencies because they interact with and stimulate their infants according to their beliefs about the infants' abilities (Snyder, Eyres, & Barnard, 1979).

The infant has the organization and ability to connect actively with the social and physical world soon after birth, preferring some stimuli over others, and is able to process novel information in a regular and predictable manner (Anders, 1994, citing Stern, 1985). In order to maintain homeostasis the infant is dependent on active participation in both biological and social regulation.

Long-term studies of individuals have shown that they have inborn characteristics that influence their responses to situations in a consistent manner, known as temperament. McClowry's (1992) review presents major concepts adhered to by temperament theorists and by nursing research on temperament.

Bell (1974) reviewed research that supported the infant's balance of control in selectively reinforcing parental behavior; he argued that the infant is in one sense more competent than the young, inexperienced parent. G. C. Anderson (1989) presented supporting research for her argument that the mother and her newborn are mutual psychophysiological caregivers. Brazelton and Als (1979) reported evidence of affective and cognitive responses by the infant in the immediate period after delivery, despite the physiological task of achieving homeostasis. They observed that the infant soon organizes reflex behavioral responses into more complex patterns of behavior.

Immediately following birth, infants alert to the human voice and track the voice, preferring rhythmic, higher-pitched voices (Brazelton, 1979). From the first day of life, the newborn is capable of precise and sustained movement in synchrony with adult speech (Condon & Sander, 1974). Infants prefer the human face over other objects and also complex patterns, moving objects, bright colors, and contour changes (Blackburn, 1983). Infants begin to imitate adult facial gestures of mouth opening and tongue protrusion within 1 to 71 hours (Meltzoff & Moore, 1983). Infants recognize milk odors over water odors at birth and within a few days have learned to recognize the mother's odor, indicated by a preference for her breast pad (Porter, Cernoch, & Perry, 1983), and breast and axillary secretions (Porter, Makin, Davis, & Christensen, 1992). Increasing evidence supports the concept that newborns begin interactive behaviors soon after birth and that this stimulation fosters their cognitive and social development.

SUMMARY

Much research supports the theory that the new mother's visual, tactile, and holding sensory experiences with her infant foster her acquaintance with her newborn through identification and claiming processes. Rubin's described touch progression has not been supported; the progression either proceeded much more rapidly or all types of touch were used initially.

Variations in identification were described in the special case of twins. The extended identification period indicates the complexity of identifying twins and the mother's problem in differentiating two infants. The one study comparing adoptive mothers with biological mothers indicates the need for further investigation as to how adoptive mothers identify and claim their infants as family members.

Research on the effects of maternal–infant contact the first hours after birth on maternal bonding behavior dominated the field for well over a decade. Although attachment behaviors were delineated for this early period, measurement of attachment as a process remains problematic. Evidence supports an ongoing process of attachment with identification and claiming. Attachment behaviors tend to vary by situation, infant state and response, cultural customs, and the mother's physical and mood state. Time samplings of behavior do not indicate the depth of emotional commitment in the attachment process. Mothers' self-reported attachment is easily obtained; however, less than ideal reliabilities of the measures may indicate that mothers are giving socially acceptable answers. The Neonatal Perception Inventories have been overused.

Qualitative research is needed to capture the mother's perceived change in her infant's interactive responses and appearance and what these changes mean to her as a mother. Why, for example, would self-reported attachment on the Feelings About My Baby scale be lower at 1 month than at 1 week?

■ 7
Working Toward Maternal Competence Early Postpartum

The cognitive work of identifying infant cues and testing behavioral skills to respond to cues builds on the cognitive restructuring begun in pregnancy of visualizing self as mother and developing feelings of competence (Deutsch et al., 1988; Leifer, 1980; Rubin, 1984). The image of the maternal self constructed during pregnancy is enlarged and refined through continued information seeking and interacting with the infant. The extent of congruity between a mother's anticipation and idealization about the mother role with her actual experiences has an impact on how smoothly her adjustment will proceed (Thornton & Nardi, 1975).

In the formal stage of maternal role identity the woman adheres largely to the expectations of social consensus in the mother role, following directives of experts until she gains some proficiency. Role models are sought, and their behavior is replicated. The role models' styles are tested against the mother's values and attitudes and in interaction with her infant. She gradually begins to differentiate her style and her behavior from that of models, moving into the informal stage of role attainment. The informal stage of role identity overlaps with the formal stage as the woman builds a repertoire of parenting behavior.

The mother's skill, sensitivity, empathic responses, and nurturing behaviors that promote the infant's health and development reflect her maternal role *competence*. Because all behavior originates in the mind (Rubin, 1984) the mother's attitudes and values influence her behavior. Achieving maternal synchrony with the infant's behavioral state and responses is central to competence. The mother's perception of her competence in the maternal role reflects her *confidence* in the mothering role.

This chapter focuses on the development of maternal role competence during the formal stage of maternal role identity, lasting about a month for most women. Informal-stage behaviors (differentiation) occur in some facets of maternal role behavior simultaneously with formal-stage (replication) behaviors in other facets. A discussion of the end of the neo-maternal period, with the mother's polarization from the infant, concludes the chapter.

SYNCHRONIZING MATERNAL BEHAVIOR WITH INFANT STATE

The success of the woman's early maternal role behaviors, such as feeding, is dependent on her responsiveness to the infant's state. The first 2 H months following birth were described as a period of initial adaptation, in which the mother learns to synchronize her mothering activities with her infant's cues of his state (Sander, 1962). The extent to which this mutuality is established depends in part on the balance the mother is able to maintain between her empathy for what she feels are the infant's needs and her objectivity in seeing the infant as a separate individual.

Infant states of consciousness or arousal range from deep sleep, light sleep, awake/drowsy to quiet alert, active alert, and crying. Infants control the quantity and type of input from the environment through their state of consciousness. During the first month, infants adapt their mobility and state behavior to a sensitive environment that meets their needs (Brazelton, 1979). The adequacy of infants' self-organization is reflected by their abilities to quiet themselves or to elicit stimulation. Mothers facilitate infants' organization of state by expanding the quiet, alert, and sleep states and by helping infants regulate transitions between states (Brazelton & Als, 1979); this requires a learned sensitivity and competence.

Development of Mother–Infant Synchrony

De Chateau's (1977) review of research focused on the neonatal period for the development of mother–infant synchrony included maternal behavior, feeding experiences, sex of infant, infant's capacities and soothability, the environment, and disadvantages at birth. He emphasized flexibility in working with families because of the vast difference in infant and parent characteristics.

> *CS:* The developed capacity to read nonverbal behavior as a message cue of the child's inner status in situational experience leads to a knowing of the child in an uncommon but highly characteristic maternal intelligence. Since all cues are direct, personal messages in communication of inarticulate feelings, there is sensitivity and responsiveness, one to the other. The maternal woman responds in ego strength with lifesaving or life-enriching actions. The child in turn responds to the maternal cues of pleasure-displeasure, approval-disapproval, within the limits of his capacities for action. (Rubin, 1984, p. 140)

H: There is an interactional effect between maternal behavior and infant responses.

At 1 and 3 months after birth, neonatal irritability (Brazelton's [1973] NBAS) was associated with required time to calm; however, fussing and crying were associated with unresponsive maternal attitudes and behavior, rather than neonatal irritability (Crockenberg & Smith, 1982). No significant predictors of fuss/cry emerged at 1 month, but neonatal irritability was linked to greater maternal responsiveness to female than to male infants. At 3 months, firstborn infants, whose mothers were less responsive and had less flexible attitudes, fussed and cried more. These circular effects were expressed by Benedek (1970); the mother "introjects the memory trace: frustrated child = inefficient, frustrating, bad mother = bad self" (p. 116).

A comparison of 12 mothers of infants with colic and 12 mothers of infants without colic at 7 weeks after birth found that mothers with colicky infants reported more bodily dysfunction, fears, disordered thinking, depression, anxiety, fatigue, hostility, and impulsive thoughts and actions and stronger feelings of personal inadequacy or inferiority (Pinyerd, 1992). Mothers with colicky infants also reported their infants' cries as more grating, urgent, distressing, and irritating and their being more angry, alarmed, and frustrated when listening to their infants' cries than did mothers of noncolicky infants.

Infant crying at 6 weeks after birth was associated with their mothers' rating them more negatively and reporting greater feelings of maternal inadequacy (Wilkie & Ames, 1986). Using a general systems theory framework, 20 mother–infant pairs were studied for stability in the mother–infant relationship at 2, 3, 4, and 5 weeks of age in areas of feeding, changing or bathing, social attention, and baby alone (measure developed for study) (Thoman, Acebo, & Becker, 1983). Maternal interactional stability was associated with low levels of infant crying during social attention but not in feeding, changing, or baby alone. Mothers of more alert and responsive newborns (measured by Brazelton NBAS) were more responsive and sensitive mothers (Osofsky, 1976). Newborn behavioral styles were consistent across situations, with male infants more responsive to auditory stimulation than females; maternal attentiveness and sensitivity toward the infant were related to infant visual, auditory, and tactile behaviors (Osofsky & Danzger, 1974).

The most frequent source of maternal confidence and uncertainty at 30 and 90 days after birth was the infant's mood—happiness or contentment (Bullock & Pridham, 1988). Other frequent sources of maternal confidence at both test periods were the infant's response to care and his physical well-being and maternal success in dealing with concerns and managing care. These findings reflect Benedek's (1970) observation, "Now, observing her child whose smile is her reward, whose crying is her punishment, her self-concept expands through the gratifying introject: good, thriving infant = good mother, good self" (p. 117).

Pridham (1987) used four facets of Lewin's (1951) life space concept—encountered change (areas of life space that are important), desired change (goals), difficult things (repelling forces), and satisfying things (attracting forces)—to study the relationship of 83 mother–newborn infant dyads. The instrument What Being the Parent of a New Baby Is Like (WPL) by Pridham and Chang (1985) was used. During the first week, life-space changes occurred most often and were largely focused on socioemotional maternal qualities such as sense of pride or fulfillment. Life-style was the second greatest change. At 1 and 3 months, life-style was the greatest change and focused on the mother's greater role at home, caretaking, and pattern of daily activities. Lack of resources, especially time, was the second greatest change at 1 month. Initially, mothers' goals included reality-bound circumstances and their socioemotional qualities, but at 1 and 3 months, themes of desired change were largely reality-bound circumstances. The attracting forces through this period were maternal perceptions of the infant's growth and development, infant care tasks, and interactions.

F. B. Roberts (1983) studied the effects of obligatory infant behavior on ease of transition to parenthood (using Hobbs's [1965] Crisis Checklist), perceived role competence, self-esteem (Rosenberg, 1965), and perception of the infant (NPI) from a theoretical framework based on role theory and symbolic interactionism. Obligatory infant behavior had negative effects on perceptions of maternal role competence (measures developed for the study), NPI, and ease of transition to the parent role. Role competence was not related to self-esteem, but perception of the infant (NPI) had positive effects on self-esteem; women who viewed their infants as above average had more positive self-esteem.

Summary

These studies reflect the mother's dependence for self-esteem on infant responses in early interactions; her self-esteem fosters her sense of competence. The mother's first few weeks of mothering are particularly vulnerable because she is still replicating much behavior and has not found the fit or mutuality with her infant.

When early mothering was viewed from Lewin's (1951) concept of psychological life space (congruent with Rubin, 1984), the attracting forces of the child's development seemed to offset the repelling forces, such as change in life-style, as women merged their earlier thinking with reality.

The scant evidence about the development of maternal–infant synchrony during the first month indicates that for the majority it had not developed yet; Sander (1962) stated that its development took up to 2H months. The development of maternal–infant synchrony depends on the mother's seeing the infant as a separate individual. In the studies of infants with colic and of infants' irritability, the mothers' symptoms are similar to the infants'; had these mothers differentiated their infants from themselves? Can this differentiation or polarization (Rubin, 1984) process be assisted by others?

Newberger's (1980) theory of parental awareness (the organized knowledge system used to make sense out of the child's responses and behavior and to decide on parental action) helps explain the mother's learning process and where she is in her first weeks in the role. Parental awareness develops in sequential stages through transformation of the cognitive structure in interaction with the environment—from initial immature stages of ability to consider only limited aspects of experience to more mature stages, characterized by the ability to utilize and recognize a more comprehensive range of information. At more mature stages, awareness of deeper facets of the child and of more complex parent–child interactions are reached, leading to greater flexibility in resolving parenthood tasks.

Mutuality of Child and Maternal Identity

As the mother gets to know her child, she becomes more comfortable in her identity as mother. The interaction between the maternal self-image and infant responses affect the evolving maternal identity.

> *CS:* In establishing the identity of the child, the maternal identity in relation to this child is established. In knowing the child there is a knowing of self in relation to the child and a more active, more securely certain behavior with or in behalf of the child. (Rubin, 1984, p. 142)

H: There is a positive relationship between maternal competence and maternal assessment of her child.

Flagler (1988) reported significant correlations between distances between primiparas' ratings of ideal mothers and themselves as mothers (measured by a semantic differential scale [Flagler, 1989]) and maternal anxiety and infant behavioral style. Mothers with less maternal competence and higher anxiety more often had infants described as difficult. One-half of the mothers received information about their infants' behavior during postpartal hospitalization; no significant differences in maternal competence or anxiety was observed by whether the mother received extra information.

Parenting confidence was central to adaptation to motherhood from pregnancy to 1 month postpartum to 2 years (Williams et al., 1987). The mother's previous experience with infants and her prenatal expectations about her ability to interpret her infant's signals predicted her postpartal confidence in mothering. Pridham and Chang (1992) found a significant relationship between mothers' competence in problem solving and their evaluation of their parenting during the first month.

Kang (1986) described a construct of parental competence operationalized by measures of cognitive and behavioral functioning. Cognitive functioning was significantly related to maternal behavior, measured by both Caldwell's (1970) Home Observation for Measurement of the Environment (HOME) and Barnard's Nursing Child Assessment Teaching Scale (NCATS). Conclusions were that knowledge may provide the foundation for maternal stimulation measured on the HOME, and that understanding children's participation in social interaction contributes to interactions during teaching observations.

Mothers' perceptions of their infants' temperaments explained 26% of the variance in their perceived problem-solving competence at 1 and 3 months (Pridham, Chang, & Chiu, 1994). Their infants' temperaments had more influence on mothers' parenting evaluations at 1 month than at 3 months. Amenability (infant's soothability, positive mood, ease of diversion from crying, and regularity of feeding and sleeping) was the most consistent temperament predictor of both parenting evaluation and problem-solving competence.

Although special teaching about neonatal behavior at 2 weeks after birth enhanced mothers' knowledge of infant behavior at 4 weeks, maternal confidence (measure developed for study) in interpreting behavioral cues of their infants was not increased (Golas & Parks, 1986). Mothers expected and had observed infant behaviors measured on the Brazelton's (1973) NBAS but were unaware of the purposeful nature of the infant behavior (e.g., response decrements to stimuli and finger sucking) (Riesch, 1979).

Although no differences were observed in adjustment to the maternal life style at 3 weeks between women who received a special teaching program at 3 days after birth and those who did not, 50% of the mothers who had fussy babies were less satisfied and more anxious about mothering than were mothers whose babies were not fussy (Brouse, 1988). Maternal concern and life-style adjustment were measured by Ellis and Hewat's (1982) revision of Schaefer and Mannheimer's (1960) Postnatal Research Inventory.

Donaldson's (1991) review of nursing intervention research to enhance maternal adaptation found that economically and educationally advantaged women appeared to benefit more than others, indicating that social and interpersonal skills are necessary to benefit when intervention occurs in groups. Individual intervention is needed to effect change in economically and educationally disadvantaged women's cognitive functioning.

Finding ways of presenting information that leads to cognitive change and maternal behavioral change is important. Twenty percent of 193 mothers responded during pregnancy that they did not know what they expected their infants to be like (Snyder et al., 1979). No relationships were found between the Brazelton NBAS and expectations of mothers on the second day postpartum or between mothers' expectations and babies' gestational age and neurological status. However, mothers who did not expect their infants to see, hear or be aware of surroundings or to need verbal stimulation from birth provided a significantly less stimulating environment at 4, 8, and 12 months (Caldwell's [1970] HOME).

Role-supplementation classes during pregnancy did not enhance role-taking skill postpartally, but mothers who had classes had less anxiety postpartally (Meleis & Swendsen, 1978). Rutledge and Pridham (1987) tested whether in-hospital preparation enhanced maternal competence for infant feeding and care during early postpartum. The preparation was beneficial for bottle-feeding mothers; however, adequate provision for rest was the greatest benefit to breast-feeding mothers. Thus, environmental effects need to be studied with teaching effects. Bull and Lawrence (1985) found that mothers were using much of the information provided in the hospital during the first 3 weeks at home. Particularly, information about physical self-care and infant feeding and behavior were useful; mothers felt they needed more information about infant behavior. Mothers of either first or male infants had many more questions during the first 6 weeks postpartum (Sumner & Fritsch, 1977).

Summary

Evidence supports the relationship between perceived maternal competence and maternal assessments of infants. However, most of the research focused on intervention measures to foster maternal competence during the puerperium. Findings about the effectiveness of these interventions were mixed. Bromwich (1976) stressed the need to work within a developmental progression in maternal behavior: the mother must first enjoy being with her infant; she may then observe and respond to cues accurately; this is followed by increased maternal action in mutually satisfying interaction that enhances communication, movement to maternal awareness of suitable stimulation for her infant's level of development, to the initiation of new experiences suggested or modeled for her, and finally, to independently developing a wide range of activities appropriate for and interesting to the infant. It seems a first intervention is to foster the mother's ability to enjoy interacting with her infant. Mothers who need help the most (those who are economically and educationally deprived) appear to benefit the least from intervention programs. This indicates that such programs have been constructed without adequate consideration of the life-space reality of these populations.

FEEDING: DEVELOPMENT OF A MATERNAL ROLE SKILL

Major concerns of mothers phoning for information during the first 4 weeks after birth were feeding, maternal problems, and infant crying (Elmer & Maloni, 1988). Pridham's (1981) review of literature on parents' adaptation in areas of infant feeding and care stressed the need for anticipatory care that fosters development of problem-solving skills. The process of feeding also involves the mother's making decision rules about patterning feedings, starting the feedings, maintaining the feeding once it is under way, terminating it, and responding to events such as the infant's drowsiness (Pridham, Knight, & Stephenson, 1989). Mothers often think of themselves as either taking charge of the feeding, accommodating to the infant's regulation of the feeding, or negotiating, with mother and infant mutually directing the feeding. Mothers of 11-week-old infants more often gave rules external to the infant as reasons for initiating feeding, but ended the feeding based on the infant's responses (Pridham, 1988).

> *CS:* The giving and receiving of food is the primary vehicle of direct action-interaction. Feeding becomes the criterion of self-esteem as mother of this child and of the goodness of fit in this relationship.
>
> In the asymmetry of the power relationship, her own capacities and competence in giving at each episode of action-interaction is critical,

and the response of the newborn serves as the basis of self-evaluation. (Rubin, 1984, p. 136)

The neomaternal woman works intensely to achieve goodness of fit in the feeding interaction.... The earnestness with which a woman approaches and works at achieving a goodness of fit feeding interaction makes her particularly sensitive to failure and rejection. The infant's refusal of the nipple, to take food, or to burp is perceived with dismay. If the infant eats well for another but does not eat well for her, this is perceived as personal rejection. (p. 137)

The third neonatal and postpartal day is not conducive to the goodness of fit in the feeding relationship. Either or both the woman and child have major physiological changes that preempt attention and militate against successful action-interaction. (p. 138)

The more personally involved the role and the more intimate the relationship, the more significantly food serves as a means of reflective, reinforced self-esteem. (Rubin, 1967c, p. 195)

H: The mother's self-esteem is positively related to the infant's feeding response. (No research.)

H: There is a relationship between maternal anxiety and infant responses.

Blank (1986) studied early psychophysiologic mother–infant interaction by assessing the relationship of maternal anxiety and perception and changes in infant satiety, anxiety, and feeding behavior among 65 bottle-feeding mothers. Mothers' perceptions of infant tenderness needs was measured by Blank's (1985) Infant Tenderness Scale (BITS); anxiety was measured by Spielberger and associates' (Spielberger, Gorsuch, Lushene, Vagg, & Jacobs, 1983) State-Trait Anxiety Inventory. Infant serum glucose was used to measure satiety and serum cortisol to measure degree of anxiety. Mild maternal anxiety levels at feeding time were associated with increased formula intake and decreased cortisol after feeding (indicative of a feeling of security). Extremely low maternal anxiety at feeding time was related to decreased formula intake and increased cortisol (indicative of a feeling of insecurity). Thus, extremely low maternal anxiety is a threat to an infant, whereas mild anxiety does not appear to pose a problem. The mother's BITS scores were not related to her infant's glucose, cortisol, or feeding behavior but were related to her own anxiety levels.

Mothers who were highly anxious had more delivery complications and babies that were more often dysmature and slow to suckle (Barnett & Parker, 1986). Both problems were interpreted as consequences of anxiety levels.

H: Competence in feeding increases after the third postpartal day and continues over the postpartum period.

Most mothers did not perceive the infant's subtle feeding cues during the first 3 days after birth (Thoman, 1975). Multiparous mothers were more sensitive than primiparous mothers, with infants of multiparous mothers nursing longer and bottle-fed infants taking more formula. Primiparous mothers breast-fed their female infants much longer than male infants were fed.

Mogan (1987) observed that mutual adaptation between mother and infant during feeding sessions increased rapidly and steadily, as indicated by feeding scores at 55–70 hours, 1–2 weeks, and 1, 2, 4, and 6 months. She questioned the validity of the in-hospital feeding session for early evaluation of mother–infant interactions. No correlation was found between mother–infant interactions during the first and second observed feedings; the 2-week observation in the mother's environment was a more optimal time to test mother–infant interactions. The infant's abilities to give clear cues and respond to the mother were low at 55–70 hours after birth but increased steadily to exceed the mother's 6-month scores. Parental age and education, infants' sex, Apgar scores, and ponderal index had no significant effect on Nursing Child Assessment Feeding Scale (NCAFS) (Barnard, 1978) scores. The first feeding session coincides with Rubin's predicted difficult period; the mother's breasts are engorged, and some infants have developed jaundice with lethargy by then.

Mothers' concerns about the infant did not differ from the third postpartal day to the first week at home (Bull, 1981). However when concerns were categorized by infant behavior and physical care of the infant, a significant decrease in concerns related to physical care of the infant occurred after the first week at home, with concerns about behavior continuing.

H: Maternal role adjustment is associated with satisfactory infant feeding experiences.

Women who were breast-feeding their infants reported less anxiety and greater mutuality at 1 month than did women who were bottle feeding their infants, measured by subscales from Cohler and associates' (Cohler, Weiss, & Grunebaum, 1970) Maternal Attitude Scale (Virden, 1988). Virden (1988) suggested that the differences may reflect a greater intensity of involvement during the role enactment by breast-feeding mothers (Sarbin & Allen, 1968). The more intense involvement may provide the woman with a greater sense of knowing her infant. However, maternal characteristics that influenced the choice to breast-feed may also influence her anxiety and mutuality with her infant. Breast-feeding mothers more often than bottle-feeding mothers initiated social interactions with their infants and shared their mother–infant experiences with their husband during the first month (Freese & Thoman, 1978). Pridham (1987) observed that mothers who breast-fed focused on different issues than women who bottle-fed.

Factors influencing the duration of breast-feeding included encouragement and sources of information, maternal uneasiness, and hospital supplementation (Duckett, Henly, & Garvis, 1993). The latter two factors may indicate a mother's lack of confidence in her ability, leading to supplementation at home and insufficient breast milk.

Thirty mother–infant pairs were studied during feeding interactions the second postpartal day using Barnard's (1978) NCAFS (Lerner, 1994). Infant behavior was assessed the same day using the BNBAS. Nine of the mothers scored below 55 on the NCAFS, a cut-off for being at risk for alterations in parenting; seven of these infants were in the transitional care nursery. No significant correlations were observed between NCAFS scores and maternal age, education, parity, ethnicity, medication during labor, complications of pregnancy, or baby in the transitional nursery. The BNBAS Regulation of State cluster correlated with the NCAFS.

Most of 59 mothers who were breast-feeding their infants reported significant difficulties during the first 2 days postpartum, with problems on the fourth to fifth postpartum days for 33% (Matthews, 1993). Problems related to infant sleepiness, poor sucking technique, and the mother's flat nipples. The better the infant's feeding score on a measure developed for the study, the higher the mother's feeding score. Nineteen percent of the infants required phototherapy for physiological jaundice. Sixteen of the 19 mothers who had not established good feeding patterns by hospital discharge had quit breast-feeding by 2 weeks after leaving the hospital.

Summary

Evidence indicates that the infant does not give clear cues and the mother does not detect subtle infant cues during feeding in the first 3 days. Findings were mixed about the improvement of mutuality in feeding situations after the third postpartal day; Mogan (1987) observed a rapid increase after that time, but Matthews (1993) observed that problems continued on the fourth to fifth postpartal days. Findings were mixed regarding feeding method and maternal role attainment behaviors. The mixed findings indicate a need for further research in this area. What is the relationship between successful feedings, self-concept, anxiety, and maternal role identity? Do mothers differ in the length of time female and male infants are breast-fed; if so, why? Are male infants stronger and able to empty the breast more quickly?

PROGRESS TOWARD MATERNAL ROLE-IDENTITY ATTAINMENT

Many factors interact to affect progress in maternal role attainment, such as the mother's physical condition, previous experience with infants, self-esteem, empathy, support system, and the infant's physical condition and responses. Validation of the mother's behavior by professionals or expert mothers, along with the infant's positive response, buoy her self-confidence.

Observed Change in Maternal Role Identity

The ongoing "incorporation into a woman's self system of a new personality dimension" proceeds by "successive and progressively refined ideal images of the self as womanly mother" (Rubin, 1984, p. 38). Development does not proceed in linear increments, but as "a spiraling, a widening in scope of capacities and experiences," leading to higher forms of mental activity and behavior (Rubin, 1994, p. 4).

> CS: The development of a maternal identity for this child is effected in a progressive series of cognitive operations that are manifest in conceptual and behavioral modes. (Rubin, 1984, p. 39)

This occurs at the end of the neomaternal-neonatal stage, about a month following delivery. There is then an operational location of the "you," the "I" in relation to the "you," and the "you" in relation to the "me." She can "read" the child's appearance and behavior with recognition. (p. 50)

H: Women progress in maternal role identity attainment over the first month.

Ruble and associates (1990) suggested that in observing change and stability in the transition to the maternal identity, instability across pregnancy and postpartum might be indicative of the occurring change in self-definition. Continuity is expected in core attitudes and beliefs. The experience of birth led to instability in attitudes about pain tolerance, interest in sex, relationship with husband, and social boredom; however, stability between pregnancy and postpartum reports were found for attitudes about relationship with mother, body image, attitude toward breastfeeding and feelings of dependency. Their findings, using their Maternal Self-Definition Questionnaire, supported the conceptualization of the transition to motherhood in four domains—role definition, interpersonal relationship, self, and peripheral aspects of the role—that may be best described by feelings rather than content.

Walker, Crain, and Thompson (1986a) operationalized maternal role self-confidence by the Pharis (1978) Self-Confidence Scale as a measure of maternal role attainment in the neonatal period and maternal identity by a semantic differential (SD) scale to measure views of self and infant that reflect the evaluative image of self as mother of the specific child. Mothers increased in self-confidence from the first week to 4 to 6 weeks later but viewed their infants less positively at the end of the postpartum period than at the beginning. Mothers maintained the same relative position within the sample on SD-Self, SD-Baby, and self-confidence. Sociodemographic variables had little or no influence on any of the variables. Mothers' views of themselves correlated with views they held of their infants, supporting Rubin's emphasis on the reciprocal nature of the "I" and "You" within the early mother–infant relationship.

The subjective components of maternal identity (on the SD scale), perceived maternal role attainment (on the Pharis Self-Confidence Scale), and objective maternal behavior (revision of Price's [1983] Maternal–Infant Adaptation Scale) during infant feedings were studied among primiparas and multiparous mothers during the first 2 days and 4 to 6 weeks following birth (Walker, Crain, & Thompson, 1986b). Significant relationships were found between observed behavior and SD-Self during the first 2 days but not at 4 to 6 weeks among all women. Thus, during this early period, the subjective components of maternal role identity were not extensively interwoven with the objective component or role behavior. As Walker et al. (1986b) noted, these findings were not surprising, considering that it takes an average of 2 H months for the mother to mesh her behaviors with infant cues. Significant relationships between SD-Self and SD-Baby were observed, however, supporting Rubin's (1984) emphasis on the reciprocity between the "I" and "You" in the early mother–infant relationship (Walker et al., 1986a). Mothers' confidence and attitudes about themselves remained relatively stable over the first month.

Mothers reported significantly lower attachment feelings at 1 month than during the first week (Mercer & Ferketich, 1994a). However, their perceived competence in the maternal role did not change significantly over that time (Mercer & Ferketich, 1995).

Reece (1992) defined self-efficacy in the parenting role as the "confidence a new mother has in her ability to meet the demands and responsibilities of parenthood" (p. 336) in her development of an instrument to measure perceived self-efficacy, the Parent Expectations Survey (PES). New mother's perceptions of self-efficacy came from past experience in caring for infants, observations of other new mothers, encouragement, and feedback from the baby or family. PES scores at 1 and 3 months postpartum were associated with greater confidence in parenting 1 year after birth and were negatively related to perceived stress.

Maternal attitudes, birthing conditions, and birthing experience explained 22% of the variance in the transition marker (Pridham & Chang's [1985] WPL) during early postpartum (Pridham, Lytton, Chang, & Rutledge, 1991). Mercer and Ferketich (1994b) reported that 51% of the variance in low-risk women's perceived maternal competence (Parental Sense of Competence measure [PSOC] by Gibaud-Wallston & Wanderman [1978]) was explained by state anxiety and self-esteem during the early postpartal hospitalization; at 1 month, 29% was explained by mastery, depression, and perceived health status. Maternal competence decreased slightly from hospitalization to 1 month after birth. High-risk women (hospitalized during pregnancy for a risk condition) did not differ in PSOC scores from low-risk women; high-risk women reported a slight decrease at 1 month. Forty-one percent of the variance in high-risk women's PSOC score the first week was predicted by state anxiety, self-esteem, fetal attachment, and mastery; at 1 month, 38% of the variance was explained by depression, self-esteem, and fetal attachment.

Parity Differences

Although the tendency is to view the experienced mother as having an advantage over the first-time mother, the former reports more stress and greater fatigue. She is concerned about her previous child's/children's acceptance of the newborn and whether she will be able to treat all children equally.

> *CS:* There is no carry-over and no transference of a maternal identity from one child to another. A woman occupies a different life space and a different self system at each childbearing experience. It is into this current and real self system and life space, rather than the archaic and no longer relevant self system and life space, that a woman originates and binds-in to a maternal identity for this child and under these circumstances. (Rubin, 1984, p. 38)

> *H:* The process of maternal role attainment proceeds for multiparous women as it does for primiparous women.

Mothers who had given birth to a second child worked at unique physical and cognitive tasks in their role transition as mother of two children (Walz & Rich, 1983). These tasks included promoting acceptance and approval of the first child, grieving the loss of the exclusive relationship with the first child, planning family life in fantasy in managing with two children, reformulating the changed relationship with the first child, identifying and claiming the second child by comparing with the first child, and assessing abilities to provide sufficient support and nurturance to both children. Ulrich (1982) observed a secundigravida who focused on gaining her husband's and older child's acceptance of the new baby and in maintaining her relationship with her husband and older child.

Second-time mothers reported, at 6 to 9 weeks after birth, that the older child's behavior had changed (no regression); they felt the change was due to their mothering capabilities (Lynch, 1982). Mothers who experienced the greatest stress were those with toddlers under 2 years of age.

At 2 to 3 weeks following birth, an increase in confrontation between mother and firstborn and a decrease in maternal playfulness occurred from the last trimester of pregnancy (Kendrick & Dunn, 1980). Although an increase in confrontation occurred when the mother was occupied with the second child, there was also an increase in positive interaction between mother and first child. The decrease in maternal attention to the firstborn occurred in contexts in which the mother was not occupied with the new baby.

Multiparas had more positive attitudes about themselves as mothers (SD-Self) than did primiparas; their attitudes became more positive from 1 to 3 days after delivery to 4 to 6 weeks postpartum (Walker et al., 1986a). Multiparas also reported greater self-confidence than did primiparas, with greater confidence reported at 4 to 6 weeks for both groups. Multiparas viewed their infants more positively than did primiparas (SD-Baby). Among primiparas a positive correlation was found between self-confidence and feelings about their infants, suggesting an interdependence between the two variables. Primiparas' observed maternal behavior and self-confidence were significantly related at 1 month, but multiparas' self-confidence was independent of observed mothering behaviors (Walker et al., 1986b).

Pridham (1987) observed that primiparas' meaning of a new infant was more related to their sense of self than that of multiparas. Primiparas reported a greater frequency of personal development or competence than did multiparas at 1 and 3 months. Primiparas reported significantly higher scores for centrality (subscale of What Being a Parent Is Like) at 1 week and 3 months than did multiparas (Pridham & Chang, 1989).

Multiparas took less time in feeding their infants than did primiparas; and although primiparas were more persistent, their infants took less formula than did multiparas' infants on the second postpartal day (Thoman, Turner, Leiderman, & Barnett, 1970). Multiparas were more efficient feeders the first 2 to 3 days after birth (Thoman, 1975).

Multiparas were not as concerned about themselves or their infants on the third postpartum day as they were about their family relationships (Moss, 1981). At 2 weeks postpartum, meeting the needs of everyone at home was the greatest concern of multiparas (Hiser, 1987). Greatest concerns of primiparas during the first postpartal week were infant crying, elimination, and routine care (Fillmore & Taylor, 1976). The baby's eyes and infant feeding were greatest concerns of primiparous Egyptian mothers during postpartal hospitalization (Govaerts & Patino, 1981). The early postpartum hospital stay was a time of fewer concerns and stresses, with the first 3 months at home generating the highest number (Larsen, 1966). Primiparas complained more about physical discomforts and were concerned about their mothering role and ability to adjust to the new baby. Multiparas with three children reported fatigue more often than did other mothers. Primiparas sought help with their problems significantly more often than did multiparas during the first 3 months after birth (Pridham, Hansen, Bradley, & Heighway, 1982). Multiparas had less help at home following birth than did primiparas (Tulman & Fawcett, 1988) and reported little or no time for themselves to pursue their interests or personal hygiene (Grubb, 1980).

Experienced mothers reported nonsignificant higher maternal competence (measured by PSOC) than did inexperienced mothers during the first week and at the first month postpartum (Mercer & Ferketich, 1995). At early postpartum, experienced mothers had 56% of the variance in their PSOC explained by mastery, self-esteem, anxiety, fetal attachment, infant health status, and depression, and 47% at 1 month by self-esteem, anxiety, educational level, pregnancy readiness, and pregnancy risk. Inexperienced mothers had 46% of the variance in their PSOC explained by anxiety, self-esteem, and educational level at early postpartum and 44% at 1 month by mastery, depression, infant health, education level, and health status. Inexperienced mothers had a significantly higher intrapartal risk score, and significantly more received support during the first 4 months following birth.

In contrast to the findings of Walker et al. (1986a), experienced mothers did not differ from inexperienced mothers by maternal infant attachment (measured by Leifer's [1980] Feelings About My Baby) at either early postpartum or 1 month (Mercer & Ferketich, 1994b), although the early scores were significantly higher than later scores for both groups. However, during pregnancy, inexperienced mothers reported significantly higher fetal attachment than did experienced mothers.

Summary

Walker and associates' test of Rubin's concept of the reciprocal relationship of the mother's subjective "I" to the "You" was supported, using the

SD measure of maternal identity (evaluation on bipolar words related to the mother's self-image as mother in relation to the ideal image of mother and of her infant and ideal infant). The early relationship between the self-image as mother and observed maternal behavior (operationalization of maternal role attainment) had disappeared at 4 to 6 weeks. Zabielski (1994) found no support for separating enacted maternal role behaviors and cognitively structured maternal identity; maternal identity was a product of cognitive, affective, and performance phenomena, with any one phenomenon able to elicit the maternal identity.

The findings showing the importance of the self system or self-esteem to self-reported maternal role competence among both primiparas and multiparas and high-risk and low-risk women support Rubin's concepts. Maternal anxiety also had significant negative effects on competence, and depression became a significant predictor at 1 month. At 1 month, both sense of mastery (ability to feel in control) and health status were important to inexperienced mothers' sense of competence.

The concerns of multiparas are different from those of primiparas. Multiparas receive less help at home than do primiparas and experience stress and fatigue in attempting to meet their family's needs. They scored higher in maternal competence than did primiparas during the puerperium but did not differ in their attachment to their infants, which decreased from 1 week to 1 month.

Care and interventions during the puerperium need to be informed by parity differences in maternal role identity behaviors. Exploration of how self-esteem may be enhanced is needed.

END OF FORMAL NEOMATERNAL STAGE

The postpartal examination represents a physical rite of passage to end the puerperium. Rubin (1984) described the woman's leaving her infant for an outing and achieving a polarization or differentiation of self from infant, to separate the "I" from the "You," to end the neomaternal period.

> *CS:* Women spontaneously effect an end point in time and space to the lying-in stage of childbearing when they have physically recovered. Independently and without awareness of the general practice, they energetically burst out into sociable space and sociable time… Postpartally it

is a sentimental reaffirmation of attachment bonds, but it is also a drive and a readiness to reenter the adult world in time and space. (Rubin, 1984, p. 99)

Relief from the oppressiveness of the puerperal situation is provided by the woman herself. As soon as body intactness is restored, a matter of three or four weeks for most women, the woman removes herself spatially from the child and from the confinement of the home and sets aside time in which to find and to be herself, the self in good continuance with her pre-pregnant, recognizable, and predictable self. (p. 124)

The distancing from the child in time, space, and objectives is a polarization (Deutsch, 1944) to form two differentiated individuals. On returning a mother perceives her child more clearly and more wholly from a refreshed and larger perspective. Moreover, there is a constancy in the child in objective reality: it is the woman who goes away and returns, appears and disappears, not the child.... There is a self and there is a child. There is polarization and a special relationship of two individuals based on, but different from the unity of mother–child as one. The neomaternal stage is completed with polarization. Third-person intermediation in the mother–child relationship is no longer necessary: there is a knowing of the baby with a reliability and predictability; there is a confidence in self as mother generated by recovery and mastery of function. (p. 126)

H: The mother's physical and functional status is significantly related to polarization or seeing the infant as separate from self. (No research.)

H: The modal time for polarization (mother no longer seeing infant as extension of self) is 1 month.

Walker and associates' (1986a) findings that the self as mother was significantly related to the evaluative component of infant (r =.69 for both multiparas and primiparas) at 4 to 6 weeks suggests that polarization may not have occurred among these populations. This finding was not surprising because Sander (1962) indicated that separation of self from infant is associated with ability to read infant cues and respond contingently and requires an average of 2H months (Sander, 1962).

H: Physical recovery is associated with expansion of the mother's social sphere.

The concept of polarization as described by Rubin has not been researched. The routine postpartal examination after birth is probably the best cultural indication that the woman is functionally ready to assume her usual activities, including sexual intercourse. However, Tulman and Fawcett's (1988) research indicated that functional status is not fully restored at this time. Women are discharged from the hospital 12 to 24 hours following birth; in some situations, they have only their partners to help them at home. Women no longer wait until 3 to 4 weeks to expand their social sphere of activities; they go grocery shopping and run errands in the first postpartal week (Stainton, 1986a). Pridham (1987) reported that 43% of mothers had returned to work during the first 3 months; the mother returned to work when the infant was from 3 to 90 days old (mean age, 39.31 days; *SD,* 22.25).

Summary

Rubin's concepts link the achievement of maternal confidence and ability to function without a third person with polarization and the end of the neomaternal period. Scientific evidence to date does not support the idea that mothers in general are able to accomplish confidence and polarization within the 1-month time frame. From the perspective of stages of maternal role identity attainment, the formal stage ends when the mother begins to try ways of meeting her infant's needs apart from the advice of experts. There is no specific time for this, and indeed, this behavior begins in some areas of infant care as soon as the mother assumes care of her infant. Some mothers are able to achieve the personal or identity stage during the puerperium, however. One-third of 242 first-time mothers described achieving the maternal role identity by 2 weeks postpartum (Mercer, 1986a).

SUMMARY

During the formal stage of maternal role identity achievement, the woman is bombarded with many demands on her time as she becomes acquainted with her infant and learns to respond to his cues. Despite her fatigue and changing body, she manages to proceed and to make progress in all areas of her tasks. Although she does not experience increased morbidity as a result of the early postpartal discharge (Norr & Nacion, 1987), little is known about the impact on her self-image and her early maternal behaviors. Does the woman who returns to her household 12 hours after birth, take on household tasks at the expense of identifying, claiming, and cueing in to her infant? Mothers are resuming other roles, such as student and work roles, without help during the first month. What difference does this make long-range in her maternal role identity and in her infant's growth and development?

Rubin's concepts regarding the neomaternal period are in general supported by research. The major exception is the end of the neomaternal stage and the polarization that occurs between mother and infant; this has not been studied. Polarization or differentiation of self from the infant is important because it is a factor in the woman's ability to develop synchronous responses to her infant's cues. What factors are involved other than the woman's need to expand her social sphere? Is polarization related to maternal characteristics and experiences, such as her ego strength, ego boundaries, and separation experiences from her own mother? In the current social context, is the differentiation of self from baby occurring earlier?

■ 8
Integrating the Maternal Self

The informal stage of role making that began in the formal stage of maternal role identity extends into the personal identity achievement stage. In the personal identity stage, the mother has synchronized her care activities with her infant's cues and differentiated her style from role models to develop her unique mothering repertoire. This ability is acquired through careful study, trial and error, and success. As the mother acquires a sense of competence, she begins a very pleasurable period of reciprocal exchange in mother–infant interactions that lasts until around 5 months after birth (Sander, 1962).

During the last half of the infant's first year, the mother's keenness in reading infant cues and her sensitive responses are as important as the initial adaptation period if the infant's spontaneity and pleasurable affect are to continue. From 5 to 9 months, the infant increasingly takes the initiative in eliciting and sustaining interaction with the mother. From 9 to 15 months, children increase their initiative in manipulating the mother to meet their needs (Sander, 1962). Thus, maternal caretaking behaviors must adapt and change over the course of the first year to maintain synchrony with the infant's developmental needs.

In this chapter, the time frame of Rubin's major observations is extended to focus on the evolving maternal identity over the first year after birth. The influences on maternal behavior, such as functional status and self-concept, maternal attitudes and traits, the interaction of maternal and spousal relationships, and maternal and infant characteristics, are first addressed. Evolving maternal role-identity behaviors—maternal competence, gratification in the role, and maternal attachment—conclude the chapter.

FUNCTIONAL STATUS AND SELF-CONCEPT/SELF-ESTEEM

The woman's body image and ability to function continue to interact with her developing identity as a mother beyond the puerperium. Yet despite not having fully recovered from childbirth, the woman attempts to balance her wife role and often her employment roles with her maternal role.

Functional and Health Status and Maternal Role Behaviors

Women expect to be able to assume their usual activities at least within a few months after birth. The decreased social support for women over the first year (Mercer & Ferketich, 1995) indicates that their families and friends may also have the same expectation.

> *CS:* The maternal identity is achieved and stabilized in some magnificent programmatic ordering even before self as a person and a woman, her own full identity of self in the world, is achieved. That sense of identity, when she feels like herself again, is achieved when her body image in action in the world is contiguous and consistent with her self-concept, about eight or nine months after childbirth. (p. 127)
>
> It takes nine months from childbirth for a woman to feel like herself again; whole, intact, functional, and in goodness of fit of self in the world. (Rubin, 1984, p. 109)

H: The woman's prepregnancy functional status is achieved around 9 months postpartum.

Mothers' functional status, measured by the Inventory of Functional Status After Childbirth (Fawcett, Tulman, & Meyers, 1988), improved from 3 weeks to 3 months after birth, but no change was observed between 3 and 6 months (Tulman et al., 1990). At 6 months, more than 80% of mothers had not fully resumed their usual self-care activities, 30% had not resumed usual levels of social and community activities, 20% had not resumed usual household activities, and 6% had not assumed their desired level of infant care activities. Of the 59% who were employed or in school by 6 months, 60% reported they had not reached their usual level of occupational activities. One-fourth did not feel as if they had recovered physically at 6 months (Tulman & Fawcett, 1991). The 6 months after birth without adequate household and child-care help was more difficult than one-half of the women had anticipated.

From 3H to 5 months, a sample of childbirth class attenders reported a decrease in physical complaints, anxiety, and depression and an increase in ego strength (Celotta, 1982). However, other childbirth class attenders reported discomfort and fatigue that interfered with sexual intercourse, less physical strength, and dissatisfaction with bodily appearance at 4 months postpartum (Fischman, Rankin, Soeken, & Lenz, 1986). Mothers drawn randomly from public records reported the following at 1 to 4 months: decreased sexual responsiveness, tiredness and fatigue, emotional distress, worry about loss of figure and personal appearance in general, interruption of sleep habits, and doubt about their worth as parents (Hobbs, 1965). A replication of the study a decade later found the same complaints around 6 months after birth (Hobbs & Cole, 1976).

Among 306 new mothers, 30% developed emotional problems postpartum, with 37% having difficulties that persisted for 6 months (Gordon, Kapostins, & Gordon, 1965). Lack of everyday help, emotional support, and encouragement were related to emotional difficulty lasting 6 months. Problems related to personal insecurity were less likely to be long-lasting than difficulties related to role conflict.

Mothers who were healthy at birth reported numerous illnesses during the second half of their infants' first year (Jones & Parks, 1990). Over one-half reported either headaches, respiratory infections, or gastrointestinal problems, with 43% reporting fatigue and 11%, gynecological problems. Life-change events were predictors of maternal illness at 6 months after birth (Lenz, Parks, Jenkins, & Jarrett, 1986). Negative life-change events had indirect effects on low-risk and high-risk women's health status at 8 months (Ferketich & Mercer, 1990). The negative life events had direct effects on self-esteem, which had direct effects on parental competence (and mastery for high-risk women), which had direct effects on health status.

Two-thirds of primiparous mothers reported a health problem at 4 and 8 months; at 1 year, three-fourths reported a health problem (Mercer, 1986a). Upper respiratory infections were most frequent, followed by gynecological problems. A decrease in general well-being at 8 months was also reported by Miller and Sollie (1980). Low-risk women reported a decrease in perceived health status at 4 and 8 months from pregnancy levels of health (Mercer et al., 1987).

Mothers with chronic illnesses experienced conflicting role expectations from health professionals and society in addition to their concerns about their performance, availability, dependency, and socialization issues (Thorne, 1990). The interrelationship between their mothering role and their illness was not recognized by the health care system.

Gjerdingen, Froberg, and Fontaine (1990) proposed a causal model, describing the relationship of the following to women's health over 12 months: social support, length of maternity leave, complications of childbirth, and exogenous variables such as income, education, occupation, age, smoking, use of alcohol, and baby's health. The model was based on the assumption that women experience many dynamic changes in mental and physical health that may persist for months following childbirth.

Strong evidence supports Rubin's concept that recuperation of at least 9 months is required to acquire a prepregnancy self-concept and body image. However, it is unclear whether prepregnancy health and physical status are achieved by 1 year after birth. Over three decades of research, reports have described health problems extending beyond the puerperium, with the problems tending to increase during the second half of the first year. Poorer physical and psychological health was reported among parents beyond the first year (McLanahan & Adams, 1987). Longitudinal research is needed to determine when women's functional and health status is fully restored following childbirth.

H: An effort to regain and establish other functions or roles apart from motherhood is evidenced around 8 months after birth.

At 8 months, primiparous, largely middle-class mothers were frustrated and impatient with the consuming nature of the mother role: "I'm me, a person who happens to be a mother.... I'm no longer a 'working woman' or a 'sexy person'"; "I'm thinking more about things I want to do than I did before, and I'm not as willing to wait" (Mercer, 1986a, p. 216). Women felt an urgent need to think of themselves and their roles apart from their infants; they found the submersion of other roles frightening. By 1 year, they had dealt with their emotional symbiosis with their infants, and most had integrated the maternal, wife, and other roles so that they were enjoying the maternal role.

This finding is congruent with Rubin's statement that it takes 8 or 9 months before the woman achieves her full identity of self in the world again. The phenomenon was called maternal individuation because it was expressed by the women in terms of regaining an adult identity and self apart from the infant; this was not accomplished at 8 months after birth (Mercer, 1986a). It could represent a higher level of the polarization process of separation of self from infant that Rubin described occurring at the end of the puerperium. Or it may reflect, in part, violated expectations in the mothering role. Mothers assumed the maternal role expecting satisfaction and fulfillment in the role much greater than gratification from other roles but were disillusioned and frustrated at 7 months when this had not happened (Liefer, 1980). Is this a commonly occurring phenomenon?

H: Mothers' health status is positively related to maternal behavior and maternal role identity.

L. O. Walker (1989b) surveyed 173 mothers between 2 and 12 months after birth; their health practices failed to buffer effects between stressors and perceived stress but contributed additively to predicted stress and to the prediction of maternal role identity. Work status and infant difficulties contributed to global stress and subsequent maternal identity. In a replication of this study when infants were aged 8 to 20 months, similar results were found, with work status and perceived stress contributing to maternal identity (Walker, L. O., 1989a). With the passage of time, the effects of early infant difficulty on maternal identity diminished.

Maternal self-reported health status was not a predictor of maternal role competence (PSOC) at 4 or 8 months among either experienced or inexperienced mothers (Mercer & Ferketich, 1995). Experienced mothers who had higher pregnancy risk scores tended to score higher on maternal competence at 4 months.

Maternal health status did not enter regressions predicting maternal role competence (PSOC) for women who had either high- or low-risk pregnancies at 4 or 8 months (Mercer & Ferketich, 1994b). However, there were significant positive relationships between health and maternal competence at 4 (.47) and 8 months (.38) among low-risk women and at 8 months among high-risk women (.31).

Health status was not a predictor of maternal–infant attachment by risk or parity status at either 4 or 8 months (Mercer et al., 1987; Mercer & Ferketich, 1994a). However, at 8 months, postpartal complications were associated with higher attachment among experienced mothers and lower attachment among inexperienced mothers; intrapartal complications were associated with greater attachment among inexperienced mothers.

Although Rubin (1984) indicated that negative effects on maternal identity of labor and delivery and of illness following birth were temporary, positive effects of postpartal complications on attachment were evident for multiparas and negative effects for primiparas at 8 months. With the passage of time and attaching to the infant, the earlier threatened risks may enhance the appreciation of the gift of a now well infant for the multipara. Further research is needed to examine whether such effects would be found in another population and whether there would be differences by parity.

Self-Concept/Self-Esteem and Maternal Role Behavior

Self-esteem is the mother's perception of how others view her and her self-acceptance of this perception (Rosenberg, 1965). There is a congruence between self and ideal self that leads to a sense of pride in self (Wylie, 1974). Self-esteem is part of the domain of self-concept, which includes the mother's global perceptions of self and her ability to function adequately in life's situations (Wylie, 1974).

H: Mothers experience an increase in self-esteem/self-concept the first year.

Leifer (1980) reported a sense of heightened self-esteem (measured by blackening smaller squares to represent self within a larger square representing ideal self) among the majority of first-time mothers at 7 months after birth. In contrast, self-concepts (Tennessee Self-Concept Scale [TSCS; Fitts, 1965]) were significantly lower at 8 months than at the first week postpartum among first-time mothers aged 20 to 42 years (Mercer 1986c).

Both high-risk and low-risk women's self-esteem (Rosenberg, 1965) was significantly lower at 8 months than at birth and 1 month; the lower self-esteem at 8 months approached the lower levels observed during pregnancy (Mercer et al., 1987). High- and low-risk mothers did not differ in reported self-esteem.

The greater the time since childbirth, the greater the possibility that one or several factors other than the maternal role have also had effects on the mother's self-concept. However, the decrease in self-concept may reflect the "disparity between the expected and the real, between the ideal image of self as woman, wife, and mother and the experience of self in body" (Rubin, 1984, p. 110). The cultural stereotype is that after the puerperal gynecological examination at 4 to 6 weeks, life returns to normal.

H: Self-concept is positively related to maternal behavior and identity.

Women who reported an easy adaptation to motherhood at 3 months after birth had higher self-concepts (TSCS), previous experience with infants and children, support from nurse and husbands, and help the first week at home (Curry, 1983). One-fourth of the 20 healthy primiparas experienced a very difficult adaptation to motherhood.

At 4 months after birth, self-concept (TSCS) was associated with largely middle-class, first-time mothers' maternal competence, measured by a revision of Blank's (1964) observer-rated Maternal Behavior Scales (MABE) (Mercer, 1986a). Women with higher self-concepts tended to handle irritating child behaviors more favorably at 1 year, measured by Disbrow, Doerr, and Caulfield's (1977) Ways of Handling Irritating Child Behaviors (WHIB) scale. Self-concept was the major predictor of a maternal role index weighted by MABE, WHIB, attachment, gratification in the mothering role, and infant's growth, at 1 year and explained 17% of the variance (Mercer, 1986b).

Although first-time, largely middle-class mothers all reported heightened self-esteem at 7 months after birth, the majority had either negative or ambivalent attitudes about the mothering role (Leifer, 1980). Mothers' self-confidence in early pregnancy was a predictor of their self-confidence at 7 months (Leifer, 1977).

Mothers with more positive personalities—measured by the self-esteem scale from the Jackson (1976) Personality Inventory and neuroticism and extraversion from the NEO-AC Personality Inventory (Costa & McCrae, 1978)—and with a higher level of education interacted more sensitively and positively with their infants, and their infants were more responsive (Fish, Stifter, & Belsky, 1993). Maternal characteristics had greater influence on dyadic relationships than infant characteristics had. Belsky's (1984) process model of determinants of parenting posits that the parent's psychological resources are more effective in buffering the parent–child relationship from stress than contextual sources of support, which are more effective than the child's characteristics.

Self-esteem (Rosenberg, 1965) was a major predictor of maternal competence (PSOC) at 4 and 8 months after birth among largely middle-class high-risk women hospitalized during pregnancy for a complication, explaining 6% and 34% of the variance, respectively (Mercer & Ferketich, 1994b). Among low-risk women, self-esteem explained 8% of the variance in maternal competence at 4 months and 6% at 8 months.

Self-esteem (Rosenberg, 1965) predicted substantial amounts of variance among multiparous mothers' maternal competence at 4 months (31%) and 8 months (34%) (Mercer & Ferketich, 1995). Self-esteem was less explanatory of primiparous mothers' maternal competence, explaining 11% at 4 months and 9% at 8 months.

Scientific evidence provides strong support for the positive relationship between self-concept and maternal role behavior. The effects are interactive, however, with each influencing the other. According to Rubin, being knowledgeable, learning new facts, abilities, and skills, leads to positive self-evaluations; this characterizes the mother and her drive to know.

EFFECTS OF MATERNAL ATTITUDES AND TRAITS

The mother's ability to adapt her responses to the developing infant is affected by her maternal attitudes and traits in addition to her functional status and self-esteem. How she reads the infant's developing assertiveness and exploratory behavior affects how she feels about her competence in mothering and her enjoyment in the role.

> *CS:* Maternal attitudes and behaviors change in relation to age, condition, and situation of the child. (Rubin, 1984, p. 2)

The intimacy of sensory experience, the exclusive communication, and the hidden nature of the child promote a romantic love for this child.... And although romanticism is hardly characteristic of a maternal identity, the propensity to see the ideal in the real child persists and endures to become characteristic of the maternal woman. (p. 64)

H: Maternal attitudes and traits are related to maternal behavior.

Mothers with more rigid child-rearing attitudes derived less enjoyment from the mothering role; rigid attitudes explained 4% of the variance in gratification in the mothering role at 4 months after birth (Mercer, 1986a). A significant negative relationship between rigid attitudes and a maternal role attainment index was found at 1 year, but rigidity did not enter the regressions as a predictor.

Maternal rigidity as a personal characteristic had no significant effect on the quality of maternal infant interaction at 3 months after birth (Butcher, Kalverboer, Minderaa, van Doormaal, & ten Wolde, 1993). However, rigid attitudes toward child rearing were associated with less responsiveness to the infant's feelings and behavior. Rigid mothers were less active, vocalized less, and expressed fewer positive emotions to their infants. Lack of empathy was associated with attitude rigidity, and this formed the basis for the association between rigid attitudes and maternal insensitivity. Infant responsivity was related to maternal attitude rigidity and sensitivity, but infant attachment at 13 months was not related to maternal rigidity.

Mothers with infants up to 10 months of age reported less psychological distress when they were classified as either androgynous or masculine (Bem Sex-Role Inventory) than did women classified as feminine or undifferentiated (Bassoff, 1984). Women who attributed masculine qualities such as assertiveness, independence, and leadership to themselves had better mental health. These findings are congruent with Breen's (1975). Effective caretaking requires assertiveness and independent decision making.

Mothers with poor social skills (interactive and community) were able to improve their skills in a special intervention program (Booth, Mitchell, Barnard, & Spieker, 1989). Posttreatment social skills were positively related to the quality of mother–child interaction.

Maternal attitudes about child rearing were predictors of maternal gratification, feelings of attachment, and the infant's growth and development at 4 months (Mercer, 1986a). At 1 year, maternal attitudes explained 10% of the variance in a maternal role attainment index that included infant growth and development.

There is strong evidence that attitudes as part of the mother's cognitive structure for parenting are related to maternal behavior. Rigidity as a trait had no effect on maternal–child interactions, but rigid attitudes had negative effects.

H: There are negative relationships between maternal mood states (e.g., anxiety and hostility) and maternal behavior.

The mother's personality integration (prenatal and 3 months postnatal) was the strongest differentiator, among 267 mothers receiving public health nursing care, of whether they provided inadequate care or excellent care for their infants at 3 months after birth (Brunnquell, Crichton, & Egeland, 1981). When age and education were controlled, the mothers' hostility/suspiciousness score was the best discriminator of inadequate or excellent care. Mothers providing excellent care had higher intelligence, positive expectations of their children, a better understanding of their relationship with their children, and a positive reaction to pregnancy. The converse was true for inadequate mothers who were also more aggressive and suspicious and described themselves negatively; their aggression, use of defenses, and anxiety scores increased from pregnancy levels.

Highly anxious mothers interacted less skillfully and communicated less with female infants at 3 and 6 months after birth; the infants were less active and alert (Farber, Vaughn, & Egeland, 1981). Anxiety predicted 3% of the variance in low-risk mothers' maternal competence at 4 months; depression predicted 10% of the variance in high-risk women's maternal competence at 8 months (Mercer & Ferketich, 1994b). Anxiety predicted 4% of experienced mothers' competence at 4 months but did not predict inexperienced mothers' competence (Mercer & Ferketich, 1995).

Although most mothers have some anxiety, high anxiety was associated with less competence in mothering. Hostility, which Rubin (1964) described as self-hate, was associated with inadequate mothering.

H: Maternal attitudes and behaviors differ by age, condition, and situation of the child.

Although attitudes may change, some continuity has been observed. Maternal attitudes during pregnancy were significantly related to anxiety, depression, and an unfavorable maternal–child relationship at 8 months after birth (Davids, Holden, & Gray, 1963). A relationship between depressive attributional style during pregnancy and postpartum depression 2 to 3 months after delivery was observed (O'Hara et al., 1982).

Maternal attitudes of 78 low-SES primiparas were measured when infants were 1, 6, and 12 months of age, with a modification of Roth's (1961) Mother-Child Relationship Evaluation (Young, 1986). No significant change in maternal attitudes occurred over the year. Mothers' attitudes on acceptance, overindulgence, and overprotection correlated positively with their own mothers' attitudes. Mothers referred for help with parenting skills scored significantly higher on the rejection scale than did unreferred mothers.

Others observed that maternal responsiveness to their infants' cues changed remarkably during the first year; early behavior was not associated with later behavior (Crockenberg & McCluskey, 1986). The change was associated with characteristics of the mother, infant, and their social environment. Unresponsive maternal attitudes were associated with maternal insensitivity at 12 months only for infants who were irritable during the neonatal period. Maternal behavior at 3 months predicted infant crying during separation in the Strange Situation (Ainsworth, 1979) at 12 months. Early unresponsiveness predicted crying at 12 months only for infants who were less irritable.

Home observations of mother–infant dyads at 6, 8, and 12 months after birth validated that, with increasing age, infants initiated interactions more often and mothers increased their initiation of games, redirections of infants' activities, and verbal requests (Green, J. A., Gustafson, & West, 1980). During this period, mothers decreased caretaking activities and repositioning their infants. Directed behavior initiated by the mother was stable across infant ages and made up 75% of total initiations.

Summary

Maternal attitudes and behaviors did not change over the infant's first year in some populations, and in others, appropriate change in relation to the infant's development was observed. Further research is needed to determine which attitudes and in what situations maternal attitudes and behaviors change over the year. Which attitudes (e.g., those about child rearing, children, life in general, proneness to anxiety) are more critical, and how may those more critical attitudes be changed?

Attitudes toward mothering appear to be learned in part from one's own mother and appear to be rather consistent over time. However, there was support for Rubin's concept that maternal behavior changes as infant developmental needs change.

INTERACTION OF MATERNAL AND INFANT CHARACTERISTICS

A transactional process of change occurs in both the mother and the infant, affecting both the mother's maternal role identity and the infant's growth and development, as shown in the theoretical model in chapter 1. Each brings personality traits to the interaction; the mother's more extensively developed characteristics have greater influence. Important maternal characteristics include self-concept, empathy (see chapter 2), rigidity, child-rearing attitudes, sense of control, history as a child, obstetrical history, and adaptability (Bee et al., 1994; Mercer, 1981b, 1986c). Infant characteristics include temperament, appearance, responsiveness, ability to give cues, and health.

> *CS:* It is in the self-image … that the biological experiences and the psychosocial aspirations and realities are intermediated to sustain and to promote the maternal identification and maternal bonds with the child. (Rubin, 1984, p. 11)
>
> The level of development of a maternal identity is directly related to and dependent on the development of the child. (p. 63)
>
> There are two members, partners of equal significance, in the maternal–child subsystem. Maternal identity, maternal behavior, and the quality of life, maternal and familial, is anchored in the developmental age-stage, sex, physical condition, and behavior of this child. (p. 103)
>
> The biological mother experiences the child not only as an individual but as an extension of herself. In action and particularly in feelings there is a highly permeable border between the actions and feelings of the child and the self. (p. 143)

H: Maternal characteristics are related to maternal perceptions of the infants and their behavior.

Maternal perceptions of infant fussiness/difficulty at 4 months were predicted by maternal inflexibility in child rearing (e.g., strict adherence to schedules) at 6 weeks with difficult infants (Power, Gershenhorn, & Stafford, 1990). Early inflexibility predicted the development of actual difficult infant behavior, with early unresponsive attitudes toward an irritable infant leading to insensitivity to infant cues (Crockenberg & McCluskey, 1986). First-time mothers' infants' difficult behavior also resulted from caregiving difficulty, infant's discomfort, resistance, or lack of interest (Power et al., 1990). Maternal attributions of infant difficulty, resistance, or lack of interest may lead to the belief that infants have "a mind of their own."

Maternal anxiety, social status, and mental health status were related to mothers' ratings of their infants on the Carey (1970) Infant Temperament Questionnaire (ITQ) at 4 months (Sameroff, Seifer, & Elias, 1982). Very few observed infant behaviors were related to maternal-reported ITQ scores.

At 6 months after birth the ITQ reflected maternal characteristics, attitudes, and behaviors more so than infant temperament (Vaughn, Taraldson, Crichton, & Egeland, 1981). Maternal behavior during feeding and play with the infant did not discriminate mothers who rated their infants as easy or difficult, nor did infant behavior during those sessions discriminate easy from difficult infants, raising questions about the ITQ's validity.

The mothers' prenatal characteristics, anxiety, and self-esteem were related to their diagnoses of easy and difficult infants at 6 months postpartum (Vaughn, Bradley, Joffe, Seifer, & Barglow, 1987). Mothers of easy infants had higher self-esteem, and mothers of difficult infants had higher anxiety scores. Multiparous, extraverted mothers more often rated their 4- to 6-month old infants as easy on the Infant Characteristics Questionnaire (Bates, Freeland, & Lounsbury, 1979).

Significant correlations between maternal and infant temperament traits at 4 months were observed for rhythmicity, adaptability, quality of mood, persistence, and distractibility among 20–29-year-old primiparas (Mercer, 1986a). At 8 months, significant correlations continued between maternal and infant temperament for adaptability, mood state, and persistence; the category of intensity was added. Very few significant relationships were observed between maternal and infant temperament categories for teenage or older (30–42 years) mothers, suggesting that women in their 20s may see their infants as an extension of themselves more so than older or younger mothers do.

At 1 year, mothers were more sensitive to the adaptive dimension of their infants' temperament, and fathers were more sensitive to infants' physical dimension (Jones, C., & Parks, 1983). One-year-olds described as more adaptable by mothers were more alert and better oriented and had earlier decrement to light and better interactive scores (on the BNBAS) as newborns.

A study of 164 low-income mothers found that mothers' personality characteristics during pregnancy predicted maternal perception of the child (Schaefer, E. S., Hunter, & Edgerton, 1987). The mother's external locus of control and psychosomatic symptoms, and her interactions with the interviewer at 4 and 12 months after birth correlated significantly with reports of the child's adjustment in kindergarten.

A meta-analysis of effects of maternal and child problems on the quality of infant attachment concluded that the mother played a more important role than the infant did in shaping the quality of the infant–mother attachment relationship (van Ijzendoorn, Goldberg, Kroonenberg, & Frenkel, 1992). Smith and Pederson (1988) reported that 94% of 12-month-old infants' attachment (measured by Ainsworth's [1979] Strange Situation) could be classified by self-reported maternal behavior. Mothers of insecurely attached 1-year-olds were less sensitively responsive at 1 and 4 months and more rejecting at 1 and 9 months (Isabella, 1993). These data indicated that observations of sensitivity are more robust during the early developmental period, when patterns of interaction are established.Whether temperament measures tap maternal attitudes or true infant behavioral styles from the mother's perspective, the mother responds to her infant from what she believes. The important factor is the outcome of maternal beliefs and perceptions of the infant. Research indicates maternal beliefs and traits have long-term effects.

H: There is an interaction of maternal and infant mood states (e.g., depression).

Mothers who were more content, religious, and thankful had 3-month-old infants who were higher on soothability (Ventura, 1986).

Parents who were depressed and anxious viewed their infants as less soothable and more easily distressed (Ventura, 1982). Difficult infant temperament was associated with postpartal depression at the second month (Mayberry & Affonso, 1993).

Depressed mothers interacted more negatively with their 2-month-old infants, who responded less positively than infants of nondepressed mothers (Cohn, Campbell, Matias, & Hopkins, 1990). Depressed mothers responded to their infants with less affection and fewer vocalizations at 1 and 3 months postpartum (Fleming et al., 1988). Depressed mothers failed to synchronize their behavior with their 3- to 4-month-old infants' behavior, were slower to respond to their infants' vocalizations, varied more in their speech, and were less likely to utilize the exaggerated intonation contours characteristic of "motherese" (Bettes, 1988).

Infants were more playful when their mothers expressed joy; they showed greater sadness, anger, and gaze aversion when their mothers expressed sadness (Termine & Izard, 1988). Infants protested and were wary following simulated maternal depression, tending to continue these responses briefly after mothers switched from depressed to normal interaction (Cohn & Tronick, 1983).

Three-month-old infants interacted with their depressed mothers a greater portion of time by showing more sadness and anger and less interest than did infants interacting with their nondepressed mothers (Pickens & Field, 1993). Depressed mothers' 3- to 6-month-old infants performed more poorly when interacting with nondepressed adults; however, they showed more head and gaze aversion when with their mothers than with nondepressed adults (Field et al., 1988). Depressed mothers and their 3-month-old infants more often shared negative behavior states and less often shared positive behavior states than did nondepressed mothers and their infants (Field, Healy, & LeBlanc, 1989; Field, Healy, Goldstein, & Guthertz, 1990).

Mothers who greatly overestimated their control in terminating their infants' crying at 5 months were more depressed and responded physiologically with signs of aversion to the cry, compared to mothers with a moderate illusion of control (Donovan & Leavitt, 1989). A disproportionate number of infants of mothers with high illusions of control were insecurely attached in the Strange Situation at 16 months.

Scientific evidence indicates that maternal depression has serious effects on the infant's behavioral style and responses. Sander's (1962) assertion that the mother's sensitive responses were important for the infant's development of spontaneity and pleasurable affect during the last half of the first year is affirmed by the research on interactive effects of maternal depression and infant behavior.

H: Maternal perceptions of infants' characteristics and behavior are related to mothering behavior.

Mothers who perceived their 3-month-old infants as more difficult (on the ITQ) were physiologically less sensitive to changes in infant expressions of smiling or crying as measured by cardiac and skin conductance responses (Donovan, Leavitt, & Balling, 1978). Mothers who had the most difficult infants were less responsive to positive infant behaviors.

The combined temperaments of Lebanese mother–infant dyads had a significant effect on maternal behaviors and mother–infant behaviors; effects were stronger when both had easy temperaments (Zahr, 1987). Mother–infant interaction was not affected by SES, infant's sex, parity, and anesthesia during childbirth.

Mothers who reported their infants as difficult interacted less and were less responsive to infant cues at 3 and 8 months after birth (Campbell, 1979). Beckwith (1972) suggested that the infant chooses to increase or decrease stimulation by initiations such as crying or smiling, confounding causality of responsiveness to infant cues.

Mothers of infants with difficult temperaments reported more problems from 3 to 9 months after birth (McKim, 1987). Just under one-half of mothers reported problems at 3, 6, and 9 months, with 37% reporting problems at 12 months. Older mothers reported more problems between 9 and 12 months than did younger mothers. Employed mothers reported more problems during the last half of the year; 47% were employed by 6 months. Leading problems were infant illness, nutrition, crying, information need, parent problems, and congenital anomalies.

Early maternal responsiveness (promptness in responding to infant crying) among 50 mother–infant dyads during the first 9 months was related to a decrease in infant crying during a later quarter (Hubbard & van Ijendoorn, 1991). Infant crying during an early quarter increased maternal unresponsiveness at later times.

At 8 months no significant differences were observed in largely middle-class mothers' maternal role behaviors of gratification, competence, or ways of handling irritating child behaviors by infant temperament clusters. However, women with slow-to-warm-up or difficult infants reported significantly lower attachment for their infants (Mercer, 1986a).

A theoretical link between mothers' perceptions of their infants' temperaments (measured by ITQ) at 8 months and mother–child attachment was found by Kemp (1987). The ITQ scores predicted infant membership in either avoidant attachment, secure attachment, or anxious attachment groups. Mothers and infants are active partners in the development of reciprocal attachment (Egeland & Farber, 1984).

Maternal–infant interactions did not vary by perceptions of infant's temperament, but cultural differences were observed (Carlile & Holstrum, 1989). Caucasian mothers differed from Chamorro (indigenous people of Guam) mothers by showing more warmth and enthusiasm during play, adjusting verbalizations to meet their infants' comprehension level, and being more creative in teaching episodes. Chamorro values include the concept of "ownership of children," firm control, maternal authority, love recognition, and strict discipline.

Summary

Maternal perceptions of infants and attitudes are part of the cognitive structure for mothering. Maternal attitudes are influenced by the culture in which the mother lives. Studies of maternal-reported infant temperament suggest that the mother's characteristics influence this evaluation. Research supports the idea that a transactional process occurs in which each partner affects the other, whether it is through mood state, behavioral style, or temperament state. Research is needed to learn more about these interactive process to offer information about how dysfunctional cycles may be interrupted. The effects of the infant's difficult temperament on both maternal and infant attachment need further investigation.

INTERACTION OF MATERNAL AND SPOUSAL RELATIONSHIPS

One of the major tasks of assuming maternal role identity is to integrate the maternal role harmoniously with the wife role identity and to assure support for the mother herself and her child from the relationship. Role integration was defined as a process of organizing multiple roles into a meaningful, larger whole; "It is the way in which parts of the interactional self are embodied with integrity and completeness, commonly referred to, and probably oversimplified, as 'having it together'" (Hall, J. M., Stevens, & Meleis, 1992, p. 450). The centrality of the wife role for a maternal sense of confidence and comfort in the transition to motherhood has been emphasized by several (Grossman, 1988).

> *CS:* The specialized mother-baby system within a family is often perceived as a wedge, intrusively disrupting the integrity of the family by its exclusivity and its usurpation of time for established lines and styles of relationships. The resentment of the displacement is experienced by every member of the family, including the woman....
>
> The exclusivity and intimacy of the mother-child subsystem is a territorial problem for the husband becoming a family man and finding the husband-wife relationship relegated to a special subsystem within the family. (Rubin, 1984, p. 101)

H: Marital relationships decline during the first year after childbirth.

Significant but modest declines in the marital relationship from pregnancy to 3 to 9 months after birth occurred among 72 well-functioning volunteer couples (Belsky, Spanier, & Rovine, 1983). The greatest impact was at 3 months. Miller and Sollie (1980) reported a decline at 8 months from a 1-month measure, indicating that the decline does not occur during the first month after birth. By 6 weeks, marital adjustment scores were lower than during pregnancy (Waldron & Routh, 1981) and continued to decline over 8 months after birth (Mercer et al., 1993). High- and low-risk mothers did not differ in marital adjustment scores, but all experienced a decrease at 4 and 8 months under earlier scores during pregnancy and 1 week and 1 month after birth, which did not differ significantly (Mercer et al., 1987).

The decline in marital satisfaction over the first 6 months was more significant among wives (Belsky, Lang, & Rovine, 1985). Women's marital relationships deteriorated less at 3 months when the division of labor changed more toward traditionalism (Belsky, Lang, & Huston, 1986). Several suggest that the marital relationship focuses more on instrumental functions and less on romance and emotional expression after birth (Belsky et al., 1985; Goldberg, Michaels, & Lamb, 1985).

Women reported a declining sexual interest from 3 to 6 months following birth (Ellis & Hewat, 1985). Leifer (1980) observed that women were torn between the roles of mother and wife and felt that they were neglecting their husbands, leading to feelings of inadequacy and guilt. Some husbands were jealous and resentful of their wives' placing the infants' needs over their needs.

Parents reporting higher marital adjustment experienced more positive change, whereas those with lower adjustment reported more negative change (Harriman, 1986; Lewis, 1988). Marital adjustment was related to the extent of change that parents perceived, with negative personal and marital change more difficult for wives. However, both parent and nonparent groups reported significant declines in love and satisfaction (McHale & Huston, 1985).

Mothers and fathers scoring higher in feminine attributes reported better marital relationships at 4 months after birth (Lenz, Soeken, Rankin, & Fischman, 1985). The implications were that persons high in femininity are more nurturing to each other and participate more actively in infant care.

Although study samples' average scores decrease over time, when examined individually, the majority do not experience negative change. Overall, feelings of love and open communication decreased and ambivalence about the marriage increased from pregnancy over 3 years after birth; 30% of couples reported fewer disagreements, and 40% reported no change (Belsky & Rovine, 1990). Lewis (1988) reported that 58% of couples had the same level of marital competence at 1 year as during pregnancy, with 37% experiencing deterioration in their relationship.

A framework of "violated expectations" has explained women's declining positive feelings about their husbands following birth (Belsky, 1985; Kalmuss, Davidson, & Cushman, 1992; Ruble, Fleming, Hackel, & Stangor, 1988). Women's satisfaction with the partner relationship decreased when experiences following birth were less positive than expected and when they were doing more of the housework and child care than they had expected.

Possibly, the greater salience of the maternal role over the wife role and declining sexual interest during the first 6 months after birth account for fewer demonstrations of romance. Although instrumental functions increase for the partner relationship, women's expectations for men's help are not met.

CS: … The woman's husband is the key contributor. The course of the pregnancy, the formation of a maternal identity, and the execution of the maternal tasks are profoundly influenced by the qualitative relationship of husband and wife. (Rubin, 1984, p. 59)

H: The woman's husband/intimate partner's support is more salient than others' support and is positively related to maternal behavior and role identity achievement.

Following birth, self-esteem was negatively associated with feelings of failure or being overwhelmed (Hobfoll & Lieberman, 1987). Women with low self-esteem and low spousal support experienced greater stress. Mothers who were more satisfied with the maternal role and who had less role strain had husbands who discussed important personal problems with them and expressed approval of their new roles as mothers (Reibstein, 1981, cited in Lieberman, 1982). Peer group relationships had little effect on maternal role satisfaction or maternal role strain. No evidence was found to indicate that other resources could substitute when husbands did not supply needed resources.

The social support network did not influence psychological distress over the first year after birth; however, the cognitive experience of social support and the extent of marital intimacy had significant independent effects (Stemp, Turner, & Noh, 1986). Others reported that intimate support was the strongest predictor of maternal satisfaction with life and parenting at 1, 8, and 18 months after birth (Crnic, Greenberg, Robinson, & Ragozin, 1984).

Women who identified their partners as most supportive had less difficulty in the transition to the maternal role (with a child aged 5 to 18 months) than did women who identified nonimmediate family members (Majewski, 1986, 1987). Partners provided physical assistance as well as intimate interaction. The spouses' participation in family life had positive effects on mothers' sensitivity to infant cues at 3 months (Broom, 1994).

Mothers' social support from husband, family, and others at 3 months was associated with mother–infant interactions as reflected by security of the infant–mother attachment at 12 months (Crockenberg, 1981). The effects of social support were greatest among irritable infants.

Mothers of 13-month-old infants reported support primarily from husbands and next from their mothers (Levitt, Weber, & Clark, 1986).

Support from and satisfaction with their husbands were related to maternal affect, life satisfaction, and infant difficulty. The infant's anxious/resistant attachment was related to negative maternal affect.

Emotional marital support and network support were positively related to maternal well-being and marital interaction but not to parental competence at 3 and 9 months after birth (Wandersman, Wandersman, & Kahn, 1980). No relationship was found between parenting group, instrumental marital, emotional marital, and network supports, indicating the importance of specificity in asking whether a person has support.

Compared to adult mothers, mostly single, Caucasian teenage mothers received less help from their male partners and relied on their mothers for major help with caretaking at 4 months (Coll, Hoffman, & Oh, 1987). Teenagers from a lower-SES family also tended to rely on other teenagers for help in caring for their infants. Teenagers who moved into the maternal role more easily had both supportive mates and supportive mothers (Mercer, 1980). Supportive mates contributed to the mother's self-esteem and morale, reaffirmed their feminine identity, and were attentive to the infant.

The partner relationship and perceived support were significantly related to maternal role competence among high- and low-risk mothers at 1, 4, and 8 months after birth but failed to enter the regressions predicting maternal competence (Mercer & Ferketich, 1994b). Network size and received support had no significant relationships with maternal competence.

Emotional support was the best predictor of satisfaction with the parenting role and infant care, measured by Lederman and Lederman's (1981) Prenatal Self-evaluation Questionnaire (PSQ), for both mothers and fathers at 6 weeks after birth (Lederman et al., 1982). Access to emotional support was important for women whose social network was 71% relatives. Multiparous mothers' satisfaction with the maternal role was related to their relationship with their husbands and their identification with a motherhood role.

Marital adjustment was related to adjustment to parenthood in model testing of primiparous mothers but not among multiparous mothers (Kirkpatrick, 1978). Attitudes were more important to multiparas' adjustment to parenthood.

A study of mothers of 12 white infants admitted to the hospital with failure to thrive (FTT) found that the mothers had more marital problems and lower psychosocial asset scores than did a control group of mothers (Lobo, Barnard, & Combs, 1992). Mothers of FTT infants also had moved more often and reported higher stress scores.

Services (e.g., baby sitting and household help) from fathers and material goods from relatives and friends were positively related to proximal mother–infant behavior at 3 months after birth, independent of the infant's risk status (Feiring, Fox, Jaskir, & Lewis, 1987). Advice from relatives was related to positive maternal affect, but advice from fathers was associated with criticism and had a negative affect.

The extent of helpfulness of child care supports had positive relationships with mothers' satisfaction with the changes in her relationship with her husband (Rankin, Campbell, & Soeken, 1985). A positive relationship between household help and satisfaction with change in marital relationship was also found.

The perceived partner relationship and received support were major predictors of experienced mothers' maternal–infant attachment the first week and at 1 month but did not enter regressions at 4 and 8 months (Mercer & Ferketich, 1994a). Neither partner relationship nor support variables were predictors of inexperienced mothers' attachment.

Perceived support was a predictor of inexperienced mothers' maternal role competence at 4 months; support and partner relationship variables did not enter regressions at any other test period from 1 week through 8 months (Mercer & Ferketich, 1995). The partner relationship had positive effects on experienced mothers' maternal competence at 4 months after birth; social support or partner relationship variables did not enter regressions at any other time from 1 week through 8 months.

From pregnancy to 12 months after birth, 501 women's parenting expectations about how their lives would be affected and how they would manage in the parenting role were more positive than their actual experiences in areas of spousal relationship and assistance in caregiving, relationships with friends, physical well-being, financial well-being, desire for employment, and maternal competence (Kalmuss et al., 1992). These discrepancies seriously affected their adjustment to motherhood. An easier adjustment to motherhood was associated with younger age, infants with easier temperaments, better marital quality during pregnancy, and nonemployment at 1 year.

At 3 to 5 months after birth, parental responsibilities and restrictions, parental gratification, and marital intimacy and stability reflected three different dimensions of the transition to parenting (Steffensmeier, 1982). Role clarity had direct effects on marital intimacy, and marital intimacy was related to gratification with the mother role, but not to parental responsibilities.

Women who reported positive marital relationships also reported less anxiety and depression at 2 months and 1 year after birth (Grossman et al., 1980). Mothers in positive marital relationships had calmer reactions at 2 and 7 months after birth (Westbrook, 1978). Those reporting either positive or ambivalent relationships described greater maternal warmth. Women in ambivalent relationships during pregnancy appeared to focus on the infant as a source of satisfaction.

Marital competence predicted maternal warmth and sensitivity to infants at 3 months after birth (Lewis et al., 1988). Dysfunctional marriages were not related to maternal investment in parenting. Mothers of boys were more highly invested than were mothers of girls. Marital adjustment during the first year was related to gratification in the mothering role (Russell, 1974). Congruence of infant rhythmicity with family rhythmicity was associated with maternal perception of overall family adjustment (Sprunger, Boyce, & Gaines, 1985).

Parenting confidence was associated with maternal role conflict and the marital relationship at 1 year after birth (Williams et al., 1987). Both Japanese and American mothers' perception of support from their husbands was related to the quality of stimulation they provided for their infants at 3 to 4 months (Durrett, Richards, Otaki, Pennebaker, & Nyquist, 1986). The more support the mother perceived from her husband, the less time she spent in the presence of her baby, but she spent more time positioning and showing affection to the baby when they were together.

Summary

Despite the decrease in satisfaction with the marital relationship the year following birth, strong scientific evidence supports Rubin's concept that the husband's support influences maternal behavior and maternal role identity. Although the woman's expectations about the division of labor may be violated following birth, the marital (or partner) relationship apparently provides emotional support that enables her to provide love and nurturing to the child.

A meta-analysis of 66 studies found significant correlations between both emotional and material support and maternal behavior (Andresen & Telleen, 1992). A direct relationship between social support and child outcomes could not be made because too few studies measured specific child outcomes. Most of the studies were of white, middle-income mothers with normal children. There was a lack of studies of multiparous mothers, employed mothers, poor mothers, nonwhite ethnic groups, adolescent mothers, mothers of handicapped children and low-birth-weight infants. An excellent roundtable publication, *Social Support and Families of Vulnerable Infants* (Raff & Carroll, 1984), focused on some of the understudied populations.

MATERNAL COMPETENCE/CONFIDENCE

Maternal competence, the skill and ability to meet the infant's needs, represents the behavioral component of the maternal role. Maternal competence may be either self-rated or observed by others. When self-rated, competence reflects the mothers' confidence in her mothering skills.

> *CS:* The full sense of maternal identity involves a shift in focus from third-person models of a child or of an expert mothering person to this child and to self in relation to this child.... This occurs ... about a month following delivery. (Rubin, 1984, p. 50)
>
> The developed capacity to read nonverbal behavior as a message cue of the child's inner status in situational experience leads to a knowing of the child in an uncommon but highly characteristic maternal intelligence. (p. 140)
>
> In establishing the identity of the child, the maternal identity in relation to this child is established. In knowing the child there is a knowing of self in relation to the child and a more active, more securely certain behavior with or in behalf of the child. (p. 142)
>
> The dedifferentiation of self from models, without closure to further replicable ideal attributes, immediately precedes the establishment of a maternal identity. (p. 51)

> *H:* Maternal role competence, including the ability to respond in synchrony with infant cues, increases over time.

Primiparous mothers' observed competence (measured by Blank's [1964] scale) increased significantly at 4 months over 1-month levels; no significant change occurred between 4 and 8 months, but competence at 12 months was lower (Mercer, 1985b). Mothers reported a decrease in negative ways of handling irritating child behavior (Disbrow et al., 1977) at 8 and 12 months over 1-month levels.

Achievement of the maternal role identity measured by the self-reported PSOC among 121 high-risk women (hospitalized antepartally) and 182 low-risk women over the first 8 months found significant increases for both groups at 4 and 8 months after a minimal decrease from birth to 1 month (Mercer & Ferketich, 1994b). The failure to find group differences in the trajectory of change over the 8 months indicated that high-risk women were not impeded in attainment of the maternal role identity. The women were largely middle-class and well educated.

As Canadian mothers became more experienced over 6, 10, and 16 weeks following birth, their understanding of their infant's cry behavior increased, and their soothing became more effective (Drummond, McBride, & Wiebe, 1993). At 6 weeks, primiparas used trial and error in dealing with infant crying; crying was understood as a signal only, with total separation of crying from the uniqueness of the situation. At 10 weeks, crying was still seen as generic communication by primiparous mothers, with the possibility of bad temper, boredom, or being spoiled; however, a beginning engagement between the themes of crying and soothing was occurring. Mothers' approach was pragmatic in finding solutions that worked. By 16 weeks, primiparas defined the cry as a specific communication, with soothing interventions individualized to the cry so that the infant system was defined. Multiparous mothers knew from the beginning that their task was to determine the nature of their infants' unique temperament, and at 6 weeks, over one-half could anticipate a continuum of communication by the cry. Multiparas' soothing was theory-directed and system-anticipated. By 10 weeks, they described the infants' maturity as making it easier to define behavioral patterns. These results from women in families ranging from poverty to upper-middle-class income add to Rubin's (1977, 1984) concepts of development of maternal identity and attachment theory, wherein the mother's development of cognitive structures of infant behavior serves as "working models" (Zeanah & Anders, 1987) for providing care (Drummond et al., 1993).

Maternal role evaluation by first-time mothers on a semantic differential scale during pregnancy, at 1 month and 1 year, dropped significantly during the early transition to the role among both working and middle-class mothers (Reilly, Entwisle, & Doering, 1987). The infant's adjustment had significant effects on working-class women's maternal role evaluations. The transition took longer for middle-class than for working-class women. At 1 month, 48% of working-class women listed their infant first (the most salient) when ranking eight important things in their lives compared to 32% of middle-class women; during pregnancy, 16% of both groups had ranked the unborn baby as first. The maternal role gained immediate salience for working-class women, more so than for middle-class women. Self-perceptions were relatively stable over the first year after birth but less stable for middle-class women in the earlier transition. In the early period, middle-class women's self-perceptions were stable and unresponsive to infant influence, indicating that they delayed taking on the new role. At 1 year, self-perceptions became more responsive to infant influences but less stable. Women whose husbands did more child care saw themselves less favorably in the maternal role than did those whose husbands were less involved. Women who had cesareans felt more competent in the role at 1 year. Middle-class mothers who had cesareans viewed their infants as less well adjusted.

Older, more affluent, and highly educated mothers attending a support group preferred to talk about personal rather than infant-related issues; the presence of infants at the meetings had adverse effects on attendance (Cronenwett, 1980). Discussions related to negative feelings about parenting were most important the first 6 months after birth, and discussions about employment were most important the second half of the first year.

In a sample of both primiparas and multiparas, the child's position in the family was more important than the family's SES in determining the quality of maternal care with Blank's (1964) rating scales (Roberts & Rowley, 1972). First children received more optimal care than their siblings did, second children received less than first or later-born children, and third or later children received more than second-born but less than firstborn children.

Satisfaction with role performance (evaluation subscale of Pridham and Chang's [1989] What Being a Parent Is Like) increased across the first 6 months after birth for 76 mothers (Grace, 1993). Although primiparous mothers demonstrated the steepest increase over the 6 months, their scores were similar to those of second-time mothers. Mothers of three or more children scored significantly higher until 3 months, when differences were no longer significant. The greater the number of children, the less life change occurred with the current birth at 3, 4H, and 6 months. The greater the maternal education, the less satisfaction with role performance. Parity was associated with greater life change. The centrality of the baby to mothers (how much the baby is on their mind) and help with parenting scores both decreased over the 6 months.

Maternal role competence (PSOC)· among multiparous mothers (68% with their second child) did not change significantly over 1, 4, and 8 months after birth (Mercer & Ferketich, 1995). The trajectory of change for primiparous mothers showed a significant increase at 4 months over first-week and 1-month levels, with a small increase at 8 months. Although the experienced mothers did not show an increase in their maternal competence, they were mothering in a more complex situation, juggling mothering among two or more children.

Scientific evidence supports an increase in maternal role competence over the first year, except for Mercer's (1985b) finding of a decrease at 1 year from 4 and 8 months. Mercer's finding was interpreted as mothers needing new skills at 1 year to deal with their increasingly mobile and manipulative toddler.

Drummond and associates' (1993) research is important in its delineation of the development of maternal synchrony. Their description of the primiparous mothers at 16 weeks indicates they had achieved an initial maternal role identity, concurring with others' findings. The time frame for knowing the infant is 3 months beyond Rubin's (1984) projected "end of the neonatal–neomaternal period" (p. 50) but well within the "two trimesters following birth" described for developmental change in maternal identity and binding-in to the child in her earlier work (Rubin, 1977, p. 67).

H: Maternal competence is positively related to cognitive problem solving.

The description above of mothers' development of a cognitive structure of infant behavior as working models for providing care supports this hypothesis also (Drummond et al., 1993) and agrees with Newberger's (1980) theory of developing parental awareness. It does not, however, support the concept proposed by Rubin that the mother differentiated herself from a model, preceding maternal role identity. Rather, the maternal intelligence worked with infant responses and trial and error to achieve synchrony and competence.

Pridham (1989) assessed mothers' decision rules for problem solving, based on information-processing theory, cognitive–phenomenological theory of coping, and competence development. Data were collected by using two simulated problems. Mothers' perceived problem-solving competence did not increase from 1 to 3 months after birth, suggesting that different criteria for assessing their problem solving were used as they became more experienced. Self-evidence/intuition as a naming rule was unrelated to problem-solving confidence. During the second and third months, everyday help had significant effects on mothers' problem-solving competence, and lay help was used to deal with knowledge issues; this was not the case during the first month (Pridham & Chang, 1992).

CS: Incorporation of the maternal identity into the self system is by way of the idealized image of self as mother of this child. There is an orientation toward the ideal and a searching of the environment and of memory for models of new and desirable attitudes and abilities. (Rubin, 1984, p.39)

H: Mothers rate themselves increasingly close to their ideal mother image during maternal role development.

At 4 months, one-third or more of 250 primiparous mothers had an image of an ideal mother as one who responded to her infant's needs, taught the infant, and provided unselfish love, nourishment, cleanliness, stimulation, and an appropriate environment (Mercer, 1986a). Two-thirds of the mothers rated themselves from 7 to 9 compared with their images of an ideal mother (rating of 10); 18% rated themselves at 10. By 8 months, 72% were in the 7-to-9 range, and 19% rated themselves at 10. At 1 year, 69% rated themselves from 7 to 9 and 23% as 10. Thus, mothers increasingly saw themselves as ideal or near-ideal mothers.

At 7 months, women who felt closer to their ideal images were in the process of changing their views of their actual and ideal selves, making it difficult to relate the relationship between actual and ideal self (Leifer, 1980). The women were changing their old self-images as they used new resources in coping with the demands of mothering and had not yet solidified new images. This is congruent with Rubin's (1984) theory about the ideal image; when an ideal is reached, it is no longer in the realm of the ideal, and a new ideal must be constructed.

Summary

Working-class women defined parenting roles in more stereotypical terms, with minimal ambiguity about the role; this may have contributed to their easier transition to the role than was true of middle-class mothers (Reilly et al., 1987). More highly educated mothers had less maternal role clarity than did less well educated mothers in Steffensmeier's (1982) study. The greater the clarity of role expectations (Burr, 1972) and the greater the consensus of role expectations within the mother's social group (Abernethy, 1973), the easier it is to move into the role. Do more highly educated, middle-class mothers have adequate role models in their social group? Do they see motherhood as less of a major life role than less well educated, working-class women?

Mothers saw themselves as increasingly more competent over the first 8 months of motherhood and increasingly approached their projected images of their ideal mother. Rubin's concepts were supported; she did not address differences by SES or educational level but included variations "to highlight the one commonality of role change involved in childbearing" (1967a, p. 238).

GRATIFICATION/SATISFACTION IN THE MATERNAL ROLE

Gratification in the maternal role is the satisfaction, enjoyment, reward, and pleasure that a woman experiences in interactions with her infant and in fulfilling the tasks of the role (Mercer, 1985c). Chodorow (1978) suggested that women's total identification with their infants enables them to derive gratification from mothering and to meet the infant's needs. Thus, gratification may act as a motivational component of maternal role. Pleasurable, enjoyable maternal interactions with the infant are necessary for the infant's optimal development, as indicated by the research on maternal anxiety and depression and security of infant attachment to the mother.

CS: The binding-in process of pregnancy and the polarization following the neonatal-neomaternal phase of the relationship goes into a holding pattern during the second and third months postpartum. As the baby develops in vigor and functional capacities, his reciprocity in the relationship enhances the value of the "you," the "I," and the experience of "we." By the third month postpartally the baby's smile in recognition and in anticipation and his actively contented behaviors fulfill the ideal image of the baby of the woman's dreams and fantasies during pregnancy. (Rubin, 1984, p. 127)

H: A mothers' gratification (satisfaction) is higher at the third month than at 1 or 2 months postpartum.

A negative relationship between educational level and gratification was reported (Russell, 1974; Steffensmeier, 1982). Middle-class parents reported less gratification in parenting than did lower-SES parents (Russell, 1974). Role clarity was positively related to gratification in the role at 3 to 5 months after birth (Steffensmeier, 1982). Mothers who planned their pregnancies experienced fewer gratifications in mothering; these mothers may have had higher expectations about the role that were unmet.

Gratification in the maternal role increased significantly from 1 to 4 months, with a minimal decrease at 8 months and a significant increase at 1 year among 20- to 29-year-old, largely middle-class mothers (Mercer, 1985b). Gratification was negatively related to role strain and positively related to self-rating of mothers' self-image in relation to their image of the ideal mother at 8 months (Mercer, 1985c, 1986a). Role strain increased at 12 months over 8-month levels.

Mothers who were dissatisfied with their maternal roles showed more rejection of their child and had more children with more difficult temperaments (Lerner & Galambos, 1985). Maternal role satisfaction was significantly related to maternal rejection, which was related to child difficulty at age 4.

Summary

These findings indicate that middle-class, more highly educated women derive less satisfaction from the maternal role. Is this because the maternal role is less salient to them? Or is it because the role is more ambiguous and they are able to define the maternal role less clearly than other roles?

Gratification's negative relationship to role strain and positive relationship to self-image in relation to ideal mother image indicate the importance of satisfaction in the maternal role. With less role strain, the mother should have less difficulty in integrating her multiple roles with the maternal role.

MATERNAL ATTACHMENT

The woman's developing relationship with her infant is accompanied by a wide range of emotions. Women felt guilty about not living up to the cultural image of the all-knowing, loving, and calm good mother (Leifer, 1980).

> *CS:* The process [binding-in/attachment] is active, intermittent and accumulative…. The origin and end-point of the process are in the maternal identity itself.
>
> Maternal identity and binding-in to the child are two major developmental changes, each dependent on the other, in the three trimesters of pregnancy and the two trimesters following delivery of the child. Developmental progress in maternal identity and in binding-in is promoted or retarded on the one side by the infant itself and on the other side by society, particularly closely related family members. (Rubin, 1977, p. 67)
>
> Enduring love, altruistic self-denial, and empathy … these actions within the matrix of affinal bonds comprise the characteristics of maternal behavior which are seen as the bottom line. (Rubin, 1984, p. 2)

H: Maternal infant attachment increases over the first year after birth.

Robson and Moss (1970) reported that mothers' maternal feelings intensified toward their infants during the second month when infants began to exhibit visual fixation and to smile. By the end of the third month, maternal attachment was such that the infant's absence was unpleasant, and the imagined loss of the infant was an intolerable prospect.

Mothers' anxiety on separation from their infants remained relatively stable from early postpartum to 3 months after birth (Hock, McBride, & Gnezda, 1989). Maternal reunion behavior with the infant was more strongly associated with maternal anxiety than with departure behavior.

Maternal–infant attachment increased significantly from 1 to 4 months among primiparous mothers (Mercer, 1985b). Attachment was significantly higher at 4 months than at 8 or 12 months.

Maternal–infant attachment mean scores changed very little over 1, 4, and 8 months among high- and low-risk women (Mercer et al., 1987). Although mean scores varied very little, significantly higher attachment was reported the first week than at 1, 4, or 8 months among inexperienced mothers (Mercer & Ferketich, 1994a). Among experienced mothers, 1-week and 4-month attachment scores were significantly higher than 1- and 8-month mean scores.

Summary

There is no evidence to support the concept that self-reported maternal attachment increases after the fourth month during the first year. Findings with inexperienced mothers are mixed: one study did not find a significant decrease after the first week; another did.

MATERNAL ROLE IDENTITY ACHIEVEMENT

At the end of an in-depth study of 19 primiparous mothers over pregnancy and 7 months after birth, mothers were actively involved in the process of self-discovery (Leifer, 1980). Leifer's findings suggested that "integrating one's identity as a mother and forming a relationship with a baby have been only tentatively established at 6 months postpartum" (p.92).

When 242 primiparas were asked at 1 year when they had first felt secure and comfortable with the maternal role as part of their identity, 3% reported, since pregnancy; 33%, the first 2 weeks; 13%, at 2 months; 15%, at 4 months; 21%, by 9 months; 11%, between 9 and 12 months; 4% stated that they were still working on it (Mercer, 1986a). Thus, roughly one-half had achieved the role by 2 months, two-thirds by 4 months, 85% by 9 months, and 96% by 1 year. Maternal competence, gratification, and attachment behaviors measured at times over the first year supported the concept that the majority of first-time mothers had achieved maternal role identity in those areas by 4 months (Mercer, 1985b, 1986a).

Zabielski (1994) reported the time of recognition of a maternal identity by 42 mothers of preterm and term infants as follows: 43% by 2 weeks after delivery, 52% by 2 months, 69% by 4 months, 86% by 6 months, and 95% by 12 months. No significant difference for time of recognition was found between term and preterm mothers. Time of recognition of the maternal identity had only 10% of variance explained by length of gestation, maternal feelings about the baby, maternal role competence, and maternal role satisfaction. Maternal identity was facilitated by successful, satisfactory interactions between mother and infant; by other persons' recognition that they had achieved the role; by feelings of love, closeness, and protectiveness for the infant; by caretaking-role readiness; by self-continuity; and by recognition of role change. Achievement of a maternal identity, true to its complexity, is measured from the woman's perspective by many variables.

The timing of multiparas' achievement of maternal role identity with the new infant is less clear. Drummond et al. (1993) found that multiparous mothers had defined the dyadic system and adapted themselves by 10 weeks postpartum, having used their prior experience to anticipate their role in defining the infant's crying cues. Multiparas had expanded the dyadic system to include social activities for the infant at 16 weeks, when primiparas defined and adapted to the dyadic system in soothing infant crying.

Grace (1993) observed that second-time mothers increased in maternal confidence similarly to primiparous mothers. Mothers of three or more children scored higher but did not show a trajectory of increase and at 4H months had a slight decrease so that all three groups scored similarly but increased in confidence at 8 months. Mercer and Ferketich (1995) found virtually no change in multiparas' maternal competence over 8 months.

Walker and Montgomery (1994) studied whether mothers' maternal role indicators measured during the postpartum predicted their 8- to 10-year-old children's socioemotional development. After forced entry of SES and parity, neither perceived nor demonstrated maternal role attainment variables predicted child outcome. The women's perception of their babies at 1 to 3 days on the semantic differential added significantly to predictions of the school-age child's social competence for multiparas and primiparas; however, the direction of the relationship was negative for primiparas. The semantic differential measure of the baby and the NPI-II, made at 4 to 6 weeks, added to predictive ability of the child's behavioral problems.

SUMMARY

The slow restoration of physical and social functioning following birth, accompanied by an increase in health problems over the first year, adds to the woman's difficulty in integrating other roles with her maternal role identity. It was not surprising that a decrease in self-concept or self-esteem was found at 8 months, when a decrease in general well-being occurred.

The supportive marital relationship does not change significantly during pregnancy and the first month following birth but declines significantly over the first year after birth. The discrepancy between the mother's expectations of forthcoming spousal help and of what parenthood would be like contributed to less satisfaction with the marital relationship.

Differences were found in early role saliency for the maternal role and in role clarity between working-class and middle-class women. The lower role clarity and role salience reported among middle-class mothers suggests that the maternal role is better defined among working-class mothers.

In general, the period around 4 months was a time of much enjoyment in infant interactions, of accomplishment in being able to identify infant needs, accompanied by a feeling of initial confidence in the maternal role. When all research is considered, the initial integration of the maternal role into the self system (self-concept) seems to occur for the majority around 4 months. The achievement of harmony with other roles, a criterion of role identity achievement, was *not* achieved by then, however. The problems with wife and other roles and the desire to return to prepregnancy adult images of other roles appeared to be more than grief work as described by Rubin for the losses incurred with motherhood.

Because maternal role identity attainment is a process and the identity is bound with the age stage of infant development, the process is ongoing over childhood and adolescence. As the child develops and transmits different cues, the mother must continue her cognitive restructuring for parenting and adapt her maternal behavior to the new developmental need. In this sense, the maternal role continues to evolve until the child reaches independence in adulthood.

Leifer (1980) suggests that it is important to distinguish between maternal response to the infant and response to the maternal role in the transition to the maternal role. Women were relating lovingly to infants while feeling depressed, inadequate, and anxious about their changed life-styles. Further research is needed to distinguish whether these responses are grief work in relinquishing former life-styles or a lack of integration of the maternal role with other roles. Until harmony is achieved with other roles, the maternal role identity is not fully integrated into the self-system.

No research after the first 4 to 6 postpartal weeks, whether quantitative or qualitative, has used Rubin's cognitive operations of replication, fantasy, or dedifferentiation from role models. Would other cognitive operations or themes be more useful? Zabielski (1994) discovered 8 common themes from mothers' descriptions of their identity recognition: role expectations, role partner contact/interaction, role acknowledgment, role qualities, role actions, role readiness, self-continuity, and role change. These offer directions for research to discover more about the complex process of maternal role identity attainment.

The failure of models to explain substantial variance in maternal role identity variables suggests a need to continue to explore relevant variables and situational contexts. Koniak-Griffin's (1993) historical and empirical review of maternal role attainment and Gaffney's (1992) practice model for maternal role sufficiency suggest additional variables to consider.

■ 9
Preterm Birth: Interrupting the Process of Maternal Role Achievement

In chapters 3–8 maternal behaviors evolving over pregnancy and the months postpartum in the process of maternal role achievement were described. The focus of this chapter is on transition to the maternal role when this process is interrupted.

The anticipatory preparation for the maternal role is interrupted by the preterm birth. The mother's lack of preparedness for the untimely birth and the uncertainty of her premature infant's survival and outcome call for extraordinary cognitive restructuring in her transition to the formal stage of maternal role identity. The mother must deal with events around the birth and possible reasons for the untimeliness, reconcile the image of her preemie with her pregnancy fantasy image of a newborn as she grieves her loss, find hope for the infant's outcome, and deal with the unanticipated environment of the neonatal intensive care unit (NICU) in her first interactive behaviors with her infant.

The disproportionate number of premature infants in study samples of abused or neglected infants and knowledge about the effects of

215

mother–infant interaction on infant development have stimulated much research on the transactional effects of mother–preterm infant interactions the first year after birth. Goldberg's (1978) review of research on the effects of prematurity on parent–infant interaction found that in comparison to mothers of term infants, mothers of preterm infants were less actively involved with their babies: there was, for example, less body contact and less time face to face; the mothers smiled at, touched, and talked to their infants less. Most of the studies focused on infants less than 4 months of age. Because practices in NICUs and care and survival of premature infants have changed tremendously in the past 2 decades, the focus here is on research since 1980.

Preterm infants have not achieved control over their autonomic, motoric, and state regulation and must develop their physical integrity and internal stability before they are able to use caregiver input and support or interact responsively (Gorski, Davison, & Brazelton, 1979). A comparison of behavioral organization (BNBAS) of preterm infants, term infants in NICU, healthy term infants with prolonged hospitalization because of maternal illness, and healthy control infants found differences between preterm and healthy control infants in areas of interactive and motoric processes and state organization, with preterm infants having less motor maturity, more deviant reflexes, and a general flattening of state (Holmes et al., 1982). Preterm infants' performance was more like full-term infants in the NICU than other groups, indicating that early behavioral deficits also result from other factors associated with preterm birth, such as hospitalization, illness, and obstetric complication.

Preterm infants' inabilities to give clear distress signals, difficulties with state modulation, and slow attendance to visual and auditory stimuli make it particularly difficult for their unprepared parents, who are frightened, worried, and feeling incompetent.

THE PRETERM LABOR

Although obstetric factors (e.g., pregnancy-induced hypertension and incompetent cervical os), medical factors (e.g., maternal diabetes, acute infections), and socioeconomic factors (e.g., low SES, absence of prenatal care) contribute to preterm birth; in the absence of such factors, the etiology remains largely unknown. Rubin (1984) hinted at limited, indirect cognitive control over labor.

> *CS:* A woman starts and stops in labor frequently. The uterus is as tense and as irritable as she is. But the image of an incompletely formed baby, the hazards awaiting such a baby, and the dangers to the intactness and wholeness of her own body in childbirth help her to "hold on" to the baby and the pregnancy. (Rubin, 1984, p. 58)
> The uterine muscle contractility is not under voluntary controls, but it is responsive to the involuntary inputs of the reticular system and limbic or survival system of the brain. (p. 92)
> It takes a strong ego or, more correctly, a strongly formed maternal identity to withstand the pressures for an early termination of the pregnancy. (p. 63)

H: Women hold back (hesitate to let go) when they are fearful or ambivalent about the birth and or outcome.

McKay and Barrows (1991) videotaped 20 women during the second stage of labor. When women viewed the tapes postpartally, they recognized their hesitation and emotional conflict about delivering. Their reasons for hesitating were their unreadiness to be mothers, not wanting to care for another baby, waiting for a husband or midwife to arrive, fear of the intense sensation and pain, embarrassment, and fear for their infant (previous loss of infant).

H: Women may avoid premature delivery by cognitive control.

Seventy percent of women admitted to the hospital for preterm labor were able to carry their infants to term (Mackey & Coster-Schulz, 1992). Thirty percent of the women had waited from 2 days to 2 weeks before seeking care for the preterm labor symptoms. Their waiting was related to previous experience with preterm labor, difficulty in accessing care, and feeling that the changes occurring within their bodies were a normal part of pregnancy. Causes of the preterm labor were attributed to physical activity, emotional stress, or fate. Women remained on bedrest at home after their discharge from the hospital and reported using cognitive approaches to prevent further preterm labor. Cognitive approaches included focusing on the baby, determination not to return to the hospital until ready to deliver, and optimistic thoughts. Women who had more nurturing tended to deliver at term; those who delivered early had little support at home or in other social situations. This is supportive of findings discussed in chapter 4 about the potential effects of mother–father relationships on pregnancy outcome.

Self-diagnostic confusion was observed among women who experienced preterm labor about "the ambiguous symptoms, absence of a meaningful label to attach to symptoms, and the context of pregnancy with its expected discomforts," to the extent that it was unclear about the appropriate action to take (Patterson, Douglas, Patterson, & Bradle, 1992, p. 372). Attempts to make sense of and deal with the symptoms of preterm labor delayed seeking care. Thus, women were cognitively unaware of the preterm labor at onset.

Although onset of contractions is not under cognitive control, cognitive and other behaviors were associated with managing to carry the infant to term along with medical treatment after hospitalization. Confusion about the symptoms of preterm labor does not support any initial cognitive control to stop the labor.

IMPACT OF THE NICU ON MATERNAL RESPONSES

The aura of the NICU and the preterm infants' conditions and appearance are frightening under the best of circumstances. But to the newly delivered mother, the NICU is overwhelming.

> *CS:* The woman traumatized by delivery ... or exhaustion from labor has little unbound energy for either fantasy imagery or direct visualization of the child.... In the configurational gestalt, the background delineates the unfamiliar object in the foreground and the child itself is not seen in the isolette, under the treatment lamp, or in the midst of intravenous tubing on initial viewing. The background paraphernalia has to be dealt with and separated out from the image of the child before the child can be seen, identified, or recognized. (Rubin, 1984, p. 134)
>
> There is remarkably little pleasurable smiling in the woman observing her newborn child. The smile is a product of recognition and there is little that is recognizable in the neonate to the neomaternal woman. (p. 134)

H: Early maternal behavior, such as identifying and claiming the infant, is interrupted by the stress of dealing with the NICU environment.

Miles and Mathes (1991) ascertained that the child's behavior, emotional response, and parental role alterations were the most stressful facets of an intensive care unit. This research and the Pediatric ICU scale (Carter & Miles, 1989) led to the development of a Parental Stressor Scale: Neonatal Intensive Care Unit (PSS:NICU), with three subscales—parental role alterations, sights and sounds of the unit, and infant behavior and appearance—to be used for either research or clinical intervention (Miles, Funk, & Carlson, 1993). Alterations in the parental role, measured by the PSS:NICU, were stressful for both parents but significantly more stressful for mothers than for fathers (Miles, Funk, & Kasper, 1992).

Based on Ajzen and Fishbein's (1980) theory of reasoned action, Kurtz and associates (Kurtz, Perez-Woods, Tse, & Snyder, 1992) developed an instrument based on a cognitive processing model to measure antecedents of parents' behavior with newborns in the NICU. Beliefs about events have an evaluative component and are related to individual's attitudes. Parents have beliefs about the admission of their infant to the NICU and perceptions about social norms for NICU admission. Attitudes and norms affect behavioral intentions and behavior. When events in the NICU are positive or negative, these tend to influence subsequent parental behavior. Belief statements derived from parents completing the statement "The admission of my baby to the NICU" included negative feelings (burdened, concerned, confused, shocked, guilty, incompetent) and positive feelings (grateful, satisfied, confident, hopeful). Soon after birth, parental beliefs about infant outcome decreased, and attitudes about outcome improved. Motivation to use a behavior increased as the influence of social norms increased. By 2 weeks after birth, the significance of relationships between beliefs and attitudes decreased, and relationships between motivations and social norms increased. As parents learned more about unit norms, the influence of their previously held beliefs decreased.

A change model to enhance parenting in the NICU, based on King's (1981) assumptions was proposed (Norris & Hoyer, 1993). The assumptions include the following: parents have a right to knowledge about their infants and to participate in decisions influencing the infants and their lives; nurses have a responsibility to share information to facilitate this end; perceptual inaccuracy may occur in nurse-parent interactions, leading to incongruent expectations; and change may not occur when parent and nurse goals are incongruent (Norris & Hoyer, 1993). A model of symbolic interactionism was also proposed for caring for parents of preterm infants in the NICU (Edwards & Saunders, 1990).

A qualitative study described an example of incongruence—mismatched caring for the infant—resulting in the nurses' labeling mothers as denying the seriousness of the situation and being inappropriately worrisome (Stainton, 1992). Mothers focused on *possibilities,* whereas caretakers focused on actual or *potential* problems. Professionals searched expertly for early warning signs of infant morbidity or mortality; mothers focused on the possibility of good outcomes, searching for information suggesting progress while remaining cognizant of the problems.

Looking for the positive has been evident in studying perceptions of the preterm neonate. Preterm mothers scored their infants more positively compared to the average preterm infant than term mothers compared their infant to an average term infant on NPI-I and NPI-II at 6 to 8 weeks postpartum (Weingarten, Baker, Manning, & Kutzner, 1990). Mothers completing Broussard's NPI-I of their preterm infants within 48 hours after birth, the NPI-II on discharge from the NICU and an NPI-III 2 to 3 weeks following hospital discharge, perceived their infants more positively than an average infant at all three test periods (Koniak, Ludington-Hoe, Chaze, & Sachs, 1985). Their perceptions were modified somewhat when they became more acquainted with their infants and assumed caretaking roles, indicating that mothers continued to identify their infants during hospitalization and the weeks after discharge.

Assumptions underlying instrument and care models verify that parents have difficulty with early acquaintance behaviors in the NICU. Koniak and associates' (1985) findings that mothers viewed their infants more positively in the NICU may reflect a means of maintaining their hope or an avoidance of tempting fate. Stainton's (1992) findings indicate that mothers' focus on the positive may be a coping mechanism.

MATERNAL IDENTITY DIFFUSION DURING UNCERTAINTY

No research is reported on maternal identity diffusion. However, based on the definition of adolescents' identity diffusion as having no set occupational or ideological direction (Marcia, 1980), *maternal identity diffusion* at birth of a preterm infant is defined as having no cognitive set or direction for proceeding with maternal role behaviors. Because maternal identity is established in relation to the infant as role partner, knowing the infant helps to know directions for role identity behaviors. Anticipatory behaviors formulated during pregnancy are no longer applicable, and directives from experts in the formal stage of maternal role identity are also uncertain about infant outcome, especially for very low birthweight (VLBW) preterms. Thus, a maternal identity in relation to a preterm infant in the NICU is tenuous at best. The mother remains trapped in the formal stage dependent on directives from professional experts. She is handicapped not only in acquaintance with her infant but also in gathering cognitive information to begin informal maternal role stage behaviors of experimenting with what works best for her frail infant.

> *CS:* The mother of a premature has a very incomplete delivery with an incomplete infant. There is no end of one phase of childbearing and the beginning of another. There is identity diffusion and a continuance of the pregnancy as if still awaiting delivery. There is constricted energy and space for action and the images of the child are of nightmarish quality. (Rubin, 1984, p. 104)

> *H:* The mother of a premature remains in a state of maternal identity diffusion as long the infant remains critical in the NICU.

Maternal physical and emotional responses are considered reflective of the mother's lack of any directions for proceeding with her maternal role. Predominant for preterm mothers were emotional distress (sadness, shock, anxiety, crying, guilt, insomnia), psychosomatic symptoms (physical illness at the thought of visiting infant in NICU, feelings of faintness, heart palpitations), disappointment (expected a cute cuddly baby; the baby did not look like a baby), alienation from the infant, resentment and anger, inconvenience and financial difficulties in traveling to the hospital to visit, and uncertainty about the infant's survival and long-term prognosis (Pederson, Bento, Chance, Evans, & Fox, 1987). Mothers reported a need for special preparation for caring for infants after discharge from the hospital, indicating that they had an inadequate knowledge base; the usual formal stage of role achievement was extended. Grandparents, frequent sources of help, were also distressed and responded similarly to parents to the infant's appearance and the NICU (Blackburn & Lowen, 1986).

Mothers of 41 preterm infants, matched with mothers of term infants on parity, type of delivery, age, and race, were significantly more anxious and depressed than were mothers of term infants during the first postpartal week (Gennaro, 1988). Anxiety and depression did not vary by the infant's level of illness. At 2 through 7 weeks, both groups of mothers experienced a similar affective response.

The preterm mothers' major concerns during the first week were the infant's health, weight, and development and discharge from the hospital, in that order (Gennaro, Zukowsky, Brooten, Lowell, & Visco, 1990). More concerns were expressed the first week and after discharge from the hospital; however, the number of concerns were consistent at 40 weeks adjusted gestational age and every month through 6 months.

During the first week after birth, mothers of preterm infants cried more, felt more helpless, worried more about future pregnancies and their ability to cope, felt guilty about their baby's condition, and worried more that they were losing touch with reality than did mothers of term infants (Trause & Kramer, 1983). One month after the infants were home, mothers of preterm infants were adjusting to the realities of caring for their infants, and mothers of term infants reported significantly more crying and not wanting to be left alone.

Mothers of VLBW infants ($\leq$ 1500 g) reported higher anxiety and depression than did mothers of low birthweight infants (LBW, 1,501–2,500 g) until their infants were at 3 months adjusted gestational age (Gennaro, York, & Brooten, 1990). Mothers of LBW infants reported higher anxiety and depression at 3 and 4 months adjusted age.

In contrast, Aradine and Ferketich (1990) reported no significant differences in anxiety levels of women who had preterm infants and either high- or low-risk women who delivered full-term infants at 1 week, 1 or 4 months; mean state anxiety scores for mothers of preterm infants did not differ from those reported by Gennaro (1988). During the first postpartal week, 40% of all mothers and 45% of mothers with preterm births had depression scores greater than 16, the cut-off point for clinical depression on the CES-D (Radloff, 1977). By 4 months, mothers with premature births had depression scores similar to those of low-risk women delivering term infants.

Casteel (1990) reported parents' affective and cognitive responses during the first week their preterm infants were in the NICU and the first week after their discharge. Negative affective responses included anxiety, fear, helplessness, and sadness; positive affective responses included amazement, confidence, love, and parental well-being. Cognitive responses included protection, provision, and attachment themes. Significantly more negative feelings were reported in the NICU, and more positive feelings were reported in the home setting. A greater proportion of mothers' cognitive responses were reported in the home setting. The quality of mothers' cognitive responses differed from fathers'; mothers were more specific about their parenting behaviors.

A case study of a mother of a preterm, chronically ill infant in the NICU described a process of maternal rehearsal for caregiving at home (Hayes, Stainton, & McNeil, 1993) that illustrates work to overcome maternal role diffusion. The meaning of the mother's experience fell into the categories of uncertainty, experiencing the baby as powerful in the mother–infant relationship, working to gain acceptance from the baby, blurred territory in initiating care practices, and being alone and vulnerable.

Research supports general maternal identity diffusion while the infant is in the NICU. Uncertainty and worry about the infant's survival, health, and developmental outcome render it impossible to define a maternal identity in relation to the unknown preterm partner. In addition, mothers' emotional response to the reality of the situation and their lengthy separation from the infant in the NICU deters accurate information processing. Huckabay (1987) found that mothers who received pictures of their preterm infants upon mothers' discharge from the hospital demonstrated more bonding behavior when they visited their infants in the NICU than did mothers who did not receive pictures. The early "worry work" of mothers of preterm infants seems to decrease their anxiety and depression their first month at home, in contrast to term mothers, who experienced more anxiety at that time. Being able to interact with their infants at any time and the greater convenience of not having to leave their family to visit the infant in the NICU may have also decreased anxiety and depression from previous levels.

PROGRESS TOWARD MATERNAL ROLE IDENTITY

With the formal and informal stages of maternal role identity achievement extended and mothers' cognitive work handicapped by a tenuous role partner who contributes to maternal identity diffusion, a delay in achievement of a maternal role identity is expected. Does she catch up? Are there problematic periods? How does the mother achieve synchrony in mother–infant interactions when the infant gives only subtle and inconsistent cues?

H: Mothers of preterm infants will not progress in maternal competence, maternal gratification, and maternal attachment, at the same rate as mothers of full-term infants.

MATERNAL COMPETENCE

Family Relationships and Maternal Competence

Mothers who demonstrated low activity with their preterm infants in the NICU were identified with 44% accuracy by their relationship with their own mothers and with the infants' fathers and by whether they had previous abortions (Minde, Marton, Manning, & Hines, 1980). Maternal–infant interactions were related to infants' responsivity and remained consistent at 3 months; NICU activity was predictive of caretaking patterns at home.

During the third to fifth weeks after birth, satisfaction with the partner relationship had direct effects on maternal affect; affect had direct effects on mothers' attitudes toward their infants in the NICU (Coffman, Levitt, Deets, & Quigley, 1991). Mothers in difficult marriages tended to have negative perceptions of their infants. As the number of previous preterm births increased, the marital adjustment of mothers of preterm infants with severe respiratory distress syndrome decreased (Lamm, 1983). Others found no relationship between the quality of spousal relationship and mothers' perceptions of their infants at 2 days and 6 to 8 weeks postpartum (Weingarten et al., 1990).

Formal/Informal Stage

Videotapes of parents visiting their preterm infant in an NICU showed that mothers touched their infants 43.4% of the time during three visits

(Harrison, L. L., & Woods, 1991). Mothers touched their infants more than either grandmothers or fathers did; infants were touched infrequently on their legs, feet, and front of their bodies. Most infants had monitoring equipment in those areas. Infants of less than 28 weeks gestation received lighter touch and less touching than infants of more than 28 weeks gestation. Younger infants had lower mean saturation and more abnormal oxygen values during touch than did older infants, so the hesitancy to handle young infants may have been an adaptive response.

Six phases of maternal adjustment related to the mother's emotional state, perception of her baby, and family responses were observed among mothers of preterm infants weighing 1,500 g or less from 1 week to 3 months: anticipatory grief, anxious waiting, positive anticipation, anxious adjustment, exhausted accommodation, and confident caring (McHaffie, 1990). The first three phases were observed in the NICU and the last three after the baby's discharge from the hospital. Mothers who did not feel ready to take their infants home from the hospital had much difficulty in establishing and maintaining relationships and had inappropriate perceptions of the infant (e.g., angry with baby as cause of troubles, irritated by baby's behavior that was considered a deliberate thwarting of their efforts at care, and did not love the baby but concealed this from NICU staff).

Unexpectedly, no significant differences were observed among Latina mothers' perceived maternal confidence during the first week following birth, by whether they had preterm or term infants (Zahr, 1993). Observed maternal competence behaviors were not related to self-reported maternal confidence. Parity was the strongest predictor of maternal confidence, followed by the infant's health (fewer medical complications).

Within the first 6 weeks, mothers of preterm infants expressed a larger number and different types of concerns than did mothers of term infants (Goodman & Sauve, 1985; Minde, Perrotta, & Marton, 1985). Mothers of preterms were concerned about their infants' appearance, cerebral palsy, or mental retardation, in contrast to term mothers' worry about overweight or bad temper. The idiosyncratic behavior of sick preterm infants determined much of their mothers' style of interacting with them.

No mother of a preterm infant felt her infant knew her on the first day after birth, whereas 66% of mothers of term infants felt their baby knew them (Goodman & Sauve, 1985). At 28 days after discharge, 40% of preterm mothers and 17% of term mothers continued to feel that their infants did not know them. Only 40% of high-risk mothers felt that the baby was theirs when they came home from the hospital, compared to 93% of the low-risk group. Most (83%) mothers of normal infants felt their baby was really their own either during pregnancy or at birth, compared to 23% of high-risk mothers. Yet no differences in how the two groups of mothers viewed their infant, compared to an average infant, were found at 2 and 6 weeks postdischarge.

Maternal adjustment to infants weighing 1,500 g or less at birth, 3 to 6 weeks postpartum, and at 6 months corrected age was studied, using a transactional model of coping with stress within an ecological systems-theory perspective (Thompson, Oehler, Catlett, & Johndrow, 1993). Significant psychological distress occurred among 48% at birth, 33% at 3 to 6 weeks postpartum, and 41% at 6 months; distress at the time of birth was not a function of infant birthweight, gestational age, or the potential impact of neonatal illness on subsequent outcome. From birth to 6 months gestational age, stress was less related to the preterm baby and more to daily hassles, less support, and greater conflict in the family environment.

Perceiving one's baby as above average indicates that the mother has some acquaintance with her baby in relation to an average baby (Broussard's [1979] Neonatal Perception Inventories [NPI]). Mothers of preterm infants on apnea monitors reported significantly higher NPI scores 2 weeks after their discharge from the NICU than did either mothers of nonmonitored preterm infants or full-term infants (Leonard, Scott, & Erpestad, 1992). This finding was attributed to the intervention program provided for mothers of monitored infants. Mothers of nonmonitored preterm infants scored lowest on the NPI. Poorer perceptions of infants were related to maternal psychological distress; mothers most bothered by their infants reported the highest number of negative psychological symptoms. At 6 months, mothers of monitored infants rated their infants as having significantly higher intellectual and social development. Mothers who received information about preterm infants' interactive capability reported significantly more of their infants' behavior during a 10-minute feeding session (Riesch & Munns, 1984).

Establishing Synchronous Behavior with the Infant

No significant differences were found in rhythmic patterning of mother–infant pair interactions between 15 term newborns and 15 preterm infants at 40 weeks gestational age (Censullo, Lester, & Hoffman, 1985). Differences in synchrony (time spent in mutual attention) were not significant, although preterm dyads scored lower (58.8, SD = 39.4) than term dyads (82.4, SD = 59.4).

A comparison of preterm and term mother–infant dyads within 48 hours after birth and at 1, 2, and 3 months after their expected date of birth found that, at 1 month, term infants were more alert and focused during feedings and moved their legs, heads and mouths more than did preterm infants (Minde et al., 1985). Mothers of preterm infants touched and smiled at their infants less often but looked *en face* more frequently than did mothers of term infants. At 2 months, the only infant difference was term infants' greater leg movement. Mothers of preterms continued to touch and smile at their infants less frequently but vocalized more. Mothers of preterm infants spent less time with nipples in the infants' mouths at both 1 and 2 months. At 3 months, preterm infants exhibited more head and mouth movements; their mothers looked at and talked to them more but still smiled at them less. Both groups reported a large number of feeding problems at 1 and 2 months, but by 3 months, mothers of preterm infants reported more feeding problems, and more indicated that their infants' sleeping patterns were more predictable than did mothers of term infants.

Shortly after their infants' discharge from the NICU, mothers' cognitive adaptation in both primary control (how much the infant's current recovery and future developmental status depended on maternal actions and the extent to which future perinatal complications could be prevented in subsequent births) and secondary control (whether mothers had benefited from the crises and had answered the question "Why me?") were related to a measure of adaptational outcome on Lorr and McNair's (1982) Profile of Mood States (Affleck, Tennen, & Gershman, 1985). At 6 months, mothers who had done more to prevent adverse pregnancy outcomes, had been more optimistic about their pregnancy outcomes, and had seen their infants' complications as more avoidable reported greater mood disturbance and more distress since their infants' hospitalization (Affleck, Tennen, & Rowe, 1988).

A comparison of healthy term, healthy preterm, sick preterm, and sick term infants found that infant illness affected BNBAS performance and maternal behavior at 3 months (Greene, Fox, & Lewis, 1983). Sick infants were less attentive during the first month, cried more at 3 months, and received more proximal and vocal response from their mothers. Attentive and alert infants were less irritable, and their mothers used less proximal stimulation and were less attentive to them. Hazardous obstetrical and postnatal events were associated with a shorter period of preterm infant wakefulness and less irritability during time awake at 1 month corrected gestational age (Beckwith & Cohen, 1978). These infants were receiving more interactions from their caregivers than were infants who had had a more optimal preterm course.

Significant relationships between maternal mood states at hospital discharge of high-risk infants and 9 months later were found; early mood states were moderately associated with caretaking difficulty at 9 months (Affleck, Allen, McGrade, & McQueeney, 1982). Good maternal problem-solving ability was associated with higher levels of anxiety during infant stay in the NICU (Gennaro, 1986).

Anxiety and depression measured during the first postnatal week following preterm birth was positively related to the number of acute care visits infants had experienced from hospital discharge to 6 months adjusted age (Gennaro & Stringer, 1991). Although mothers who took their preterm infants to more acute care visits (either 0, 1, or >1) had higher anxiety and depression the first week, their infants had not differed by morbidity, birthweight, gestational age, or initial length of hospitalization. Thus, the mother's initial reaction to her infant's illness was related to her later use of acute care facilities, supporting the concept of a vulnerable child syndrome, also suggested by Levy (1980). Preterm mothers' anxiety and depression were significantly lower at 9 months than prior to discharge from the hospital (Brooten et al., 1988).

Maternal confidence measured by the Maternal Confidence Questionnaire (Parker & Zahr, 1985) among mothers of preterm infants at 4 and 8 months (corrected age) was unrelated to birthweight, gestational age, Apgar scores, days on the respirator, and days in the hospital (Zahr, 1991). At 4 months, the presence and severity of ventricular bleed were associated with maternal confidence. At both 4 and 8 months, maternal education, family income, social support, and previous experience with infants were significantly related to maternal confidence. Mothers who saw themselves as more confident rated their infants as less difficult, more adaptable, and more predictable at both 4 and 8 months.

Others also reported that infant risk status at birth and major or minor illnesses were unrelated to mothers' stress at 1 and 13 months after birth (Coffman, Levitt, & Guacci-Franco, 1993). The preterm infant's hospitalization after the newborn period was significantly related to maternal stress and less satisfaction and closeness with relationships.

Mothers of preterm infants scored less favorably in mother–infant interactions during a teaching task measured by the Nursing Child Assessment Teaching Scale (NCATS) (Barnard, 1978) than did mothers of term infants at 3 months after discharge from the hospital (Harrison, 1990). No relationship was found between the NCATS and maternal affect scores among mothers of toddlers, but relationships between maternal knowledge of child development and educational level, as well as significant differences between African-American, Hispanic, and white mothers, were found (Gross, Conrad, Fogg, Willis, & Garvey, 1993), indicating a need to control for these variables when using the NCATS. Others reported that the feeding scale had potential to identify increased risk of impaired mother–infant interaction related to infant case status (Farel, Freeman, Keenan, & Huber, 1991).

An intervention of demonstrating either the BNBAS or a routine physical examination to mothers of preterm infants prior to discharge from the NICU led to more positive maternal attitudes on the Cohler Maternal Attitude Scale at 6 months corrected age than among preterm mothers not observing either intervention (Szajnberg, Ward, Krauss, & Kessler, 1987). Preterm mothers adapted better than did term mothers to the symbiotic needs of the infant, indicating that they were less conflicted about issues of reciprocity, exploration, and dependency on the mother at both pre- and postintervention times. More intervention than control mothers rated their infants as easier on the Carey (1970) ITQ.

Maternal assessments of term and preterm infants with respiratory distress syndrome on a modified Brazelton scale did not differ significantly from trained clinicians' assessments prior to infants' discharge from the hospital (Field, Hallock, Dempsey, & Shuman, 1978), indicating that mothers had assimilated information about their infants' behavioral abilities at that time. Both mothers and clinicians assigned less optimal ratings to preterm infants, and the ratings correlated with Bayley motor scores at 8 months. Maternal ratings of infant temperament at 4 and 8 months were significantly correlated and also correlated significantly with clinicians' ratings on BNBAS and Bayley Scales at 8 months.

Temporal patterning was a basic property of early face-to-face mother–infant interaction, with term infants more often than preterm infants leading interaction at 3 and 5 months corrected age, and term dyads showing higher coherence (Lester, Hoffman, & Brazelton, 1985). Both term and preterm dyads were able to coordinate their behavioral cycles during interaction, but synchrony was higher among term dyads, with preterm dyads less able to coordinate their behavioral cycles of affect and attention during social interactions.

Measures of mothers' sensitivity and competence (with the Boston City Hospital Assessment of Parental Sensitivity [BCHAPS]) in interacting with their preterm infants in the NICU were predictive of mother–infant interaction scores at 8 months corrected age as measured by Egeland and associates (Egeland, Deinard, Taraldson, & Brunnquette, 1975) play scale (Zahr & Cole, 1991). The NICU measure of BCHAPS was significantly related to later maternal caretaking skills, affective behaviors, and parity.

A comparison of term and preterm mother–infant dyads at 6, 8, 10, and 14 months found that preterm infants vocalized less, played less, and were more fretful than term infants of the same chronological age; preterm infants looked at objects and the environment more (Crawford, 1982). All differences except vocalization disappeared by 14 months. With the exception of spending less time in the same room with their infants at 8 months, mothers of preterm infants demonstrated more caretaking and affectionate behavior toward their infants, and these differences decreased with increased infant age.

Differences in mother–infant interactions between term and preterm dyads persisted from 4 to 24 months after birth (Barnard, Bee, & Hammond, 1984). At 4 months, preterm infants were lower in responsiveness, but their mothers demonstrated equal or heightened levels of responsiveness compared to term mothers. At 8 months, preterm infants were comparable to term infants in task involvement, with maternal involvement either remaining stable or declining. At 24 months, preterm mothers demonstrated lower levels of positive responses during teaching and reported less involvement with the child in daily activities than did term mothers. Education was associated positively with mothers' positive messages, greater facilitation, less restriction, and more responsivity, but differences between term and preterm dyads were not attributable to either education or parity.

Maternal confidence measured by the Toddler Care Questionnaire from 12 to 36 months did not differ significantly between mothers of preterm and term infants (Gross, Rocissano, & Roncoli, 1989). Preterm maternal confidence was explained (33% of variance) by prior child-care experience, birth order, and report of the child having cerebral palsy. Maternal confidence with term infants was explained (38%) by prior child-care experience, maternal age, and child's birthweight. Findings supported Bandura's (1982) theory of self-efficacy, in which perception of prior task mastery is the most important factor in predicting confidence in future performances of the task.

No significant differences were observed between term and preterm mothers' perceived competence in their mothering at 1 year; maternal competence was measured by L. O. Walker's (1977) semantic differential scale (Zabielski, 1994). Contact with their infants and role expectations in the rights that mothers felt that they were denied were major themes that preterm mothers discussed.

Magyary's (1984) review of research concurred with Goldberg's (1978) earlier review—that mothers of preterm infants were less actively involved with their infants during the newborn period. However, during the first 6 months, a shift from maternal hypoactivity to hyperactivity occurs, with asynchronous response to infant cues, overwhelming the immature infant. During the last half of the infant's first year, the dyadic interactive pattern of a "hyperattentive-hyperresponsive mother with a hypoattentive-hyporesponsive infant" either continues or moves to mutual responsiveness similar to mothers and full-term infants; or the hyperactive mother becomes a hypoactive mother with a more responsive infant (Magyary, 1984, p. 241).

Summary

Research indicated that the preterm infant is not as interactive with the mother as the term infant is over infancy. Maternal responses were also different: preterm mothers smiled less and stimulated the infant less the first 6 months. There is no evidence to link how the interruptions in maternal role achievement may have influenced these responses. The anxiety and depression following preterm birth have long-range effects in the mother's responses to her infant and appear independent of the infant's birthweight or health status. The infants' recurring illnesses and daily hassles were added deterrents to achieving maternal competence in caring for difficult infants.

MATERNAL GRATIFICATION

Mothers of VLBW ($\leq$1,500-g) infants interviewed during the first 10 days and again 3 to 5 weeks after birth gained confidence in their mother role during this time; their pleasure in interacting with their infants increased significantly, they gained knowledge about their infants' cues, and they felt that their infants were responding to them (Oehler, Hannan, & Catlett, 1993). Feelings of anger increased over this period, but feelings of responsibility and guilt decreased for many; roughly three-fourths continued to feel sad. Only one-half of the mothers reported increased infant behaviors and used the behaviors in interacting with their infants; thus, one-half were not attributing meaning to infant behavior or using behavioral cues.

Group differences were not found in satisfaction with parenting, life satisfaction, maternal life stress, and social support between mothers of term and preterm infants at 1 and 4 months (Crnic, Greenberg, Ragozin, Robinson, & Basham, 1983). Both stress and social support predicted maternal attitudes at 1 month and mother–infant interactions at 4 months.

Mothers of preterm infants vocalized more than did term mothers at 4 months, only slightly more at 8 and 12 months; maintained the *en face* position less at 4 months, more at 8 months; and smiled at their infants less often (Crnic, Ragozin, Greenberg, Robinson, & Basham, 1983). Throughout the first year, preterm infants displayed less positive affect than did term infants and scored lower on four of five measures of cognitive and motor development, even though they were equal to term infants in gestational age. Asynchronous mother–infant interactions persisted over 12 months; both mothers and preterm infants responded less positively to each other and enjoyed their interactive time less than did mothers and term infants. These differences were more vivid at 12 months.

In contrast, Zabielski (1994) found no significant differences between preterm and term mothers' satisfaction in the maternal role at 1 year after birth. Successful, satisfying interactions between mother and infant facilitated achieving a maternal identity.

Professional support predicted preterm mothers' infant stimulation on HOME scores, maternal satisfaction with parenting at 8 months, and mothers' global affect ratings at 12 months (Crnic, Greenberg, & Slough, 1986). Stress and support measures at 1 month were associated with mother and infant functioning at 8 and 12 months.

Summary

Satisfaction with the maternal role was associated with support and perceived competence in mothering the preterm infant. The preterm mother's lack of smiling noted in the section on competence does not reflect enjoyment in caretaking activities. Rubin noted that lack of smiling indicated not knowing the infant; this agrees with the association of maternal satisfaction with maternal competence.

MATERNAL ATTACHMENT

A comparison of 17 parents of preterm infants with 17 parents of term infants (matched for parity and with no differences in social, ethnic, and educational backgrounds) at 6 to 20 months after birth found that preterm mothers had delays in attachment, negative perception of the baby (on NPI), and continuing anxiety about leaving the infant with a babysitter (Jeffcoate, Humphrey, & Lloyd, 1979a). Two preterm children had been abused or neglected. One-half of the preterm mothers stated that it took longer than 2 months to feel love for their infants (Jeffcoate, Humphrey, & Lloyd, 1979b). Preterm mothers reported significantly greater stress, which was attributed to different role expectations and subsequent loss of self-confidence and self-esteem after a period of enforced separation from the baby. Mothers described caring and nurturing as their major roles.

Rubin (1963a) suggested that type and extent of touch represented emotional commitment. Mothers of preterm infants touched their infants less at 4 months, more at 8 months, and less at 12 months, compared to mothers of term infants (Crnic, Ragozin et al., 1983).

No significant differences were found in maternal affective perception of the infant between preterm and term mothers at 1 year after birth; this was measured by Leifer's (1980) How I Feel About My Baby scale

(Zabielski, 1994). Of 21 mothers of preterms, 1 said that she still had not formed an attachment with her infant, and 2 others expressed doubts that they had established bonds at 1 year. The two mothers who had doubts suggested that their inability to hold their infants following birth had contributed to their feelings.

Summary

Interruptions in the early acquaintance process and uncertainty about the preterm infant's survival may delay or interfere with the attachment process; however, there is insufficient scientific evidence to support this supposition. Longitudinal, qualitative research is needed to describe the early development of attachment among mothers of preterm infants. Under what conditions does the mother begin to know and attach to her preterm infant?

EVENTS TRIGGERING RECOGNITION OF A MATERNAL IDENTITY

In the comparison of 21 first-time mothers of preterm infants with 21 first-time mothers of term infants, eight themes were associated with triggering women's maternal identity recognition (the situation in which the woman first really felt like a mother): role partner contact/ interaction, role qualities, role actions, role expectations, role acknowledgment, self-continuity, role readiness, and role change (Zabielski, 1994). No preterm mother described a maternal identity recognition event in the delivery room or during pregnancy or role readiness. Only preterm mothers worried that they had not formed an attachment with their infants.

Role partner contact or interaction was the main theme discussed most often by preterm mothers but least discussed by term mothers (Zabielski, 1994). Role qualities was the main theme most often discussed by term mothers but least often discussed by preterm mothers. The median time for maternal identity recognition for term mothers occurred at 1 week postpartum, and for preterm mothers it was 11 weeks after birth; 62% of term mothers experienced maternal identity recognition within 2 weeks after birth, but only 24% of preterm mothers reported maternal recognition within 2 weeks. This finding suggests that as many as three-fourths of mothers of preterm infants experience maternal identity diffusion for at least 2 weeks. The more positive the mother's affective view of her infant, the earlier she recognized a maternal identity. All three preterm mothers who doubted that they had formed an attachment with their infants experienced some delay in maternal identity recognition.

LONG-TERM EFFECTS OF PRETERM BIRTH ON PARENTING

A follow-up of parents of preterm infants several years after their discharge found that parental anxiety when their infant was in the NICU had no relationship to current perceptions of their children (Philipp, 1983). Parents of preterm children older than 3.5 years viewed a videotape of a preterm infant on an apnea monitor and then completed ratings of premature infant behavior, attractiveness, general health, and caregiving (Epps, 1993). Information about infant health status did not bias perceptions in areas other than health; significant main effects were found only on the general health scale. Women who had severe complications of pregnancy reported more postpartal depression, a relationship that persisted when controlled for preterm birth with neonatal hospitalization and demographic factors (Burger, Horwitz, Forsyth, Leventhal, & Leaf, 1993). Many mothers who have preterm infants are hospitalized and treated for long periods prior to birth.

The vulnerable child syndrome, first described by Green and Solnit (1964), following parental reactions to the threatened loss of a child and associated with later child behavior or development, has been observed by several (Escalona, 1982; McCormick, Shapiro, & Starfield, 1982). Miles and Holditch-Davis (in press) reported that 24 mothers of 3-year-old prematurely born children had adopted a "compensatory parenting style" in which they provided special experiences and voided other experiences to compensate their preterm children for their earlier experiences. The compensatory parenting style involved protection, stimulation, attention, and reduced demands for their children who were viewed as both "special" and "normal," with both positive and negative outcomes.

SUMMARY

The effects of preterm birth in interrupting the anticipatory stage and delaying achievement of subsequent stages of maternal role identity are well documented. Preterm mothers' concerns are real, but their emotional response to preterm birth is not dependent on infant illness, birthweight, or gestational age. How much of the emotional response is due to the mother's self-concept and coping abilities, unreadiness for the birth, spousal and family support, previous experiences with loss, or other factors?

Scientific evidence indicates a *vulnerable mother syndrome* (Randell, personal communication, May 22, 1994) in the situation of preterm birth with long-term sequelae. As role partners, premature infants' behavioral deficits are an enormous challenge for the mother in developing sensitive responses to cues; there appears to be a struggle for the mother to create a cognitive structure for providing care. In her efforts to achieve competence she may overreact, as research shows her overstimulation of the infant during observations.

The preterm mother was not able to achieve the same level of competence that term mothers were able to achieve over the first year. Mothers lacked synchrony with their preterm infants for as long as 2 years and reported a compensatory parenting style at 3 years. The positive relationship of maternal confidence with easier preterm infants indicates the impact of preterm infants who are difficult to care for and/or sick on maternal role competence.

Maternal attachment also seems to develop more slowly when infants are preterm. Although mothers correctly identified their infants' physical conditions near discharge from the NICU in one study, the early identifying and claiming behaviors demonstrated by mothers of term infants were not reported.

Consistent in all research was the report of mothers smiling less at their preterm infants during interactions, indicating that they were enjoying their maternal role behaviors less. Rubin (1984) suggested that mothers do not smile at what they do not recognize in the neonate; mothers apparently do not recognize their infant's cues and may be concentrating so heavily on the mothering act that they do not see, as was suggested by Rubin (1961a) in early feeding behaviors of mothers of term infants. Mothers' flat affect may also reflect maternal depression. Regardless of the cause, effects of negative or flat maternal response on the preterm infants were observed.

The preterm mothers' better adaptation to their infants' symbiotic needs in one study may reflect the effects of having a critically ill infant at birth and current gratefulness for the gift of a live infant. Practically, mothers' inability to have their infants at home for several weeks after birth leaves a feeling of early deprivation and emptiness.

By examining the maternal role in different situations, concepts that have remained vague or abstract may be illuminated or amplified. Were facets of the process of maternal role identity achievement vividly illustrated by the situation of preterm birth in such a way that new information was obtained? The *centrality of the role partner, the infant,* to the process of maternal role identity was strongly reaffirmed. Scientific evidence supported the theory that there is an early diffusion of maternal role identity with uncertainty about the infant's outcome, and inability to hold and care for the infant for an extended period is associated with feelings of denial of parental rights and stressors in the NICU. Cognitive restructuring for assuming motherhood is difficult or impossible in moment-by-moment change in infant function, rendering identifying and claiming impossible. No wonder that one-half of mothers were not recognizing their preterm's cues at 3 to 5 weeks.

McHaffie's (1990) identification of phases of preterm mothers' adaptation suggests a *different trajectory of maternal identity achievement* for preterm mothers. The phases of anticipatory grief, anxious waiting, and positive anticipation while the infant was in the NICU were evident in research reports. The last three phases occurring after the infant's discharge are descriptive, but research reports have not revealed information about the process occurring in anxious adjustment and exhausted accommodation to achieve confident caring. This missing information about the preterm mothers' process of anxious adjustment and exhausted accommodation is critical. When do preterm mothers identify and claim their infants in a basic way? Does the long period of very little response from the infant condition the mother so that she must make decisions without infant input, such as in feeding, thus leading to noncontingent behavior? Is the motivation to achieve competence so great that she pushes herself ahead without the usual information other mothers have? Without positive input or smiles, she does not smile, and a transactional process begins between the mother–infant dyad that interactions are not enjoyable, compounding the problem.

How much of the preterm's mother's difficulty is due to her inability to finish the cognitive tasks of pregnancy? Research has documented the importance of the mental rehearsals for motherhood and attaching to the unborn infant. Within the context of a frail infant who may not survive, what are the effects of the interruption of the usual trajectory of maternal role identity on the ultimate achievement of a maternal identity?

Professional support to preterm mothers has been highly effective in all reports. Thorough preparation of mothers for taking their infants home and a thorough assessment of their readiness and social environment for having the infant at home are imperative.

■ 10
Transition to the Maternal Role Following Birth of an Infant with Anomalies or Chronic Illness

To wish for a well, normal infant during pregnancy and have an imperfect infant with a defect or chronic illness at birth is a profound loss for the mother. The maternal role is the only role in which one partner creates or produces the other partner. The mother's self-concept (how imperfect is she to produce an imperfect child, the child as an extension of herself), her goals and plans (a child requiring special treatment, surgery), her perceived social status (tendency for less than "normal" to be stigmatized), and her family are threatened.

The pregnancy task of finding social acceptance and support for her child has to be renewed and reworked to find acceptance and support for a handicapped child. Ensuring safe passage is extended in efforts to assure the best health and the best situation possible for her infant. Attaching to the handicapped child while grieving the loss of her fantasied child requires giving of herself and commitment more far-reaching than ever anticipated. A parent of a normal child expects to fulfill the role in an active capacity until the child reaches adulthood; in situations of mental retardation and severe handicap, the parental role is never diminished and may become increasingly difficult.

GRIEF PROCESS

No loss is relinquished willingly. The mother experiences a painful withdrawal of attachment from her lost image of her infant to be.

> *CS:* The mother of a child with a congenital defect feels denied and rejected in her wishes and expectations and confronted with her own defectiveness in making a child. There is a devastating shock and a profound bereavement (Lindemann, 1944) for a remarkably short period of time. The bereavement seems to stop at the protest stage, in vehement denial that a defect should be met with rejection. The resultant energy and activity of a mother in securing remediation or compensatory adaptive modalities for her child and the close, firm durable bond with this child of hers is awesome testimony to the capacity for courage and altruism of the human spirit.... The painful uniqueness is relieved in experience with other mothers whose situations are as bad as or worse than her own and in finding people of goodwill whose consideration and help reduce her burden. (Rubin, 1984, p. 104)
>
> Identification of the child organizes maternal behavior and maternal attitudes.... Disappointments take time to overcome and the identification and other binding-in measures are delayed or limited.... The condition of the baby, particularly its wholeness and intactness, is essential to determine before acting or interacting in relation to the child. From antepartal fantasies of the unborn child and her own misgivings about being able to produce anything desirable or perfect out of her own body, each mother has an expectancy of an imperfect or deformed child.... With supportive adults, the identification process is operationally complete by four weeks with a normal, healthy baby. (Rubin, 1977, pp. 68–69)

H: The mother of a child with a defect experiences shock and a grief process.

Parental reaction to a child's disability has been described within either a time-bound or chronic sorrow model (Clubb, 1991). Stages within the time-bound model include impact or shock, beginning at the time of diagnosis; denial behavior, occurring briefly as parents look for a second diagnosis and gradually face reality; grief demonstrated through feelings of anger, guilt, and sadness; focusing outward when realistic adaptation begins; and closure when the child's diagnosis is accepted as a disruption to family life that will continue. Shock was a time-specific phase over the first 6 days after the birth of a handicapped infant; however, protest and yearning, disorganization, and reorganization phases were neither time- nor phase-specific over 3 months after birth (Mercer, 1977a, 1990). Mothers were faced with the necessity of reformulating their wishes, hopes, and expectations in accord with the handicapped infant's situation. Decisions had to be made in the reorganization of family plans as mothers prepared to take their infants home to their families.

In situations of Down syndrome and mental retardation, from 68% to 75% of mothers reported a series of ups and downs with no general upward course, as opposed to a steady, gradual adaptation (Damrosch & Perry, 1989; Wikler, Wascow, & Hatfield, 1981). The failure to mourn when an infant was diagnosed with defects led to rejection of the child; inability to deal with these feelings of rejection negatively affected maternal and child behavior (Naylor, 1982). A case study of a mother who expressed deep grief following the birth of her son with Apert's syndrome illustrated how negative feedback was used to cope (Mercer, 1973). The mother controlled information input by refusing to see, touch, or interact with her infant until she felt emotionally ready; she then began with small doses, gradually increasing her involvement until she was strongly attached to the infant.

Although all mothers grieved, only one-fifth of their behavioral responses reflected grief (shock, anger, fear, guilt, withdrawal, depression); social behaviors (evaluation of others' responses to the infant, appraisals of self, responses to others' support) made up 45% of responses and cognitive behaviors (planning for the future, reviewing the past, wishes, dissonance, search for cause) made up 35% (Mercer, 1975). The percentage of grief responses remained constant from the first week, to 1, 2, and 3 months after birth, while social behaviors increased slightly and cognitive behaviors decreased. The latter finding supports the concept that much cognitive restructuring must occur at birth in order to proceed with establishing a maternal identity.

H: Mothers of infants with defects report feeling or fearing this outcome during pregnancy. (*H* supported, see "Fantasy" in chapter 3.)

H: A mother's bereavement process stops at the stage of protest.

Rubin (1954) defined bereavement as a behavioral syndrome resulting from the loss or denial of love; its course is dependent upon the bereaved person's past experience in forming love relationships and coping with deprivation, the degree of sorrow producing stimulus, and the extent of emotional energy the person has available to resist sorrow. In the situation of irreparable birth defects, such as mental retardation, the maternal deprivation is permanent as long as either she or the child lives. Parkes (1972) observed that both stigma and deprivation play a part in determining the overall reaction to bereavement. This may reflect why mothers search for social response to and acceptance of their infants.

Childs (1985) interviewed 50 mothers who had had a retarded child 1 year earlier; mothers were asked to focus on their feelings during the first 3 weeks after birth. Over 90% reported feelings of guilt, denial, inferiority, shame, and confusion and a questioning of their religious beliefs; 80% reported wishing they would die at some time during the first week, feeling anger, and a need to blame others. Other emotions included feeling lonely, unloved, and helpless. Forty percent of the mothers had thoughts about infanticide, although they would never have carried through with it, reasoning that it would be best for the child, the family, and mankind.

Horan (1982) used attribution theory to explain parental reactions to the birth of an infant with a defect, hypothesizing that the quicker causal attribution is made, the more rapidly the parent will move through stages of adjustment. When self-blame of a modifiable cause is made, a rapid adjustment should occur because there is control in preventing a recurrence. Nonmodifiable causes of the defect, such as genetic ones, were hypothesized to lead to greater assaults on the self-esteem. Affleck and associates' (1988) findings related to mothers of preterm infants support this hypothesis.

Schroeder (1974) reported the grief process as ongoing among mothers with handicapped children aged 1 month to 10 years. One mother of an 18-month-old with Down syndrome said while crying, "You don't ever stop thinking about it. I don't think they're [feelings] any easier to deal with" (p. 162). A review of research on mothers' grief responses after the birth of an infant with a congenital defect also reported chronic grief (Carreto, 1981).

Evidence supports the fact that chronic sorrow, manifested by a pattern of ups and downs, occurs following the birth of an infant with a defect. Parents' coping responses to the child with spina bifida (aged 2 months to 18 years; mean, 6.2 years) was positively related to marital satisfaction and the quality of the relationship between husband and wife (Van Cleve, 1989). Mothers reported using coping strategies such as crying, busying oneself with other activities, ignoring problems, and getting away, more so than fathers did. High copers (above the median coping score) used strategies of crying, talking with someone, exercising, asking for help, yelling/screaming, and slamming doors. This study, which included longtime experience with the child's handicap, indicates that bereavement behaviors are chronic. Higher income and increased age of parent were predictive of parental coping. If Rubin meant by "bereavement stops at the stage of protest" that parents continue to protest the plight of their infant, the strategies described by Van Cleve (1989) support this hypothesis.

PROGRESS TOWARD MATERNAL ROLE IDENTITY

With the extensive cognitive restructuring needed to deal with a handicapped infant and the simultaneous grief work, a period of maternal identity diffusion is expected. Until the mother identifies and accepts her infant, progress in maternal identity achievement is delayed.

> *CS:* If there is a problem in the baby's intactness, in wholeness or in function, however, there is centration [centering] on the problem and a limited extension of the radius of identification. The centration continues as long as the problem remains. (Rubin, 1984, p. 141)

H: Mothers who had an infant with a birth defect or chronic illness will not proceed through the maternal role identity process of achieving role competence, gratification, and attaching to the infant at the same rate as mothers of normal infants.

H: Mothers focus on imperfections in identifying their child.

244 ::Achieving the Maternal Identity

Maternal Role Competence

Van Riper and Selder (1989) studied parental responses to the birth of a child with Down syndrome within the framework of transition theory, noting that the major characteristic of a transition is uncertainty. Parents of infants with Down syndrome reported uncertainty about the future and the diagnosis, as well as apprehension about their parenting abilities and the professional's initial responses. The uncertainty projects into childhood, as evidenced by concerns about educational programs, the future, and the child's health. The task of a life transition is to incorporate the transitional event so that it has meaning for the person experiencing it while regaining self-integrity. This involves recognizing trigger events that cause recognition of the changed situation and identification of missed options. Reactivation of feelings and sensations at the time of the initial diagnosis is one trigger event. Irrevocability is a second trigger event, in which the parent becomes aware of the permanence of the changed reality. Information seeking and normalization were strategies used to get back to their life plans. Reaffirming identity constancy—that they remained the same persons they were prior to the birth of their child—helped decrease uncertainty.

Mothers whose newborn infants were hospitalized in a children's hospital immediately following birth, for treatment of a congenital defect, responded largely (81%) with assimilative responses (attempts to establish a sense of reality and stability about their infants, including identifying and comparing responses) (Kikuchi, 1980). Accommodative responses (attempts to deal with perceived realities, including preparing, optimizing, protesting, and avoiding responses) made up 20% of mothers' responses. The ratio of assimilative to accommodative behaviors was consistent during the first, second, third, and fourth weeks following the infant's birth. Mothers focused on those infant features that were abnormal, with 68% of assimilative responses focused on function, 22% on structural anatomical features, and 10% on medical treatment. Most of the assimilative behaviors were identifying (92%), contrasted to only 8% comparing features. Focus on the infant's defect decreased at the second week but increased again at the fourth week. Focus on function included feeding and retaining, elimination, sleeping, and problems related to the specific defect. Two-thirds of mothers' accommodative responses were preparing for possible actualization of their fears and wishes. The percentage of responses focused on infant function is consistent with that reported for mothers with normal infants (Chao, 1979, 1983).

Mothers who took their infants with birth defects home with them from the hospital expressed a different ratio of assimilative behaviors: 44% assimilative and 56% accommodative the first week and 50-50 at 1 and 3 months (Mercer, 1974b). Mothers seemed to be controlling input to a tolerable level. Depression and anger were high at 2 months, when 41% of responses were assimilating behavior and 59% of responses were accommodative.

A study of mothers with apneic infants on monitors during hospitalization and at 2 weeks and 2 months following birth found that they experienced a "severe, magnified response to parenthood" (Dean, 1986, p. 70). Five difficulties they faced included vigilance, or watchfulness; struggles about leaving the baby; restrictions imposed by the monitoring; relationships with their other children; and concerns about discontinuing the monitor. When infants are on monitors, a responsible caretaker must be within 10 seconds of response time. Monitors are a constant reminder that apnea imposes an immediate, tangible threat to their infants' lives.

A comparison of maternal responses to infants with craniofacial deformity (mean age, 17 weeks) and maternal responses to normal infants (mean age, 15 weeks) found that mothers of facially deformed infants exhibited less nurturant behavior than did mothers of normal infants (Barden, Ford, Jensen, Rogers-Salyer, & Salyer, 1989). In free-play episodes, mothers of deformed infants demonstrated less tactile–kinesthetic stimulation, touched their infants affectionately less often, were less likely to hold the infants in the *en face* position, and were less responsive to behavioral cues than were mothers of normal infants.

Holaday (1986) studied the development of the maternal conceptual set in response to chronically ill children during the first 6 months following birth, using concepts from Johnson's (1980) Behavioral System Model as a theoretical framework. The concept of a set had two components: perseveration and preparation. The perseveratory set refers to habitual or routine responses in which specific stimuli are responded to with specific patterns of behavior. The preparatory set represents what is attended to or focused on in a situation and is contingent on the perseveratory set. The perseveratory and preparatory sets are believed to come together to form the conceptual set.

The infants did not always provide clear cry signals. Because infants had been hospitalized, most of the mothers had missed out on the usual acquaintance period. Stage I, an inadequate conceptual set, lasted from 1 day to 1 month, depending on the severity of the illness, the length of infant's hospitalization, and the clarity of the cry signal. The process of developing rules for categorizing the cry was central to the development of the conceptual set; at the first observation, the mother was a "closed system" and would not or could not respond to the infant's cry. During later observations in Stage I, mothers moved to using simple but rigid categorical rules for classifying the type of cry; most mothers saw the cry as a sign of distress.

In Stage II, mothers began to develop a conceptual set; different types of cries were considered and there were degrees to a cry stimulus. Mothers responded inconsistently in the absence of fixed rules for evaluating infant cries or complex rules for integrating alternative meanings of the cry. By Stage III, mothers combined and used alternative interpretations of the cry, increasing possible interventions; even when a decision was made, the mother remained open to alternative reasons and interventions. Most mothers had developed a sophisticated conceptual set by 2 months after birth, but one (of six) had not reached this level until 6 months after the infant's birth. Drummond and associates (1993) found it took first-time mothers of normal infants 4 months to reach a sophisticated level of cry response; multiparas, 6 weeks (see chapter 8). Holaday's (1986) sample included equal numbers of primiparas and multiparas.

The median percentage of cries ignored by the mothers was 22, with the most responsive mother ignoring 16% and the least responsive ignoring only 29% (Holaday, 1981). Infants with serious chronic illnesses varied in their crying constancy, and 2 with more serious illnesses fussed as opposed to crying.

Patterns of interaction between mother–chronically ill infant dyads were often noncontingent (Holaday, 1987). Mothers used controlling or interruptive behavior patterns, with infants frequently ceasing interactive behavior. Mothers spent 90% of the time in facial gaze, compared to the infants' 44%, and 45% of time in vocalization, compared to the infants' 7%.

Mothers of 16-week-old infants with congenital heart disease (CHD) were scored significantly lower on the Social Emotional Growth Fostering subscale of the Nursing Child Assessment Feeding Scale (Barnard, 1978) than were a control group of mother–healthy infant dyads

(Lobo, 1992). Mothers of infants with CHD less often smiled, made eye contact, touched, hummed, or sang to their infants than did mothers of normal infants. Infants with CHD scored significantly lower on clarity of cues and responsiveness to parent.

The relationship between the home environment and sensorimotor development of Down syndrome and nonretarded infants at 6.5, 17, and 24 months was studied by Smith and Hagen (1984) in Norway. Medical complications of Down syndrome children were unrelated to the quality of their home environments. Growth rates for the Down syndrome infants slowed markedly as they aged. No differences were observed in maternal behavior between the two groups at 6.5 months; most mothers of Down syndrome infants thought the baby's behavior was age-appropriate. At 17 months, mothers of Down syndrome infants provided more physical stimulation and smiled more often at their infants; mothers of nonretarded children talked more about the environment, gave more definite directions, and more often provided attention to their babies. Focused exploration was a solitary activity for Down syndrome infants but an interactive process among nonretarded infants. At 6.5 months, the only environmental difference between Down syndrome and nonretarded infants was that the latter more often had household and caretaking objects provided; no differences were observed at 17 months. The inanimate environment was positively related to psychological development of the Down syndrome infants only. Maternal behavior with Down syndrome infants was not synchronous with the infants' developmental stage; thus, the different behavior was due to other qualities of the child; parity and maternal age were not factors in differences. The researchers recommended very early intervention with mothers of Down syndrome infants.

Maternal sensitivity, elaborativeness, stimulation value, and mood were intercorrelated, but stimulation value was the major maternal quality that was significantly related to 2-year-olds' with Down syndrome mental development (Crawley & Spiker, 1983). Maternal directiveness was unrelated to mental development. The transactional effects of the infant's handicap and maternal behavior was observed among deaf toddlers, who were more passive and less actively involved in interactions, whereas their mothers were always more dominant in the interactions (Wedell-Monnig & Lumley, 1980).

Mothers with children aged 4 months to 15 years in the pediatric ICU, were functioning at healthy levels in family adaptability, cohesion, and coping mechanisms (Philichi, 1989). Mothers' religious affiliations were related to overall coping and to the dimensions of reframing, passive appraisal, and seeking spiritual support.

Krulik (1980) reported that mothers of chronically ill children worked at strengthening the child's resources and coping abilities and adapting the environment to accept the child. Normalizing tactics occurred in managing diet requirements, treatments, medications, and their sequelae. Normalization has a high cost as family members attempt to balance the demands of the chronic illness with needs to parent the child as other children are parented (Deatrick, Knafl, & Walsh, 1988).

Seideman and Kleine (1995) evolved a theory of transformed parenting from a grounded theory study of the parenting process of 42 parents whose children, ages 10 months to 69 years, had developmental delay including mental retardation. Their theory of transformed parenting includes an initial entrance process and a subsequent ongoing performance process. The entrance process includes receiving and responding to the child's diagnosis. The performance process includes reality construing, contextual, and operating processes. The ongoing process of interpreting the child's problems is facilitated through deducing reality loops in the reality construing process. The earlier described maternal grief response and assimilative and accommodative responses are congruent with the entrance and beginning performance processes as described by Seideman and Kleine (1995).

Maternal Gratification

Mothers with craniofacially deformed infants reported that they were more satisfied with parenting and reported more positive life experiences following their pregnancies than did mothers of normal infants (Barden et al., 1989). Their interactional behaviors, described above, did not reflect pleasure with parenting. However, the mother's intense concentration on her tasks with a handicapped infant perhaps does not reflect her gratification in the monumental task she is accomplishing.

African-American and Latino mothers of children with spina bifida (mean age, 8 years) were significantly less satisfied with the maternal role than were white mothers (Fagan & Schor, 1993). Mothers' satisfaction in the parental role was predicted by adult companionship and social support. Family functioning was associated with perceived maternal competence and well-being.

Maternal Attachment

Behaviors of assessment, touch, and care activities of mothers with infants with birth defects were observed during the first week and at 1, 2, and 3 months and categorized as either attachment or aversion behaviors (Mercer, 1974a). Maternal assessments were appraisals of the infants' appearance or function; 68% of assessments focused on function and the remainder on appearance. Assessment responses indicative of attachment remained stable the first month (61%), increased to 70% at 2 months and to 77% at 3 months. Touch attachment behaviors changed very little over the 3-month observation period but decreased slightly from 88% the first week to 82% at 3 months. Care activities, including mothering acts indicating responsiveness or unresponsiveness to the baby's cues and seeking or avoiding care activities, decreased from 97% at 1 month, to 83% at 2 months, and to 73% at 3 months. When all attachment and aversion behaviors were summed, little variation was observed. Verbal attachment behaviors exceeded physical attachment behaviors.

Emde and Brown (1978) observed that mothers with Down syndrome infants had some difficult and tragic ups and downs in the process of developing maternal attachment. The normal upsurge of attachment when the infant smiles and interacts positively is complicated by the Down syndrome infant, who sees less well and has a more placid body. The mother needs a "solid sense of self, which includes giving, available others, and a feeling of continuity between the past and the present" (p. 319) for attachment. Possible reasons for mothers' inability to be more giving were deprivation of social affective responses during hospitalizations, prolonged or incomplete grieving, and lack of social reciprocity by infants.

A comparison of maternal–infant attachment between mothers with and without a handicapped infant, at 1, 6, and 12 months after birth, found that mothers of handicapped infants were significantly less attached at 1 month, but no differences between the two groups were found at 6 or 12 months (Capuzzi, 1989). When controlled for the effects of social support, no differences were found at 1 month, indicating that social support facilitates maternal attachment during that time. Maternal attachment among mothers of handicapped infants increased significantly at 6 months over the

1-month score, with scores remaining constant at 12 months. Among mothers with normal infants, attachment scores dropped slightly at 6 months from 1-month levels and increased again at 12 months.

Parents of children with spina bifida aged 2 months to 18 years said that they would be tested during pregnancy for possible neural tube defects if they became pregnant again (Van Cleve, 1993). However, one-half replied that they would not consider an abortion if neural tube defects were diagnosed, although they were already caring for one child with spina bifida. These findings indicate much emotional investment in their handicapped child.

H: Role models of other mothers of children with defects facilitate transition to the role of mother of an infant with a defect.

A significant positive relationship was observed between parental coping with a child with spina bifida and parental attendance at an organizational meeting related to the handicap (Van Cleve, 1989). The time from birth until a woman can identify with other mothers with an infant with a defect varies; until the mother accepts her identity as a mother of a child with a defect, she will not attend organizational meetings (Mercer, 1990).

SUMMARY

Despite the maternal identity diffusion at birth described by Van Riper and Selder (1989), mothers giving birth to an infant with a defect moved quickly to gain knowledge they needed in restructuring their cognitive plans for mothering. They demonstrated acquaintance behavior of identifying the infant's function during the formal stage of maternal role identity similar to that of mothers of normal infants, despite their profound shock and grief process. Kikuchi's (1980) interviews with mothers whose infants were transferred immediately following birth for treatment in a children's hospital revealed that mothers were seeking information and identifying the infant at a much greater rate than were mothers who had taken their defective infants home (Mercer, 1974b). Mothers' focus on their infants' problems were evident, supporting Rubin's theory.

Scientific evidence in the situation of the birth of an infant with a defect or chronic health problem indicates that mothers respond to unforeseen crises by seeking additional information. Perhaps all later maternal behaviors with a defective infant are also intensified and magnified, as Dean (1986) observed among mothers with apneic infants on monitors.

The development of a conceptual or cognitive set to respond to infant crying proceeded similarly among mothers with infants born with chronic illness (Holaday, 1986) as described among mothers of normal infants (Drummond et al., 1993). This reflects the extraordinary cognitive work of mothers of handicapped infants, because the handicapped infants' cries were less clear.

However, despite the great assimilation of information during the formal stage of maternal role identity, longitudinal research indicates noncontingent and less positive maternal responses in feeding and play situations at infant ages when mothers of normal infants respond skillfully and demonstrate pleasurable interaction.

Mothers' attachment to their defective infants increased over time; although mothers of handicapped infants expressed less attachment during the first month, by 6 months these differences disappeared. It remains unclear when mothers with infants with congenital defects achieve a maternal role identity. The uncertainty of handicapped infants' functioning continues for many over a lifetime; this may lend such a degree of diffuseness that the mother in some instances is unable to experience the clear-cut self-confidence that mothers of normal infants experience.

One wonders whether the mother of an infant with a handicap is able to begin assimilating knowledge more vigorously and earlier than the mother of a preterm infant in part because she completed the anticipatory stage of maternal role identity. The maturity of the handicapped infant and the specific handicap allows a firmer diagnosis than is possible for the immature preterm infant (who may or may not have a ventricular bleed, cerebral palsy, or other complication) so that some uncertainty about prognosis in general is removed earlier for the mother with a handicapped infant. Regardless of how bad the prognosis, the mother can begin to construct her framework for parenting her infant with a birth defect.

Research reviews report that research in this area has been largely descriptive (Kazak, 1986), without control groups (Murphy, 1982), and has included parents of children over a wide age range (Austin, 1991). Diagnostic labels do not differentiate areas of concern among families with a chronically ill child (Stein & Jessop, 1989). Diagnostic groups differ mainly by differences in family interaction with the health care system.

Many theoretical papers offer insights for sensitive intervention with families with a handicapped infant (Bernier, 1990; Freitag-Koontz, 1988; McElheny, 1989; Revell & Liptak, 1991; Van Riper et al.,1992).

The chronic grief process that is reported and the association of support with satisfaction in parenting handicapped children demand more longitudinal research focused on the trajectory of maternal role identity achievement from birth through school years. Early and ongoing health care intervention is especially critical for this population, which is deprived of parenting a healthy, well-developed child and faces daily stigma and hassles.

three

THE MOTHER IN SOCIAL CONTEXT

■ 11
Life Circumstance and Teenage, Older, and Single Mothers: Maternal Role Attainment

At each phase in life, the person's life space, self system, and environment are different. The life space refers to the psychological environment as it exists for the person at any given time; knowledge of both the psychological and physical environment is important in understanding behavior (Lewin, 1951). The mother's goals, needs, values, dreams, ideals, and fears, interacting with environmental forces that may be friendly, helpful, hostile, or restraining, will influence her ability to provide warm, nurturing care for her infant and achieve a maternal identity.

In 1992 55% of all live births were to women in their twenties, 13% to adolescents, and 32% to women aged 30 to 44 years (Ventura, Martin, Taffel, Mathews, & Clarke, 1994). Examining maternal role attainment by the two groups outside the peak childbearing years, the teenager and the woman aged 30 and older, contrasts the impact of the life space on maternal behavior. Many variables other than level of maturity affect each group's work in becoming mothers.

In this chapter, these two groups of mothers are contrasted, followed by a review of the unmarried or single mother's maternal role transition. How does each of these situations alter, enhance, impede, or magnify, the process of internalizing the maternal role identity?

> CS: The ideal theory or theories should explain the phenomenological and subjective experience of women becoming mothers in validatable terms and in a way sufficient to provide testable hypotheses for the variations in the human experience of mothering.... This would also include the woman who herself is a young teenager or an "elderly" primipara or multipara. (Rubin, 1984, p. 3)

THE MATERNAL ROLE AND THE TEENAGE MOTHER

In 1992, 505,415 births were to teenage mothers; 12,220 were to mothers under 15 years (Ventura, Martin, Taffel, Mathews, & Clarke, 1994). Although 1992 birth rates had declined 1%–2% for teenagers aged 15 to 17 years, rates for those aged 10–14 years and 18–19 years had almost no change.

When compared to their nonpregnant peers with similar demographic backgrounds, teenage mothers had more often experienced foster care, family violence, parental substance abuse, lower educational achievements, violence, and alcohol abuse from their less-well-educated boyfriends (Oz & Fine, 1988); poorer relationships with their parents; and greater isolation and less interest in work or school (Rogeness, Ritchey, Alex, Zuelzer, & Morris, 1981). These findings portray a profile of very needy young women, who have relatively little power in a hostile environment. In addition to the increased vulnerability of the young woman's child, these psychological, sociocultural, economic, family, and health variables interact with the teenagers' developmental level to create a context in which motherhood can be an inhibitor or an enhancer of their own maturation (Buchholz & Gold, 1986).

Comparisons of Personality Traits and Attitudes

The maternal role creates new stressors for the already stressed and less mature teenager. Teenage mothers reported stressors related to family interactions, body image, finances, others' relationships with their infants, the infant's father and his family, their health, living arrangements, and lack of time for homework during their first month home from the hospital (Panzarine, 1986). These are enormous stresses for an immature person.

H: Teenagers are less mature in personality and social development and in child-rearing attitudes associated with maternal role identity achievement.

Less mature personality traits and child-rearing attitudes may affect all teenagers' transitions to the maternal role because psychosocial development does not always parallel chronological age or biological development. The early adolescent ($\leq$15 years) is adapting to the abrupt body-image changes of puberty. If she has moved from the concrete stage of cognitive functioning, she remains largely present-oriented and inconsistent in using her newly acquired logic (Mercer, 1990). She does not consider future effects of current behavior. She is highly egocentric, which makes it difficult for her to give of self in behalf of her infant. Middle adolescents (15–17 years) are able to consider consequences of their behavior but do not routinely do so; they tend to be idealistic and inconsistently altruistic in their new intellectual prowess. Although they are less egocentric than early adolescents, egocentrism continues at a high level.

Teenagers had poor self-concepts as persons but good self-concepts as parents (Abrums, 1980). However, they reported positive child-rearing attitudes, handled irritating child behaviors positively, and perceived good communication with their children. Teenagers more often than adults focused on the concrete tasks of parenting, such as feeding and keeping the infant clean, in defining an ideal parent, whereas adult mothers focused more on developmental needs, such as cognitive stimulation and social interaction (Mercer, 1986a). Thus, the standard against which the adolescent rates herself in the mothering role is different and may be inadequate in fostering the infant's psychosocial development.

Pregnant adults surpassed both pregnant adolescent and nonpregnant adolescent groups in cognitive preparation for parenting (Sommer et al., 1993). However, when IQ, SES, race, and educational level were controlled, differences between pregnant adolescents and pregnant adults were no longer significant.

Pond and Kemp (1992) did not find any differences between adolescents' (ages 13–16) and adults' (ages 21–33) state and trait anxiety and self-confidence. Negative relationships between anxiety and self-confidence were observed in both groups.

A study of 204 mothers aged 18 years or younger found that their cognitive functioning and ego development were average for their age (Camp & Morgan, 1984). They tended toward authoritarian attitudes and agreed with the view that children are irritating and a nuisance and that conflictual interpersonal relationships are normal. However, the young mothers had more positive than negative attitudes toward their infants (aged 2 weeks to 4 months), but their attitudes were somewhat less positive than those of a sample of older women. Whites had higher vocabulary scores than did blacks and Hispanics, and blacks scored higher than did whites and Hispanics on parental attitudes of control.

At 1 and 12 months after birth, Caucasian adolescent mothers scored significantly lower on empathy toward children's needs but did not differ in other attitude constructs from older mothers (Baranowski, Schilmoeller, & Higgins, 1990). Teenagers' (aged 15 to 19) empathy at 4 months after birth and self-concept and personality integration on the Tennessee Self Concept Scale (TSCS) (Fitts, 1965) at 1 and 8 months were significantly lower than those of older mothers (Mercer, 1986c). Teenagers' temperament traits of adaptability, intensity, mood, persistence, and distractibility were also less positive than older mothers'. At 8 months after birth, personality integration, empathy, and temperament activity level, intensity, and threshold to stimulus were significantly related to observed maternal competence.

TEENAGERS' MATERNAL ROLE IDENTITY ATTAINMENT

The teenage mother's ecological environment and life space place her at a handicap in maternal role identity attainment. This is especially true for the younger teenager (<15 years).

H: Teenage mothers will score lower than adult mothers will on maternal competence, maternal gratification, and maternal attachment and will experience greater difficulty in achieving a maternal role identity.

The Early Adolescent (<15 Years)

CS: The family of the thirteen to fifteen-year-old biological mother is neither structurally nor functionally equipped to rear a child as a mother. Sexual play and reproductive capacities at a child's level of mental, moral, and social development are a preposterous claim for maternal capability.... The young biological mother's task is centered on being a good, acceptable daughter, not a mother. There is no formation of a maternal identity in relation to this child and no assumption of other maternal tasks. (Rubin, 1984, pp. 59–60)

H: The life space of adolescents 15 years or younger prevents their assumption of a maternal identity.

Mothers 16 years or less were significantly more depressed than those aged 17 to 19 years or adult mothers (infants' age not given) (Reis, 1989). Using the criterion of 16 as a cut-off for clinical depression on the CES-D scale, 67% of the younger adolescents were depressed, 53% of older adolescents, and 35% of adult mothers. In addition to their depression, adolescents were also more punitive and less knowledgeable and had less social support than the older mothers (Reis, 1988).

Mothering behavior of black teenagers, 13 to 15 and 16 to 17 years, was compared during the postpartal hospitalization, using Rubin's concepts (Hardman, 1975). At first contact with their infants, younger mothers responded less positively and paid less attention to their infants over 3 days than did older mothers. Younger teens did not proceed in maternal touch as rapidly as did older teens. Younger mothers were also inept during feeding observations, making no attempts to entice their infants to suck.

Of 12 teenage mothers studied from their infants' births through 12 months, two 14-year-olds did not achieve the maternal role, whereas teenagers aged 16 to 19 were able to do so (Mercer, 1980). The 14-year-olds were unable to place their infants' needs above their own at any time during the first year and described their infants as being like siblings. The grandmothers were caring for the infants as the teenagers' siblings. Of 44 teenagers aged 14 to 18 years, mothers aged 14 to 15 spent significantly less time looking at their infants, vocalized less, and maintained less physical contact with them, from 1 month to 1 year after birth (LeResche, Strobino, Parks, Fischer, & Smeriglio, 1983).

Adolescents 16 years or younger (mean, 15 years) had nonsignificant, higher means in maternal–fetal attachment than did adults aged 20 years or older and nonsignificant higher maternal–infant adaptation scores (on Price's [1983] measure) during the first 2 postpartal days (Kemp, Sibley, & Pond, 1990). Adults rated their pregnancies as good experiences more often and rated their labors as more difficult, but the young adolescents perceived themselves as more prepared to be mothers than adults did. Adolescents' views of good mothering differed from those of older mothers (Mercer, 1986a); during the postpartal hospitalization, adolescents were particularly unrealistic about the responsibilities of motherhood (Mercer, 1979a). Very few teenagers said they were looking forward to motherhood during hospitalization (Mercer, 1986a).

Rubin's concept about the early adolescent's inability to move into the maternal role has scientific support. The high rate of depression found in one study is alarming. The majority of adolescent mothers are living with their mothers and/or family members; this is beneficial when the families are not dysfunctional. The grandmother or surrogate may serve as a replacement or supplement mother, supporter, or mentor to the daughter in an apprentice role as mother (Apfel & Seitz, 1991). Grandmothers who had more knowledge about infant care had adolescent daughters who had more knowledge about mothering (Stevens, 1984). Grandmothers fulfilled roles of managing, caretaking, coaching, assessing, nurturing, assigning, and patrolling, fostering growth of their adolescent daughters and grandchildren (Flaherty, M. J., 1988). The early adolescent especially needs a mother–person to mother her and to provide guidance in order to learn to provide nurturant behaviors and meet her infant's needs (Mercer, 1979a, 1990).

Achievement of Maternal Role Competence by Middle and Late Teenagers

Teenagers' fantasies about their infants' appearances and personalities during pregnancy carried over at 1 month in their ratings of their infants' temperament (Zeanah et al., 1986) and at 4 months (Zeanah, Keener, Anders, & Vieira-Baker, 1987). At 4 months, the teenage mothers demonstrated more nurturing and cognitive stimulation with infants they perceived as less rhythmic, attempted more distress-relieving strategies and provided more cognitive stimulation with infants they perceived as more intense, and tried to relieve distress with infants perceived as more fussy or difficult (Zeanah et al., 1987). The young mothers developed rather stable cognitive representations or working models of their infants during pregnancy, which were only partially altered by experience over the first 4 months.

Mothers aged 17 to 18 years scored lower on maternal responsiveness than did mothers 19 and older during the postpartal hospitalization; race and marital status were unrelated to responsiveness (Jones, Green, & Krauss, 1980). Although teenagers interacted with their infants in similar patterns as did older mothers for the first three months, teenagers were less aware of and less responsive to their infants' signals than older mothers were (Roosa, Fitzgerald, & Carson, 1982).

Newly delivered adolescent mothers' responses to their infants were positively related to their age and grade in school (Ruff, 1987). Their scores on fostering cognitive, social, and emotional growth (NCAFS) were low. Over 6 to 12 weeks postpartum, these scores improved significantly; however, teen mothers responded less to their infants' distress. Maternal responses were associated negatively with maintaining a relationship with the baby's father the first week. Maternal responses with male infants declined at 6 to 12 weeks.

During the first 24 hours following delivery no relationship between observed maternal behaviors (de Chateau's Observation of Mother and Infant Behavior [OMIB]) and self-reported competence (Gibaud-Wallston & Wandersman's [1978] PSOC) was found among teenage mothers (Julian, 1983). Their PSOC mean score of 75.5 (*SD*, 10.7) was similar to that reported by low-risk first-time adult mothers (mean, 76.3; *SD*, 9.41) (Mercer & Ferketich, 1994b).

Black low-income primiparas aged 15 to 24 demonstrated encompassing behaviors during first contacts with their infants as they reached out for infants using both their hands and arms (Bampton, Jones, & Mancini, 1981). The majority held and gazed *en face* at their infants; over one-half verbalized to their infants, and all made positive statements about the infant's appearance and behavior.

During the first 2 to 3 days after birth, mothers aged 17 to 19 years underestimated infants' developmental rate and viewed some infant behaviors less optimally than did single adult mothers but did not differ in levels of stress (Becker, 1987). The older the mother, the more likely she was to view her infant as able to modulate behavioral state. Adolescents were as aware of their newborn's interactive behaviors as were adult mothers. Others reported that rural Caucasian adolescents knew as much about infant development and had attitudes as positive as adult mothers at 3 months after birth (Schilmoeller & Baranowski, 1985). Adolescents provided less stimulation for their infants as measured on the HOME and relied more on their relatives and mothers for help and information about child care than adults did.

Teenagers' NPI scores did not differ from adults'; 31% perceived their infants negatively, compared to 38.8% reported by Broussard and Hartner (1971) and 23% reported by Palisin (1980) (LeResche et al., 1983). Teenagers who perceived their infants negatively had less physical contact with their infants than did those who rated their infants positively.

Homeless adolescents in a special support program were observed during infant feeding (NCAFS) the first month and at 1–3 months and 4–6 months (Rich, 1990). Parenting behaviors did not differ significantly from an NCAST sample greater than 25 years of age, indicating that the homeless teens were sensitive to infant cues, responded to infant distress, and demonstrated behaviors that were growth-fostering for their infants. Their infants responded with significantly less clear cues and less responsiveness than did infants in the adult sample, however. The mothers as a group did not have a sense of feeding times contingent to their infants' needs and appeared to have a limited ability to help the infants organize their behavior.

Teenage mothers who had high levels of support and higher self-esteem and who used direct action as their method of coping reported less stress (Colletta & Gregg, 1981). Teenagers' major coping strategy was to ask for help (Colletta, Hadler, & Gregg, 1981). Emotional support and amount of support had an inverse relationship with maternal rejection of the infant (Colletta, 1981). Support networks need to be evaluated for their support or interference; family members and friends who provided support also interfered with the adolescent's sense of autonomy (Richardson, Barbour, & Bubenzer, 1991). Support from friends and relatives was associated with greater stress and distress, whereas support from a male partner was related to less stress (Thompson, 1986). Teenage mothers with a supporting partner were less rejecting and punitive with their infants (Unger & Wandersman, 1988).

Black teenage mothers' support was related to a decrease in their stress and an increase in their self-esteem (Colletta & Lee, 1983). Black teenage mothers who sought help with child-rearing problems from family members were more skillful parents (Stevens, 1988). Perceived support, social network resources, and support interventions were related to better postpartum adjustment for teenage mothers (80% black) and their infants' improved health and development (Unger & Wandersman, 1985). Latina adolescent mothers who identified mentors/role-models were more skilled in utilizing support resources and in dealing with relationship problems than were mothers without mentors (Rhodes, Contreras, Mangelsdorf, 1994). Mothers with mentors were also less depressed and anxious. An excellent model depicting the effects of the social support system on the teenage mother, her parenting, and child development was proposed by Nath, Borkowski, Whitman, and Schellenbach (1991).

Mothers aged 15 through 17 years scored significantly lower on acceptance and control than did mothers aged 18 to 21 at 6 months (Jarrett, 1982). Teenage mothers showed high warmth and physical interaction but lower verbalization in interacting with their 6-month-old infants than did women aged 20 and older (Landy, Clark, Schubert, & Jillings, 1983). Only three differences were observed in mothering skills: older mothers looked at their baby's faces, engaged in mutual face-to-face interaction, and smiled at their babies more often. The amount of time in social interaction did not differ by maternal age of dyads. The infants did not differ at birth on Apgar or BNBAS scores or at 6 months in observed behavior.

Adolescent mothers did not differ from adults in improvement of cognitive readiness for parenting at 6 months after birth, despite their demographic deficits and experiencing greater stress (Sommer et al., 1993). Adolescent cognitive readiness during pregnancy was a predictor of infant distractibility, infant reinforcement to mother, restriction of maternal roles, and maternal attachment at 6 months.

Adolescent mothers (aged 15–17 years, 45% black and 55% white) demonstrated less expressiveness, delight, and positive regard, fewer positive attitudes, and fewer and poorer-quality vocalizations than did adult mothers during feeding periods at 6 months after birth (Culp, Culp, Osofsky, & Osofsky, 1991). Adolescents were less inventive and less patient and had fewer positive attitudes than did adult mothers.

A test of Belsky's (1984) prioritized determinants of parenting (parent's psychological resources most effective in buffering mother–child relationship from stress, followed by contextual sources of stress and support, with the child's characteristics having least effects) among 157 teenage mothers (73% black and 27% white) at 1 year after birth was supported (McKenry, Kotch, & Browne, 1991). Bavolek's (1984) Adult–Adolescent Parenting Inventory was used to assess parenting and child-rearing attitudes. Inappropriate expectations were related negatively to self-esteem and positively to passive appraisal. Lack of empathic awareness was predicted by black race, greater depression, and passive appraisal. Strong belief in corporal punishment was predicted by lower self-esteem and greater passive appraisal. Less education and black race predicted role reversal. Black race was not highly related to dysfunctional parenting attitudes, nor did it serve as a buffer, as suggested by the belief of greater family support; black race was significantly related to poverty ($r = .448$). Lack of empathy was associated with low self-esteem and the infant's developmental delays. Corporal punishment was associated with a combination of negative life events during the past year and being unmarried.

Cognitive and motor development of teenage and adult mothers' infants were compared at early postpartum and at 6 and 12 months after birth (Carlson, Labarba, Sclafani, & Bowers, 1986). No maternal age differences were found in maternal and infant complications; however, black infants weighed less, and black mothers experienced more problems during childbirth. Infants did not differ on the Bayley Mental Development Index by age group; black infants performed significantly more poorly than white infants did. Adolescent mothers had a less stimulating environment, as measured on the HOME, than did adult mothers, and HOME scores were lower for blacks than for whites. Adolescence did not present a risk factor when race, parity, SES, and quality of prenatal care were controlled.

Teenagers aged 15 to 19 scored significantly lower on observed maternal competence at 1, 4, 8, and 12 months than did women aged 20 to 29 years and 30 to 42 years (Mercer, 1985b; Mercer, Hackley, & Bostrom, 1984). The observer-rated maternal competence correlated significantly with teenagers' self-reported ways of handling irritating child behaviors at 1 and 12 months. Teenagers handled their infants' irritating behaviors less positively at 12 months than at 1 month.

Barnard (1986) also reported less competence among younger mothers during infant feeding on the Nursing Child Assessment Feeding Scale (NCAFS) and teaching the infant on the Nursing Child Assessment Teaching Scale (NCATS), and less stimulation in the home environment

(HOME). Maternal age correlated more positively with the interactive score for males than for females at 12 months.

Summary

Research findings indicate the magnitude of interactional effects of the teenager's ecological environment and life space on maternal behavior. Although the teenagers did not differ from adults in their early perceptions of their infant, they were less responsive to their infants. Infants were less responsive in the study of homeless adolescents; these mothers provided less contingent care. Does the cycle of turmoil that leads to homelessness begin during infancy, as expressed by the infants' flat affect?

Future research needs to clarify more about the teenagers' ecological environment in relation to their mothering. Is it possible that mixed findings about teenagers' knowledge and interactions with their infants are related to different ecological contexts? Rural adolescents did not differ from adults in these areas, yet inner-city and stressed adolescents did.

Gratification in the Maternal Role

Many mothers under 18 were frustrated with parenting responsibilities, saw the infants as an intrusion in their lives, and expressed little pleasure in the role (Jarrett, 1982). Pregnancy data were the most powerful predictors of attitude toward the infant and parental attitudes of hostility between 2 weeks to 4 months (Camp & Morgan, 1984). Over 75% of teenagers described the first few weeks after birth as pleasurable and exciting; this was in contrast to adult mothers' intense fatigue (Mercer, 1986a).

Teenagers' postpartal hospitalization was marked by an aura of unreality as they received attention, praise, and gifts and viewed their infants as "cute" and "precious" (Mercer, 1979a, p. 375). By 2 weeks postpartum, a phase of reality shock occurred; the mother's deprivations in the role far outweighed her gratifications in the formal stage of maternal role identity (Mercer, 1980). Between 3 to 5 months a balance of maternal give-and-take occurred, with a balance between deprivations and gratification; mothers made decisions about their lives in relation to what they were willing to give and intended to take. From 6 to 8 months, an internalization of the maternal role occurred among 75%; gratification in the role far outweighed deprivations, and feelings of role competency emerged.

Younger maternal age among mothers aged 16 to 38 was associated with less satisfaction with parenting at 4 months (Ragozin, Basham, Crnic, Greenberg, & Robinson, 1982). In contrast to these findings, teenagers 15–19 years old reported significantly higher gratification in the mothering role than did women aged 30 and older but did not differ significantly from 20–29-year-old mothers at 1, 4, and 8 months after birth (Mercer, 1985b). Teenagers' gratification decreased significantly at 12 months, not differing from older mothers, but was less than that of mothers in their 20s.

Adolescents, more so than older mothers, demonstrated more positive maternal behavior and greater satisfaction with life and the maternal role when they had better family support and quality interactions in their social network (Schilmoeller, Bavanowski, & Higgins, 1991). Older mothers reported more family support than did adolescents, but adolescents reported the same number of social contacts as did older mothers.

Summary

Findings are mixed about the teenagers' enjoyment and gratification in the maternal role. Again, this may very well relate to the feelings of acceptance and support in the young mother's life space. In order to be helpful to young mothers, events in the woman's ecological environment and her psychological life space must be known. Researchers must compare teenage mothers in different situations with different assets, controls, and needs.

Development of Maternal Attachment

The discussion in chapter 4 about the pregnancy task of attaching to the fetus included research on adolescent mothers. Findings were mixed about the relationship of teenagers' self-esteem and social support to fetal attachment.

Anglo and Hispanic adolescent mothers were observed during feeding interactions the first week and first month following birth, using de Chateau's (1976) OMIB; mothers completed the NPI-I and NPI-II (Feller, Henson, Bell, Wong, & Bruner, 1983). During the first week, roughly one-half rated their infants as above average on NPI-I; by 1 month 94% rated their infants as above average. Although mothers held their infants closely during the first 10 days, they demonstrated few affectionate, touching, and loving behaviors or *en face* position. Affectionate, loving behaviors increased from Day 1 to Day 30 for all mothers, but the OMIB mean scores had decreased at Day 30. At 6 months, teenage mothers showed greater affection toward their infants than did adult mothers (Landy et al., 1983).

Age, race, social class, education, and previous pregnancies had no significant effects on the psychological adaptation or medical status of teenagers aged 14 to 19 years (63% black, 27% white, 10% Hispanic) (Wise & Grossman, 1980). At 6 weeks postpartum, adolescents who were more separate from their families were doing more child care, were less depressed, and felt more positively about their pregnancies and their infants. The teenagers' ego strength was explicit in their adaptation to pregnancy, and their infant's health status and temperament were more strongly related to adaptation to motherhood than their female identification and relationships with others. Ego strength measured during pregnancy was associated with anticipating motherhood more realistically and positively and developing attachment to the newborn more quickly.

Adolescents 17 years or younger talked less about and showed less positive affect toward their infants at 8 months after birth than did adult mothers (Levine, Coll, & Oh, 1985). Differences during face-to-face interactions were related more to maternal ego development, support, and educational level; teaching interactions were related to maternal age. Teenage mothers with lower ego development, education, and support were at greater risk of not providing optimal caregiving environments for their infants. Fewer attachment behavior were observed during in-hospital feedings among teenage mothers than among adult mothers (Norr & Roberts, 1991).

Teenage mothers' self-reported attachment to their infants did not differ significantly from older mothers' attachment at 1, 4, 8, or 12 months after birth (Mercer, 1985b). At 4 months, attachment scores were significantly higher than at any other test period for all mothers.

Teenagers' infants' attachment to them (Strange Situation Behavior) was predicted best by the teenagers' social network, living with the grandmother, and financial aid (Frodi et al., 1984). Adolescent mothers of infants who were securely attached at 14 months were providing more care for them at age 6 months than were mothers whose infants demonstrated avoidant attachment behavior (Lamb, Hopps, & Elster, 1987). Significantly more teenagers' infants were in avoidant and resistant groups than were samples of adult mothers' infants.

Summary

Research supports the hypothesis that teenage mothers' more active interactions with their infants were associated with greater attachment to their infants, as is the case with adult mothers. The association of increased attachment with teenagers functioning independently of their families indicates both greater maturity and possibly avoidance of conflict in problem families. There is no research that provides insight about how the development of the attachment process may differ among teenagers in different ecological environments. What is the relationship of the development of maternal attachment to empathy, egocentrism, locus of control, and flexibility among teenagers?

Summary

No research was found indicating that the early adolescent of less than 15 years of age achieves a maternal identity. The immature middle and older teenager, who is in the throes of evolving her identity as an adult capable of psychosocial independence from her family, is handicapped in achieving a maternal role identity. Although she achieves the role, she functions at a lower level of competence than do older women.

Research on teenage mothering has been confounded by failure to control for ecological variables such as poverty, family support and relationships, relationships with father of infant, and school achievement. Although the mother's ego development and educational level are strong indicators of her responsiveness to her infant, her SES or that of her parents in large part dictates how stimulating the environment for her infant will be. Despite the teenager's pattern of less vocalization to her infant, the infant's cognitive development proceeds similarly to that of adult mothers' infants during the first year after birth.

The concurrent social and economic disadvantages of teenage parenting have increasingly greater effects on the child's intellectual development as the child ages; small differences between teenagers' and adults' children were found during preschool years, with larger differences found by elementary school years (Brooks-Gunn & Furstenberg, 1986). Behavioral differences (activity levels, hostility, and undercontrol of behavior) were reported more often than intellectual differences during the early years, with boys affected more than girls. Ruff's (1987) findings that teenage mothers' responses to males declined at 6 to 12 months may be related to this. Research is needed to replicate this work and to explore whether this would occur in other populations, and if so, why.

The teenagers' fewer verbalizations and, in some studies, fewer smiles and fewer contingent responses may also lead to less secure attachment for their infants as they enter toddlerhood. The teenagers' lower gratification in mothering after 8 months may reflect difficulty in dealing with an infant moving into toddlerhood and seeking the autonomy that she herself desires.

How the teenager deals with the first stage of maternal role identity achievement during pregnancy forecasts later behaviors, largely because her level of development affects both. However, intervention to enhance maternal role identity among 12- to 19-year-olds during pregnancy did not show significant differences at 4 to 6 weeks postpartum in maternal identity, self-confidence, or scores on the NCAFS; only an increase in maternal–fetal attachment occurred (Koniak-Griffin & Verzemnieks, 1991). The inclusion of such young mothers with near-adult mothers may have confounded the findings because most research has indicated the profound difficulty young adolescents ($\leq$15 years) have in the mothering role. Mothers 16 years and older who participated in a model demonstration program increased in responsive, engaging, and elaborative styles of behavior with their infants, but those younger than 16 did not change these behaviors (Cooper, Dunst, & Vance, 1990).

Success has been demonstrated in programs geared to prevent repeat pregnancies, foster the return to school of mothers 17 or younger, and improve the record of immunizations (O'Sullivan & Jacobsen, 1992). An excellent summary of primary, secondary, and tertiary prevention with adolescent mothers and their families is found in a report of a roundtable, *Adolescent Pregnancy: Nursing Perspectives on Prevention* (Humenick, Wilkerson, & Paul, 1991).

MATERNAL ROLE IDENTITY AND THE WOMAN AGED 30 AND OLDER

The woman who delays motherhood until her 30s has usually achieved a higher level of education and an established career and has become accomplished in many roles. Women in their 30s may take longer to become pregnant, but most have healthy pregnancies and healthy babies. From 1980 to 1990, births to women from 30 to 34 years increased by 33%, and births to women 35 to 39 years old increased by 39%; estimates are that, by the year 2000, 1 in every 12 babies will be born to women aged 35 and older (March of Dimes Birth Defects Foundation, 1993).

Personality and Psychosocial Characteristics of the Woman Aged 30 and Older

Roosa (1988) compared middle-class women younger than 28 years (M = 23.6) with women 28 years and older (M = 31.5) as delayed child bearers; the older group were better educated, had a better occupation rank and higher income, and had married later. The two groups did not differ by marital adjustment, internal locus of control, self-esteem, and masculinity and femininity at pregnancy, or at 3, 6, or 12 months following birth. Both groups reported a significant decrease in marital adjustment at 3 months. No differences were observed in the percentage who were employed or who returned to employment after childbirth. Roosa questioned whether delayed child bearers were a distinct group apart from demographic characteristics.

First-time mothers aged 30 to 42 had significantly higher self-concepts and personality integration than did mothers younger than 30 years the first week and at 8 months after birth (Mercer, 1986a, 1986c). Older mothers had significantly greater flexibility in child-rearing attitudes but did not differ in empathy from women in their 20s. Their attitudes in regard to appropriate control of the child's aggression, encouragement of reciprocity, and acceptance of complexities of childrearing (Cohler's Maternal Attitude Scale [MAS]) were significantly more optimal than younger women's (Mercer et al., 1982). Self-concept and maternal attitudes were predictors of maternal role behavior consistently over the first year of motherhood. Two-thirds of the older women had baccalaureates or higher degrees, compared to one-third of the women in their 20s (Mercer, 1985b).

Others compared Canadian primiparas 35 years or older with a group 31 years or younger and reported no significant differences in the percentages for university education, income, or nature of employment (Robinson, Olmsted, Garner, & Gare, 1988). Older women reported a higher degree of total autonomy, and younger women reported greater social dependence and social investment. Although older women's level of distress increased as pregnancy progressed, they continued to be better adjusted at third trimester than the younger group (Robinson, Garner, Gare, & Crawford, 1987).

Autonomy is a precondition for effective mothering (Guttman, 1983). Older women continued to report greater autonomy at 12 months after birth than during pregnancy, but both groups reported a decrease over that time related to autonomous achievement and freedom from others' control and less attachment to other people (Robinson et al., 1988). Younger women had a more traditional sex role orientation than did older women both before and after birth. At 1 year, older women were less satisfied with their financial status and material assets than were younger women.

Cost of the Maternal Role at 30 Years and Older

More mature women have assets beyond their stronger sense of comfort with self. Their greater financial security enables better health care, better nutrition, and more stimulating environments. All of these assets forecast success in achieving a maternal role identity, but at what cost?

> *CS:* The prospect of becoming the bearer and giver in pregnancy, in labor, and in delivery is a costly and hazardous prospect. This giving involves giving up or giving away of the physical, mental, and social self. The more intellectually and experientially mature the woman, the more the subjective side of the equation predominates to increase the costliness of having a child. (Rubin, 1984, p. 8)

> *H:* The older the woman, the greater the cost perceived in the transition to motherhood.

Winslow (1987) derived a conceptual framework of "pregnancy as a project" from interview data with women aged 35 to 44. The women, who were experienced in planning and directing their lives, used the same approach to pregnancy that they used in previous life experiences; many described their pregnancies as projects. They progressed through four phases: planning for pregnancy (preconception), seeking safe passage (dominant up to 20 weeks gestation), the reality of now (goal to savor the moment), and anticipating the future (goal to integrate motherhood with other important parts of previous life). The latter two phases occurred over the last half of pregnancy. Their controlled planning for conception and later cognitive work of savoring the experience indicate that the mature population carefully weighs costs and benefits for motherhood in advance.

Pickens (1982) identified 6 cognitive processes in identity reformulation of Caucasian women aged 30 or older, who had been in a professional career for 7 years or more, at 13–26 days and 16–17 weeks postpartum. Women were reviewing attachments to career and former prepregnant self, projecting a model as an ideal for future self, planning, cost accounting in costs and rewards in becoming a mother, weighing alternatives or priorities in maternal versus career roles, and assessing their knowledge and performance in the mother role. Reviewing processes predominated at 13 to 26 days but had diminished to the least prominent at 4 months. Projecting and planning decreased over time; weighing remained the same, but cost accounting and assessing processes doubled. At 4 months, costs and rewards of motherhood were even; however, during early postpartum, the costs were four times greater than rewards. Teenage mothers viewed motherhood as almost twice as costly as rewarding at both 2 and 4 weeks, but at 5 months, costs equaled rewards (Mercer, 1980). Pickens's sample described the costs as deprivation of time for physical rest and sleep and for reading and relaxing, the strain motherhood placed on the marriage, disorganization caused by the infant's lack of schedule, lack of adult stimulation, and isolation and aloneness. The loss of employment was a cost to their self-esteem. See chapter 3 for additional discussion of the older first-time mother's cognitive work during pregnancy.

MATERNAL ROLE ATTAINMENT BY MOTHERS 30 AND OLDER

In contrast to teenagers, the older mother has many assets in her maturity and life space. Giving is basic to motherhood. Is the older mother able to give more than the younger mother?

H: The older the woman, the greater her maternal competence and the greater her attachment to her infant.

H: The older the woman, the lower her gratification in the maternal role.

Maternal Competence

The social network of primiparas 35 years and older changed to include mothers with children under 2 but became smaller from the last trimester of pregnancy to 1 month postpartum (Reece, 1993). This suggests that role models were sought for their new role, and other members were dropped. Mothers' mean scores for self-evaluation in parenting (WPL-R; Pridham & Chang, 1989) differed little from Pridham and Chang's normative data for primiparas with an average age of 27. The centrality of the infant subscale means for older mothers was 5.08 (*SD,* 1.03), compared to Pridham and Chang's sample, 4.78 (*SD,* .90). Unexpectedly, life-change averages differed very little between older and younger mothers. Functional and parenting support from the partner was related to self-evaluation in parenting but did not buffer postpartum stress.

Ragozin and associates (1982) reported that with increased maternal age (age range, 16–38), greater commitment to time in the role, more optimal maternal behavior, and greater satisfaction with parenting were observed. In contrast, younger mothers ($\leq$ 31 years) tended to adapt more quickly to the mothering role and reported a greater decrease in psychological and physical symptoms at 6 months than did mothers 35 years and older (Robinson et al., 1988). Younger women had reported more symptoms during early pregnancy, with no differences at third trimester and postpartum. The older women's symptoms did not decrease until 1 year; it took that long for them to integrate their career and mother roles. Only one-third of younger mothers who had careers during pregnancy were employed at 1 year, whereas all of the older mothers who had careers were employed. Mercer (1986a) observed a reorganization of activities and priorities among all age groups at 1 year, as women wished to establish firmer boundaries between self and infant and regain prepregnancy facets of the former self.

Interviews with two groups of first-time, white, college-educated mothers (one aged $\geq$33 years; the other, 23 to 29 years) revealed that the younger mothers felt less in control of their lives and were less conscious of planning time of child bearing (Frankel & Wise, 1982). Forty percent of older mothers gave up their careers for a period, with 60% continuing to work part-time or more, in contrast to 20% of younger mothers giving up their careers and 80% continuing to work part-time or more. Their pediatricians reported that late mothers had greater maturity, sense of competence, capacity for restraint and discipline, and capacity to enjoy their infants; mothers who had difficult infants felt that their maturity helped them to manage. Younger mothers reported sacrifices, isolation, and restlessness and were less ready to relinquish their earlier life-style to accommodate the child.

Although mothers 30 years and older had higher mean scores in observed maternal competence at 1, 4, 8, and 12 months than did women in their 20s, the differences were not significant (Mercer, 1985b). Their competence increased at 4 months over the 1-month level, with no significant change at 8 and 12 months. Older mothers also reported handling irritating child behaviors more positively over the first year, although differences were not significant. No significant differences were observed in role strain by maternal age at 4, 8, or 12 months after birth.

Summary

Older mothers achieved competence at the same or higher levels than those of younger mothers. Unexpectedly, their reported life changes were similar to those of women in their 20s. Further, they utilized their more mature skills in competent mothering.

Gratification in the Mothering Role

Women 30 years and older did not differ significantly in gratification in the mothering role from women in their 20s at 1, 4, and 8 months but reported significantly less gratification than did teenagers; however, at 12 months, women in their 20s reported significantly more gratification in the role than did older mothers. All mothers increased in gratification at 4 months over 1-month levels, with little change at 8 months. Women in their 20s increased, teenagers decreased, and women 30 and older did not change in reported gratification in the maternal role (Mercer, 1985b). Gratification among older mothers at 8 months was positively associated with self-rating in the maternal role, partner relationship, and previous experience in caring for infants; gratification was negatively associated with educational level (Mercer, 1985c). Thirty-two percent of older women's gratification was predicted at 8 months by educational level, age, and social support. Similar percentages of women 30 and older and women in their 20s were employed (59% and 55%, respectively).

Maternal competence, infant temperament, and father support were predictors of maternal satisfaction among women older than 28 years (mean, 32 years) (Coady, 1983). Many reported that motherhood turned out to be more fulfilling than expected and planned to repriortize their lives.

Women 30 and older did not derive less gratification in mothering than did women in their 20s until 1 year after birth. Their extensive cognitive preparation during pregnancy in weighing the costs of motherhood, along with their delay of motherhood, suggests that they were prepared to enjoy the role. However, the more highly educated woman enjoyed the role less; more highly educated women may be in fulfilling professions that compete more with the maternal role.

Attachment to the Infant

No research focused on older mothers' attachment to their infants was found except for Mercer's (1985b, 1986a). Self-reported maternal attachment did not differ between older mothers and younger mothers at any time over the first year. Attachment was significantly higher at 4 months than either at 1, 8, or 12 months after birth.

Summary

Although the older primigravida has an increased likelihood of chronic disease that may adversely affect pregnancy outcome, such as hypertension, midlife pregnancy is currently associated with healthy middle-class women (Mansfield & McCool, 1989). With a paucity of research funds, it is understandable that this population, with positive assets and outcomes, has lower research priority than populations with multiple problems.

The more mature woman is better equipped psychosocially to assume the maternal role identity. Although her overall performance was stellar, it was not significantly so. Her planning for the pregnancy was far more sophisticated, but the ratio of her assessed costs and rewards following birth was similar to the teenager's perceived costs and rewards in the mother role.

The older mother's progression in assuming the maternal role identity was similar to that of the woman in her 20s. She reported a greater number of health problems until 1 year after birth; this was related to difficulty in integrating career and maternal roles. The negative relationship between gratification and educational level among older mothers agrees with findings by Russell (1974) and Steffensmeier (1982) for mothers not differentiated by age group. Thus, it was not maternal age per se but level of education that was related to less gratification in the mother role.

THE ADULT UNMARRIED OR SINGLE WOMAN AND MATERNAL ROLE IDENTITY

Only 5% of all births in the United States were to unmarried mothers in 1960; by 1988 this proportion had increased to 26% (Carnegie Task Force, 1994). In 1992, there were 1,224,876 nonmarital births in the United States, 30% of all births (Ventura et al., 1994). Nonmarital birth rates per 1,000 births were highest for women 20 to 24 years (68.5), followed by women aged 18 to 19 years (67.3) and women 25 to 29 years (56.5). The nonmarital birth rate for women 30–34 years was 37.9, the highest level ever recorded.

Many of the single adult mothers have more education and better-paying positions than women nationally have (Pakizegi, 1990); however, the most common problem experienced by single mothers is economic (Macklin, 1987). Economic insecurity was high in single-mother families because of low earning capacity, lack of child support from nonresidential parents, and few public benefits (McLanahan & Booth, 1989). Single mothers' children were more likely to be poor as adults and to become single parents themselves as a result of economic deprivation, parental practices, and neighborhood conditions.

Mothers who choose single parenthood go through two main decision-making processes: whether or not to become a single mother and how (Pakizegi, 1990). For some, pregnancy is unplanned, but the decision is made to have a child rather than an abortion. Although attitudes toward the family and marriage have changed during the past 3 decades, the majority of Americans continue to value marriage, parenthood, and family life (Thornton, 1989), and single mothers continue to face stigmatization (Mercer, 1990).

Psychosocial Characteristics of the Single Mother

Considering the deliberateness of some single mothers' decisions to become mothers, at times through an unknown sperm donor, the motivation to assume a maternal role identity may be considered high. When the single woman refuses to consider an abortion, her motivation in assuming a maternal role identity may be more variable, as her decision may also reflect religious or right-to-life beliefs. These decisions may or may not include anticipation of the responsibilities and commitment necessary for motherhood.

Despite the shift in societal attitudes and the greater acceptance of alternative family structures, a study of 654 low-income women (72% single) reported that 35% of the adult mothers in the group were depressed (Reis, 1988). Low social support was significantly correlated with greater depression.

Different events triggered high anxiety among largely single (86%), poor African-American women than among middle-class, largely married (78%) whites (Green, 1990). African-American women were stressed by external issues of lack of money, mate/spouse issues, family and job or school; whites were stressed by internal events such as anticipatory fear or concern. These findings indicate that adequate resources and partner support facilitate the woman's cognitive work on maternal role concerns.

High depressive symptoms (CES-D) were reported by 60% of single-parent families with a child aged 1 to 4 years (Hall, Gurley, Sachs, & Kryscio, 1991). Employed mothers reported lower depression and more positive parenting attitudes than did nonemployed mothers. Higher depressive symptoms were predicted by poorer family functioning, less tangible support, higher everyday stressors, and greater use of avoidance coping.

A comparison of single mothers, 75% divorced and median age 34, and of married mothers, median age 32 (ages of children not given), found that single mothers' self-esteem was not significantly different from that of married mothers (Keith & Schafer, 1982). Unmarried mothers were more depressed, committed to work, spent more hours in the labor force, and had greater work–family role strain.

Single mothers with children aged 2 to 11 years were trapped in the difficult situation of feeling they were failures at not reaching the dream of a "normal" family, in relinquishing education, and accepting employment in typical female jobs (Quinn & Allen, 1989). This led to low-paid, inflexible, dead-end employment situations that caused worries about money, time, child care, and their children's quality of life.

White single mothers (two-thirds divorced or separated) with pre-school children were a great deal poorer than a comparison group selected by stratified random sampling (Richards, 1989). Single mothers had moved three times more frequently during the past 3 years, had smaller functional networks, were younger (mean, 29 years; range, 20–42), and had had their first child at a younger age than did married mothers. Single mothers survived by swapping child care, eating with relatives, and receiving occasional or regular cash donations from family and friends. Some viewed single parenthood as a challenge or as a relief (to be free of a conflictual relationship), whereas others viewed it as "an all-encompassing burden"; in addition to financial burdens, part of their problems was the lack of a backup person in emergencies or on a day-to-day basis (p. 399).

Studies of characteristics and SES of single mothers that included divorced women with children of older ages may be biasing descriptions of the single mother having a first child. The emotions, stress, and depressive symptoms as a result of the transition from a wife role to an ex-wife role would not be a part of the life space of most single mothers.

Maternal Role Identity Achievement and the Adult Single Mother

Scant evidence was found to describe the process of maternal role identity achievement among single adult women. If the unmarried woman is unpartnered or lacks an intimate adult partner, mothering is hypothesized to be more difficult because of the lack of diffusion of tension between mother and child and the interactional support, as shown in the theoretical model in chapter 1.

> *CS:* The single woman has a complex problem in social acceptance to having a child and becoming a mother. There is no one who wants or needs her child and no one who cares particularly about the sacrifices she must make in childbearing, childbirth, and childrearing.... As long as she hopes that the partner in conception can or will accept the child, the woman pursues all maternal tasks. If the partner in conception is unacceptable to her, or is rejecting of her and the child, the woman can-

not support and pursue the maternal tasks of pregnancy. She tends particularly to avoid binding-in to the child. (Rubin, 1984, p. 60)

In conversation with Dr. Rubin (January 8, 1994), she said that in her reference to the single woman's inability to pursue maternal tasks during pregnancy she was thinking more of women who were rape victims. She deferred sharing thoughts about the single parent in the 1990s because she lacked data on this population.

H: Single mothers have less social support than partnered mothers.

Finding acceptance for their pregnancy was difficult for single, unpartnered women; families and the infants' fathers responded negatively, contributing to single women's feelings of anxiety and depression and lowered self-esteem (Tilden, 1983a). Single women were aware of the need to seek out support and listed their mothers, sisters, or friends as major supports; their emotional and informational support did not differ from partnered women's, but they had less tangible support (Tilden, 1984).

A comparison of married, single/partnered, and single/unpartnered women during pregnancy found a significant negative relationship between severity of problems and complaints and number of close relationships among the single/unpartnered group (Liese, Snowden, & Ford, 1989). Among both married and single/unpartnered groups, the greater the number of household tasks performed by the woman, the greater the number of problems and complaints. No psychological losses or gains in task sharing were found for single women with partners.

Nonmarried, heterosexual, first-time mothers aged 20 to 39 years reported inadequate help and/or care during their recuperation from birth, for continuing birth problems, and for physical health 1 month after birth (Mercer, 1990). Their concerns focused on lack of money, going back to work, and their relationship with the infant's father. One-half had a high school education, 22% had not finished high school, 21% had some college, and 7% did not report education. They reported five different living arrangements: alone with infant, with a male partner, with parents, with other relatives, and with another woman who shared expenses.

Another variation in nonmarried mothers from a legal perspective is the partnered lesbian relationship (Pennington, 1990). The lesbian couple, although very supportive of each other, is faced with harassment, hostility, judgmental attitudes, and anger from persons normally within a parental support system.

A study of functional and dysfunctional single, low-income black mothers found that less adaptive mothers provided emotional and instrumental support more frequently to their relatives than did adaptive mothers (Lindblad-Goldberg & Dukes, 1985). These findings point out the importance of a functional family microsystem in which support is exchanged equitably.

Single mothers of preschool children were more socially isolated than married mothers; in addition to working longer hours, they received less emotional and parental support (Weinraub & Wolf, 1983). Single mothers' social networks were also less stable over time than married mothers'. Single mothers tended to report more life changes, with stresses from changes in employment or responsibilities, living conditions, and personal goals, whereas married women's stresses centered on home and family. The single mothers also were less likely than married mothers to confide in the persons whom they saw most frequently and rated their friends and relatives as less supportive.

The absence of a close friend and persons to call on contributed to problems in single parenting (Norbeck & Sheiner, 1982). Two parents and older siblings moderate stress experienced by poor children (Sandler, 1980).

Long-term single parenting was found to be a chronic stressor (Thompson & Ensminger, 1989). At the child's adolescence, those mothers who had been single parents since the child was school-age had higher levels of psychological distress than did mothers who lived with another adult or with a spouse. Mothers who had less distress reported emotional support, having a friend as a confidant, and attending church frequently.

Evidence supports the hypothesis that the single mother has less support. Although some single parents were aware of the importance of seeking out support, others were apparently unable to do this.

H: Maternal tasks of pregnancy differ in the situation of the single woman.

A comparison of single and partnered women during the anticipatory stage of pregnancy found that all women worked on all of the pregnancy tasks (Tilden, 1983a). Single women spent more time in deciding whether or not to continue their pregnancy (give of self); two-thirds had gotten pregnant by accident, compared to one-fourth of the partnered group. Their decision was made independent of the father of the baby but was influenced by their financial situation and their age (60% were approaching 30). Role models for the decision of single motherhood were their mothers or surrogate mothers, who had reared them and their siblings alone.

Single women had to ensure the future safety of their unborn children through legal avenues (Tilden, 1983a, 1984). In addition to determining the baby's last name, whether to name the father on the birth certificate, and the father's legal rights and responsibilities, legal guardianship had to be determined in the event something happened to the mother.

The lesbian woman faces social stigma and hassles in finding supportive caretakers in seeking safe passage. (See chapter 4.)

Tilden's important research indicates that the single mother works at usual pregnancy tasks. Her pregnancy tasks were more complex due to legal ramifications and lack of an intimate partner who would automatically be a legal guardian in the event she was incapacitated.

H: There is a positive association between the single mother's relationship with the father of the baby (or intimate partner) and maternal attachment to the baby. (No research.)

H: The unpartnered or single mother experiences greater difficulty in maternal role achievement than the partnered mother does.

Unmarried first-time mothers studied at 1, 6, and 12 months after birth scored significantly higher on Overprotection and Rejection scales and lower on the Acceptance scale (measured by Roth's [1961] Mother–Child Evaluation Scale) than did married mothers (Young, 1986). Unmarried mothers had less often planned their pregnancies. Mothers who were referred for help with infant care scored higher on rejection.

Single mothers living apart from their parents or other relatives demonstrated more emotional and verbal responsivity and greater involvement with their infants on the HOME (Caldwell & Bradley, 1984) than did those living with family members at 4 months after birth (Barratt, Roach, & Colbert, 1991). The older the mother, the greater was her responsivity, organization of the environment, and involvement with the child. Significant negative relationships were found between psychological symptoms and mothers' organization of the environment, involvement with the child, and provision of age-appropriate activities and toys. Predictors of parenting included disruption in family of origin (single or step-parent), current residence, maternal age, psychological symptoms, and infant difficulty. Mothers who viewed their infants as more difficult were less responsive to and less involved with them and provided fewer age-appropriate activities. Single mothers exhibited significantly less involvement with their young infants and less emotional and verbal responsivity than did mothers from two-parent families. Egocentrism (although subclinical) was associated with the mother's impaired mental health and appeared to interfere with the mother's ability to make optimal choices for her infant.

Black grandmothers were much more actively involved with dual parenting when they shared a home with the adult single mother than when daughters lived in the community (Wilson, 1984). They were also less critical of the single daughter's parenting when they shared a home.

Single mothers were worried about their competencies as mothers, and family members were critical of their mothering in some instances (Mercer, 1990). At 4 months, being married was significantly related to maternal competence among women in their 20s ($r = .34$). Single mothers were enjoying their infants but continued to be concerned about their care. They viewed motherhood as fostering their growth in giving up bad habits and in becoming more organized and more responsible as adults. Those not living with their parents or a family member were more often dealing with problems with the infant's father.

Two-thirds of the single mothers reported achieving a maternal identity prior to 6 months after birth (Mercer, 1990). At 8 months, the relationship between marital status and maternal competence was significant but much lower ($r = .20$ among women aged 20 to 29 and .24 among women aged 30 and older). Four of the 28 single mothers were pregnant with a second child at 1 year. Some single mothers reported physical and/or emotional abuse by male partners; one male partner molested the woman's daughter. Despite their struggles, the women enjoyed their infants and their interactions with them; their self-image was enhanced through their maternal identity over the year.

Higher depressive symptoms and a poorer primary intimate relationship were predictive of less positive parenting attitudes; parenting attitudes predicted child behavior (Hall et al., 1991). Less favorable parenting attitudes, higher everyday stressors, and greater use of active-cognitive coping were associated with more child behavior problems. Others reported no significant differences on measures of parenting by single or married mothers of preschool-age children (Weinraub & Wolf, 1983).

The most powerful predictor of psychological adjustment among low-income single mothers of preschoolers was perception of childhood familial adversity (Olson, Kieschnick, Banyard, & Ceballo, 1994). Women's perceptions of their childhood nurturant relationships were related to actual and perceived social support. There was a relationship between women's mothers being viewed as harsh disciplinarians and their perceived ability to cope with child care as effectively as others. Women who reported good relationships with one or both parents reported better emotional health and higher self-evaluations of their coping ability.

Summary

There is scant research on becoming a mother among this population, which had 30% of all infants born in 1992. Research to date indicates that the majority of single mothers are vulnerable in their lack of consistent, reliable support from family and friends and their economic problems. Their ecological environment in many situations is as hostile as that of the teenage mother. Their life space is often troubled. In what situations are family members nonsupportive of the single mother? How may dysfunctional families can be identified and helped early during the single mother's pregnancy? Do more unpartnered mothers than partnered mothers have histories of poor relationships with their parents? Early relationships with parents become internalized and are thought to have enduring effects on the adult's social interactions and ability to seek and receive support (Flaherty, J. A., & Richman, 1986; Sarason, Sarason, & Pierce, 1990).

Thus far, data support the fact that although the single mother has a difficult time, she feels as rewarded by her infant and her enhanced self-image as do other mothers. The two reports of overprotectiveness observed among single mothers need further investigation. Is this a result of their being the only parent and feeling total responsibility for the child? Studies of single mothers beyond the first year indicate that they face greater difficulties than do partnered parents and that those difficulties affect their child into adulthood.

No research was found to illuminate how the achievement of maternal role identity may differ for the single/unpartnered adult, except Tilden's research during pregnancy. Longitudinal studies gathering information, such as described by Tilden during pregnancy, are needed during formal, informal, and personal identity stages of maternal role identity. Who does the single mother select as a major support for herself during this transition? Who in addition to her mother does she select for role models?

The number of single women becoming mothers, and their problems described in the few studies, place this as a research priority. The profound negative effects of the life space and ecological environments of many of the nonmarried mothers on their ability to mother and on their children demand examination if they and their children are to be helped. The proportion of research focused on the single mother in relation to the numbers of single mothers suggests that perhaps society thus far has not cared enough about the single mother's plight as observed earlier by Rubin.

SUMMARY

The contrasts of the younger and older and nonmarried mothers highlight the impact of the woman's life space and ecological environment on maternal role achievement. However, the woman who became a mother at 30 or older was not significantly different from the woman in her 20s in her work toward maternal role achievement.

The older woman's cognitive work prior to and during her pregnancy amplified this process; the research in this area reaffirms this cognitive work's importance to early mothering. The cost of motherhood did not appear greater for the older woman, but she had postponed motherhood until she felt the timing was right.

The cost of motherhood appears to be greater for the more highly educated woman. This may be a socialization pattern that has evolved over the past 2 decades. The more highly educated woman may have been socialized more strongly toward career than toward motherhood.

The theoretical model proposed in chapter 1 was strongly supported by the interactional effects between mother, infant, and supportive partner, and the interactional effects of the microsystem and macrosystem on the developing maternal role.

■ 12
Employment and the Maternal Role

One of the greatest changes in the social setting affecting young families during the past 3 decades has been the increasing number of working mothers of infants. In 1965, 17% of mothers of 1-year-olds worked full-time; by 1991, 53% were in the work force (Carnegie Task Force, 1994).

The woman who is developing a maternal role identity may be spending up to one-third of her time in an employment setting and a few minutes each day in a day-care setting. The mother performs specific activities and roles in each of the settings; her wife, maternal, employment, day-care (if applicable), and other roles have effects on each other and on maternal role achievement.

CORRELATES OF MATERNAL EMPLOYMENT

Early reviews of maternal employment focused largely on the effects of maternal employment on the child (Etaugh, 1974; Hoffman, 1974;

Murray, 1975; Stolz, 1960). Siegel and Haas (1963) sought to identify knowledge about the correlates of maternal employment through their review. The only differences found between employed and nonemployed mothers' were that employed mothers had smaller families and a tendency toward more egalitarian attitudes concerning division of authority and labor in the home. The popular literature portrayed employed mothers as deviant, with many guilt-inducing indictments into the late 1970s (Zambrana, Hurst, & Hite, 1979). Fathers did not help more with child care, and parental role specialization was not significantly changed in families when the mother was employed (Stuckey, McGhee, & Bell, 1982).

Women who returned to full-time employment following the birth of a child had greater commitment to work during pregnancy (Amstey & Whitbourne, 1988). Women who were employed more often had mothers who worked when they were young than did nonemployed women.

Almost two-thirds of women who returned to work within the first 3 months after childbirth gave financial need as the reason (Volling & Belsky, 1993). Women who had more prestigious occupations and higher levels of education gave career development and personal enjoyment as reasons for returning to work. Full-time employed mothers reported less commitment to their maternal role during pregnancy than did consistent homemakers (planned to stay home and did) but were equally as committed to their infants and their maternal role as were part-time employed and inconsistent homemakers (planned to return to work but stayed home).

Employed mothers of preterm infants at 3 months postpartum were significantly more employment-oriented and reported less choice and satisfaction with employment status than did nonemployed mothers (Youngblut, Loveland-Cherry, & Horan, 1990, 1991). Employed mothers were employed more hours during pregnancy and reported plans to return to employment sooner after birth than did nonemployed mothers. Higher employment orientation was associated with higher educational level, fewer children, more hours employed, greater total support for employment, greater financial necessity, and less choice and satisfaction with employment status. At 3 months, 50% of the mothers were nonemployed, 36.4% were employed, and 13.6% were on a leave of absence.

MOTHER–CARETAKER AND SEPARATION ANXIETY

When Dr. Rubin (personal communication, January 8, 1994) was queried about her thoughts on the effects of employment on maternal identity achievement, she declined to comment, stating that she had not researched this area. Her earlier work, however, made reference to the spatial distancing that occurs with maternal employment.

> *CS:* Each increment in spatial distancing between a woman and her child evokes resistance, anxiety, and self-discipline in accommodation to the maturing child's enlarging sphere of physical space. Whether the spatial distancing is for starting school, going to camp, evenings or over-nights with friends, or for leaving home for college, work, or marriage, there is maternal pain and anxiety. (Rubin, 1984, p. 142)

H: Employed mothers experience anxiety in leaving their infants with other caretakers.

Employed mothers, in contrast to nonemployed mothers, did not doubt other caregivers' competence or express anxiety about leaving their infants and did not perceive that their infants were distressed by their leaving them (Hock, 1978). The greater the career orientation of nonemployed mothers, the greater their personal offense at their infants' discontent and the greater their perceptions of infant distress at their leaving them.

Older, well-educated mothers, who preferred employment, decreased in anxiety about separation (sadness and guilt) from their infants earlier and to a greater extent than did mothers who preferred to stay at home, at 2 days, 7 weeks, 8 and 13.5 months after birth (DeMeis, Hock, & McBride, 1986). No group differences in separation anxiety were observed during the first 7 weeks, suggesting that both groups were focusing more on the maternal role. All mothers who preferred employment had returned to employment within 12 months, with 92% returning within 4 months; 44% of mothers who preferred to stay at home if given a choice were employed by 10 months. There were no differences in anxiety about separation between mothers who stayed home and those who preferred to stay home but were employed.

Employed mothers reported less anxiety on the Maternal Separation Anxiety Scale (MSAS) when their second-born infant was 7 months old than they had reported for their firstborn at 7 months (Pitzer & Hock, 1989). However, mothers' employment-related separation anxiety subscale scores did not differ between first- and second-born infants. No differences in MSAS were observed by sex of the infant, but an interview schedule revealed that mothers of second-born sons were significantly more anxious about separation (Pitzer & Hock, 1992). Symptoms of depression (CES-D) were unrelated to anxiety on the MSAS when children were 8 months and 3.5 years of age, but when children were 6 years old, mothers with higher MSAS scores had more symptoms of depression, fewer coping skills, lower self-esteem, and perception of themselves as poorer wives than did mothers with low MSAS scores (Hock & Schirtzinger, 1992). This finding suggests more maternal separation anxiety effects when the child leaves the mother to enter school than when the mother leaves the infant and preschooler for employment or other reasons.

Employed mothers who reported high separation anxiety more often exhibited intrusive behaviors with their infant at 10 months (Strange Situation) (Stifter, Coulehan, & Fish, 1993). Although mothers' employment was not directly related to attachment, infants of high-anxiety employed mothers developed anxious-avoidant attachments, indicating that the link between maternal employment and mother–infant attachment may be through the mother's separation anxiety and its effect on mother–infant interactions.

Shuster (1993) identified a typology of maternal responses to integrating parenting and employment during infancy; the typology was based on interviews and questionnaires when the infant was 4 to 6 weeks old and at 4 to 5 months after the mother had returned to work. The *enamored* mother believed in her supremacy as caregiver, her expectations for the infant's caregiver was supplemental to her care, her interactions with her infant were sensitive, and her caregiving was contingent. The *manager* mother was the organizer, with the caregiver as an equal partner; her interactions with her infant were acceptable, and her caregiving was responsive. The *distressed* mother believed in the exclusivity of the primary caregiver, and the caregiver was a competitor; she preferred to be at home with the baby; mother–infant interactions were responsive caregiving, coupled with distancing, avoidance, and inappropriate independence expectations. The *disengaged* mother was angry, rejected motherhood, and saw the caregiver as primary provider who had replaced her; her caregiving was insensitive and noncontingent, and she was disconnected from the parenting role. All four groups reported positive perceptions of their child care expectations and experiences. The manager and disengaged groups expressed a positive desire to return to work.

ROLE CONFLICT AND ROLE STRAIN

Role conflict and role strain are expected outcomes of multiple role identities; however, Thoits (1983) found that persons with more identities had less psychological distress. Isolated persons gained more from multiple identities and were harmed more by identity losses than were persons more socially integrated.

During postpartal hospitalization and at 3 months after birth, 77% and 78% of 317 mothers agreed that motherhood was the major fulfillment in a woman's life; 66% planned to return to work prior to their infant's first birthday (Hock et al., 1984). If given a choice, 69% of mothers said they would rather stay home during the early postpartum, compared to 76% at 3 months. At early postpartum, 46%, contrasted to 34% at 3 months, agreed that a career gave much personal satisfaction, but 75% agreed that they would not regret postponing their careers to stay home with their children.

When mothers continue employment roles as they develop their maternal roles, their responsibilities in the household usually continue. Regardless of mothers' employment status, mothers gave the majority of infant care across 1, 6, and 12 months (Jones & Heermann, 1992). Although fathers' proportion of caregiving increased as maternal employment hours increased, fathers never assumed a majority of any type of caregiving. Fathers became more involved in caregiving at 1 year when mothers were employed full-time.

H: Employed mothers will report greater role conflict or role strain than nonemployed mothers will.

A study of potential role conflict between worker, spouse, parent, and self as a self-actualizing person roles found that women who were in jobs not viewed as careers reported greater role conflict than did women in careers (Holahan & Gilbert, 1979). Differences were between the self role and spouse and parent roles. When spouse support was controlled, the differences disappeared. Despite the longer hours and increased demand in careers, the life satisfaction scores were higher among the career group in all four roles; satisfaction with career may offset role conflict.

Mothers with high commitments to both work and parenting had lower role strain when they had professional/managerial jobs (O'Neil & Greenberger, 1994). Women with low-work–low-parenting commitment had significantly less role strain when employed in lower-status jobs than did women in professional or managerial positions.

No differences in role conflict, marital satisfaction, employment role attitude, or ease of transition to the maternal role were found between employed and nonemployed mothers with children aged 5 to 18 months of age (Majewski, 1986). Mothers with careers reported more conflict on subscale measures of worker versus self and worker versus spouse than did mothers in jobs not viewed as careers. Regardless of employment status, mothers who reported greater role conflict in spouse, parent, or self roles had greater difficulty in their transition to the maternal role.

Role conflict problems were significant concerns among families with firstborn infants, studied at 3, 7, 9 and/or 12 months (McKim, 1987). Mothers working outside the home reported more problems in the last half of the first year of motherhood, and older mothers reported more problems between 9 and 12 months than younger mothers. Parents reported dissatisfaction with the existing social networks.

Employed second-time mothers had significantly fewer relatives and neighbors in their social networks than did nonemployed mothers, whereas employed mothers listed more coworkers during pregnancy; there were no differences in perceived support by employment group during pregnancy, at 6 weeks, or at 6 months after birth (Jordan, 1987). Marital satisfaction was high among both groups over all test periods. Nonemployed mothers reported more support for the parental role from friends and family following birth.

Professional women combine their multiple roles in unique patterns (Cartwright, 1987). Common patterns among a sample of largely white women physicians were "superwoman," "career of limited ambition," and "medicine is my lust." The superwoman orchestrated and drove herself through diverse and competing timetables, giving equal importance to roles of doctor, mother, and wife. The woman with a career of limited ambitions placed her family first and selected a less taxing role in medicine; she did not appear stressed and found time to garden. The "medicine is my lust" woman put medicine first and decided to forgo family. If she had a relationship, it was secondary; juggling roles was not a problem because her profession was first.

Women (37% with high school education) experienced a three-phase process in redefining their roles as mothers, wives, and workers (Hall, 1987, 1992). The first phase included factors influencing their decisions to resume employment, such as societal and work role expectations, spouse's response, adequate child care, and finances. In the second phase, role strain was experienced in the form of guilt, loss, exhaustion, ambivalence, resentment, and anger, as they tried to meet their expectations and responsibilities. Unmet needs, difficulties with household maintenance, and lack of time for family activities were identified and weighed with the consequences of unrelieved role strain, including marital conflict, illness, and dissatisfaction. During the third phase, reducing role strain, several steps were taken to regain control of their lives: letting go of myths, expectations, and feelings; setting priorities; organizing and planning; negotiating and delegating responsibilities to spouses; and establishing new expectations.

Role strain was not related to age, educational level, occupation, or schedule flexibility at 10 to 12 months after birth; women in income categories of less than $19,999 and $40,000 to $59,999 had greater role strain than those with incomes of $20,000 to $39,999 and more than $60,000 (Hemmelgarn & Laing, 1991). Women who were employed full-time had significantly greater role strain than did those who worked part-time or in not regularly scheduled positions.

At 12 months after birth, mothers aged 30 and older who had adequate social support experienced less maternal role strain than did mothers without adequate support (Smith, 1994a). Employment status (nonemployed, part-time, or full-time) had no effect on role strain. Type of child care (paid or reciprocal) had effects on role strain at 4 months and on observed maternal behavior at 8 months (Smith, 1994b). Mothers with paid child care had less role strain.

Summary

Type of employment (career vs. short-time job), social support, and type of child care appear more related to role strain than does employment alone. Employed mothers reduced their role strain by reorganizing their cognitive structure for parenting and their priorities and delegating more household tasks.

HEALTH STATUS OF EMPLOYED VERSUS NONEMPLOYED MOTHERS

Employed ($\geq$40 hours per week) mothers reported significantly more stress and less self-actualization, exercise, nutrition, interpersonal support, and stress management than did nonemployed mothers with infant children (Walker & Best, 1991). Major sources of stress, in order of frequency, for employed mothers were conflicts about returning to work, lack of time, fatigue and sleep disturbance, work overload, and infant illness. Major sources of stress for nonemployed mothers were fatigue and sleep disturbance, work overload, lack of time, other unclassified sources, and infant behaviors. Although employed mothers managed their responsibilities in ways that enabled them to have positive images of themselves as mothers, it may have been at the expense of their own well-being.

Mothers who preferred employment but stayed home had higher levels of depression than did mothers who stayed home because of their preference (Hock & DeMeis, 1990). Mothers who preferred to and stayed home reported significantly more separation-related anxiety than did employment-preferred employed mothers. In a follow-up study, employment-preferred employed mothers and employment-preferred stay-at-home women had higher scores in career salience than did home-preferred stay-at-home and home-preferred employed groups. Employment-preferred employed women reported lower investment in the maternal role than did the home-preferred stay-at-home women. Employment-preferred stay-at-home mothers were more stressed and reported significantly higher depressive symptoms than did other groups.

Employment status and infant difficulty were related to reported stress among mothers of infants aged 2 to 12 months; neither had direct effects on maternal identity (Walker, L. O., 1989b). A health-promotive life-style was negatively related to perceived stress. Stressors, perceived stress, and health-promotive life-style subscales of self-actualization, nutrition, interpersonal support, and stress management contributed additively in explaining maternal identity.

In interviews between 3 and 5 months after birth, only 35% of employed mothers, in contrast to 64% of fathers, described stress related to multiple role demands (Ventura, 1987). Financial issues were related to the stress of multiple roles. Infant care was also a major stress, reported by 35% of mothers and 20% of fathers; 14% of mothers and

11% of fathers were stressed with their spouses.

Killien (1993) reported 70% of employed study participants worked to within 1 week of delivery, with over one-third taking no leave before childbirth. By 4 months postpartum, 80% had returned to employment, with 15% having returned by 6 weeks postpartum. More than one reason for returning to work was sometimes given and included financial (76.3%), self-fulfilling (30.5%), workplace policy (30.5%), work-motivated (25.4%), and family/baby-motivated (1.7%). One-half of the mothers felt that they were working too many hours at 4 months; among those who were employed at the time, 23.9% had missed work days due to their own illness during the past month, and 28.4% had missed work because of the infant's illness. An additional 38% reported that their poor health interfered with their work performance, although they had not been absent. These women with many resources were faced with trying to meet financial needs or their career demands at some cost to their health.

Because fatigue is a problem for mothers during the first year, one would expect employment to be a factor; however, neither the number of hours worked per week nor the spouse's equitable sharing of housework were predictors of fatigue (Killien & Jarrett, 1994). By 8 months, 85% of the mothers were employed. A study of Finnish mothers found that they reported experiencing fatigue over the first year, although their mean frequency was lower than that reported by U.S. mothers (Fetrick & Killien, 1994). Finland provides 80% of earnings to employed women while on maternity leave during the first 10–12 months after birth.

Employed mothers reported managing fatigue by strategies to get more sleep, such as trading off, getting used to it, and working around the baby's schedule (Jarrett, Olshansky, & Fetrick, 1994).

IMPACT OF MATERNAL EMPLOYMENT ON MATERNAL BEHAVIOR

Maternal Competence

Brazelton (1986) observed that parents who were concerned about having to return to work prior to 3 months after birth tended to talk about their future role as parents as opposed to the future baby as a person. He suggested that the younger the infant and more inexperienced the mother upon returning to employment, the more likely the mother is to deny that her leaving has consequences for the infant or herself, to project important caregiving issues onto the substitute caregiver, and to tend to distance her feelings of responsibility and of intense attachment. During the first 4 months after birth, employed parents and substitute care providers should be helped with the infant's achievement of homeostatic control over input and output systems, attending to and using social cues to extend attention states and to assimilate more complex trains of messages, beginning to press limits with the parent in taking in and responding to information in the reciprocal feedback system, and being allowed to demonstrate and incorporate a sense of autonomy within the dyad or triad (Brazelton, 1986).

At 8 months after birth, 55.3% of first-time mothers were employed (Mercer & Hackley, 1984). No differences were found between employed and nonemployed mothers for number of stressors, health status, help with mothering, mate's help with baby, regularity of infant's schedule, perception of self in mothering role, role strain, maternal attitudes, attachment to the infant, maternal behaviors, and ways of handling irritating infant behaviors. Employed mothers' infants scored lower in growth and development. When examined by age group (teens, 20–29 years, and 30–42 years), employed teens scored higher on maternal competency than did nonemployed teens, but the converse was true for the women aged 20–29 years; no differences were observed among older employed mothers (Mercer, 1985b).

Mothers who were employed full-time and had paid child care exhibited more competent maternal behavior at 8 months after birth (Smith, 1994b). Yet mothers employed part-time demonstrated more competent maternal behavior when they had reciprocal child care.

Slesinger (1981) observed that the mother's work experience was an important measure of secondary integration (living with family or male partner provided primary integration) for skilled mothering. Employed women had to keep schedules, maintain commitments, arrange for child care, and be able to communicate with others; these factors contributed to their better mothering skills.

Summary

Very little research has addressed maternal role competence by employment status. Findings are mixed about the effects of maternal employment on maternal role competence. The interactive effects of multiple settings and multiple roles with the woman's life space need examining.

The single mother (see chapter 11) had difficulty managing mother and employment roles.

Gratification in Mothering Role

No significant differences were found between employed and nonemployed first-time mothers' gratification in the mothering role at 8 months after birth (Mercer, 1986a). Despite employed women in their 20s reporting significantly greater role strain, their gratification in mothering did not differ from nonemployed mothers.

Brazilian mothers with clerical jobs identified having 12 roles, such as wife, mother, daughter, employer, student, and housekeeper, but described pleasure in the intimacy and reciprocation, caring, and energy generation of the maternal role (Meleis, Kulig, Arruda, & Beckman, 1990). However, the maternal role was also stressful in depleting their energy, the worries created about the present and future, the responsibilities, and lack of resources for child care. All of the women expressed a sense of gratification, fulfillment, and accomplishment at being able to conceive and give and receive love.

Women who adapted well to employment also adapted well to early motherhood (Jimenez & Newton, 1982). Women who worked longer during pregnancy had significantly higher job satisfaction, and the sooner they planned to return to work, the higher was their job satisfaction. Work satisfaction scores correlated negatively with anxiety, guilt, depression, repression, and fatigue and positively with extroversion and arousal at 1 to 2 months after birth. Virtually no relationship was found between reported maternal behaviors or attitudes toward the infant and job satisfaction, but women who rocked their infants more were also more satisfied with their coworkers.

High work involvement (importance of job to life prior to pregnancy) was associated with nonemployed mothers feeling more irritable, less important, and more depressed at 5 to 9 months after birth (Pistrang, 1984). Their self-esteem was lower, motherhood was more costly and less satisfying, and more negative changes had occurred in their marriages. Among employed mothers, low work involvement was related to feeling more important and to greater satisfaction with motherhood. Most of the women, regardless of previous work involvement, were working part-time. Effects of employment were related to previous work involvement.

Employed mothers with infants aged 10 to 12 months, who scored higher on maternal identity measured by L. O. Walker's (1982) SDS, also reported less role strain (Hemmelgarn & Laing, 1991).

Summary

Although there is gratification in the maternal role when multiple roles are involved, the cost of the maternal role is identified. The mother's values about employment appear to be more important to her satisfaction with the maternal role than role strain or fatigue.

MATERNAL ATTACHMENT

A positive relationship was found between occupational commitment and the quality of maternal–infant interaction (measured by Price's [1983] AMIS) during postpartal hospitalization but not at 6 weeks postpartum (Riesch, 1984). Women whose mothers worked when they were children tended to have a lower quality of interaction with their newborn infants than did women whose mothers had not worked during their childhood. A higher quality of interaction was observed among mothers who either did not intend to return to work at all nor to resume work after 4 months than among mothers who intended to return by 4 months. A higher quality of maternal interaction was directed toward male infants than toward female infants.

Employed mothers aged 30–42 years reported significantly higher infant attachment than did nonemployed mothers (Mercer, 1986a). However, women in their 20s and teenagers reported no differences in attachment by employment status.

The system of care received by the infant in the family was the focus of a research review of the attachment relationship between mother and infant and maternal employment (Schachere, 1990). The link between maternal caregiving characteristics and quality of infant attachment was verified as well established. Marital quality had effects on the parent–infant relationship regardless of mothers' employment status but was more critical when mothers were employed. Qualitative differences in attachment relationships between employed mothers and their infants were influenced by maternal characteristics, paternal involvement in child rearing, and the marital relationship.

No differences were found in the quality of the infant's attachment to the mothers in the Strange Situation by hours of maternal employment at 6 and 12 months, reason for return to work, or ease of maternal return to work (Wille, 1992). Mothers who worked more hours at both 6 and 12 months after birth were more autonomous on departure from their infant. Mothers who returned to work for financial reasons or found the return to work difficult, demonstrated less autonomous behavior and more anxiety on reunion with their infants. A greater proportion of infants of employed mothers were insecure–avoidant, compared to infants of nonemployed mothers over the first year (Barglow, Vaughn, & Molitor, 1987). The relationship between attachment quality and work status was significant only for firstborn infants of mothers who were employed full-time.

An analysis of 13 studies (N = 897) examined the security of infant–mother attachment (Strange Situation at 11–24 months) by experience of, extent of, and onset of nonmaternal care (Lamb, Sternberg, & Prodromidis, 1992). Secure attachments were found significantly more often among infants who had exclusive maternal care than among infants who experienced regular nonmaternal care for more than 5 hours per week. Ratings of avoidance were higher among infants receiving nonmaternal care. A small but significant relationship between age of enrollment in nonmaternal care and attachment insecurity was found. Insecure attachments were more likely when children were cared for in centers rather than in family day-care homes or with in-home baby-sitters.

Summary

Employed women aged 30 and older reported greater attachment to their infants than did younger mothers. This may relate to their greater integration of self and values toward both roles. Interactive effects of wife roles and type of day care appear important to developing maternal attachment among employed women.

SUMMARY

Women continue employment after childbirth for many reasons; however, financial need is the major reason. One study's findings suggested that their own mothers' employment influenced whether they continued employment along with the maternal role. Employed women did not demonstrate greater separation anxiety; this may be a protective mechanism, as suggested by Brazelton (1986).

For whatever reason the woman opts for employment, her spouse is not inclined to share the child care equally. Conflict and role strain were associated more with spousal and family roles than with the employment role. The mother seems to deal with the strain of employment by altering her ideal images of self in the multiple roles and negotiating for more support.

The employed mother's health may be adversely affected by the long working hours of employment and maternal roles during the early months after birth. There is apparently less time for the working mother to pursue health-promoting activities. However, employment status was not related to fatigue or to maternal role strain.

Little is known about the cognitive process that is ongoing in the development of the maternal identity as the woman juggles the employment role with other roles. Shuster's (1993) delineation of the relationship between the mothers' distress in integrating maternal and employment roles and the quality of mother–infant interaction is an important beginning. Evidence indicates that the well-integrated woman who is committed to both roles and does well in the employment role also does well in the mothering role.

Although some studies report differences in infant–mother attachment between children cared for by their mothers at home and children in substitute child care, the interaction of family and child care systems, along with family and maternal variables, have not been considered (McCartney & Galanopoulos, 1988). McCartney and Galanopoulos proposed an ecological model based on Bronfenbrenner's (1977) theory for considering the effects of the cultural macrosystem on interactions of the family and child care and assessment of the microsystems on adaptive attachment.

The large percentage of mothers returning to the work force during the period of infancy merits more research on transition to the maternal role while continuing employment. Are there long-range effects? Only through close examination of interactive variables can sufficient data be derived for use in preventive health measures for both mother and infant. The economic status of families in the United States is not apt to change in the near future so that mothers who prefer not to resume employment following childbirth will have that choice. Even the career woman who excels in both career and maternal roles would profit by guidelines to promote her and her child's mental health.

■ **four**

CONCLUSIONS

■ 13
Conclusions

Reva Rubin's contributions to maternity nursing and to the theories related to the process of maternal identity achievement are substantial. Her work set the study of early maternal behavior and maternal role attainment on its scientific course. Her reported theories made the process of maternal role identity amenable to empirical study. She relied on participant observation of maternal behavior in the natural context of clinic, hospital, and home environments in her course of study. Her analyses of these observations have informed maternity nursing practice and provided theories for testing and further elaboration through qualitative research.

A criterion for a good theory is not so much that its predictions are confirmed but that useful and important data are generated from it (Grusec, 1992). Not only have Rubin's theories in large part been supported, but their usefulness has been demonstrated in clinical practice and research; they have stimulated the production of much important data.

Rubin's identification of the woman's cognitive reformulation of her self-identity and family-subsystem relationships in assuming the maternal identity have been confirmed by researchers from several disciplines. Her concept of the infant's centrality to the woman's maternal identity has been illustrated in all situational contexts, with the situation of the preterm birth highlighting the maternal identity diffusion that occurs when the woman's process of maternal identity is interrupted for the period she is unable to hold and identify her infant. There is very strong evidence to support Rubin's concept that maternal behaviors are uncertain and oscillating in direction without feedback from the child in the situation of the preterm infant. (OR – - - transport?)

Rubin's identification of women's cognitive and psychosocial work in maternal tasks of pregnancy—ensuring safe passage, seeking support for herself and the infant, binding-in to her infant, and learning to give for the benefit of her dependent infant—have proved fruitful avenues for identifying mothers who experience vulnerability in later mothering. The accomplished work on pregnancy tasks as the basic structure that becomes elaborated following birth in mothering has been demonstrated in many situations.

LIMITATIONS

Although Rubin blended somewhat disparate symbolic interactionist, field, cognitive, and psychoanalytic theories, her blend was one of congruence; however, these theories seem to have influenced the language she chose to use in some of her theoretical concepts. The terminology used may have delimited the use of some of her concepts because of their different meanings in different theoretical contexts. Moral masochism, the willingness to postpone self-gratification and to place another's welfare above oneself, is central to achievement of a maternal identity. Giving of oneself is a clearer derivative, but her references to moral masochism may be objectionable to those who are not psychoanalytically oriented. The term "fantasy," as opposed to the more commonly used "mental rehearsal for the maternal role," has been misinterpreted by some. Dedifferentiation by the woman from role models by formulating her own style and behavior for the role is somewhat clumsier than differentiation; her definition does not show any difference between the two terms. Polarization is used as the mother's early differentiation of self from infant; the borrowing from Deutsch (1945) of the illustration of cell division as an analogy of a psychological mother–child division is clear, and although it is applied to a specific situation, it may confuse the novice. These very important theoretical concepts are also the least researched and least used in practice.

Many of Rubin's concepts reflect the historical context in which they were formulated, and this cannot be called a limitation. What is important was her vision in identifying those maternal behaviors that have continued to be identified as universal, although with variations deriving from a different social and technological context. Examples of these concepts include the progression of maternal touch and taking-in and taking-hold behaviors during the first 3 days.

MAJOR GAPS IN KNOWLEDGE ABOUT THE TRANSITION TO THE MATERNAL ROLE

Although numerous theoretical frameworks have been used to study the transition to the maternal role, the intricate process continues to be elusive in many respects. The cognitive restructuring process for a maternal identity encompassing competence in mothering is dependent on the woman's cognitive abilities: to project into the future, to consider alternatives and problem-solve, to know what information she needs and where to obtain it, to communicate effectively, to trust others, and to establish nurturing relationships with others. Evidence indicates that the latter two abilities become a part of the woman's cognitive schemata during her early years of being mothered. We don't know *whether or how* a woman may be aided in directing her cognitive work toward specific tasks that professionals identify that she is neglecting. Because the woman is operating from her psychological life space with resources available to her, this information is critical for effective intervention.

When the process of maternal role achievement is interrupted, how can assistance or "makeup" cognitive work be facilitated? Or is this possible? In situations of maternal identity diffusion with an infant whose situation is fixed, how may the woman be helped to move to a cognitive reformulation that allows her to make the decision to progress toward an altered (from her pregnancy-projected ideal mother, ideal baby) self-image and identity?

How does the woman achieve differentiation of self from baby? Does this proceed in stages, with birth being a first stage and polarization a second stage? Research reports do not indicate that psychological separation of mother from baby is completed by the end of the first month. Research documents that lack of a firm ego boundary between mother and child leads to the mother's projecting her negative life events and/or characteristics on the baby. Is the daughter–mother relationship related to the firmness of the daughter's ego boundary? Does the reconciliation process of the woman with her mother during pregnancy, when she begins to identify with her mother as an adult, facilitate her ability to also establish clearer boundaries between self and child?

Because psychological separation of mother from infant is necessary for her to be able to establish contingent behavior and be responsive to infant cues, this is a critical link in the maternal role identity. How can psychological separation be facilitated so that the mother sees the infant empathically from the infant's needs rather than from her projection of his needs?

These are very critical questions in the face of the complexities inherent in the large populations of women in extremely vulnerable childbearing situations. Since Kempe and associates' (Kempe, Silverman, Steele, Droegemuller, & Silver, 1962) publication of "The Battered Child Syndrome" around the same time as Rubin's earliest publications, a large multidisciplinary focus has been directed to research on parenting and early mothering to identify the etiology of child abuse and neglect. Strong evidence has been provided to shift the mid-century mentality of "mother blaming" for children's problems to placing the crisis of young children's neglect within an ecological framework.

The Carnegie Task Force on Meeting the Needs of Young Children (1994) identified federal, state, local, and private agencies and communities as having failed in ameliorating poverty and in providing adequate prenatal and child care, help for isolated parents, and programs to help parents in providing necessary resources and stimulation for their infants and young children. Cultural, family-structural, and economic changes during the last half of the 20th century have led to one-fourth of young children living in poverty. Maternal employment is a necessity for many mothers, but inadequate day care and family leave policies increase their burdens. During this same time, advanced technology has enabled women with chronic illnesses and fertility problems to become mothers and has allowed the survival of ill and very immature infants.

PRIORITIES

As the 21st century nears, the development of mothering is occurring within the context of many social problems that have increased societal awareness about the critical roles of parenting and the families that nurture these roles. Mothers of preterm infants have voiced to researchers that they were denied their rights as mothers and as decision makers during their NICU experience. Enormous strides have been made in the past 25 years in NICU environments, socially and technically; in the early 1970s, parents weren't allowed in NICUs. But the technological advances may have taken over from the social advances: How can mothers be denied their rights? How is this related to their maternal identity diffusion during their NICU experience? The number of preterm births and evidence documenting sequelae in mothers developing contingent behavior with these infants place research focused on interruptions in maternal identity as a major priority. The mother's inability to establish contingent behavior with the infant in the situation of preterm birth (even after the infant has caught up developmentally) *may not* be related to early psychological separation of mother from infant. Many VLBW infants are born at the beginning of the third trimester; it is during this time that mothers share a lot of interactional experiences with the fetus and are actively visualizing their future interactions with a healthy term infant. Thus, the preterm infant may be born before a psychological tie is firmed and the mother gets to know the infant's sleep–wake periods in utero or to experience the displaced body space. The inability to hold or to see the infant, apart from equipment, for days or weeks following birth delays the acquaintance-attachment process. How do the missed experiences of third trimester alter the development of mother–infant interactions over the first year?

Rubin's (1984) concepts about the experience of time and space in the physical and social space, relative to the childbearing woman's body, have not been explored. She hypothesized that the woman's experience during the third trimester afforded her greater sympathy and tolerance for the infant. Qualitative data are needed to explicate more clearly the third-trimester experiences of the mother with her infant. Then research could focus on whether a link exists between mother–preterm infant interaction over the first year and missed third-trimester experiences.

Another neglected area of research concerns a large population: roughly one-fourth of mothers are single. Evidence to date from samples biased by low SES and from divorced and separated mothers indicates that the unpartnered woman in particular (unmarried and without an intimate partner) has many problems in achieving a maternal identity. The one research report on her pregnancy tasks revealed a greater complexity in the context of less family support. Research indicated maternal overprotectiveness during infancy. Does the unpartnered woman have greater difficulty in the psychological separation from her infant? The situational context for the unpartnered mother's achievement of a maternal identity may contain extraordinary stressors, such as fighting for everyday survival (Smith-Battle, 1993) and living necessities (Green, N. L., 1990).

Mothering in the 21st century will continue to involve the necessity of integrating employment roles with maternal roles. Evidence suggests that commitment to and success in the roles facilitate the role integration. At what cost to the mother? Type of day care and support are emerging as important variables.

Technological achievements will continue to enable mothers in a variety of situations to move into the maternal role. Continuing to research the process in a variety of situations may lead to greater understanding of the process as it occurs more universally.

The need for a shift in society's priorities to place a greater value on mothers and their children by providing more extensive support and health care during childbearing and child rearing has never been more urgent. For the care to be received and utilized by mothers, current knowledge about the maternal role must be utilized. Current knowledge must be extended through allocation of research funds to continue work on clarification of the complex process of achievement of maternal role identity.

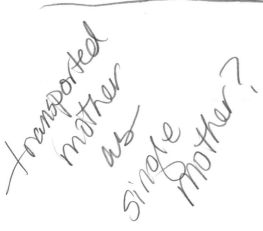

References

Aaronson, L. S. (1989). Perceived and received support: Effects on health behavior during pregnancy. *Nursing Research, 38,* 4–9.

Abbink, C., Dorsel, S., Flores, J. E., Meyners, J. E., & Walker, C. J. (1982). Bonding as perceived by mothers of twins. *Pediatric Nursing, 8,* 411–413.

Abernethy, V. D. (1973). Social network and response to the maternal role. *International Journal of Sociology, 3,* 86–92.

Abrums, M. E. (1980). Adolescent pregnancy and parenthood. *Communicating Nursing Research, 13,* 42–43.

Affleck, G., Allen, D. A., McGrade, B. J., & McQueeney, M. (1982). Maternal caretaking perceptions and reported mood disturbance at hospital discharge of a high risk infant and nine months later. *Mental Retardation, 20,* 220–225.

Affleck, G., Tennen, H., & Gershman, K. (1985). Cognitive adaptations to high-risk infants: The search for mastery, meaning, and protection from future harm. *American Journal of Mental Deficiency, 89,* 653–656.

Affleck, G., Tennen, H., & Rowe, J. (1988). Adaptational features of mothers' risk and prevention appraisals after the birth of high-risk infants. *American Journal on Mental Retardation, 92,* 360–368.

Affonso, D. D. (1977). "Missing pieces": A study of postpartum feelings. *Birth and the Family Journal, 4*(4), 159–164.

Affonso, D. D. (1992). Postpartum depression: A nursing perspective on women's health and behaviors. *Image: Journal of Nursing Scholarship, 24*, 215–221.

Affonso, D. D., & Arizmendi, T. G. (1986). Disturbances in postpartum adaptation and depressive symptomatology. *Journal of Psychosomatic Obstetrics and Gynaecology, 5*, 15–32.

Affonso, D. D., & Domino, G. (1984). Postpartum depression: A review. *Birth, 11*, 232–235.

Affonso, D., Lovett, S., Paul, S., Arizmendi, T., Nussbaum, R., Newman, L., & Johnson, B. (1991). Predictors of depression symptoms during pregnancy and postpartum. *Journal of Psychosomatic Obstetrics and Gynaecology, 12*, 255–271.

Affonso, D. D., Lovett, S., Paul, S. M., & Sheptak, S. (1990). A standardized interview that differentiates pregnancy and postpartum symptoms from perinatal clinical depression. *Birth, 17*, 121–130.

Affonso, D. D., Lovett, S., Paul, S., Sheptak, S., Nussbaum, R., Newman, L., & Johnson, B. (1992). Dysphoric distress in childbearing women. *Journal of Perinatology, 12*, 325–332.

Affonso, D. D., & Mayberry, L. J. (1990). Common stressors reported by a group of childbearing American women. *Health Care for Women International, 11*, 331–345.

Affonso, D. D., Mayberry, L. J., Graham, K., Shibuya, J., Kunimoto, J., & Kuramoto, M. (1992). Adaptation themes for prenatal care delivered by public health nurses. *Public Health Nursing, 9*, 172–176.

Affonso, D. D., Mayberry, L. J., & Sheptak, S. (1988). Multiparity and stressful events. *Journal of Perinatology, 8*(4), 312–317.

Affonso, D. D., & Sheptak, S. (1989). Maternal cognitive themes during pregnancy. *Maternal–Child Nursing Journal, 18*, 147–166.

Affonso, D. D., & Stichler, J. F. (1978) Exploratory study of women's reactions to having a cesarean birth. *Birth and Family Journal, 3*(4), 149–155.

Affonso, D. D., & Stichler, J. F. (1980). Cesarean birth: Women's reactions. *American Journal of Nursing, 80*, 468–480.

Ainslie, R. C., Solyom, A. E., & McManus, M. E. (1982). On the infant's meaning for the parent: A study of four mother–daughter pairs. *Child Psychiatry and Human Development, 13*, 97–110.

Ainsworth, M. D. S. (1973). The development of mother–infant attachment. In B. M. Caldwell & H. N. Riccuiti (Eds.), *Review of child development research*, (pp. 1–94). Chicago: University of Chicago Press.

Ainsworth, M. D. S. (1979). Infant–mother attachment. *American Psychologist, 34*, 932–937.

Ali, Z., & Lowry, M. (1981). Early maternal–child contact: Effects on later behavior. *Developmental Medicine Child Neurology, 23,* 337–345.

Ament, L. A. (1990). Maternal tasks of the puerperium reidentified. *Journal of Obstetric, Gynecologic, and Neonatal Nursing, 19,* 330–335.

Amstey, F. H., & Whitbourne, S. K. (1988). Work and motherhood: Transition to parenthood and women's employment. *Journal of Genetic Psychology, 149,* 111–118.

Anders, R. F. (1994). Infant sleep, nighttime relationships, and attachment. *Psychiatry, 57,* 11–21.

Anderson, A., & Anderson, B. (1987). Mothers' beginning relationship with twins. *Birth, 14,* 94–98.

Anderson, A., & Anderson, B. (1990). Toward a substantive theory of mother–twin attachment. *MCN, the American Journal of Maternal Child Nursing, 15,* 373–377.

Anderson, G. C. (1989). Risk in mother–infant separation postbirth. *Image: Journal of Nursing Scholarship, 21*(4), 196–199.

Andresen, P. A., & Telleen, S. L. (1992). The relationship between social support and maternal behaviors and attitudes: A meta-analytic review. *American Journal of Community Psychology, 20,* 753–774.

Anisfeld, E., & Lipper, E. (1983). Early contact, social support, and mother–infant bonding. *Pediatrics, 72,* 79–83.

Apfel, N. H., & Seitz, V. (1991). Four models of adolescent mother–grandmother relationships in black inner-city families. *Family Relations, 40,* 421–429.

Aradine, C. R., & Ferketich, S. (1990). The psychological impact of premature birth on mothers and fathers. *Journal of Reproductive and Infant Psychology, 8,* 75–86.

Arizmendi, T. G., & Affonso, D. D. (1984). Research on psychosocial factors and postpartum depression: A critique. *Birth, 11,* 237–245.

Arizmendi, T. G., & Affonso, D. D. (1987). Stressful events related to pregnancy and postpartum. *Journal of Psychosomatic Research, 31,* 743–756.

Austin, J. K. (1991). Family adaptation to a child's chronic illness. *Annual Review of Nursing Research, 9,* 103–120.

Avant, K. C. (1981). Anxiety as a potential factor affecting maternal attachment. *Journal of Obstetric, Gynecologic, and Neonatal Nursing, 10,* 416–419.

Avant, P. K. (1982). A maternal attachment assessment strategy. In S. S. Humenick (Ed.), *Analysis of current assessment strategies in the health care of young children and childbearing families* (pp. 171–190). Norwalk, CT: Appleton-Century-Crofts.

Ball, J. A. (1987). *Reactions to motherhood.* Cambridge: Cambridge University Press.

Ballinger, C. B., Buckley, D. E., Naylor, G. J., & Stansfield, D. A. (1979). Emotional disturbance following childbirth: Clinical findings and urinary excretion of cyclic AMP (adenosine 3'5' cyclic monophosphate). *Psychological Medicine, 9,* 293–300.

Ballou, J. W. (1978a). *The psychology of pregnancy.* Lexington, MA: Lexington Books.

Ballou, J. W. (1978b). The significance of reconciliative themes in the psychology of pregnancy. *Bulletin of the Menninger Clinic, 42,* 383–413.

Bampton, B., Jones, J., & Mancini, J. (1981). Initial mothering patterns of low-income black primiparas. *Journal of Obstetric, Gynecologic, and Neonatal Nursing, 10,* 174–178.

Bandura, A. (1982). Self-efficacy mechanism in human agency. *American Psychologist, 37,* 122–147.

Baranowski, M. D., Schilmoeller, G. L., & Higgins, B. S. (1990). Parenting attitudes of adolescent and older mothers. *Adolescence, 25,* 781–790.

Barden, R. C., Ford, M. E., Jensen, A. G., Rogers-Salyer, M., & Salyer, K. E. (1989). Effects of craniofacial deformity in infancy on the quality of mother–infant interactions. *Child Development, 60,* 819–824.

Barglow, P., Vaughn, B. E., & Molitor, N. (1987). Effects of maternal absence due to employment on the quality of infant–mother attachment in a low-risk sample. *Child Development, 58,* 945–954.

Barnard, K. (1978). *The nursing child assessment satellite training manual.* Seattle: University of Washington.

Barnard, K. E. (1986). Screening variable: Maternal age. *NCAST National News 2*(3), 1.

Barnard, K. E., Bee, H. L., & Hammond, M. A. (1984). Developmental changes in maternal interactions with term and preterm infants. *Infant Behavior and Development, 7,* 101–113.

Barnard, K. E., Magyary, D., Sumner, G., Booth, C. L., Mitchell, S. K., & Spieker, S. (1988). Prevention of parenting alterations for women with low social support. *Psychiatry, 51,* 248–253.

Barnett, B., & Parker, C. (1986). Possible determinants, correlates and consequences of high levels of anxiety in primiparous mothers. *Psychological Medicine, 16,* 177–185.

Barnes, J. E., Leggett, J. C., & Durham, T. W. (1993). Breastfeeders versus bottlefeeders: Differences in femininity perceptions. *Maternal–Child Nursing Journal, 21,* 15–19.

Barratt, M. S., Roach, M. A., & Colbert, K. K. (1991). Single mothers and their infants: Factors associated with optimal parenting. *Family Relations, 40,* 448–454.

Bassoff, E. S. (1984). Relationship of sex-role characteristics and psychological adjustment in new mothers. *Journal of Marriage and the Family, 46,* 449–454.

Bates, J. E., Freeland, C. A. B., & Lounsbury, M. L. (1979). Measurement of infant difficultness. *Child Development, 50,* 794–803.

Bavolek, S. J. (1984). *Handbook for the Adult–Adolescent Parenting Inventory.* Schaumburg, IL: Family Development Associates.

Beck, A. (1978). *Beck Depression Inventory.* Philadelphia: Center for Cognitive Therapy.

Beck, A., Ward, C., Mendelson, M., Mock, J., & Erbaugh, J. (1961). An inventory for measuring depression. *Archives of General Psychiatry, 4,* 561–571.

Beck, C. T. (1987). Vaginal and cesarean birth mothers' temporal experiences during the postpartum period. *Journal of Obstetric, Gynecologic, and Neonatal Nursing, 16,* 366–367.

Beck, C. T. (1991). Maternity blues research: A critical review. *Issues in Mental Health Nursing, 12,* 291–300.

Beck, C. T. (1992). The lived experience of postpartum depression: A phenomenological study. *Nursing Research, 41,* 166–170.

Beck, C. T. (1993). Teetering on the edge: A substantive theory of postpartum depression. *Nursing Research, 42,* 42–48.

Beck, C. T., Reynolds, M. A., & Rutowski, P. (1992). Maternity blues and postpartum depression. *Journal of Obstetric, Gynecologic, and Neonatal Nursing, 21,* 287–293.

Becker, P. T. (1987). Sensitivity to infant development and behavior: A comparison of adolescent and adult single mothers. *Research in Nursing and Health, 10,* 119–127.

Beckwith, L. (1972). Relationships between infants' social behavior and their mothers' behavior. *Child Development, 43,* 397–411.

Beckwith, L., & Cohen, S. E. (1978). Preterm birth: Hazardous obstetrical and postnatal events as related to caregiver–infant behavior. *Infant Behavior and Development, 1,* 403–411.

Bee, A. M., Legge, D., & Oetting, S. (1994). Ramona T. Mercer: Maternal role attainment. In A. Marriner-Tomey (Ed.), *Nursing theorists and their work* (pp. 390–405). St. Louis: Mosby.

Behrends, R. S., & Blatt, S. J. (1985). Internalization and psychological development throughout the life cycle. *Psychoanalytic Study of the Child, 40,* 11–39.

Bell, R. Q. (1974). Contributions of human infants to caregiving and social interaction. In M. Lewis & L. S. Rosenblum (Eds.), *The effect of the infant on its caregiver* (pp. 1–19). New York: John Wiley & Sons.

Belle, D. (1982). *Lives in stress: Women and depression.* Beverly Hills, CA: Sage Publications.

Belsky, J. (1984). The determinants of parenting: A process model. *Child Development, 55,* 83–96.

Belsky, J. (1985). Exploring individual differences in marital change across the transition to parenthood: The role of violated expectations. *Journal of Marriage and the Family, 47,* 1037–1044.

Belsky, J., Lang, M., & Huston, T. L. (1986). Sex typing and division of labor as determinants of marital change across the transition to parenthood. *Journal of Personality and Social Psychology, 50,* 517–522.

Belsky, J., Lang, M. E., & Rovine, M. (1985). Stability and change in marriage across the transition to parenthood: A second study. *Journal of Marriage and the Family, 47,* 855–865.

Belsky, J., & Rovine, M. (1990). Patterns of marital change across the transition to parenthood: Pregnancy to three years postpartum. *Journal of Marriage and the Family, 52,* 5–19.

Belsky, J., Spanier, G. B., & Rovine, M. (1983). Stability and change in marriage across the transition to parenthood. *Journal of Marriage and the Family, 45,* 567–577.

Bem, S. L. (1981). *Bem Sex Role Inventory professional manual.* Palo Alto, CA: Consulting Psychologist Press.

Benedek, T. (1949). The psychosomatic implications of the primary unit: Mother–child. *American Journal of Orthopsychiatry, 19,* 642–654.

Benedek, T. (1956). Psychobiological aspects of mothering. *American Journal of Orthopsychiatry, 26,* 272–278.

Benedek, T. (1959). Parenthood as a developmental phase. *Journal of the American Psychoanalytic Association, 7,* 389–417.

Benedek, T. (1970). The family as a psychologic field. In E. J. Anthony & T. Benedek (Eds.), *Parenthood: Its psychology and psychopathology* (pp. 109–136). Boston: Little, Brown.

Berkowitz, G. S., & Kasl, S. V. (1983). The role of psychosocial factors in spontaneous preterm delivery. *Journal of Psychosomatic Research, 27,* 283–290.

Bernier, J. C. (1990). Parental adjustment to a disabled child: A family-systems perspective. *Families in Society: The Journal of Contemporary Human Services, 71,* 589–596.

Berry, K. H. (1983). The body image of a primigravida following cesarean delivery. *Issues in Health Care of Women, 6,* 367–376.

Bettes, B. A. (1988). Maternal depression and motherese: Temporal and intonational features. *Child Development, 59,* 1089–1096.

Bibring, G. L. (1965). Some specific psychological tasks in pregnancy and motherhood. In *1 Congress International de Medecine Psychosomatique et Maternite* (pp. 21–26). Paris: Gauthier-Villars.

Bibring, G. L., Dwyer, T. F., Huntington, D. S., & Valenstein, A. F. (1961). A study of the psychological processes in pregnancy and of the earliest mother–child relationship. *Psychoanalytic Study of the Child, 16,* 9–24.

Bibring, G. L., & Valenstein, A. F. (1976). Psychological aspects of pregnancy. *Clinical Obstetrics and Gynecology, 19,* 357–371.

Birdsong, L. S. (1981). Loss and grieving in cesarean mothers. In C. F. Kehoe (Ed.), *The cesarean experience* (pp. 187–209). New York: Appleton-Century-Crofts.

Biringen, Z. (1990). Direct observation of maternal sensitivity and dyadic interactions in the home: Relations to maternal thinking. *Developmental Psychology, 26,* 278–284.

Bishop, B. E. (1992). Congratulations Reva! *MCN, the American Journal of Maternal Child Nursing, 17,* 231.

Blackburn, S. (1983). Fostering behavioral development of high-risk infants. *Journal of Obstetric, Gynecologic, and Neonatal Nursing, 12,* May/June (Suppl.), 76s–86s.

Blackburn, S., & Lowen, L. (1986). Impact of an infant's premature birth on the grandparents and parents. *Journal of Obstetric, Gynecologic, and Neonatal Nursing, 15,* 173–178.

Blank, D. M. (1985). Development of the Infant Tenderness Scale. *Nursing Research, 34,* 211–216.

Blank, D. M. (1986). Relating mothers' anxiety and perception to infant satiety, anxiety, and feeding behavior. *Nursing Research, 35,* 347–351.

Blank, M. (1964). Some maternal influences on infants' rates of sensorimotor development. *Journal of the American Academy of Child Psychiatry, 3,* 668–687.

Bliss-Holtz, V. J. (1988). Primiparas' prenatal concern for learning infant care. *Nursing Research, 37,* 20–24.

Blumberg, N. L. (1980). Effects of neonatal risk, maternal attitude, and cognitive style on early postpartum adjustment. *Journal of Abnormal Psychology, 89,* 139–150.

Booth, C. L., Mitchell, S. K., Barnard, K. E., & Spieker, S. J. (1989). Development of maternal social skills in multiproblem families: Effects on the mother–child relationship. *Developmental Psychology, 25,* 403–412.

Boudreaux, M. (1981). Maternal attachment of high-risk mothers with well newborns. *Journal of Obstetric, Neonatal, and Gynecologic Nursing, 10,* 366–369.

Bowlby, J. (1969). *Attachment and loss: Attachment* (Vol. 1). New York: Basic Books.

Bowlby, J. (1973). *Attachment and loss: Separation and anger* (Vol. 2). New York: Basic Books.

Boyd, C. (1990). Testing a model of mother–daughter identification. *Western Journal of Nursing Research, 12*(4), 448–461.

Bradley, C. F. (1983). Psychological consequences of intervention in the birth process. *Canadian Journal of Behavioural Science, 15,* 422–438.

Bradley, C. F., Ross, S. E., & Warnyca, J. (1983). A prospective study of mothers' attitudes and feelings following cesarean and vaginal births. *Birth: Issues in Perinatal Care and Education, 10*(2), 79–83.

Bramadat, I. J., & Driedger, M. (1993). Satisfaction with childbirth: Theories and methods of measurement. *Birth, 20,* 22–29.

Brazelton, T. B. (1973). *Neonatal behavioral assessment scale.* Philadelphia: J. B. Lippincott.

Brazelton, T. B. (1979). Behavioral competence of the newborn infant. *Seminars in Perinatology, 3,* 35–43.

Brazelton, T. B. (1986). Issues for working parents. *American Journal of Orthopsychiatry, 56,* 14–25.

Brazelton, T. B., & Als, H. (1979). Four early stages in the development of mother–infant interaction. *Psychoanalytic Study of the Child, 34,* 349–369.

Breen, D. (1975). *The birth of a first child: Towards an understanding of femininity.* London: Tavistock Publications.

Bretherton, I. (1992). The origins of attachment theory: John Bowlby and Mary Ainsworth. *Developmental Psychology, 28,* 759–775.

Brodish, M. S. (1982). Relationship of early bonding to initial infant feeding patterns in bottle-fed newborns. *Journal of Obstetric, Gynecologic, and Neonatal Nursing, 11,* 248–252.

Brody, S. (1956). *Patterns of mothering.* New York: International Universities Press.

Bromwich, R. M. (1976). Focus on maternal behavior. *American Journal of Orthopsychiatry, 46,* 439–446.

Bronfenbrenner, U. (1977). Toward an experimental ecology of human development. *American Psychologist, 32,* 513–531.

Bronfenbrenner, U. (1986). Ecology of the family as a context for human development: Research perspectives. *Developmental Psychology, 22,* 723–742.

Bronfenbrenner, U. (1989). Ecological systems theory. *Annals of Child Development, 6,* 185–246.

Brooks-Gunn, J., & Furstenberg, F. F., Jr. (1986). The children of adolescent mothers: Physical, academic, and psychological outcomes. *Developmental Review, 6,* 224–251.

Broom, B. L. (1994). Impact of marital quality and psychological well-being on parental sensitivity. *Nursing Research, 43,* 138–143.

Brooten, D., Gennaro, S., Brown, L. P., Butts, P., Gibbons, A. L., Bakewell-Sachs, S., & Kumar, S. P. (1988). Anxiety, depression, and hostility in mothers of preterm infants. *Nursing Research, 37,* 213–216.

Brouse, A. J. (1988). Easing the transition to the maternal role. *Journal of Advanced Nursing, 13,* 167–172.

Brouse, S. H. (1985). Effect of gender role identity on patterns of feminine and self-concept scores from late pregnancy to early postpartum. *Advances in Nursing Science, 7*(3), 32–48.

Broussard, E. R. (1979). Assessment of the adaptive potential of the mother–infant system: The Neonatal Perception Inventories. *Seminars in Perinatology, 3,* 91–100.

Broussard, E. R., & Hartner, M. S. S. (1971). Further considerations regarding maternal perception of the first born. In J. Hellmuth (Ed.), *Exceptional Infant: Vol. 2. Studies in Abnormalities* (pp. 432–446). New York: Brunner/Mazel.

Brown, M. A. (1986a). Marital support during pregnancy. *Journal of Obstetric, Gynecologic, and Neonatal Nursing, 15,* 475–483.

Brown, M. A. (1986b). Social support, stress, and health: A comparison of expectant mothers and fathers. *Nursing Research, 35,* 72–76.

Brown, M. A. (1987a). Employment during pregnancy: Influences on women's health and social support. *Health Care for Women International, 8*(2–3), 151–167.

Brown, M. A. (1987b). How fathers and mothers perceive prenatal support. *MCN, the American Journal of Maternal Child Nursing, 12,* 414–418.

Brunnquell, D., Crichton, L., & Egeland, B. (1981). Maternal personality and attitude in disturbances of child rearing. *American Journal of Orthopsychiatry, 51,* 680–691.

Bryce, R. L., Stanley, F. J., & Enkin, M. W. (1988). The role of social support in the prevention of preterm birth. *Birth, 15,* 19–23.

Buchholz, E. S., & Gold, B. (1986). More than playing house: A developmental perspective on the strengths in teenage motherhood. *Journal of Orthopsychiatry, 56,* 347–359.

Budd, K. W. (1986). Perinatal risk designation, self-coherence, coping, and mood: Relationships to psychosocial health during pregnancy. *Dissertation Abstracts International, 46,* 3780B.

Bull, M. J. (1981). Change in concerns of first-time mothers after one week at home. *Journal of Obstetric, Gynecologic, and Neonatal Nursing, 10,* 391–394.

Bull, M., & Lawrence, D. (1985). Mothers' use of knowledge during the first postpartum weeks. *Journal of Obstetric, Gynecologic, and Neonatal Nursing, 14,* 315–320.

Bullock, C. B., & Pridham, K. F. (1988). Sources of maternal confidence and uncertainty and perceptions of problem-solving competence. *Journal of Advanced Nursing, 13,* 321–329.

Burger, J., Horwitz, S. M., Forsyth, W. C., Leventhal, J. M., & Leaf, P. J. (1993). Psychological sequelae of medical complications during pregnancy. *Pediatrics, 91,* 566–571.

Burke, B. M., & Kolker, A. (1993). Clients undergoing chorionic villus sampling versus amniocentesis: Contrasting attitudes toward pregnancy. *Health Care for Women International, 14,* 193–200.

Burke, P. J., & Tully, J. C. (1977). The measurement of role identity. *Social Forces, 55,* 881–897.

Burr, W. R. (1972). Role transitions: A reformulation of theory. *Journal of Marriage and the Family, 34,* 407–416.

Burr, W. R., Leigh, G. K., Day, R. D., & Constantine, J. (1979). Symbolic interactionism and the family. In W. R. Burr, R. Hill, F. I. Nye, & I. L. Reiss (Eds.), *Contemporary theories about the family* (Vol. 2, pp. 42–111). New York: Free Press.

Burritt, J., & Fawcett, J. (1980). Body experience during pregnancy. *Issues in Health Care of Women, 2,* 1–10.

Butcher, P. R., Kalverboer, A. F., Minderaa, R. B., van Doormaal, E. F., & ten Wolde, Y. (1993). Rigidity, sensitivity and quality of attachment: The role of maternal rigidity in the early socioemotional development of premature infants. *Acta Psychiatrica Scandinavica, 88* (Suppl. 375), 5–38.

Caldwell, B. M. (1962). The usefulness of the critical period hypothesis in the study of filiative behavior. *Merrill-Palmer Quarterly, 8,* 229–242.

Caldwell, B. (1970). *Home inventory for infants.* Unpublished manuscript. University of Arkansas, Center for Early Development in Education, Little Rock.

Caldwell, B. M., & Bradley, R. H. (1984). *Manual for the home observation for measurement of the environment.* Little Rock: University of Arkansas. (Original work published 1978.)

Camp, B. W., & Morgan, L. J. (1984). Child-rearing attitudes and personality characteristics in adolescent mothers: Attitudes toward the infant. *Journal of Pediatric Psychology, 9,* 57–63.

Campbell, S. B. G. (1979). Mother–infant interaction as a function of maternal ratings of temperament. *Child Psychology and Human Development, 10,* 67–76.

Campbell, S. B. G., & Taylor, P. M. (1979). Bonding and attachment: Theoretical issues. *Seminars in Perinatology, 3,* 3–13.

Cannon, R. B. (1977). The development of maternal touch during early mother–infant interaction. *Journal of Obstetric, Gynecologic, and Neonatal Nursing, 6*(2), 28–33.

Caplan, G. (1959). *Concepts of mental health and consultation.* Washington, DC: U.S. Department of Health, Education and Welfare.

Capuzzi, C. (1989). Maternal attachment to handicapped infants and the relationship to social support. *Research in Nursing and Health, 12,* 161–167.

Carek, D. J., & Capelli, A. J. (1981). Mothers' reactions to their newborn infants. *Journal of the American Academy of Child Psychiatry, 20,* 16–31.

Carey, W. B. (1970). A simplified method for measuring infant temperament. *Journal of Pediatrics, 77,* 188–194.

Carey, W. B., & McDevitt, S. C. (1978). Revision of the infant temperament questionnaire. *Pediatrics, 61,* 735–738.

Carlile, K. S., & Holstrum, W. J. (1989). Parental involvement behaviors: A comparison of Chamorro and Caucasian parents. *Infant Behavior and Development, 12,* 479–494.

Carlson, D. B., Labarba, R. C., Sclafani, J. D., & Bowers, C. A. (1986). Cognitive and motor development in infants of adolescent mothers: A longitudinal analysis. *International Journal of Behavioral Development, 9,* 1–13.

Carlson, S. E. (1976). The irreality of postpartum: Observations on the subjective experience. *Journal of Obstetric, Gynecologic, and Neonatal Nursing, 5*(5), 28–30.

Carnegie Task Force. (1994). *Starting points: Meeting the needs of our youngest children.* New York: Carnegie Corporation of New York.

Carreto, V. (1981). Maternal responses to an infant with cleft lip and palate: A review of literature. *Maternal–Child Nursing Journal, 10,* 197–205.

Carroll, J. S. (1978). The effect of imagining an event on expectations for the event: An interpretation in terms of availability heuristic. *Journal of Experimental Social Psychology, 14,* 88–96.

Carson, K., & Virden, S. (1984). Can prenatal teaching promote maternal attachment? Practicing nurses test Carter-prenatal attachment intervention. *Health Care for Women International, 5,* 355–369.

Carter, M. C., & Miles, M. S. (1989). Parental Stressor Scale: Pediatric intensive care unit. *Maternal–Child Nursing Journal, 18,* 187–198.

Carter-Jessop, L. (1981). Promoting maternal attachment through prenatal intervention. *MCN, the American Journal of Maternal Child Nursing, 6,* 107–112.

Cartwright, L. K. (1987). Role montage: Life patterns of professional women. *Journal of American Medical Women's Association, 42*(5), 142–148.

Casteel, J. K. (1990). Affects and cognitions of mothers and fathers of preterm infants. *Maternal–Child Nursing Journal, 19,* 211–220.

Caulfield, C., Disbrow, M. A., & Smith, M. (1977). Determining indicators of potential for child abuse and neglect: Analytical problems in methodological research. *Communicating Nursing Research, 10,* 141–162.

Celotta, B. (1982). New motherhood: A time of crisis? *Birth, 9,* 21–23.

Censullo, M., Lester, B., & Hoffman, J. (1985). Rhythmic patterning in mother–newborn interaction. *Nursing Research, 34,* 342–346.

Chao, Y. M. (1979). Cognitive operations during maternal role enactment. *Maternal–Child Nursing, 8,* 211–274.

Chao, Y. M. (1983). Conceptual behaviour of Chinese mothers in relation to their newborn infants. *Journal of Advanced Nursing, 8,* 303–310.

Chertok, L. (1969). *Motherhood and personality.* London: Tavistock.

Childs, R. E. (1985). Maternal psychological conflicts associated with the birth of a retarded child. *Maternal–Child Nursing Journal, 14,* 175–181.

Chinn, P. L., & Jacobs, M. K. (1983). *Theory and nursing: A systematic approach.* St. Louis: C.V. Mosby.

Chodorow, N. (1978). *The reproduction of mothering.* Berkeley: University of California Press.

Choi, E. C. (1986). Unique aspects of Korean-American mothers. *Journal of Obstetric, Gynecologic, and Neonatal Nursing, 15,* 394–400.

Choi, E. S. C., & Hamilton, R. K. (1986). The effects of culture on mother–infant interaction. *Journal of Obstetric, Gynecologic, and Neonatal Nursing, 15,* 256–261.

Clubb, R. L. (1991). Chronic sorrow: Adaptation patterns of parents with chronically ill children. *Pediatric Nursing, 17,* 461–466.

Coady, S. S. (1983). Delayed childbearing: Correlates of maternal satisfaction at one year postpartum. *Dissertations Abstract International, 43,* 3199-B.

Coffman, S. (1992). Parent and infant attachment: Review of nursing research 1981–1990. *Pediatric Nursing, 18,* 421–425.

Coffman, S., Levitt, M. J., Deets, C., & Quigley, K. L. (1991). Close relationships in mothers of distressed and normal newborns: Support, expectancy confirmation, and maternal well-being. *Journal of Family Psychology, 5,* 93–107.

Coffman, S., Levitt, M. J., & Guacci-Franco, N. (1993). Mothers' stress and close relationships: Correlates with infant health status. *Pediatric Nursing, 19,* 135–140.

Cogan, R., & Edmunds, E. P. (1980). Pronominalization: A linguistic facet of the maternal–paternal sensitive period. *Nursing Research, 29,* 225–227.

Cohler, B. J., Grunebaum, H. U., Weiss, J. L., & Moran, D. L. (1971). The childcare attitudes of two generations of mothers. *Merrill-Palmer Quarterly, 17,* 3–17.

Cohler, B. J., Weiss, J. L., & Grunebaum, H. U. (1970). Child-care attitudes emotional disturbance among mothers of young children. *Genetic Psychology Monographs, 82,* 3–47.

Cohn, J. F., Campbell, S. B., Matias, R., & Hopkins, J. (1990). Face-to-face interactions of postpartum depressed and nondepressed mother–infant pairs at 2 months. *Developmental Psychology, 26,* 15–23.

Cohn, J. F., & Tronick, E. Z. (1983). Three-month-old infants' reaction to simulated maternal depression. *Child Development, 54,* 185–193.

Coleman, M., Ryan, R., & Williamson, J. (1989). Social support and the alcohol consumption patterns of pregnant women. *Applied Nursing Research, 2,* 154–160.

Coll, C. T. G., Hoffman, J., & Oh, W. (1987). The social ecology and early parenting of Caucasian adolescent mothers. *Child Development, 58,* 955–963.

Colletta, N. D. (1981). Social support and the risk of maternal rejection by adolescent mothers. *Journal of Psychology, 109,* 191–197.

Colletta, N. D., & Gregg, C. H. (1981). Adolescent mothers' vulnerability to stress. *Journal of Nervous and Mental Disease, 169,* 50–54.

Colletta, N. D., Hadler, S., & Gregg, C. H. (1981). How adolescents cope with the problems of early motherhood. *Adolescence, 16,* 499–512.

Colletta, N. D., & Lee, D. (1983). The impact of support for black adolescent mothers. *Journal of Family Issues, 4,* 127–143.

Colman, A. D., & Colman, L. L. (1973–1974). Pregnancy as an altered state of consciousness. *Birth and the Family Journal, 1,* 7–11.

Condon, J. T. (1987). Altered cognitive functioning in pregnant women: A shift toward primary process thinking. *British Journal of Medical Psychology, 60,* 329–334.

Condon, J. T., & Watson, T. L. (1987). The maternity blues: Exploration of a psychological hypothesis. *Acta Psychiatrica Scandinavica, 76,* 164–171.

Condon, W. S., & Sander, L. W. (1974). Neonate movement is synchronized with adult speech: Interactional participation and language acquisition. *Science, 183,* 99–101.

Cooper, C. S., Dunst, C. J., & Vance, S. D. (1990). The effect of social support on adolescent mothers' styles of parent–child interaction as measured on three separate occasions. *Adolescence, 25,* 49–57.

Corbin, J. M. (1987). Women's perceptions and management of a pregnancy complicated by chronic illness. *Health Care for Women International, 8,* 317–337.

Costa, P., & McCrae, R. (1978). *The NEO personality inventory.* Odessa, FL: Psychological Assessment Resources.

Cox, B. E., & Smith, E. C. (1982). The mother's self-esteem following cesarean delivery. *MCN, the American Journal of Maternal Child Nursing, 7,* 309–314.

Cox, J. L., Connor, Y., & Kendell, R. E. (1982). Prospective study of psychiatric disorders of childbirth. *British Journal of Psychiatry, 140,* 111–117.

Cox, J. L., Holden, J. M., & Sagovsky, R. (1987). Detection of postnatal depression: Development of the Edinburgh Postnatal Depression Scale. *British Journal of Psychiatry, 150,* 782–786.

Cox, M. J., Owen, M. T., Lewis, J. M., Reidel, C., Scalf-McIver, L., & Suster, A. (1985). *Journal of Family Issues, 6,* 543–564.

Cranley, M. S. (1981a). Development of a tool for the measurement of maternal attachment during pregnancy. *Nursing Research, 30,* 281–284.

Cranley, M. S. (1981b). Roots of attachment: The relationship of parents with their unborn. *Birth Defects: Original Article Series, 17*(6), 59–83.

Cranley, M. S. (1984). Social support as a factor in the development of parents' attachment to their unborn. *Birth Defects: Original Article Series, 20,* 99–124.

Cranley, M. S. (1992). Response to "A critical review of prenatal attachment research." *Scholarly Inquiry for Nursing Practice: An International Journal, 6,* 23–26.

Cranley, M. S. (1993). The origins of mother–child relationship: A review. *Physical and Occupational Therapy in Pediatrics, 12*(2–3), 39–51.

Cranley, M. S., Hedahl, K. J., & Pegg, S. H. (1983). Women's perceptions of vaginal and cesarean deliveries. *Nursing Research, 32,* 10–15.

Crawford, J. W. (1982). Mother–infant interaction in premature and full-term infants. *Child Development, 53,* 957–962.

Crawley, S. B., & Spiker, D. (1983). Mother–child interactions involving two-year-olds with Down syndrome: A look at individual differences. *Child Development, 54,* 1312–1323.

Crittenden, P. M., & Bonvillian, J. D. (1984). The relationship between maternal risk status and maternal sensitivity. *American Journal of Orthopsychiatry, 54,* 250–262.

Crnic, K. A., Greenberg, M. T., Ragozin, A. S., Robinson, N. M., & Basham, R. B. (1983). Effects of stress and social support on mothers and premature and full-term infants. *Child Development, 54,* 209–217.

Crnic, K. A., Greenberg, M. T., Robinson, N. M., & Ragozin, A. S. (1984). Maternal stress and social support: Effects on the mother–infant relationship from birth to eighteen months. *American Journal of Orthopsychiatry, 54,* 224–235.

Crnic, K. A., Greenberg, M. T., & Slough, N. M. (1986). Early stress and social support influences on mothers' and high-risk infants' functioning in late infancy. *Infant Mental Health Journal, 7,* 19–33.

Crnic, K. A., Ragozin, A. S., Greenberg, M. T., Robinson, N. M., & Basham, R. B. (1983). Social interaction and developmental competence of preterm and full-term infants during the first year of life. *Child Development, 54,* 1199–1210.

Crockenberg, S. B. (1981). Infant irritability, mother responsiveness, and social support influences on the security of infant–mother attachment. *Child Development, 52,* 857–865.

Crockenberg, S., & McCluskey, K. (1986). Change in maternal behavior during the baby's first year of life. *Child Development, 57,* 746–753.

Crockenberg, S. B., & Smith, P. (1982). Antecedents of mother–infant interaction and infant irritability in the first three months of life. *Infant Behavior and Development, 5,* 105–119.

Croft, C. A. (1982) Lamaze childbirth education: Implications for maternal infant attachment. *Journal of Obstetric, Gynecologic and Neonatal Nursing, 11,* 333-336.

Cronenwett, L. R. (1980). Elements and outcomes of a postpartum support group program. *Research in Nursing and Health, 3,* 33–41.

Cronenwett, L. R. (1985). Network structure, social support, and psychological outcomes of pregnancy. *Nursing Research, 34,* 93–99.

Cropley, C., Lester, P., & Pennington, S. (1976). Assessment tool for measuring maternal attachment behaviors. In L. K. McNall & J. T. Galeener (Eds.), *Current practice in obstetric and gynecologic nursing.* (Vol. 1, pp. 16–28). St. Louis: C. V. Mosby.

Crowell, J. A., & Feldman, S. S. (1991). Mothers' working models of attachment relationships and mother and child behavior during separation and reunion. *Developmental Psychology, 27,* 597–605.

Culp, R. E., Culp, A. M., Osofsky, J. D., & Osofsky, H. J. (1991). Adolescent and older mothers' interaction patterns with their six-month-old infants. *Journal of Adolescence, 14,* 195–200.

Culp, R. E., & Osofsky, H. J. (1989). Effects of cesarean delivery on parental depression, marital adjustment, and mother–infant interaction. *Birth, 16,* 53–57.

Curry, M. A. H. (1979). Contact during the first hour with the wrapped or naked newborn: Effect on maternal attachment behaviors at 36 hours and three months. *Birth and the Family Journal, 6,* 227–235.

Curry, M. A. (1982). Maternal attachment behavior and the mother's self-concept: The effect of early skin-to-skin contact. *Nursing Research, 31,* 73–78.

Curry, M. A. (1983). Variables related to adaptation to motherhood in "normal" primiparous women. *Journal of Obstetric, Gynecologic, and Neonatal Nursing, 12,* 115–121.

Curry, M. A. (1987). Maternal behavior of hospitalized pregnant women. *Journal of Psychosomatic Obstetrics and Gynaecology, 7,* 165–182.

Curtis, A. (1991). Perceived similarity of mothers and their early adolescent daughters and relationship to behavior. *Journal of Youth and Adolescence, 20,* 381–397.

Cutrona, C. E., & Troutman, B. (1986). Social support, infant temperament, and parenting self-efficacy: A mediational model of postpartum depression. *Child Development, 57,* 1507–1518.

Damrosch, S. P., & Perry, L. A. (1989). Self-reported adjustment, chronic sorrow, and coping of parents of children with Down syndrome. *Nursing Research, 38,* 25–30.

Davids, A., Holden, R. H., & Gray, G. B. (1963). Maternal anxiety during pregnancy and adequacy of mother and child adjustment eight months following childbirth. *Child Development, 34,* 993–1002,

Davids, A., & Rosengren, W. R. (1962). Social stability and psychological adjustment during pregnancy. *Psychosomatic Medicine, 24,* 579–583.

Davis, B., & Jones, L. C. (1992). Differentiation of self and attachment among adult daughters. *Issues in Mental Health Nursing, 13,* 321–331.

Davis, M. S., & Akridge, K. M. (1987). The effect of promoting intrauterine attachment in primiparas on postdelivery attachment. *Journal of Obstetric, Gynecologic, and Neonatal Nursing, 16,* 430–437.

Dean, P. G. (1986). Monitoring an apneic infant: Impact on the infant's mother. *Maternal–Child Nursing Journal, 15,* 65–76.

Deatrick, J. A., Knafl, K. A., & Walsh, M. (1988). The process of parenting a child with a disability: Normalization through accommodations. *Journal of Advanced Nursing, 13,* 15–21.

de Chateau, P. (1976). The influence of early contact on maternal and infant behaviour in primiparae. *Birth and the Family Journal, 3*(4), 149–155.

de Chateau, P. (1977). The importance of the neonatal period for the development of synchrony in the mother–infant dyad: A review. *Birth and the Family Journal, 4*(1), 10–22.

de Chateau, P., & Wiberg, B. (1977a). Long-term effect on mother–infant behaviour of extra contact during the first hour post partum: 1. First observations at 36 hours. *Acta Paediatrica Scandinavica, 66,* 137–143.

de Chateau, P., & Wiberg, B. (1977b). Long-term effect on mother–infant behaviour of extra contact during the first hour post partum: 2. A follow-up at three months. *Acta Paediatrica Scandinavica, 66,* 145–151.

DeMeis, D. K., Hock, E., & McBride, S. L. (1986). The balance of employment and motherhood: Longitudinal study of mothers' feelings about separation from their first-born infants. *Developmental Psychology, 22,* 626–632.

Depression Guideline Panel. (1993). *Depression in primary care: Vol. 1. Detection and diagnosis.* Rockville, MD: Agency for Health Care Policy and Research. (AHCPR Publication No. 93-0550)

Deutsch, F. M., Ruble, D. N., Fleming, A., Brooks-Gunn, J., & Stangor, C. (1988). Information-seeking and maternal self-definition during the transition to motherhood. *Journal of Personality and Social Psychology, 55,* 420–431.

Deutsch, H. (1945). *Psychology of women, Vol. 2: Motherhood.* New York: Grune & Stratton.

Dickerson, P. S. (1981). Early postpartum separation and maternal attachment to twins. *Journal of Obstetric, Gynecologic, and Neonatal Nursing, 10,* 120–123.

Dignan, M. H. (1965). Ego identity and maternal identification. *Journal of Personality and Social Psychology, 1,* 476–483.

DiIorio, C., Van Lier, D., & Manteuffel, B. (1992). Patterns of nausea during the first trimester of pregnancy. *Clinical Nursing Research, 1,* 127–140.

DiMatteo, M. R., Kahn, K. L., & Berry, S. H. (1993). Narratives of birth and the postpartum: Analysis of the focus group responses of new mothers. *Birth, 20,* 204–211.

Disbrow, M. A., & Doerr, H. (1982). *Measures to predict child abuse: A validation study* (Report No. MC-R-530351). Rockville, MD: USDHHS, Public Health Service, Bureau of CHSA.

Disbrow, M. A., Doerr, H., & Caulfield, C. (1977). Measuring the components of potential for child abuse and neglect. *Journal of Child Abuse and Neglect, 1,* 279–296.

Donaldson, N. E. (1991). A review of nursing intervention research on maternal adaptation in the first 8 weeks postpartum. *Journal of Perinatal and Neonatal Nursing, 4*(4), 1–11.

Donley, M. G. (1993). Attachment and the emotional unit. *Family Process, 32,* 3–20.

Donovan, W. L., & Leavitt, L. A. (1989). Maternal self-efficacy and infant attachment: Integrating physiology, perceptions, and behavior. *Child Development, 60,* 460–472.

Donovan, W. L., Leavitt, L. A., & Balling, J. D. (1978). Maternal physiological response to infant signals. *Psychophysiology, 15,* 68–74.

Drake, M. L., Verhulst, D., Fawcett, J., & Barger, D. F. (1988). Spouses' body image changes during and after pregnancy: A replication in Canada. *Image: Journal of Nursing Scholarship, 20,* 88–92.

Driscoll, J. W. (1990). Maternal parenthood and the grief process. *Journal of Perinatal and Neonatal Nursing, 4*(2), 1–10.

Drummond, J. E., McBride, M. L., & Wiebe, C. F. (1993). The development of mothers' understanding of infant crying. *Clinical Nursing Research, 2,* 396–413.

Duckett, L., Henly, S. J., & Garvis, M. (1993). Predicting breast-feeding duration during the postpartum hospitalization. *Western Journal of Nursing Research, 15*(2), 177–198.

Duncan, H. A. (1989). *Duncan's dictionary for nurses* (2nd ed.). New York: Springer Publishing Co.

Dunnington, R. M., & Glazer, G. (1991). Maternal identity and early mothering behavior in previously infertile and never infertile women. *Journal of Obstetric, Gynecologic, and Neonatal Nursing, 20,* 309–318.

Durrett, M. E., Richards, P., Otaki, M., Pennebaker, J. W., & Nyquist, L. (1986). Mother's involvement with infant and her perception of spousal support, Japan and America. *Journal of Marriage and the Family, 48,* 187–194.

Edwards, L. D., & Saunders, R. B. (1990). Symbolic interactionism: A framework for the care of parents of preterm infants. *Journal of Pediatric Nursing, 5,* 123–128.

Egeland, B., Breitenbucher, M., & Rosenberg, D. (1980). Prospective study of the significance of life stress in the etiology of child abuse. *Journal of Consulting and Clinical Psychology, 48,* 195–205.

Egeland, B., Deinard, A., Taraldson, B., & Brunnquette, D. (1975). *Manual for feeding and play observation scales.* Minneapolis: University of Minnesota.

Egeland, B., & Farber, E. A. (1984). Infant–mother attachment: Factors related to its development and changes over time. *Child Development, 55,* 753–771.

Ehlert, U., Patalla, U., Kirschbaum, C., Piedmont, E., & Hellhammer, D. H. (1990). Postpartum blues: Salivary cortisol and psychological factors. *Journal of Psychosomatic Research, 34,* 319–325.

Eidelman, A. I., Hoffmann, N. W., & Kaitz, M. (1993). Cognitive deficits in women after childbirth. *Obstetrics & Gynecology, 8,* 764–767.

Ellis, D., & Hewat, R. (1982). Assisting women with breastfeeding: The implementation and evaluation of a program to augment nursing interventions. In G. Zilm, A. Hilton, & M. Richmond (Eds.), *Nursing research:*

A base for practice, service and education (pp. 258–268). Vancouver: University of British Columbia.

Ellis, D. J., & Hewat, R. J. (1985). Mothers' postpartum perceptions of spousal relationships. *Journal of Obstetric, Gynecologic, and Neonatal Nursing, 14,* 140–146.

Elmer, E., & Maloni, J. A. (1988). Parent support through telephone consultation. *Maternal–Child Nursing Journal, 17,* 13–23.

Emde, R. N., & Brown, C. (1978). Adaptation to the birth of a Down's syndrome infant: Grieving and maternal attachment. *Journal of American Academy of Child Psychiatry, 17,* 299–323.

Entwisle, D. R., & Doering, S. G. (1981). *The first birth: A family turning point.* Baltimore: Johns Hopkins University Press.

Epps, S. (1993). Effects of labels of infant health and gender on parent ratings of a preterm infant. *Children's Health Care, 22,* 273–285.

Escalona, S. (1982). Babies at double hazard: Early development of infants at biologic and social risk. *Pediatrics, 70,* 670–676.

Etaugh, C. (1974). Effects of maternal employment on children: A review of recent research. *Merrill-Palmer Quarterly, 20,* 71–98.

Fagan, J., & Schor, D. (1993). Mothers of children with spina bifida: Factors related to maternal psychosocial functioning. *American Journal of Orthopsychiatry, 63,* 146–152.

Farber, E. A., Vaughn, B., & Egeland, B. (1981). The relationship of prenatal maternal anxiety to infant behavior and mother–infant interaction during the first six months of life. *Early Human Development, 5,* 267–277.

Farel, A. M., Freeman, V. A., Keenan, N. L., & Huber, C. J. (1991). Interaction between high-risk infants and their mothers: The NCAST as an assessment tool. *Research in Nursing and Health, 14,* 109–118.

Fawcett, J. (1977). The relationship between identification and patterns of change in spouses' body images during and after pregnancy. *International Journal of Nursing Studies, 14,* 193–213.

Fawcett, J. (1978). The "what" of theory development. In *Theory development: What, why, how?* (pp. 17–33) (NLN Publication No. 15–1708). New York: National League for Nursing.

Fawcett, J., Bliss-Holz, V. J., Haas, M. B., Leventhal, M., & Rubin, M. (1986). Spouses' body image changes during and after pregnancy: A replication and extension. *Nursing Research, 35,* 220–223.

Fawcett, J., Pollio, N., & Tully, A. (1992). Women's perceptions of cesarean and vaginal delivery: Another look. *Research in Nursing and Health, 15,* 439–446.

Fawcett, J., Pollio, N., Tully, A., Baron, M., Henklein, J. C., & Jones, R. C. (1993). Effects of information on adaptation to cesarean birth. *Nursing Research, 42,* 49–53.

Fawcett, J., Tulman, L., & Myers, S. T. (1988). Development of the inventory of functional status after childbirth. *Journal of Nurse-Midwifery, 33,* 252–260.

Fawcett, J., & Weiss, M. E. (1993). Cross-cultural adaptation to cesarean birth. *Western Journal of Nursing Research, 15,* 282–297.

Feiring, C., Fox, N. A., Jaskir, J., & Lewis, M. (1987). The relation between social support, infant risk status and mother–infant interaction. *Developmental Psychology, 23,* 400–405.

Feller, C. M., Henson, D., Bell, L., Wong, S., & Bruner, M. (1983). Assessment of adolescent mother–infant attachment. *Issues in Health Care of Women, 4,* 237–250.

Ferketich, S. L., & Mercer, R. T. (1990). Effects of antepartal stress on health status during early motherhood. *Scholarly Inquiry for Nursing Practice: An International Journal, 4,* 127–149.

Fetrick, A., & Killien, M. (1994). Postpartum fatigue among Finnish women. *Communicating Nursing Research, 27*(2), 286.

Field, T. M., Hallock, N. F., Dempsey, J. R., & Shuman, H. H. (1978). Mothers' assessments of term and pre-term infants with respiratory distress syndrome: Reliability and predictive validity. *Child Psychiatry and Human Development, 9*(2), 75–85.

Field, T., Healy, B., Goldstein, S., & Guthertz, M. (1990). Behavior-state matching and synchrony in mother–infant interactions of nondepressed versus depressed dyads. *Developmental Psychology, 26,* 7–14.

Field, T., Healy, B., Goldstein, S., Perry, S., Bendell, D., Schanberg, S., Zimmerman, E. A., & Kuhn, C. (1988). Infants of depressed mothers show "depressed" behavior even with nondepressed adults. *Child Development, 59,* 1569–1579.

Field, T., Healy, B., & LeBlanc, W. G. (1989). Sharing and synchrony of behavior states and heart rate in nondepressed versus depressed mother–infant interactions. *Infant Behavior and Development, 12,* 357–376.

Field, T., Morrow, C., & Adlestein, D. (1993). Depressed mothers' perceptions of infant behavior. *Infant Behavior and Development, 16,* 99–108.

Field, T., Sandberg, D., Garcia, R., Vega-Lahr, N., Goldstein, S., & Guy, L. (1985). Pregnancy problems, postpartal depression, and early mother–infant interactions. *Developmental Psychology, 21,* 1152–1156.

Fillmore, C. J., & Taylor, K. W. (1976). Infant care concerns of primigravida mothers and nursing practice: Two models. *Nursing Papers, 8,* 15–25.

Fischer, L. R. (1981). Transitions in the mother–daughter relationship. *Journal of Marriage and the Family, 43*, 613–622.

Fischman, S. H., Rankin, E. A., Soeken, K. L., & Lenz, E. R. (1986). Changes in sexual relationships in postpartum couples. *Journal of Obstetric, Gynecologic, and Neonatal Nursing, 15*, 58–63.

Fish, M., Stifter, C. A., & Belsky, J. (1993). Early patterns of mother-infant dyadic interaction: Infant, mother, and family demographic antecedents. *Infant Behavior and Development, 16*, 1–18.

Fisher, S. (1968). Body boundary and perceptual vividness. *Journal of Abnormal Psychology, 73*, 392–396.

Fitts, W. H. (1965). *Tennessee Self Concept Scale manual.* Nashville, TN: Counselor Recordings and Tests.

Flagler, S. (1988). Maternal role competence. *Western Journal of Nursing Research, 10*(3), 274–290.

Flagler, S. (1989). Semantic differentials and the process of developing one to measure maternal role competence. *Journal of Advanced Nursing, 14*, 190–197.

Flagler, S. (1990). Relationships between stated feelings and measures of maternal adjustment. *Journal of Obstetric, Gynecologic, and Neonatal Nursing, 19*, 411–416.

Flagler, S., & Nicoll, L. (1990). A framework for the psychological aspects of pregnancy. *NAACOG's Clinical Issues in Perinatal and Women's Health Nursing, 1*(3), 267–278.

Flaherty, J. A., & Richman, J. A. (1986). Effects of childhood relationships on the adult's capacity to form social supports. *American Journal of Psychiatry, 143*, 851–855.

Flaherty, M. J., Sr. (1973). Feminine masochism: A review of the literature. *Maternal–Child Nursing Journal, 2*, 135–141.

Flaherty, M. J. (1988). Seven caring functions of black grandmothers in adolescent mothering. *Maternal–Child Nursing, 17*, 191–207.

Fleming, A. S., Ruble, D. N., Flett, G. L., & Shaul, D. L. (1988). Postpartum adjustment in first-time mothers: Relations between mood, maternal attitudes, and mother–infant interactions. *Developmental Psychology, 24*, 71–81.

Fleming, A. S., Ruble, D. N., Flett, G., & Van Wagner, V. (1990). Adjustment in first-time mothers: Changes in mood and mood content during the early postpartum months. *Developmental Psychology, 26*, 137–143.

Fogel, C. I., (1993). Pregnant inmates: Risk factors and pregnancy outcomes. *Journal of Obstetric, Gynecologic, and Neonatal Nursing, 22*, 33–39.

Foley, G. & Hobin, M. (1981). *The attachment-separation-individuation (A-S-I) scale.* Reading, MA: Family Centered Resource Project.

Franck, K., & Rosen, E. (1948). Projective test of masculinity–femininity. *Journal of Consulting Psychology, 13*, 247–256.

Frankel, S. A., & Wise, M. J. (1982). A view of delayed parenting: Some implications of a new trend. *Psychiatry, 45*, 220–225.

Fraser, E. B. (1977). The work of a multigravida in becoming the mother of twins. *Maternal–Child Nursing Journal, 6*, 87–105.

Freda, M. C., Andersen, H. F., Damus, K., & Merkatz, I. R. (1993). What pregnant women want to know: A comparison of client and provider perceptions. *Journal of Obstetric, Gynecologic, and Neonatal Nursing, 22*, 237–244.

Freese, M. P., & Thoman, E. B. (1978). The assessment of maternal characteristics for the study of mother–infant interactions. *Infant Behavior and Development, 1*, 95–105.

Freitag-Koontz, M. J. (1988). Parents' grief reaction to the diagnosis of their infant's severe neurologic impairment and static encephalopathy. *Journal of Perinatal Neonatal Nursing, 2*(2), 45–57.

Freud, S. (1949). *The ego and the id*. London: Hogarth Press.

Frodi, A., Keller, B., Foye, H., Liptak, G., Bridges, L., Grolnick, W., Berko, J., McAnarney, E., & Lawrence, R. (1984). Determinants of attachment and mastery motivation in infants born to adolescent mothers. *Infant Mental Health Journal, 5*, 15–23.

Frommer, E. A., & O'Shea, G. (1973a). Antenatal identification of women liable to have problems in managing their infants. *British Journal of Psychiatry, 123*, 149–156.

Frommer, E. A., & O'Shea, G. (1973b). The importance of childhood experience in relation to problems of marriage and family-building. *British Journal of Psychiatry, 123*, 157–160.

Fuld Theorists Video Project. (1988). Reva Rubin: The theory of maternal identity. Oakland, CA: Samuel Merritt College Studio Three.

Fuller, J. R. (1990). Early patterns of maternal attachment. *Health Care for Women International, 11*, 433–446.

Funke, J., & Irby, M. I. (1978). An instrument to assess the quality of maternal behavior. *Journal of Obstetric, Gynecologic, and Neonatal Nursing, 7*(5), 19–22.

Funke-Furber, J. (1979). Predictive study of early mother–child relationships. *Child Abuse and Neglect, 3*, 259–267.

Gaffney, K. F. (1986). Maternal–fetal attachment in relation to self-concept and anxiety. *Maternal–Child Nursing Journal, 15*, 91–101.

Gaffney, K. F. (1988). Prenatal maternal attachment. *Image: Journal of Nursing Scholarship, 20*, 106–109.

Gaffney, K. F. (1992). Nursing practice model for maternal role sufficiency. *Advances in Nursing Science, 15*(2), 76–84.

Gage, M. G., & Christensen, D. H. (1991). Parental role socialization and the transition to parenthood. *Family Relations, 40,* 332–337.

Gara, E. O., & Tilden, V. P. (1984). Adjusted control: An explanation for women's positive perceptions of their pregnancies. *Health Care for Women International, 5,* 427–436.

Gardner, R. A. (1970). The use of guilt as a defense against anxiety. *Psychoanalytic Review, 57,* 124–136.

Gay, J. (1981). A conceptual framework of bonding. *Journal of Obstetric, Gynecologic, and Neonatal Nursing, 10,* 440–444.

Gay, J. R., Edgil, A. E., & Douglas, A. B. (1988). Reva Rubin revisited. *Journal of Obstetric, Gynecologic, and Neonatal Nursing, 18,* 394–399.

Gennaro, S. (1986). Anxiety and problem-solving ability in mothers of premature infants. *Journal of Obstetric, Gynecologic, and Neonatal Nursing, 15,* 160–164.

Gennaro, S. (1988). Postpartal anxiety and depression in mothers of term and preterm infants. *Nursing Research, 37,* 82–85.

Gennaro, S., & Stringer, M. (1991). Stress and health in low birthweight infants: A longitudinal study. *Nursing Research, 40,* 308–310.

Gennaro, S., York, R., & Brooten, D. (1990). Anxiety and depression in mothers of low birthweight and very low birthweight infants: Birth through 5 months. *Issues in Comprehensive Pediatric Nursing, 13,* 97–109.

Gennaro, S., Zukowsky, K., Brooten, D., Lowell, L., & Visco, A. (1990). Concerns of mothers of low birthweight infants. *Pediatric Nursing, 16,* 459–462.

Gibaud-Wallston, J., & Wandersman, L. P. (1978, August). *Development and utility of the parenting sense of competence scale.* Paper presented at American Psychological Association Meeting, Toronto.

Giblin, P. T., Poland, M. L., Waller, J. B., Jr., & Ager, J. W. (1988). Correlates of parenting on a neonatal intensive care unit: Maternal characteristics and family resources. *Journal of Genetic Psychology, 149,* 505–514.

Gilligan, C. (1982). *In a different voice.* Cambridge, MA: Harvard University Press.

Gillman, R. D. (1968). The dreams of pregnant women and maternal adaptation. *American Journal of Orthopsychiatry, 38,* 688–692.

Gjerdingen, D. K., Froberg, D. G., & Fontaine, P. (1990). A causal model describing the relationship of women's postpartum health to social support, length of leave, and complications of childbirth. *Women and Health, 16,* 71–87.

Gjerdingen, D. K., Froberg, D. G., & Fontaine, P. (1991). The effects of social support on women's health during pregnancy, labor and delivery, and the postpartum period. *Family Medicine, 23,* 370–375.

Gladieux, J. D. (1978). Pregnancy—the transition to parenthood: Satisfaction with the pregnancy experience as a function of sex role conceptions, marital relationship, and social network. In W. B. Miller & L. F. Newman (Eds.), *The first child and family formation* (pp. 275–295). Chapel Hill: University of North Carolina.

Glass, J. (1983). Pre-birth attitudes and adjustment to parenthood: When "preparing for the worst" helps. *Family Relations, 32,* 377–386.

Glazer, G. (1980). Anxiety levels and concerns among pregnant women. *Research in Nursing and Health, 3,* 107–113.

Gloger-Tippelt, G. (1983). A process model of the pregnancy course. *Human Development, 26,* 134–148.

Gloger-Tippelt, G. (1988). *The development of the mother's conceptions of the child before birth.* Paper presented at the Sixth Biennial International Conference on Infant Studies, Washington, DC.

Golas, G. A., & Parks, P. (1986). Effect of early postpartum teaching on primiparas' knowledge of infant behavior and degree of confidence. *Research in Nursing and Health, 9,* 209–214.

Goldberg, S. (1978). Prematurity: Effects on parent–infant interaction. *Journal of Pediatric Psychology, 3*(3), 137–144.

Goldberg, S. (1983). Parent–infant bonding: Another look. *Child Development, 54,* 1355–1382.

Goldberg, W. A., Michaels, G. Y., & Lamb, M. E. (1985). Husbands' and wives' adjustment to pregnancy and first parenthood. *Journal of Family Issues, 6,* 483–503.

Gonik, B., & Creasy, R. K. (1986). Preterm labor: Its diagnosis and management. *American Journal of Obstetrics and Gynecology, 154,* 3–8.

Goodman, J. R., & Sauve, R. S. (1985). High risk infant: Concerns of the mother after discharge. *Birth, 12,* 235–242.

Gordon, R. E., Gordon, K. K., Gordon-Hardy, L., Hursch, C. J., & Reed, K. G. (1986). Predicting postnatal emotional adjustment with psychosocial and hormonal measures in early pregnancy. *American Journal of Obstetrics and Gynecology, 155,* 80–82.

Gordon, R. E., Kapostins, E. E., & Gordon, K. K. (1965). Factors in postpartum emotional adjustment. *Obstetrics and Gynecology, 25,* 158–166.

Gorski, P. A., Davison, M. F., & Brazelton, T. B. (1979). Stages of behavioral organization in the high-risk neonate: Theoretical and clinical considerations. *Seminars in Perinatology, 3,* 61–72.

Gotlib, I. H., Whiffen, V. E., Mount, J. H., Milne, K., & Cordy, N. I. (1989). Prevalence rates and demographic characteristics associated with depression in pregnancy and the postpartum. *Journal of Consulting and Clinical Psychology, 57,* 269–274.

Gottesman, M. M. (1992). Maternal adaptation during pregnancy among adult early, middle, and late childbearers: Similarities and differences. *Maternal–Child Nursing Journal, 20,* 93–110.

Gottlieb, L. (1978). Maternal attachment in primiparas. *Journal of Obstetric, Gynecologic, and Neonatal Nursing, 7*(1), 39–44.

Govaerts, K., & Patino, E. (1981). Attachment behavior of the Egyptian mother. *International Journal of Nursing Studies, 18,* 53–60.

Grace, J. T. (1984). Does a mother's knowledge of fetal gender affect attachment? *MCN, the American Journal of Maternal Child Nursing, 9,* 42–45.

Grace, J. T. (1989). Development of maternal–fetal attachment during pregnancy. *Nursing Research, 38,* 228–232.

Grace, J. T. (1993). Mothers' self-reports of parenthood across the first 6 months postpartum. *Research in Nursing and Health, 16,* 431–439.

Green, J. A., Gustafson, G. E., & West, M. J. (1980). Effects of infant development on mother–infant interactions. *Child Development, 51,* 199–207.

Green, M., & Solnit, A. J. (1964). Reactions to the threatened loss of a child: A vulnerable child syndrome. *Pediatrics, 34,* 58–66.

Green, N. L. (1990). Stressful events related to childbearing in African-American women. *Journal of Nurse–Midwifery, 35,* 231–236.

Greene, J. G., Fox, N. A., & Lewis, M. (1983). The relationship between neonatal characteristics and three-month mother–infant interaction in high-risk infants. *Child Development, 54,* 1286–1296.

Griffith, S. (1976). Pregnancy as an event with crisis potential for marital partners: A study of interpersonal needs. *Journal of Obstetric, Gynecologic, and Neonatal Nursing, 5,* 35–38.

Gross, D. (1989). Implications of maternal depression for the development of young children. *Image: Journal of Nursing Scholarship, 21,* 103–107.

Gross, D., Conrad, B., Fogg, L., Willis, L., & Garvey, C. (1993). What does the NCATS measure? *Nursing Research, 42,* 260–265.

Gross, D., Rocissano, L., & Roncoli, M. (1989). Maternal confidence during toddlerhood: Comparing preterm and fullterm groups. *Research in Nursing and Health, 12,* 1–9.

Grossman, F. K. (1988). Strain in the transition to parenthood. In R. Palkovitz & J. B. Sussman (Eds.), *Transitions to parenthood* (pp. 85–104). New York: Haworth Press.

Grossman, F. K., Eichler, L. S., Winickoff, S. A., Anzalone, M. K., Gofsey-eff, M. H., & Sargent, S. P. (1980). *Pregnancy, birth, and parenthood.* San Francisco: Jossey Bass.

Grubb, C. A. (1980). Perceptions of time by multiparous women in relation to themselves and others during the first postpartal month. *Maternal–Child Nursing Journal, 9,* 225–331.

Gruis, M. (1977). Beyond maternity: Postpartum concerns of mothers. *MCN, the American Journal of Maternal Child Nursing, 2,* 182–188.

Grusec, J. E. (1992). Social learning theory and developmental psychology: The legacies of Robert Sears and Albert Bandura. *Developmental Psychology, 28,* 776–786.

Guttman, H. A. (1983). Autonomy and motherhood. *Psychiatry, 46,* 230–235.

Hall, J. M., Stevens, P. E., & Meleis, A. I. (1992). Developing the construct of role integration: A narrative analysis of women clerical workers' daily lives. *Research in Nursing and Health, 15,* 447–457.

Hall, L. A. (1980). Effect of teaching on primiparas' perceptions of their newborn. *Nursing Research, 29,* 317–322.

Hall, L. A., Gurley, D. N., Sachs, B., & Kryscio, R. J. (1991). Psychosocial predictors of maternal depressive symptoms, parenting attitudes, and child behavior in single-parent families. *Nursing Research, 40,* 214–220.

Hall, W. (1987). The experience of women returning to work following the birth of their first child. *Midwifery, 3,* 187–195.

Hall, W. A. (1992). Comparison of the experience of women and men in dual-earner families following the birth of their first infant. *Image: The Journal of Nursing Scholarship, 24,* 33–38.

Hansen, C. H. (1990). Baby blues: Identification and intervention. *NAA-COG's Clinical Issues in Perinatal and Women's Health, 1*(3), 369–374.

Hardman, M. (1975). *The younger vs. the older adolescent black mother taking on nurturing-mothering role* (Clinical Conference Papers, 1973). No. G-94 3M 2/75 (pp. 133–141). Kansas City, MO: American Nurses Association.

Harriman, L. C. (1986). Marital adjustment as related to personal and marital changes accompanying parenthood. *Family Relations, 34,* 233–239.

Harrison, L. L., & Woods, S. (1991). Early parental touch and preterm infants. *Journal of Obstetric, Gynecologic, and Neonatal Nursing, 20,* 299–306.

Harrison, M. J. (1990). A comparison of parental interactions with term and preterm infants. *Research in Nursing and Health, 13,* 173–179.

Harvey, S. M., Carr, C., & Bernheine, S. (1989). Lesbian mothers: Health care experiences. *Journal of Nurse-Midwifery, 34,* 115–119.

Hassan, S. A. (1990). Maternal behaviors and initial maternal–infant interaction of vaginally and cesarean delivered mothers. *Maternal–Child Nursing Journal, 19,* 177–178.

Hayes, E. E. (1983). Assessment of early mothering: A tool. *Issues in Health Care of Women, 6,* 361–366.

Hayes, N., Stainton, M. C., & McNeil, D. (1993). Caring for a chronically ill infant: A paradigm case of maternal rehearsal in the neonatal intensive care unit. *Journal of Pediatric Nursing, 8,* 355–360.

Hees-Stauthamer, J. C. (1985). *The first pregnancy: An integrating principle in female psychology.* Ann Arbor, MI: UMI Research Press.

Heffner, E. (1978). *Mothering.* Garden City, NY: Doubleday.

Heidrich, S. M., & Cranley, M. S. (1989). Effect of fetal movement, ultrasound scans, and amniocentesis on maternal–fetal attachment. *Nursing Research, 38,* 81–84.

Heinstein, M. I. (1967). Expressed attitudes and feelings of pregnant women and their relations to physical complications of pregnancy. *Merrill-Palmer Quarterly, 13,* 217–236.

Hemmelgarn, B., & Laing, G. (1991). The relationship between situational factors and perceived role strain in employed mothers. *Family Community Health, 14,* 8–15.

Herbert, M., Sluckin, W., & Sluckin, A. (1982). Mother-to-infant bonding. *Journal Child Psychology and Psychiatry, 23,* 205–221.

Highley, B. L. (1967). Maternal role identity. In *Defining clinical content in graduate nursing programs in maternal and child health nursing* (pp. 31–34). Boulder, CO: Western Interstate Commission for Higher Education.

Hiser, P. L. (1987). Concerns of multiparas during the second postpartum week. *Journal of Obstetric, Gynecologic, and Neonatal Nursing, 16,* 195–203.

Hobbs, D. F., Jr. (1965). Parenthood as crisis: A third study. *Journal of Marriage and the Family, 27,* 367–372.

Hobbs, D. F., Jr., & Cole, S. P. (1976). Transition to parenthood: A decade replication. *Journal of Marriage and the Family, 38,* 723–731.

Hobfoll, S., & Leiberman, J. (1987). Personality and social resources in immediate and continued stress resistance among women. *Journal of Personality and Social Psychology, 52,* 18–26.

Hock, E. (1978). Working and nonworking mothers with infants: Perceptions of their careers, their infants' needs, and satisfaction with mothering. *Developmental Psychology, 14,* 37–43.

Hock, E., & DeMeis, D. K. (1990). Depression in mothers of infants: The role of maternal employment. *Developmental Psychology, 26,* 285–291.

Hock, E., Gnezda, M. T., & McBride, S. L. (1984). Mothers of infants: Attitudes toward employment and motherhood following birth of the first child. *Journal of Marriage and the Family, 46,* 425–431.

Hock, E., McBride, S., & Gnezda, M. T. (1989). Maternal separation anxiety: Mother–infant separation from the maternal perspective. *Child Development, 60,* 793–802.

Hock, E., & Schirtzinger, M. G. (1992). Maternal separation anxiety: Its developmental course and relation to maternal mental health. *Child Development, 63,* 93–102.

Hock, E., Schirtzinger, M.G., & Lutz, W. (1992). Dimensions of family relationships associated with depressive symptomatology in mothers of young children. *Psychology of Women Quarterly, 16,* 229–241.

Hoffman, L. W. (1974). Effects of maternal employment on the child: A review of the research. *Developmental Psychology, 10,* 204–228.

Holaday, B. (1981). Maternal response to their chronically ill infants' attachment behavior of crying. *Nursing Research, 30,* 343–348.

Holaday, B. (1986). Maternal conceptual set development: Identifying patterns of maternal response to chronically ill infant crying. *Maternal–Child Nursing Journal, 15,* 47–59.

Holaday, B. (1987). Patterns of interaction between mothers and their chronically ill infants. *Maternal–Child Nursing Journal, 16,* 29–43.

Holahan, C. K., Gilbert, L. A. (1979). Interrole conflict for working women: Careers versus jobs. *Journal of Applied Psychology, 64,* 86–90.

Holden, J. M. (1991). Postnatal depression: Its nature, effects, and identification using the Edinburgh Postnatal Depression Scale. *Birth, 18,* 211–221.

Holmes, D. L., Nagy, J. N., Slaymaker, F., Sosnowski, R. J., Prinz, S. M., & Pasternak, J. F. (1982). Early influence of prematurity, illness, and prolonged hospitalization on infant behavior. *Developmental Psychology, 18,* 744–750.

Hopkins, J., Marcus, M., & Campbell, S. B. (1984). Postpartum depression: A critical review. *Psychological Bulletin, 95,* 498–515.

Horan, M. L. (1982). Parental reaction to the birth of an infant with a defect: An attributional approach. *Advances in Nursing Science, 5*(1), 57–68.

Hott, J. R. (1980). Best laid plans: Pre- and postpartum comparison of self and spouse concept in primiparous Lamaze couples who share delivery and those who do not. *Nursing Research, 29,* 20–27.

Hubbard, F. O. A., & van Ijzendoorn, M. H. (1991). Maternal unresponsiveness and infant crying across the first 9 months: A naturalistic longitudinal study. *Infant Behavior and Development, 14,* 299–312.

Huckabay, L. M. D. (1987). The effect on bonding behavior of giving a mother her premature baby's picture. *Scholarly Inquiry for Nursing Practice: An International Journal, 1,* 115–129.

Humenick, S. S. (1981). Mastery: The key to childbirth satisfaction? A review. *Birth and the Family Journal, 8*(2), 79–83.

Humenick, S. S., & Bugen, L. A. (1981). Mastery: The key to childbirth satisfaction? A study. *Birth and the Family Journal, 8*(2), 84–90.

Humenick, S. S., & Bugen, L. A. (1987). Parenting roles: Expectation versus reality. *MCN, the American Journal of Maternal Child Nursing, 12,* 36–39.

Humenick, S. S., Wilkerson, N. N., & Paul, N. W. (Eds.). (1991). *Adolescent pregnancy: Nursing perspectives on prevention.* White Plains, NY: March of Dimes Birth Defects Foundation. (Birth Defects: Original Article Series, No. 27.)

Hwang, C. P. (1987). Cesarean childbirth in Sweden: Effects on the mother- and father–infant relationship. *Infant Mental Health Journal, 8,* 91.

Imle, M. A. (1990). Third trimester concerns of expectant parents in transition to parenthood. *Holistic Nursing Practice, 4*(3), 25–36.

Imle, M. A., & Atwood, J. R. (1988). Retaining qualitative validity while gaining quantitative reliability and validity: Development of the transition to Parenthood Concerns Scale. *Advances in Nursing Science, 11*(1), 61–75.

Isabella, R. A. (1993). Origins of attachment: Maternal interactive behavior across the first year. *Child Development, 64,* 605–621.

Istvan, J. (1986). Stress, anxiety, and birth outcomes: A critical review of the evidence. *Psychological Bulletin, 100,* 331–348.

Jackson, D. (1976). *Jackson Personality Inventory.* Gaslen, NY: Research Psychologists Press.

Janis, I. L. (1958). *Psychological stress.* New York: John Wiley.

Jarrahi-Zadeh, A., Kane, F. J., Van de Castle, R. L., Lachenbruch, P. A., & Ewing, J. A. (1969). Emotional and cognitive changes in pregnancy and early puerperium. *British Journal of Psychiatry, 115,* 797–805.

Jarrett, G. E. (1982). Childrearing patterns of young mothers: Expectations, knowledge, and practices. *MCN, the American Journal of Maternal Child Nursing, 7,* 119–124.

Jarrett, M., Olshanky, E., & Fetrick, A. (1994). Constructing patterns to manage fatigue in working parents with infants. *Communicating Nursing Research, 27*(2), 288.

Jeffcoate, J. A., Humphrey, M. E., & Lloyd, J. K. (1979a). Disturbance in parent–child relationship following preterm delivery. *Developmental Medicine and Child Neurology, 21,* 344–352.

Jeffcoate, J. A., Humphrey, M. E., & Lloyd, J. K. (1979b). Role perception and response to stress in fathers and mothers following pre-term delivery. *Social Sciences and Medicine, 13A,* 139–145.

Jenkins, P. W. (1976). Conflicts of a secundigravida. *Maternal–Child Nursing Journal, 5,* 117–126.

Jimenez, M. H., & Newton, N. (1982). Job orientation and adjustment to pregnancy and early motherhood. *Birth, 9,* 157–163.

Johnson, D. E. (1980). The behavioral system model for nursing. In J. P. Riehl & C. Roy (Eds.), *Conceptual models for nursing practice* (2nd ed., pp. 207–216). New York: Appleton-Century-Crofts.

Jones, C., & Parks, P. (1983). Mother-, father-, and examiner-reported temperament across the first year of life. *Research in Nursing and Health, 6,* 183–189.

Jones, F. A., Green, V., & Krauss, D. R. (1980). Maternal responsiveness of primiparous mothers during the postpartum period: Age differences. *Pediatrics, 65,* 579–584.

Jones, L. C. (1986). A meta-analytic study of the effects of childbirth education on the parent–infant relationship. *Health Care for Women International, 7,* 357–370.

Jones, L. C., & Heermann, J. A. (1992). Parental division of infant care: Contextual influences and infant characteristics. *Nursing Research, 41,* 228–234.

Jones, L. C., & Parks, P. (1990). Frequency of illness in mother–infant dyads. *Health Care for Women International, 11,* 461–475.

Jordan, P. L. (1987). Differences in network structure, social support, and parental adaptation associated with maternal employment status. *Health Care for Women International, 8,* 133–150.

Josselson, R. (1987). *Finding herself: Pathways to identity development in women.* San Francisco: Jossey-Bass.

Josten, L. (1981). Prenatal assessment guide for illuminating possible problems with parenting. *MCN, the American Journal of Maternal Child Nursing, 6,* 113–117.

Josten, L. (1982). Contrast in prenatal preparation for mothering. *Maternal–Child Nursing Journal, 11,* 65–73.

Julian, K. C. (1983). A comparison of perceived and demonstrated maternal role competence of adolescent mothers. *Issues in Health Care of Women, 4,* 223–236.

Kalmuss, D., Davidson, A., & Cushman, L. (1992). Parenting expectations, experiences, and adjustment to parenthood: A test of the violated expectations framework. *Journal of Marriage and the Family, 54,* 516–526.

Kang, R. R. (1986). A model of parental competence. *NCAST National News*, *2*(1), 1–2.

Kaplan, B. J. (1986). A psychobiological review of depression during pregnancy. *Psychology of Women Quarterly*, *10*, 35–48.

Kapp, K. T., Hornstein, S., & Graham, V. T. (1963). Some psychologic factors in prolonged labor due to inefficient uterine action. *Comprehensive Psychiatry*, *4*, 9–18.

Karmel, R. (1975). Body image characteristics of late pregnancy and changes observed at the postnatal period. In *The Family, 4th International Congress of Psychosomatic Obstetrics and Gynecology, Tel Aviv, 1974*. Basel: Karger.

Kazak, A. E. (1986). Families with physically handicapped children: Social ecology and family systems. *Family Process*, *25*, 265–281.

Kearney, M., & Cronenwett, L. R. (1989). Perceived perinatal complications and childbirth satisfaction. *Applied Nursing Research*, *2*, 140–142.

Keefe, M. R. (1988). The impact of infant rooming-in on maternal sleep at night. *Journal of Obstetric, Gynecologic, and Neonatal Nursing*, *18*, 122–126.

Keith, L., & Luke, B. (1991). The association between women's work, working conditions, and adverse pregnancy outcomes: A review of the literature and directions for future research. *Women's Health Issues*, *1*, 113–119.

Keith, P. M., & Schafer, R. B. (1982). A comparison of depression among employed single-parent and married women. *Journal of Psychology*, *110*, 239–247.

Kemp, V. H. (1987). Mothers' perceptions of children's temperament and mother–child attachment. *Scholarly Inquiry for Nursing Practice: An International Journal*, *1*, 51–68.

Kemp, V. H., & Hatmaker, D. D. (1989). Stress and social support in high-risk pregnancy. *Research in Nursing and Health*, *12*, 331–336.

Kemp, V. H., & Hatmaker, D. D. (1993). Health practices and anxiety in low-income, high- and low-risk pregnant women. *Journal of Obstetric, Gynecologic, and Neonatal Nursing*, *22*, 266–272.

Kemp, V. H., & Page, C. K. (1987). Maternal prenatal attachment in normal and high-risk pregnancies. *Journal of Obstetric, Gynecologic, and Neonatal Nursing*, *16*, 179–184.

Kemp, V. H., Sibley, D. E., Pond, E. F. (1990). A comparison of adolescent and adult mothers on factors affecting maternal role attainment. *Maternal–Child Nursing Journal*, *19*, 63–75.

Kempe, C. H., Silverman, F. N., Steele, B. B., Droegemueller, W., & Silver, H. K. (1962). The battered child syndrome. *Journal of the American Medical Association*, *18*, 17–24.

Kendell, R., McGuire, R., Connor, Y., & Cox, J. (1981). Mood changes in the first three weeks after childbirth. *Journal of Affective Disorders, 3,* 317–326.

Kendrick, C., & Dunn, J. (1980). Caring for a second baby: Effects on interaction between mother and firstborn. *Developmental Psychology, 16,* 303–311.

Kennedy, J. C. (1973). The high-risk maternal–infant acquaintance process. *Nursing Clinics of North America, 8*(3), 549–556.

Kennell, J., Jerauld, R., Wolfe, H., Chesler, D., Kreger, N., McAlpine, W., Steffa, M., & Klaus, M. (1974). Maternal behavior one year after early and extended post-partum contact. *Developmental Medicine and Child Neurology, 16,* 172–179.

Kennerley, H., & Gath, D. (1989). Maternity blues: 3. Associations with obstetric, psychological, and psychiatric factors. *British Journal of Psychiatry, 155,* 367–373.

Kikuchi, J. F. (1980). Assimilative and accommodative responses of mothers to their newborn infants with congenital defects. *Maternal–Child Nursing Journal, 9,* 141–221.

Killien, M. G. (1993). Returning to work after childbirth: Considerations for health policy. *Nursing Outlook, 41,* 73–81.

Killien, M., & Jarrett, M. (1994). Predictors of postpartum fatigue. *Communicating Nursing Research, 27*(2), 287.

King, I. M. (1981). *A theory for nursing: Systems, concepts, process.* New York: Wiley.

Kirkpatrick, S. W. (1978). Adjustment to parenthood: A structural model. *Genetic Psychology Monographs, 98,* 51–82.

Klatskin, E. H., & Eron, L. D. (1970). Projective test content during pregnancy and postpartum adjustment. *Psychosomatic Medicine, 32,* 487–493.

Klaus, M. H., Jerauld, R., Kreger, N. C., McAlpine, W., Steffa, M., & Kennell, J. H. (1972). Maternal attachment: Importance of the first post-partum days. *New England Journal of Medicine, 286,* 460–463.

Klaus, M. H., Kennell, J. H., Plumb, N., & Zuehlke, S. (1970). Human maternal behavior at the first contact with her young. *Pediatrics, 46,* 187–192.

Klaus, M. H., & Kennell, J. H. (1982). *Parent–infant bonding.* St. Louis: C. V. Mosby.

Koepke, J. E., Austin, J., Anglin, S., & Delesalle, J. (1991). Becoming parents: Feelings of adoptive mothers. *Pediatric Nursing, 17,* 333–336.

Kohn, C. L., Nelson, A., & Weiner, S. (1980). Gravidas' responses to real-time ultrasound fetal image. *Journal of Obstetric, Gynecologic, and Neonatal Nursing, 9,* 77–79.

Koniak, D., Ludington-Hoe, S., Chaze, B. A., & Sachs, S. M. (1985). The impact of preterm birth on maternal perception of the neonate. *Journal of Perinatology, 5*(3), 29–35.

Koniak-Griffin, D. (1988a). The relationship between social support, self-esteem, and maternal–fetal attachment in adolescents. *Research in Nursing and Health, 11,* 269–278.

Koniak-Griffin, D. (1993). Maternal role attainment. *Image: Journal of Nursing Scholarship, 25,* 257–262.

Koniak-Griffin, D., Lominska, S., & Brecht, M. (1993). Social support during adolescent pregnancy: A comparison of three ethnic groups. *Journal of Adolescence, 16,* 43–56.

Koniak-Griffin, D., & Verzemnieks, I. (1991). Effects of nursing intervention on adolescents' maternal role attainment. *Issues in Comprehensive Pediatric Nursing, 14,* 121–138.

Kontos, D. (1978). A study of the effects of extended mother–infant contact on maternal behavior at one and three months. *Birth and the Family Journal, 5*(3), 133–140.

Krulik, T. (1980). Successful "normalizing" tactics of parents of chronically-ill children. *Journal of Advanced Nursing, 5,* 573–578.

Kruse, J., Zweig, S., & LeFevre, M. (1988). Health locus of control and behaviors related to pregnancy. *Family Medicine, 20,* 422–425.

Kumar, R. (1990). An overview of postpartum psychiatric disorders. *NAACOG's Clinical Issues in Perinatal and Women's Health, 1*(3), 351–358.

Kumar, R., Robson, K. M., & Smith, A. M. R. (1984). Development of a self-administered questionnaire to measure maternal adjustment and maternal attitudes during pregnancy and after delivery. *Journal of Psychosomatic Research, 28,* 43–51.

Kurtz, M. M., Perez-Woods, R. C., Tse, A. M., & Snyder, D. J. (1992). Antecedents of behavior: Parents of high-risk newborns. *Care of Children in Hospitals, 21,* 213–223.

Labs, S. M., & Wurtele, S. K. (1986). Fetal health locus of control scale: Development and validation. *Journal of Consulting and Clinical Psychology, 54,* 814–819.

Laizner, A. M., & Jeans, M. E. (1990). Identification of predictor variables of a postpartum emotional reaction. *Health Care for Women International, 11,* 191–207.

Lamb, M. E., Hopps, K., & Elster, A. A. (1987). Strange situation behavior of infants with adolescent mothers. *Infant Behavior and Development, 10,* 39–48.

Lamb, M. E., Sternberg, K. J., & Prodromidis, M. (1992). Nonmaternal care and the security of infant–mother attachment: A reanalysis of the data. *Infant Behavior and Development, 15,* 71–83.

Lamm, N. H. (1983). The second high-risk birth: Impact on maternal dyadic adjustment. *Issues in Health Care of Women, 4,* 251–259.

LaMonica, E. L. (1981). Construct validity of an empathy instrument. *Research in Nursing and Health, 4,* 384–400.

Landy, S., Clark, C., Schubert, J., & Jillings, C. (1983). Mother–infant interactions of teenage mothers as measured at six months in a natural setting. *Journal of Psychology, 115,* 245–258.

Landy, S., Montgomery, J., & Walsh, S. (1989). Postpartum depression: A clinical view. *Maternal–Child Nursing Journal, 18,* 1–29.

Lantican, L. S. M., & Corona, D. F. (1992). Comparison of the social support networks of Filipino and Mexican-American primigravidas. *Health Care for Women International, 13,* 329–338.

LaRossa, R. (1983). The transition to parenthood and the social reality of time. *Journal of Marriage and the Family, 45,* 579–589.

Larsen, V. L. (1966). Stresses of the childbearing year. *American Journal of Public Health, 56,* 32–56.

Laughlin, H. P. (1967). *The neuroses.* Washington, DC: Butterworths.

Layton, J. M., & Wykle, M. H. (1990). A validity study of four empathy instruments. *Research in Nursing and Health, 13,* 319–325.

Leatherman, J., Blackburn, D., & Davidhizar, R. (1990). How postpartum women explain their lack of obtaining adequate prenatal care. *Journal of Advanced Nursing, 15,* 256–267.

Lebe, D. (1982). Individuation of women. *Psychoanalytic Review, 69,* 63–73.

Lederman, R. P. (1984b). *Psychosocial adaptation in pregnancy.* Englewood Cliffs, N J: Prentice-Hall.

Lederman, R. P. (1984a). Anxiety and conflict in pregnancy: Relationship to maternal health status. *Annual Review of Nursing Research, 2,* 27–61.

Lederman, R. P. (1986). Maternal anxiety in pregnancy: Relationship to fetal and newborn health status. *Annual Review of Nursing Research, 4,* 3–19.

Lederman, R., & Lederman, E. (1981, September). *The prenatal self-evaluation questionnaire.* Poster presentation at the Council of Nurse Researchers Meeting, Washington, DC.

Lederman, E., Lederman, R. P., & Kutzner, S. (1982, August). *Prediction of multiparous mothers' satisfaction with infant care.* Paper presented at the Ninetieth Annual Convention of the American Psychological Association, Washington, DC.

Lee, G. L. (1982). Relationship of self-concept during late pregnancy to neonatal perception and parenting profile. *Journal of Obstetric, Gynecologic, and Neonatal Nursing, 11,* 186–190.

Lee, K. A., & DeJoseph, J. F. (1992). Sleep disturbances, vitality, and fatigue among a select group of employed childbearing women. *Birth, 19,* 208–213.

Leeman, C. P. (1970). Dependency, anger, and denial in pregnant diabetic women: A group approach. *Psychiatric Quarterly, 44,* 1–25.

Leifer, M. (1977). Psychological changes accompanying pregnancy and motherhood. *Genetic Psychology Monographs, 95,* 55–96.

Leifer, M. (1980). *Psychological effects of motherhood.* New York: Praeger.

Lemmer, C. M., Sr. (1987). Early discharge: Outcomes of primiparas and their infants. *Journal of Obstetric, Gynecologic, and Neonatal Nursing, 16,* 230–236.

Lentz, M. J., & Killien, M. G. (1991). Are you sleeping? Sleep patterns during postpartum hospitalization. *Journal of Perinatal and Neonatal Nursing, 4*(4), 30–38.

Lenz, E. R., Parks, P. L., Jenkins, L. S., & Jarrett, G. E. (1986). Life change and instrumental support as predictors of illness in mothers of 6-month-olds. *Research in Nursing and Health, 9,* 17–24.

Lenz, E. R., Soeken, K. L., Rankin, E. A., & Fischman, S. H. (1985). Sex-role attributes, gender, and postpartal perceptions of the marital relationship. *Advances in Nursing Science, 7*(3), 49–62.

Leonard, B. J., Scott, S. A., & Erpestad, N. (1992). Maternal perception of first-born infants: A controlled comparative study of mothers of premature and full-term infants. *Journal of Pediatric Nursing, 7,* 90–96.

Leonard, L. G. (1981). Postpartum depression and mothers of infant twins. *Maternal–Child Nursing Journal, 10,* 99–109.

LeResche, L., Strobino, D., Parks, P., Fischer, P., & Smeriglio, V. (1983). The relationship of observed maternal behavior to questionnaire measures of parenting knowledge, attitudes, and emotional state in adolescent mothers. *Journal of Youth and Adolescence, 12,* 19–31.

Lerner, H. (1994). The relationship between demographics, perinatal events, neonatal behavior and the feeding interaction during the early postpartum period. *NCAST National News, 10*(1), 4–5.

Lerner, J. V., & Galambos, N. L. (1985). Maternal role satisfaction, mother–child interaction, and child temperament: A process model. *Developmental Psychology, 21,* 1157–1164.

Lerum, C. W., & LoBiondo-Wood, G. (1989). The relationship of maternal age, quickening, and physical symptoms of pregnancy to the development of maternal–fetal attachment. *Birth, 16,* 13–17.

Lester, B. M., Hoffman, J., & Brazelton, T. B. (1985). The rhythmic structure of mother–infant interaction in term and preterm infants. *Child Development, 56,* 15–27.

Levin, J. S. (1991). The factor structure of the Pregnancy Anxiety Scale. *Journal of Health and Social Behavior, 32*, 368–381.

Levine, L., Coll, C. T. G., & Oh, W. (1985). Determinants of mother–infant interaction in adolescent mothers. *Pediatrics, 75*, 23–29.

Levitt, M. J., Weber, R. A., & Clark, M. C. (1986). Social network relationships as sources of maternal support and well-being. *Developmental Psychology, 22*, 310–316.

Levy, J. (1980). Vulnerable children: Parent's perspectives and the use of medical care. *Pediatrics, 65*, 956–963.

Levy, V. (1987). The maternity blues in postpartum and post-operative women. *British Journal of Psychiatry, 151*, 368–372.

Lewin, K. (1951). *Field theory in social science.* New York: Harper & Row.

Lewis, J. M. (1988). The transition to parenthood: 2. Stability and change in marital structure. *Family Process, 27*, 273–283.

Lewis, J. M., Owen, M. T., & Cox, M. J. (1988). The transition to parenthood: 3. Incorporation of the child into the family. *Family Process, 27*, 411–421.

Lia-Hoagberg, B., Rode, P., Skovholt, C. J., Oberg, C. N., Berg, C., Mullett, S., & Choi, T. (1990). Barriers and motivators to prenatal care among low-income women. *Social Science Medicine, 30*, 487–495.

Lieberman, M. A. (1982). The effects of social supports on responses to stress. In L. Goldberger & S. Breznitz (Eds.), *Handbook of stress: Theoretical and clinical aspects* (pp. 764–783). New York: The Free Press.

Liese, L. H., Snowden, L. R., & Ford, L. K. (1989). Partner status, social support, and psychological adjustment during pregnancy. *Family Relations, 38*, 311–316.

Lindblad-Goldberg, M., & Dukes, J. L. (1985). Social support in black, low-income, single-parent families: Normative and dysfunctional patterns. *American Journal of Orthopsychiatry, 55*, 42–58.

Lindemann, E. (1944). Symptomatology and management of acute grief. *American Journal of Psychiatry, 101*, 141–148.

Linder, E. A. (1984). Maternal–fetal attachment in the pregnant adolescent, self-esteem, relationship with mother, and the decision to keep or release the infant for adoption. *Dissertation Abstracts International, 46*, 1521-A-1522A. (University Microfilms No. 85-00, 832).

Lips, H. M. (1982). Somatic and emotional aspects of the normal pregnancy experience: The first 5 months. *American Journal of Obstetrics and Gynecology, 142*, 524–529.

Lips, H. M. (1985). A longitudinal study of the reporting of emotional and somatic symptoms during and after pregnancy. *Social Science Medicine, 21*, 631–640.

Litchfield, L. (1981). Feminine masochism as a component of psychoanalytic femininity. *Issues in Health Care of Women, 3*, 129–137.

Little, B. C., Hayworth, J., Carter, S. M. B., Dewhurst, J., Raptopoulos, P., Sandler, M., & Priest, R. G. (1981). Personal and psychophysiological characteristics associated with puerperal mental state. *Journal of Psychosomatic Research, 25*, 385–393.

Lobar, S. L., & Phillips, S. (1992). A clinical assessment strategy for maternal acquaintance-attachment behaviors. *Issues in Comprehensive Pediatric Nursing, 15*, 249–259.

Lobo, M. L. (1992). Parent–infant interaction during feeding when the infant has congenital heart disease. *Journal of Pediatric Nursing, 7*, 97–105.

Lobo, M. L., Barnard, K. E., & Combs, J. B. (1992). Failure to thrive: A parent–infant interaction perspective. *Journal of Pediatric Nursing, 7*, 251–261.

Loos, C., & Julius, L. (1989). The client's view of hospitalization during pregnancy. *Journal of Obstetric, Gynecologic and Neonatal Nursing, 18*, 52–56.

Lorr, M., & McNair, D. (1982). *Profile of Mood States–B*. San Diego, CA: Educational and Industrial Testing Service.

Lotas, M. B., & Willging, J. M. (1979). Mothers, babies, perception. *Image: Journal of Nursing Scholarship, 11*(2), 45–51.

Lowe, N. K. (1993). Maternal confidence for labor: Development of the childbirth self-efficacy inventory. *Research in Nursing and Health, 16*, 141–149.

Lubin, B., Gardener, S. H., & Roth, A. (1975). Mood and somatic symptoms during pregnancy. *Psychosomatic Medicine, 37*, 136–146.

Lumley, J. (1980). The image of the fetus in the first trimester. *Birth and the Family Journal, 7*(1), 5–14.

Lumley, J. M. (1982). Attitudes to the fetus among primigravidae. *Australian Paediatric Journal, 18*, 106–109.

Lumley, J., & Brown, S. (1993). Attenders and nonattenders at childbirth education classes in Australia: How do they and their births differ? *Birth, 20*, 123–131.

Lynch, A. (1982). Maternal stress following the birth of a second child. In M. H. Klaus & M. O. Robertson (Eds.), *Birth, interaction and attachment* (pp. 60–66). Skillman, NJ: Johnson & Johnson.

Mackey, M. C., & Coster-Schulz, M. A. (1992). Women's views of the preterm labor experience. *Clinical Nursing Research, 1*, 366–384.

Macklin, E. D. (1987). Nontraditional family forms. In M. B. Sussman & S. K. Steinmetz (Eds.), *Handbook of marriage and the family* (pp. 317–353). New York: Plenum Press.

344 ::*References*

MacMullen, N., Dulski, L. A., & Pappalardo, B. (1992). Antepartum vulnerability: Stress, coping, and a patient support group. *Journal of Perinatal and Neonatal Nursing, 6*(3), 15–25.

Magyary, D. (1984). Early social interactions: Preterm infant–parent dyads. *Issues in Comprehensive Pediatric Nursing, 7,* 233–254.

Mahler, M. S., Pine, F., & Bergman, A. (1975). *The psychological birth of the human infant.* New York: Basic Books.

Main, M. (1990). Cross-cultural studies of attachment organization: Recent studies, changing methodologies, and the concept of conditional strategies. *Human Development, 33,* 48–61.

Majerus, P. W., Guze, S. B., Delong, W. B., & Robins, E. (1960). Psychologic factors and psychiatric disease in hyperemesis gravidarum: A follow-up study of 69 vomiters and 66 controls. *American Journal of Psychiatry, 117,* 421–428.

Majewski, J. L. (1986). Conflicts, satisfactions, and attitudes during transition to the maternal role. *Nursing Research, 35,* 10–14.

Majewski, J. (1987). Social support and the transition to the maternal role. *Health Care for Women International, 8,* 397–407.

Malnory, M. E. (1982). A prenatal assessment tool for mothers and fathers. *Journal of Nurse-Midwifery, 27,* 26–34.

Maloni, J. A. (1994). The content and sources of maternal knowledge about the infant. *Maternal–Child Nursing Journal, 22,* 111–120.

Maloni, J. A., Chance, B., Zhang, C., Cohen, A. W., Betts, D., & Gange, S. J. (1993). Physical and psychosocial side effects of antepartum hospital bed rest. *Nursing Research, 42,* 197–203.

Maloni, J. A., & Kasper, C. E. (1991). Physical and psychosocial effects of antepartum hospital bedrest: A review of the literature. *Image: The Journal of Nursing Scholarship, 23*(3), 187–192.

Mansfield, P. K., & McCool, W. (1989). Toward a better understanding of the "advanced maternal age" factor. *Health Care for Women International, 10,* 395–415.

March of Dimes Birth Defects Foundation. (1993). Pregnancy after age 30. *Public Health Education Information Sheet* (09-407-00). White Plains, NY.

Marcia, J. E. (1980). Identity in adolescence. In J. Adelson (Ed.), *Handbook of adolescent psychology* (pp. 159–187). New York: John Wiley & Sons.

Martell, L. K. (1990a). The mother–daughter relationship during daughter's first pregnancy: The transition experience. *Holistic Nursing Practice, 4*(3), 47–55.

Martell, L. K. (1990b). Perceptions of equity by mothers and daughters during daughters' first pregnancy. *Family Relations, 39,* 305–310.

Martell, L. K., & Mitchell, S. K. (1984). Rubin's "puerperal change" reconsidered. *Journal of Obstetric, Gynecologic, and Neonatal Nursing, 13,* 145–149.

Martone, D. J., & Nash, B. R. (1988). Initial differences in postpartum attachment behavior in breastfeeding and bottle-feeding mothers. *Journal of Obstetric, Gynecologic, and Neonatal Nursing, 17,* 212–213.

Marut, J. S. (1978). The special needs of the cesarean mother. *MCN, the American Journal of Maternal Child Nursing, 3,* 202–206.

Marut, J. S., & Mercer, R. T. (1979). A comparison of primiparas' perceptions of vaginal and cesarean birth. *Nursing Research, 28,* 260–266.

Matsuhashi, Y., & Felice, M. E. (1991). Adolescent body image during pregnancy. *Journal of Adolescent Health, 12,* 313–315.

Matthews, M. K. (1993). Experiences of primiparous breast-feeding mothers in the first days following birth. *Clinical Nursing Research, 2,* 309–326.

Mauri, M. (1990). Sleep and the reproductive cycle: A review. *Health Care for Women International, 11,* 409–421.

Mayberry, L. J., & Affonso, D. D. (1993). Infant temperament and postpartum depression: A review. *Health Care for Women International, 14,* 201–211.

McBride, A. B. (1973). *The growth and development of mothers.* New York: Harper & Row.

McBride, S., & Belsky, J. (1988). Characteristics, determinants and consequences of maternal separation anxiety. *Developmental Psychology, 24,* 407–414.

McCartney, K., & Galanopoulos, A. (1988). Child care and attachment: A new frontier the second time around. *American Journal of Orthopsychiatry, 58,* 16–24.

McClowry, S. G. (1992). Temperament theory and research. *Image: Journal of Nursing Scholarship, 24,* 319–325.

McConnell, O. L., & Daston, P. G. (1961). Body image changes in pregnancy. *Journal of Projective Techniques, 25,* 451–455.

McCormick, M. C., Shapiro, S., & Starfield, B. (1982). Factors associated with maternal opinion of development: Clues to the vulnerable child? *Pediatrics, 69,* 537–543.

McDonald, R. L. (1965). Fantasy and the outcome of pregnancy. *Archives of General Psychiatry, 12,* 602–606.

McElheny, J. E. (1989). Parental adaptation to a child with bronchopulmonary dysplasia. *Journal of Pediatric Nursing, 4,* 346–352.

McFarlane, J. (1993). Battered and pregnant. *Council Perspectives, 2*(1), 1, 5.

McGrath, M. M., & Meyer, E. C. (1992). Maternal self-esteem: From theory to clinical practice in a special care nursery. *Care of Hospitalized Children, 21,* 199–205.

McHaffie, H. E. (1990). Mothers of very low birthweight babies: How do they adjust? *Journal of Advanced Nursing, 15,* 6–11.

McHale, S. M., & Huston, T. L. (1985). The effect of the transition to parenthood on the marriage relationship: A longitudinal study. *Journal of Family Issues, 6,* 409–433.

McIntosh, J. (1993). Postpartum depression: Women's help-seeking behaviour and perceptions of cause. *Journal of Advanced Nursing, 18,* 178–184.

McKay, S., & Barrows, T. (1991). Holding back: Maternal readiness to give birth. *MCN, the American Journal of Maternal Child Nursing, 16,* 251–254.

McKay, S., & Barrows, T. L. (1992). Reliving birth: Maternal responses to viewing videotape of their second stage labors. *Image, Journal of Nursing Scholarship, 24,* 27–31.

McKenry, P. C., Kotch, J. B., & Browne, D. H. (1991). Correlates of dysfunctional parenting attitudes among low-income adolescent mothers. *Journal of Adolescent Research, 6,* 212–234.

McKim, M. K. (1987). Transition to what? New parents' problems in the first year. *Family Relations, 36,* 22–25.

McLanahan, S., & Adams, J. (1987). Parenthood and psychological well-being. *Annual Review of Immunology, 5,* 237–257.

McLanahan, S. S., & Booth, K. (1989). Mother-only families: Problems, prospects, and politics. *Journal of Marriage and the Family, 51,* 557–580.

Mead, G. H. (1934). *Mind, self, and society.* Chicago: University of Chicago Press.

Mead-Bennett, E. (1990). The relationship of primigravid sleep experience and select moods on the first postpartum day. *Journal of Obstetric, Gynecologic, and Neonatal Nursing, 19,* 146–152.

Medinnus, G. R., & Curtis, F. J. (1963). The relation between maternal self-acceptance and child acceptance. *Journal of Consulting Psychology, 27,* 524–544.

Meleis, A. I., Kulig, J., Arruda, E. N., & Beckman, A. (1990). Maternal role of women in clerical jobs in southern Brazil: Stress and satisfaction. *Health Care for Women International, 11,* 369–382.

Meleis, A. I., & Swendsen, L. A. (1978). Role supplementation: An empirical test of a nursing intervention. *Nursing Research, 27,* 11–18.

Melges, F. T. (1968). Postpartum psychiatric syndromes. *Psychosomatic Medicine, 30,* 95–108.

Meltzoff, A. N., & Moore, M. K. (1983). Newborn infants imitate adult facial gestures. *Child Development, 54,* 702–709.

Mendelson, M. J. (1990). *Becoming a brother.* Cambridge, MA: MIT Press.

Mercer, R. T. (1973). One mother's use of negative feedback in coping with her defective infant. *Maternal–Child Nursing Journal, 2,* 29–37.

Mercer, R. T. (1974a). Mothers' responses to their infants with defects. *Nursing Research, 23,* 133–137.

Mercer, R. T. (1974b). Responses of five multigravidae to the event of the birth of an infant with a defect (Doctoral dissertation, University of Pittsburgh, 1973). *Dissertation Abstracts International, 34* (10).

Mercer, R. T. (1975). Responses of mothers to the birth of an infant with a defect. In *ANA clinical sessions: American Nurses' Association,* 1974, *San Francisco* (pp. 57–68). New York: Appleton-Century-Crofts.

Mercer, R. T. (1977a). *Nursing care for parents at risk.* Thorofare, NJ: C. B. Slack.

Mercer, R. T. (1977b). Postpartum: Illness and acquaintance-attachment process. *American Journal of Nursing, 77,* 1174–1178.

Mercer, R. T. (1979a). *Perspectives on adolescent health care.* Philadelphia: J. B. Lippincott.

Mercer, R. T. (1979b). "She's a multip .... she knows the ropes." *MCN, the American Journal of Maternal Child Nursing, 4,* 301–304.

Mercer, R. T. (1980). Teenage motherhood: The first year. Part 1. The teenage mother's views and responses; Part 2: How the infants fared. *Journal of Obstetric, Gynecologic, and Neonatal Nursing, 9,* 16–27.

Mercer, R. T. (1981a). The nurse and maternal tasks of early postpartum. *MCN, the American Journal of Maternal Child Nursing, 6,* 341–345.

Mercer, R. T. (1981b). Potential effects of anesthesia and analgesia on the maternal–infant attachment process of cesarean mothers. In C. F. Kehoe (Ed.), *The cesarean experience* (pp. 59–76). New York: Appleton-Century-Crofts.

Mercer, R. T. (1981c). A theoretical framework for studying factors that impact on the maternal role. *Nursing Research, 30,* 73–77.

Mercer, R. T. (1983). Parent–infant attachment. In L. J. Sonstegard, K. M. Kowalski, & B. Jennings (Eds.). *Women's health: Childbearing* (Vol. 2., pp. 17–42). New York: Grune & Stratton.

Mercer, R. T. (1985a, May). *Daughters and mothers: Comparison of mothering behaviors.* Paper presented at the Eighteenth Annual Communicating Nursing Research Conference, Western Society for Research in Nursing, Seattle.

Mercer, R. T. (1985b). The process of maternal role attainment over the first year. *Nursing Research, 34,* 198–204.

Mercer, R. T. (1985c). The relationship of age and other variables to gratification in mothering. *Health Care for Women International, 6,* 295–308.

Mercer, R. T. (1985d). The relationship of the birth experience to later mothering behavior. *Journal of Nurse Midwifery, 30,* 204–211.

Mercer, R. T. (1986a). *First-time motherhood: Experiences from teens to forties.* New York: Springer Publishing Co.

Mercer, R. T. (1986b). Predictors of maternal role attainment at one year post-birth. *Western Journal of Nursing Research, 8*(1), 9–32.

Mercer, R. T. (1986c). The relationship of developmental variables to maternal behavior. *Research in Nursing and Health, 9,* 25–33.

Mercer, R. T. (1990). *Parents at risk.* New York: Springer Publishing Co.

Mercer, R. T. (1991). Second births: The myths and the realities. *Nurseweek, 4* (8), 12–13.

Mercer, R. T., & Ferketich, S. L. (1988). Stress and social support as predictors of anxiety and depression during pregnancy. *Advances in Nursing Science, 10*(2), 26–39.

Mercer, R. T., & Ferketich, S. L. (1990a). Predictors of family functioning eight months following birth. *Nursing Research, 39,* 76–82.

Mercer, R. T., & Ferketich, S. L. (1990b). Predictors of parental attachment during early parenthood. *Journal of Advanced Nursing, 15,* 268–280.

Mercer, R. T., & Ferketich, S. L. (1994a). Maternal–infant attachment of experienced and inexperienced mothers during infancy. *Nursing Research, 43,* 344–351.

Mercer, R. T., & Ferketich, S. L. (1994b). Predictors of maternal role competence by risk status. *Nursing Research, 43,* 38–43.

Mercer, R. T., & Ferketich, S. L. (1995). Experienced and inexperienced mothers' maternal competence during infancy. *Research in Nursing and Health, 18,* 333–343.

Mercer, R. T., Ferketich, S. L., & DeJoseph, J. F. (1993). Predictors of partner relationships during pregnancy and infancy. *Research in Nursing and Health, 16,* 45–56.

Mercer, R. T., Ferketich, S. L., May, K. A., DeJoseph, J., & Sollid, D. (1987). *Antepartum stress: Effect on family health and functioning* (Report No. R01 NR 01064). Bethesda, MD: National Center for Nursing Research, NIH.

Mercer, R. T., Ferketich, S. L., May, K., DeJoseph, J., & Sollid, D. (1988). Further exploration of maternal and paternal fetal attachment. *Research in Nursing and Health, 11,* 83–95.

Mercer, R. T., & Hackley, K. C. (1984). A comparison of employed and unemployed mothers' responses and attitudes. *Western Journal of Nursing Research, 6*(3), 61.

Mercer, R. T., Hackley, K. C., & Bostrom, A. (1982). *Factors having an impact on maternal role attainment the first year of motherhood* (Report No.

MC-R-05-060435). Bethesda, MD: Maternal and Child Health (Social Security Act, Title V).

Mercer, R. T., Hackley, K. C., & Bostrom, A. G. (1983). Relationship of psychosocial and perinatal variables to perception of childbirth. *Nursing Research, 32,* 202–207.

Mercer, R. T., Hackley, K. C., & Bostrom, A. (1984). Adolescent motherhood: Comparisons of outcome with older mothers. *Journal of Adolescent Health Care, 4,* 7–13.

Mercer, R. T., & Marut, J. S. (1981). Comparative viewpoints: Cesarean versus vaginal childbirth. In D. D. Affonso (Ed.), *Impact of cesarean birth* (pp. 63–84). Philadelphia: F. A. Davis.

Mercer, R. T., Nichols, E. G., & Doyle, G. C. (1988). Transitions over the life cycle: A comparison of mothers and nonmothers. *Nursing Research, 37,* 144–151.

Mercer, R. T., Nichols, E. G., & Doyle, G. C. (1989). *Transitions in a woman's life.* New York: Springer Publishing Co.

Mercer, R. T., & Stainton, M. C. (1984). Perceptions of the birth experience: A cross-cultural comparison. *Health Care for Women International, 5,* 28–47.

Merilo, K. F. (1988). Is it better the second time around? *MCN, the American Journal of Maternal Child Nursing, 13,* 200–204.

Meyers, B. J. (1984). Mother–infant bonding: The status of this critical-period hypothesis. *Developmental Review, 4,* 240–274.

Miles, M. S., Funk, S. G., & Carlson, J. (1993). Parental Stressor Scale: Neonatal intensive care unit. *Nursing Research, 42,* 148–152.

Miles, M. S., Funk, S. G., & Kasper, M. A. (1992). The stress response of mothers and fathers of preterm infants. *Research in Nursing and Health, 15,* 261–269.

Miles, M. S., & Holditch-Davis, D. (In press). Compensatory parenting: How mothers perceive their parenting of 3-year-old prematurely born children. *Journal of Pediatric Nursing.*

Miles, M. S., & Mathes, M. (1991). Preparation of parents for the ICU experience: What are we missing? *Care of Hospitalized Children, 20,* 132–137.

Miller, B. C., & Sollie, D. L. (1980). Normal stresses during the transition to parenthood. *Family Relations, 29,* 459–465.

Millot, J. L., Filiatre, J. C., & Montagner, H. (1988). Maternal tactile behaviour correlated with mother and newborn infant characteristics. *Early Human Development, 16,* 119–129.

Milne, L. S., & Rich, O. J. (1981). Cognitive and affective aspects of the responses of pregnant women to sonography. *Maternal–Child Nursing Journal, 10,* 15–39.

Minde, K. K., Marton, P., Manning, D., & Hines, B. (1980). Some determinants of mother–infant interaction in the premature nursery. *Journal of the American Academy of Child Psychiatry, 19*, 1–21.

Minde, K., Perrotta, M., & Marton, P. (1985). Maternal caretaking and play with full-term and premature infants. *Journal of Child Psychology and Psychiatry, 26*, 231–244.

Mogan, J. (1987). What can nurses learn from structured observations of mother–infant interactions? *Issues in Comprehensive Pediatric Nursing, 10*, 67–73.

Moore, D. (1978). The body image in pregnancy. *Journal of Nurse-Midwifery, 22*, 17–27.

Moore, D. (1983). Prepared childbirth and marital satisfaction during the antepartum and postpartum periods. *Nursing Research, 32*, 73–79.

Moore, L. (1987). Effects of mediated instruction, the cesarean experience, and infant characteristics on maternal attachment behavior. *Journal of Obstetric, Gynecologic, and Neonatal Nursing, 16*, 366.

Moss, J. R. (1981). Concerns of multiparas on the third postpartum day. *Journal of Obstetric, Gynecologic, and Neonatal Nursing, 10*, 421–424.

Mpoke, S., & Johnson, K. E. (1993). Baseline survey of pregnancy practices among Kenyan Maasai. *Western Journal of Nursing Research, 15*(3), 298–313.

Muller, M. E. (1990). Binding-in: Still a relevant concept? *NAACOG's Clinical Issues in Perinatal and Women's Health Nursing, 1*(3), 297–302.

Muller, M. E. (1992). A critical review of prenatal attachment research. *Scholarly Inquiry for Nursing Practice: An International Journal, 6*, 5–22.

Muller, M. E. (1993). Development of the prenatal attachment inventory. *Western Journal of Nursing Research, 15*(2), 199–215.

Murphy, M. A. (1982). The family with a handicapped child: A review of the literature. *Developmental and Behavioral Pediatrics, 3*(2), 73–82.

Murray, A. D. (1975). Maternal employment reconsidered: Effects on infants. *American Journal of Orthopsychiatry, 45*, 773–790.

Mutryn, C. S. (1993). Psychosocial impact of cesarean section on the family: A literature review. *Social Sciences Medicine, 37*, 1271–1281.

Nath, P. S., Borkowski, J. G., Whitman, T. L., & Schellenbach, C. J. (1991). Understanding adolescent parenting: The dimensions and functions of social support. *Family Relations, 40*, 411–420.

Naylor, A. (1982). Premature mourning and failure to mourn: Their relationship to conflict between mothers and intellectually normal children. *American Journal of Orthopsychiatry, 52*, 679–687.

Newberger, C. M. (1980). The cognitive structure of parenthood: Designing a descriptive measure. *New Directions for Child Development, 7*, 45–67.

Newcomb, T. (1961). *The acquaintance process.* New York: Holt, Rinehart, and Winston.

Newton, N., & Newton, M. (1962). Mothers' reactions to their newborn babies. *Journal of American Medical Association, 181,* 206–210.

Nicoll, L. H. (1988). Factors influencing prefatory maternal response in the primigravida. *Dissertation Abstracts International, 49,* 9B (University Microfilms No. 8811234).

Niemela, P. (1980). Working through ambivalent feelings in woman's life transitions. *Acta Psychologica Fennica* (Suppl. 220), 99–107.

Nilsson, A., & Almgren, P. (1970). Para-natal emotional adjustment: A prospective investigation of 165 women, Part II. *ACTA Psychiatrica Scandinavica* (Suppl. 220), 65–141.

Norbeck, J. S., & Anderson, N. J. (1989a). Life stress, social support, and anxiety in mid- and late-pregnancy among low income women. *Research in Nursing and Health, 12,* 281–287.

Norbeck, J. S., & Anderson, N. J. (1989b). Psychosocial predictors of pregnancy outcomes in low-income black, Hispanic, and white women. *Nursing Research, 38,* 204–209.

Norbeck, J. S., & Sheiner, M. (1982). Sources of social support related to single-parent functioning. *Research in Nursing and Health, 5,* 3–12.

Norbeck, J. S., & Tilden, V. P. (1983). Life stress, social support, and emotional disequilibrium in complications of pregnancy: A prospective, multivariate study. *Journal of Health and Social Behavior, 24,* 30–46.

Norr, K. L., Block, C. R., Charles, A., Meyering, S., & Meyers, E. (1977). Explaining pain and enjoyment in childbirth. *Journal of Health and Social Behavior, 18,* 260–275.

Norr, K. F., & Nacion, K. (1987). Outcomes of postpartum early discharge, 1960–1986: A comparative review. *Birth, 14,* 135–141.

Norr, K. F., Nacion, K. W., & Abramson, R. (1989). Early discharge with home follow-up: Impacts on low-income mothers and infants. *Journal of Obstetric, Gynecologic, and Neonatal Nursing, 18,* 33–144.

Norr, K. F., & Roberts, J. E. (1991). Early maternal attachment behaviors of adolescent and adult mothers. *Journal of Nurse-Midwifery, 36,* 334–342.

Norr, K. F., Roberts, J. E., & Freese, U. (1989). Early postpartum rooming-in and maternal attachment behaviors in a group of medically indigent primiparas. *Journal of Nurse-Midwifery, 34*(2), 85–91.

Norris, D. M., & Hoyer, P. J. (1993). Dynamism in practice: Parenting within King's framework. *Nursing Science Quarterly, 6,* 79–85.

Nuckolls, K. B., Cassel, J., & Kaplan, B. H. (1972). Psychological assets, life crisis and the prognosis of pregnancy. *American Journal of Epidemiology, 95,* 431–441.

Oates, D. S., & Heinicke, C. M. (1985). Prebirth prediction of the quality of the mother–infant interaction the first year of life. *Journal of Family Issues, 6*, 523–542.

O'Brien, B., & Naber, S. (1992). Nausea and vomiting during pregnancy: Effects on the quality of women's lives. *Birth, 19*, 138–143.

O'Connell, M. E. (1983). Locus of control specific to pregnancy. *Journal of Obstetric, Gynecologic, and Neonatal Nursing, 12*, 161–164.

O'Connor, S., Vietze, P. M., Sherrod, K. B., Sandler, H. M., & Altemeier, W. A. III. (1980). Reduced incidence of parenting inadequacy following rooming-in. *Pediatrics, 66*, 176–182.

Oehler, J. M., Hannan, T., & Catlett, A. (1993). Maternal views of preterm infants' responsiveness to social interaction. *Neonatal Network, 12*(6), 67–74.

O'Hara, M. W., Neunaber, D. J., & Zekoski, E. M. (1984). Prospective study of postpartum depression: Prevalence, course, and predictive factors. *Journal of Abnormal Psychology, 93*, 158–171.

O'Hara, M. W., Rehm, L. P., & Campbell, S. B. (1982). Predicting depressive symptomatology: Cognitive-behavioral models and postpartum depression. *Journal of Abnormal Psychology, 91*, 457–461.

O'Hara, M. W., Rehm, L. P., & Campbell, S. B. (1983). Postpartum depression: A role for social network and life stress variables. *Journal of Nervous and Mental Disease, 171*, 336–341.

Olsen, L. C. (1982). Observations of early mother–infant interaction in Liberia. *Journal of Nurse-Midwifery, 27*, 9–14.

Olson, S. L., Kieschnick, E., Banyard, V., & Ceballo, R. (1994). Socioenvironmental and individual correlates of psychological adjustment of low-income single mothers. *American Journal of Orthopsychiatry, 64*, 317–331.

Omar, M. A., & Schiffman, R. F. (1993). Prenatal vitamins: A rite of passage? *MCN, the American Journal of Maternal Child Nursing, 18*, 322–324.

O'Neil, R., & Greenberger, E. (1994). Patterns of commitment to work and parenting: Implications for role strain. *Journal of Marriage and the Family, 56*, 101–118.

Osofsky, J. D. (1976). Neonatal characteristics and mother–infant interaction in two observational situations. *Child Development, 47*, 1138–1147.

Osofsky, J. D., & Danzger, B. (1974). Relationships between neonatal characteristics and mother–infant interaction. *Developmental Psychology, 10*, 124–130.

O'Sullivan, A. L., & Jacobsen, B. S. (1992). A randomized trial of a health care program for first-time adolescent mothers and their infants. *Nursing Research, 41*, 210–215.

Oz, S., & Fine, M. (1988). A comparison of childhood backgrounds of teenage mothers and their non-mother peers: A new formulation. *Journal of Adolescence, 11,* 251–261.

Padawer, J. A., Fagan, C., Janoff-Bulman, R., Strickland, B. R., & Chorowski, M. (1988). Women's psychological adjustment following emergency cesarean versus vaginal delivery. *Psychology of Women Quarterly, 12,* 25–34.

Pakizegi, B. (1990). Emerging family forms: Single mothers by choice: Demographic and psychosocial variables. *Maternal–Child Nursing Journal, 19,* 1–19.

Palisin, H. (1980). The neonatal perception inventory: Failure to replicate. *Child Development, 51,* 737–742.

Palisin, H. (1981). The neonatal perception inventory: A review. *Nursing Research, 30,* 285–289.

Panzarine, S. (1986). Stressors, coping, and social supports of adolescent mothers. *Journal of Adolescent Health Care, 7,* 153–161.

Parker, B., McFarlane, J., Soeken, K., Torres, S., & Campbell, D. (1993). Physical and emotional abuse in pregnancy: A comparison of adult and teenage women. *Nursing Research, 42,* 173–178.

Parker, S., & Zahr, L. (1985). *The Maternal Confidence Questionnaire.* Boston, MA: Boston City Hospital.

Parkes, C. M. (1972). *Bereavement: Studies of grief in adult life.* New York: International Universities Press.

Parsons, C., & Redman, S. (1991), Self-reported cognitive change during pregnancy. *Australian Journal of Advanced Nursing, 9*(1), 20–29.

Partridge, S. E. (1988). The parental self-concept: A theoretical exploration and practical application. *American Journal of Orthopsychiatry, 58,* 281–287.

Patterson, E. T., Douglas, A. B., Patterson, P. M., & Bradle, J. B. (1992). Symptoms of preterm labor and self-diagnostic confusion. *Nursing Research, 41,* 367–372.

Patterson, E. T., Freese, M. P., & Goldenberg, R. L. (1986). Reducing uncertainty: Self-diagnosis of pregnancy. *Image: Journal of Nursing Scholarship, 18,* 105–109.

Patterson, E. T., Freese, M. P., Goldenberg, R. L. (1990). Seeking safe passage: Utilizing health care during pregnancy. *Image: Journal of Nursing Scholarship, 22,* 27–31.

Paykel, E. S., Emms, E. M., Fletcher, J., & Rassaby, E. S. (1980). Life events and social support in puerperal depression. *British Journal of Psychology, 136,* 339–346.

Pederson, D. R., Bento, S., Chance, G. W., Evans, B., & Fox, A. M. (1987). Maternal emotional responses to preterm birth. *American Journal of Orthopsychiatry, 57,* 15–21.

Pellegrom, P., & Swartz, L. (1980). Primigravidas' perceptions of early postpartum. *Pediatric Nursing, 6*(6), 25–27.

Pennington, S. B. (1990). The lesbian mother. In R. T. Mercer, (Ed.), *Parents at risk* (pp. 226–243). New York: Springer Publishing Co.

Perry, S. E. (1983). Parents' perceptions of their newborn following structured interactions. *Nursing Research, 32,* 208–212.

Peterson, G. H., & Mehl, L. E. (1978). Some determinants of maternal attachment. *American Journal of Psychiatry, 135,* 1168–1173.

Pharis, M. E. (1978). *Age and sex differences in expectations for infants and the parenting among couples in a first pregnancy and among university students.* Unpublished doctoral dissertation, the University of Texas at Austin.

Philichi, L. M. (1989). Family adaptation during a pediatric intensive care hospitalization. *Journal of Pediatric Nursing, 4,* 268–276.

Philipp, C. (1983). The role of recollected anxiety in parental adaptation to low birthweight infants. *Child Psychiatry and Human Development, 13,* 239–248.

Phillips, C. A. (1992). Vulnerability in family systems: Application to antepartum. *Journal of Perinatal and Neonatal Nursing, 6*(3), 26–36.

Pickens, D. S. (1982). The cognitive processes of career-oriented primiparas in identity reformulation. *Maternal–Child Nursing Journal, 11,* 135–164.

Pickens, J., & Field, T. (1993). Facial expressivity in infants of depressed mothers. *Developmental Psychology, 29,* 986–988.

Pinyerd, B. J. (1992). Infant colic and maternal mental health: Nursing research and practice concerns. *Journal of Comprehensive Pediatric Nursing, 15,* 155–167.

Pistrang, N. (1984). Women's work involvement and experience of new motherhood. *Journal of Marriage and the Family, 46,* 433–447.

Pitt, B. (1968). Atypical depression following childbirth. *British Journal of Psychiatry, 114,* 1325–1335.

Pitt, B. (1973). Maternity blues. *British Journal of Psychiatry, 122,* 431–433.

Pitzer, M. S., & Hock, E. (1989). Employed mothers' concerns about separation from the first- and second-born child. *Research in Nursing and Health, 12,* 123–128.

Pitzer, M. S., & Hock, E. (1992). Infant gender and sibling dyad influences on maternal separation anxiety. *Maternal–Child Nursing Journal, 20,* 65–80.

Pond, E. F., & Kemp, V. H. (1992). A comparison between adolescent and adult women on prenatal anxiety and self-confidence. *Maternal–Child Nursing Journal, 20,* 11–20.

Pop, V. J. M., Essed, G. G. M., deGeus, C. A., van Son, M. M., & Komproe, I. H. (1993). Prevalence of post partum depression: Or is it postpuerperium depression? *Acta Obstetrica Gynecologica Scandinavica, 72,* 354–358.

Porter, L. S., & Demeuth, B. R. (1979). The impact of marital adjustment on pregnancy acceptance. *Maternal–Child Nursing Journal, 8,* 103–113.

Porter, R. H., Cernoch, J. M., & Perry, S. (1983). The importance of odors in mother–infant interactions. *Maternal–Child Nursing Journal, 12,* 147–154.

Porter, R. H., Makin, J. W., Davis, L. B., & Christensen, K. M. (1992). Breast-fed infants respond to olfactory cues from their own mother and unfamiliar lactating females. *Infant Behavior and Development, 15,* 85–93.

Power, T. G., Gershenhorn, S., & Stafford, D. (1990). Maternal perceptions of infant difficultness: The influence of maternal attitudes and attributions. *Infant Behavior and Development, 13,* 421–437.

Price, G. M. (1983). Sensitivity in mother–infant interactions: The AMIS scale. *Infant Behavior and Development, 6,* 353–360.

Pridham, K. F. (1981). Infant feeding and anticipatory care: Supporting the adaptation of parents to their new babies. *Maternal–Child Nursing Journal, 10,* 111–126.

Pridham, K. F. (1987). The meaning for mothers of a new infant: Relationship to maternal experience. *Maternal–Child Nursing Journal, 16,* 103–122.

Pridham, K. F. (1988). Structures of maternal information processing for infant feeding. *Western Journal of Nursing Research, 10,* 566–575.

Pridham, K. F. (1989). Mothers' decision rules for problem solving. *Western Journal of Nursing Research, 11,* 60–74.

Pridham, K. F., & Chang, A. S. (1985). Parents' beliefs about themselves as parents of a new infant: Instrument development. *Research in Nursing and Health, 8,* 19–29.

Pridham, K. F., & Chang, A. S. (1989). What being the parent of a new baby is like: Revision of an instrument. *Research in Nursing and Health, 12,* 323–329.

Pridham, K. F., & Chang, A. S. (1992). Transition to being the mother of a new infant in the first 3 months: Maternal problem solving and self-appraisals. *Journal of Advanced Nursing, 17,* 204–216.

Pridham, K. F., Chang, A. S., & Chiu, Y. (1994). Mothers' parenting self-appraisals: The contribution of perceived infant temperament. *Research in Nursing and Health, 17,* 381–392.

Pridham, K. F., Hansen, M. F., Bradley, M. E., & Heighway, S. M. (1982). Issues of concern to mothers of new babies. *Journal of Family Practice, 14,* 1079–1085.

Pridham, K., Knight, C. B., & Stephenson, G. (1989). Decision rules for infant feeding: The influence of maternal expertise, regulating functions, and feeding method. *Maternal–Child Nursing Journal, 18,* 31–48.

Pridham, K. F., Lytton, D., Chang, A. S., & Rutledge, D. (1991). Early postpartum transition: Progress in maternal identity and role attainment. *Research in Nursing and Health, 14,* 21–31.

Priel, B., Gonik, N., & Rabinowitz. (1993). Appraisals of childbirth experience and newborn characteristics: The role of hardiness and affect. *Journal of Personality, 61*(3), 299–315.

Pritham, U. A., & Sammons, L. N. (1993). Korean women's attitudes toward pregnancy and prenatal care. *Health Care for Women International, 14,* 145–153.

Quinn, M. M. (1991). Attachment between mothers and their Down syndrome infants. *Western Journal of Nursing Research, 13*(3), 382–396.

Quinn, P., & Allen, K. R. (1989). Facing challenges and making compromises: How single mothers endure. *Family Relations, 38,* 390–395.

Radloff, L. (1977). The CES-D Scale: A self-report depression scale for research in the general population. *Journal of Applied Psychological Measurement, 1,* 385–401.

Raff, B. S., & Carroll, P. (Eds.) (1984). Social support and families of vulnerable infants. *Birth Defects: Original Article Series, 20*(5).

Ragozin, A. S., Basham, R. B., Crnic, K. A., Greenberg, M. T., & Robinson, N. M. (1982). Effects of maternal age on parenting role. *Developmental Psychology, 18,* 627–634.

Randell, B. P. (1988). *Older primiparous women: The evolution of maternal self perception within the context of mother–daughter and spousal relationships.* Unpublished doctoral dissertation, University of California, San Francisco.

Randell, B. P. (1993). Growth versus stability: Older primiparous women as a paradigmatic case for persistence. *Journal of Advanced Nursing, 18,* 518–525.

Rankin, E. A. D., & Campbell, N. D. (1983). Perception of relationship changes during the third trimester of pregnancy. *Issues in Health Care of Women, 6,* 351–359.

Rankin, E. A. D., Campbell, N. D., & Soeken, K. L. (1985). Adaptation to parenthood: Differing expectations of social supports for mothers versus fathers. *Journal of Primary Prevention, 5,* 145–153.

Reading, A. E. (1983). The influence of maternal anxiety on the course and outcome of pregnancy: A review. *Health Psychology, 2,* 187–202.

Reading, A. E., Cox, D. N., Sledmere, C. M., & Campbell, S. (1984). Psychological changes over the course of pregnancy: A study of attitudes toward the fetus/neonate. *Health Psychology, 3,* 211–221.

Reece, S. M. (1992). The parent expectations survey: A measure of perceived self-efficacy. *Clinical Nursing Research, 1,* 336–346.

Reece, S. M. (1993). Social support and the early maternal experience of primiparas over 35. *Maternal–Child Nursing Journal, 21,* 91–98.

Rees, B. L. (1980a). Maternal identification and infant care: A theoretical perspective. *Western Journal of Nursing Research, 2*(4), 686–706.

Rees, B. L. (1980b). Measuring identification with the mothering role. *Research in Nursing and Health, 3,* 49–56.

Reeves, N., Potempa, K., & Gallo, A. (1991). Fatigue in early pregnancy: An exploratory study. *Journal of Nurse-Midwifery, 36,* 303–308.

Reichert, J. A., Baron, M., & Fawcett, J. (1993). Changes in attitudes toward cesarean birth. *Journal of Obstetric, Gynecologic, and Neonatal Nursing, 22,* 159–167.

Reilly, T. W., Entwisle, D. R., & Doering, S. G. (1987). Socialization into parenthood: A longitudinal study of self-evaluations. *Journal of Marriage and the Family, 49,* 295–308.

Reis, J. (1988). Correlates of depression according to maternal age. *Journal of Genetic Psychology, 149,* 535–545.

Reis, J. (1989). The structure of depression in community based young adolescent, older adolescent, and adult mothers. *Family Relations, 38,* 164–168.

Revell, G. M., & Liptak, G. S. (1991). Understanding the child with special health care needs: A developmental perspective. *Journal of Pediatrics, 6,* 258–268.

Rhodes, J. E., Contreras, J. M., & Mangelsdorf, S. C. (1994). Natural mentor relationships among Latina adolescent mothers: Psychological adjustment, moderating processes, and the role of early parental acceptance. *American Journal of Community Psychology, 22,* 211–227.

Rich, O. J. (1969). Hospital routines as rites of passage in developing maternal identity. *Nursing Clinics of North America, 4*(1), 101–109.

Rich, O. J. (1973). Temporal and spatial experience as reflected in the verbalizations of multiparous women during labor. *Maternal–Child Nursing Journal, 2,* 239–325.

Rich, O. J. (1990). Maternal–infant bonding in homeless adolescents and their infants. *Maternal–Child Nursing Journal, 19,* 195–210.

Richards, L. N. (1989). The precarious survival and hard-won satisfactions of white single-parent families. *Family Relations, 38,* 396–403.

Richardson, P. (1981). Women's perceptions of their important dyadic relationships during pregnancy. *Maternal–Child Nursing Journal, 10,* 159–174.

Richardson, P. (1983a). Women's perceptions of change in relationships shared with children during pregnancy. *Maternal–Child Nursing Journal, 12,* 75–88.

Richardson, P. (1983b) Women's perceptions of change in relationships shared with their husbands during pregnancy. *Maternal–Child Nursing Journal*, 12, 1–19.

Richardson, P. (1987). Women's important relationships during pregnancy and the preterm labor event. *Western Journal of Nursing Research*, 9(2), 203–222.

Richardson, P. (1990). Women's experiences of body change during normal pregnancy. *Maternal–Child Nursing Journal*, 19, 93–111.

Richardson, R. A., Barbour, N. B., & Bubenzer, D. L. (1991). Bittersweet connections: Informal social networks as sources of support and interference for adolescent mothers. *Family Relations*, 40, 430–434.

Riesch, S. (1979). Enhancement of mother–infant social interaction. *Journal of Obstetric, Gynecologic, and Neonatal Nursing*, 8, 242–246.

Riesch, S. K. (1984). Occupational commitment and the quality of maternal infant interaction. *Research in Nursing and Health*, 7, 295–303.

Riesch, S. K., & Munns, S. K. (1984). Promoting awareness: The mother and her baby. *Nursing Research*, 33, 271–276.

Ringler, N. M., Kennell, J. H., Jarvella, R., Navojosky, B. J., & Klaus, M. H. (1975). Mother-to-child speech at 2 years: Effects of early postnatal contact. *Journal of Pediatrics*, 86, 141–144.

Robarge, J. P., Reynolds, Z. B., & Groothuis, J. R. (1982). Increased child abuse in families with twins. *Research in Nursing and Health*, 5, 199–203.

Roberts, C. J., & Rowley, J. R. (1972). A study of the association between quality of maternal care and infant development. *Psychological Medicine*, 2, 42–49.

Roberts, F. B. (1983). Infant behavior and the transition to parenthood. *Nursing Research*, 32, 213–217.

Robinson, G. E., Garner, D. M., Gare, D. J., & Crawford, B. (1987). Psychological adaptation to pregnancy in childless women more than 35 years of age. *American Journal of Obstetrics and Gynecology*, 156, 328–333.

Robinson, G. E., Olmsted, M., Garner, D. M., & Gare, D. J. (1988). Transition to parenthood in elderly primiparas. *Journal of Psychosomatic Obstetrics and Gynaecology*, 9, 89–101.

Robson, K. (1967). The role of eye-to-eye contact in maternal–infant attachment. *Journal of Child Psychology and Psychiatry*, 8, 13.

Robson, K. M., & Kumar, R. (1980). Delayed onset of maternal affection after childbirth. *British Journal of Psychiatry*, 136, 347–353.

Robson, K. S., & Moss, H. A. (1970). Patterns and determinants of maternal attachment. *Journal of Pediatrics*, 77, 976–985.

Rogeness, G. A., Ritchey, S., Alex, P. L., Zuelzer, M., & Morris, R. (1981). Family patterns and parenting attitudes in teenage parents. *Journal of Community Psychology, 9*, 239–245.

Romito, P. (1990). Postpartum depression and the experience of motherhood. *Acta Obstetrica Gynecologica Scandinavica* (Suppl. 69), *154*, 5–37.

Roosa, M. W. (1988). The effect of age in the transition to parenthood: Are delayed childbearers a unique group? *Family Relations, 37*, 322–327.

Roosa, M. W., Fitzgerald, H. E., & Carson, N. A. (1982). Teenage and older mothers and their infants: A descriptive comparison. *Adolescence, 17*, 1–17.

Rosenberg, M. (1965). *Society and the adolescent self image.* Princeton, NJ: Princeton University Press.

Roth, R. M. (1961). *The mother–child relationship evaluation manual.* Los Angeles: Western Psychological Services.

Rothman, B. K. (1986). *The tentative pregnancy: Prenatal diagnosis and the future of motherhood.* New York: Viking Penguin.

Rothman, B. K. (1989). *Recreating motherhood: Ideology and technology in a patriarchal society.* New York: W. W. Norton.

Rubin, R. (1954). Bereavement. Unpublished manuscript.

Rubin, R. (1961a). Basic maternal behavior. *Nursing Outlook, 9*, 683–686.

Rubin, R. (1961b). Puerperal change. *Nursing Outlook, 9*, 753–755.

Rubin, R. (1963a). Maternal touch. *Nursing Outlook, 11*, 828–831.

Rubin, R. (1964). Behavioral definitions in nursing therapy. In *Conference on maternal and child nursing: Current concepts in nursing care.* Columbus, OH: Ross Laboratories.

Rubin, R. (1967a). Attainment of the maternal role: Part 1. Processes. *Nursing Research, 16*, 237–245.

Rubin, R. (1967b). Attainment of the maternal role: Part 2. Referrants. *Nursing Research, 16*, 342–346.

Rubin, R. (1967c). Food and feeding: A matrix of relationships. *Nursing Forum, 6*(2), 195–205.

Rubin, R. (1967d). The neomaternal period. In M. Duffey, E. H. Anderson, B. S. Bergersen, M. Lohr, & M. H. Rose (Eds.), *Current concepts in clinical nursing* (Vol. 1, pp. 388–391). St. Louis: C. V. Mosby.

Rubin, R. (1968a). Body image and self-esteem. *Nursing Outlook, 16*, 20–23.

Rubin, R. (1968b). A theory of clinical nursing. *Nursing Research, 17*, 210–212.

Rubin, R. (1970). Cognitive style in pregnancy. *American Journal of Nursing, 70*, 502–508.

Rubin, R. (1972). Fantasy and object constancy in maternal relationships. *Maternal–Child Nursing Journal, 1*, 101–111.

Rubin, R. (1975). Maternal tasks in pregnancy. *Maternal–Child Nursing Journal, 4,* 143–153.

Rubin, R. (1977). Binding-in in the postpartum period. *Maternal–Child Nursing Journal, 6,* 67–75.

Rubin, R. (1983). Two psychological aspects of the postpartum period. In L. J. Sonstegard, K. M. Kowalski, & B. Jennings (Eds.), *Women's health: Childbearing* (Vol. 2, pp. 245–254). New York: Grune & Stratton.

Rubin, R. (1984). *Maternal identity and the maternal experience.* New York: Springer Publishing Co.

Rubin, R. (1992). Reflections on the gift of birth. *Clinical Nursing Research, 1,* 315–316.

Rubin, R., & Erickson, F. (1977). Research in clinical nursing. *Maternal–Child Nursing Journal, 6*(3), 151–164.

Rubin, R., & Erickson, F. (1978). Research in clinical nursing. *Journal of Advanced Nursing, 3,* 131–144.

Ruble, D. N. (1987). The acquisition of self-knowledge: A self-socialization perspective. In N. Eisenberg (Ed.), *Contemporary topics in developmental psychology* (pp. 243–270). New York: Wiley.

Ruble, D. N., Brooks-Gunn, J., Fleming, A. S., Fitzmaurice, G., Stangor, C., & Deutsch, F. (1990). Transition to motherhood and the self: Measurement, stability, and change. *Journal of Personality and Social Psychology, 58,* 450–463.

Ruble, D. N., Fleming, A. S., Hackel, L. S., & Stangor, C. (1988). Changes in the marital relationship during the transition to first time motherhood: Effects of violated expectations concerning division of household labor. *Journal of Personality and Social Psychology, 55,* 78–87.

Ruff, C. C. (1987). How well do adolescents mother? *MCN, the American Journal of Maternal Child Nursing, 12,* 249–253.

Russell, C. S. (1974). Transition to parenthood: Problems and gratifications. *Journal of Marriage and the Family, 36,* 294–301.

Rutledge, D. L., & Pridham, K. F. (1987). Postpartum mothers' perceptions of competence for infant care. *Journal of Obstetric, Gynecologic, and Neonatal Nursing, 16,* 185–194.

Salisbury, M. H. (1993). *Seeking safe passage: Health behaviors of pregnant adolescents.* Unpublished doctoral dissertation, University of Texas, Austin.

Salmon, P., & Drew, N. C. (1992). Multidimensional assessment of women's experience of childbirth: Relationship to obstetric procedure, antenatal preparation and obstetric history. *Journal of Psychosomatic Research, 36,* 317–327.

Sameroff, A. J., Seifer, R., & Elias, P. K. (1982). Sociocultural variability in infant temperament ratings. *Child Development, 53,* 164–173.

Samko, M. R., & Schoenfeld, L. S. (1975). Hypnotic susceptibility and the Lamaze childbirth experience. *American Journal of Obstetrics and Gynecology, 121,* 631–636.

Sammons, L. N. (1990). Psychological aspects of second pregnancy. *Clinical Issues in Perinatal and Women's Health Nursing, 1*(3), 317–324.

Sandelowski, M., & Black, B. P. (1994). The epistemology of expectant parenthood. *Western Journal of Nursing Research, 16*(6), 601–622.

Sandelowski, M., & Bustamante, R. (1986). Cesarean birth outside the natural childbirth culture. *Research in Nursing and Health, 9,* 81–88.

Sandelowski, M., Harris, B. G., & Holditch-Davis, D. (1990). Pregnant moments: The process of conception in infertile couples. *Research in Nursing and Health, 13,* 273–282.

Sander, L. W. (1962). Issues in early mother–child interaction. *Journal of American Academy of Child Psychiatry, 1,* 141–166.

Sandler, I. N. (1980). Social support resources, stress, and maladjustment of poor children. *American Journal of Community Psychology, 8,* 41–52.

Sarason, B. R., Sarason, I. B., & Pierce, G. R. (Eds.). (1990). *Social support: An interactional view.* New York: John Wiley.

Sarbin, T. R., & Allen, V. L. (1968). Role theory. In Lindzey, G., & Aronson, E. (Eds.), *Handbook of social psychology* (2nd ed., Vol. 1, pp. 488–567). Menlo Park, CA: Addison-Wesley.

Sargent, C., & Stark, N. (1987). Surgical birth: Interpretations of cesarean delivery among private hospital patients and nursing staff. *Social Science and Medicine, 25,* 1269–1276.

Schachere, K. (1990). Attachment between working mothers and their infants: The influence of family processes. *American Journal of Orthopsychiatry, 60,* 19–34.

Schaefer, E. S., Hunter, W. M., & Edgerton, M. (1987). Maternal prenatal, infancy and concurrent predictors of maternal reports of child psychopathology. *Psychiatry, 50,* 320–330.

Schaefer, E., & Manheimer, H. (1960). *Dimensions of perinatal adjustment.* Paper presented at the Eastern Psychological Association annual meeting, New York.

Schafer, P. J. (1987). Philosophic analysis of a theory of nursing. *Maternal–Child Nursing Journal, 16,* 289–368.

Schafer, P. J. (1990). Philosophic analysis of a theory of nursing. *Maternal–Child Nursing Journal, 19,* 175–176.

Schilder, P. (1950). *The image and appearance of the human body.* New York: International Universities Press.

Schilmoeller, G. L., & Baranowski, M. D. (1985). Childrearing of firstborns by adolescent and older mothers. *Adolescence, 20,* 805–822.

Schilmoeller, G. L., Baranowski, M. D., & Higgins, B. S. (1991). Long-term support and personal adjustment of adolescent and older mothers. *Adolescence, 26,* 787–797.

Schodt, C. M. (1989). Parental–fetal attachment and couvade: A study of patterns of human–environment integrality. *Nursing Science Quarterly, 2,* 88–97.

Schroeder, E. (1974). The birth of a defective child: A cause for grieving. In J. E. Hall & B. R. Weaver (Eds.), *Nursing of families in crisis* (pp. 158–170). Philadelphia: J. B. Lippincott.

Schroeder, M. A. (1977). Is the immediate postpartum period crucial to the mother–child relationship? *Journal of Obstetric, Gynecologic, and Neonatal Nursing, 6*(3), 37–40.

Schroeder, M. A. (1985). Development and testing of a scale to measure locus of control prior to and following childbirth. *Maternal–Child Nursing Journal, 14,* 11–121.

Schroeder-Zwelling, E., & Hock, E. (1986). Maternal anxiety and sensitive mothering behavior in diabetic and nondiabetic women. *Research in Nursing and Health, 9,* 249–255.

Sears, R. R., Maccoby, E. E., & Levin, H. (1957). *Patterns of Child Rearing.* New York: Harper & Row.

Seideman, R. Y., & Kleine, P., F., (1995). A theory of transformed parenting: Parenting a child with developmental delay/mental retardation. *Nursing Research, 44,* 38–42.

Shearer, E. L. (1989). Commentary: Does cesarean delivery affect the parents? *Birth, 16,* 57–58.

Sheehan, F. (1981). Assessing postpartum adjustment: A pilot study. *Journal of Obstetric, Gynecologic, and Neonatal Nursing, 10,* 19–23.

Shereshefsky, P. M., Liebenberg, B., & Lockman, R. F. (1973). *Maternal adaptation.* In P.M. Shereshefsky & L. J. Yarrow (Eds.), *Psychological aspects of a first pregnancy and early postnatal adaptation* (pp. 165–180). New York: Raven Press.

Sherwen, L. N. (1981). Fantasies during the third trimester of pregnancy. *MCN, the American Journal of Maternal Child Nursing, 6,* 398–401.

Sherwen, L. N. (1987). *Psychosocial dimensions of the pregnant family.* New York: Springer Publishing Co.

Sholomskas, D., & Axelrod, R. (1986). The influence of mother–daughter relationships on women's sense of self and current role choices. *Psychology of Women Quarterly, 10,* 171–182.

Shuster, C. (1993). Employed first-time mothers: A typology of maternal responses to integrating parenting and employment. *Family Relations, 42,* 13–20.

Siegel, A. E., & Haas, M. B. (1963). The working mother: A review of research. *Child Development, 34,* 513–542.

Siegel, E., Bauman, K. E., Schaefer, E. S., Saunders, M. M., & Ingram, D. D. (1980). Hospital and home support during infancy: Impact on maternal attachment, child abuse and neglect, and health care utilization. *Pediatrics, 66,* 183–190.

Silvestre, D., & Fresco, N. (1980). Reactions to prenatal diagnosis: An analysis of 87 interviews. *American Journal of Orthopsychiatry, 50,* 610–617.

Slade, P. D. (1977). Awareness of body dimensions during pregnancy: An analogue study. *Psychological Medicine, 7,* 245–252.

Slavazza, K. L., Mercer, R. T., Marut, J. S., & Shnider, S. M. (1985). Anesthesia, analgesia for vaginal childbirth: Differences in maternal perceptions. *Journal of Obstetric, Gynecologic, and Neonatal Nursing, 14,* 321–329.

Slesinger, D. P. (1981). *Mothercraft and infant health.* Lexington, MA: Lexington Books.

Smith, C. (1994a). Effects of social support and employment on first-time older mothers. *Communicating Nursing Research, 27*(2), 243.

Smith, C. M. (1994b). *Effects of employment and social support on first-time mothers age 30 and older the first year of motherhood.* Unpublished doctoral dissertation, University of California, San Francisco.

Smith, J. A. (1990). Transforming identities: A repertory grid case study of the transition to motherhood. *British Journal of Medical Psychology, 63,* 239–253.

Smith, L., & Hagen, V. (1984). Relationship between the home environment and sensorimotor development of Down syndrome and nonretarded infants. *American Journal of Mental Deficiency, 89,* 124–132.

Smith, P. B., & Pederson, D. R. (1988). Maternal sensitivity and patterns of infant–mother attachment. *Child Development, 59,* 1097–1101.

Smith-Battle, L. (1993). Mothering in the midst of danger. In S. L. Feetham, S. B. Meister, J. M. Bell, & C. L. Gilliss (Eds.), *The nursing of families* (pp. 235–246). Newbury Park, CA: Sage Publications.

Snowden, L. R., Schott, T. L., Awalt, S. J., & Gillis-Knox, J. (1988). Marital satisfaction in pregnancy: Stability and change. *Journal of Marriage and the Family, 50,* 325–333.

Snyder, C., Eyres, S. J., & Barnard, K. (1979). New findings about mothers' antenatal expectations and their relationship to infant development. *MCN, the American Journal of Maternal Child Nursing, 4,* 354–357.

Sommer, K., Whitman, T. L., Borkowski, J. G., Schellenbach, C., Maxwell, S., & Keogh, D. (1993). Cognitive readiness and adolescent parenting. *Developmental Psychology, 29,* 389–398.

Sostek, A. M., Scanlon, J. W., & Abramson, D. C. (1982). Postpartum contact and maternal confidence and anxiety: A confirmation of short-term effects. *Infant Behavior and Development, 5*, 323–329.

Spielberger, C., Gorsuch, R., & Lushene, R., Vagg, P. R., & Jacobs, G. A. (1983). *The state-trait anxiety inventory.* Palo Alto, CA: Consulting Psychologists Press.

Sprunger, L. W., Boyce, W. T., & Gaines, J. A. (1985). Family–infant congruence: Routines and rhythmicity in family adaptations to a young infant. *Child Development, 56*, 564–572.

Stainton, M. C. (1985). The fetus: A growing member of the family. *Family Relations, 34*, 321–326.

Stainton, M. C. (1986a). Origins of attachment: Culture and cue sensitivity. *Dissertation Abstracts International, 46*(11), 3786-B.

Stainton, M. C. (1986b). Parent–infant bonding: A process, not an event. *Dimensions in Health Service, 63*(3), 19–20.

Stainton, M. C. (1990). Parents' awareness of their unborn infant in the third trimester. *Birth, 17*, 92–96.

Stainton, M. C. (1992). Mismatched caring in high-risk perinatal situations. *Clinical Nursing Research, 1*, 35–49.

Stainton, M. C., NcNeil, D., & Harvey, S. (1992). Maternal tasks of uncertain motherhood. *Maternal–Child Nursing Journal, 20*(3,4), 113–123.

Steffensmeier, R. H. (1982). A role model of the transition to parenthood. *Journal of Marriage and the Family, 44*, 319–334.

Stein, G. (1980). The pattern of mental change and body weight change in the first postpartum week. *Journal of Psychosomatic Research, 24*, 165–171.

Stein, R. E. K., & Jessop, D. J. (1989). What diagnosis does not tell: The case for a noncategorical approach to chronic illness in childhood. *Social Sciences Medicine, 29*, 769–778.

Steinberg, M. C. (1984). The relationship between anticipated life change and nausea and vomiting of the first trimester of pregnancy of primiparas. *Journal of Perinatology, 4*(3), 24–28.

Stemp, P. S., Turner, R. J., & Noh, S. (1986). Psychological distress in the postpartum period: The significance of social support. *Journal of Marriage and the Family, 48*, 271–277.

Stern, D. (1985). *The interpersonal world of the child.* New York: Basic Books.

Stern, P. N., Tilden, V. P., & Maxwell, E. K. (1980). Culturally-induced stress during childbearing: The Filipino-American experience. *Issues in Health Care of Women, 2*, 67–81.

Stevens, J. H., Jr. (1984). Black grandmothers' and black adolescent mothers' knowledge about parenting. *Developmental Psychology, 20*, 1017–1025.

Stevens, J. H., Jr. (1988). Social support, locus of control, and parenting in three low-income groups of mothers: Black teenagers, black adults, and white adults. *Child Development, 59,* 635–642.

Stifter, C. A., Coulehan, C. M., & Fish, M. (1993). Linking employment to attachment: The mediating effects of maternal separation anxiety and interactive behavior. *Child Development, 64,* 1451–1460.

Stolte, K. (1986). Postpartum "missing pieces": Sequela of a passing obstetrical era? *Birth, 13,* 100–103.

Stolz, L. M. (1960). Effects of maternal employment on children: Evidence from research. *Child Development, 31,* 749–782.

Stotland, E., Mathews, K. E., Jr., Sherman, S. E., Hansson, R. O., & Richardson, B. Z. (1978). *Empathy, fantasy, and helping.* Beverly Hills: CA: Sage Publications.

Strang, V. R., & Sullivan, P. L. (1985). Body image attitudes during pregnancy and the postpartum period. *Journal of Obstetric, Gynecologic, and Neonatal Nursing, 14,* 332–337.

Stryker, S. (1968). Identity salience and role performance. *Journal of Marriage and the Family, 4,* 558–564.

Stuckey, M. F., McGhee, P. E., & Bell, N. J. (1982). Parent–child interaction: The influence of maternal employment. *Developmental Psychology, 18,* 635–644.

Sullivan, D. A., & Beeman, R. (1981). Satisfaction with postpartum care: Opportunities for bonding, reconstructing the birth and instruction. *Birth, 8,* 153–159.

Sumner, G., & Fritsch, J. (1977). Postnatal parental concerns: The first six weeks of life. *Journal of Obstetric, Gynecologic, and Neonatal Nursing, 6*(3), 27–32.

Svejda, M. J., Campos, J. J., & Emde, R. N. (1980). Mother–infant "bonding": Failure to generalize. *Child Development, 51,* 775–779.

Swann, W. B., Jr. (1990). Role change. *Annual Review of Sociology, 16,* 87–110.

Sweeney, J., & Bradbard, M. R. (1988). Mothers' and fathers' changing perceptions of their male and female infants over the course of pregnancy. *Journal of Genetic Psychology, 149,* 393–404.

Szajnberg, N., Ward, M. J., Krauss, A., & Kessler, D. B. (1987). Low birthweight prematures: Preventive intervention and maternal attitude. *Child Psychiatry and Human Development, 17,* 152–165.

Taylor, S. E. (1983). Adaptation to threatening events: A theory of cognitive adaptation. *American Psychologist, 38,* 1161–1173.

Tcheng, D. M. (1984). Emotional response of primary and repeat cesarean mothers to the cesarean method of childbirth. *Health Care for Women International, 5,* 323–333.

ten Bensel, R. W., & Paxson, C. L. (1977). Child abuse following early postpartum separation. *Journal of Pediatrics, 90,* 490–491.

Termine, N. T., & Izard, C. E. (1988). Infants' responses to their mothers' expressions of joy and sadness. *Developmental Psychology, 24,* 223–229.

Thoits, P. A. (1983). Multiple identities and psychological well-being: A reformulation and test of the social isolation hypothesis. *American Sociological Review, 48,* 174–187.

Thoman, E. B. (1975). Development of synchrony in mother–infant interaction in feeding and other situations. *Federation Proceedings, 34,* 1587–1592.

Thoman, E. B., Acebo, C., & Becker, P. T. (1983). Infant crying and stability in the mother–infant relationship: A systems analysis. *Child Development, 54,* 653–659.

Thoman, E. B., Turner, A. M., Leiderman, P. H., & Barnett, C. R. (1970). Neonate–mother interaction: Effects of parity on feeding behavior. *Child Development, 41,* 1103–1111.

Thomas, R. B. (1987). Methodological issues and problems in family health care research. *Journal of Marriage and the Family, 49,* 65–70.

Thompson, M. S. (1986). The influence of supportive relations on the psychological well-being of teenage mothers. *Social Forces, 64,* 1006–1024.

Thompson, M. S., & Ensminger, M. E. (1989). Psychological well-being among mothers with school age children: Evolving family structures. *Social Forces, 67,* 715–730.

Thompson, R. J., Jr., Oehler, J. M., Catlett, A. T., & Johndrow, D. Q. (1993). Maternal psychological adjustment to the birth of an infant weighing 1500 grams or less. *Infant Behavior and Development, 16,* 471–485.

Thorne, S. E. (1990). Mothers with chronic illness: A predicament of social construction. *Health Care for Women International, 11,* 209–221.

Thornton, A. (1989). Changing attitudes toward family issues in the United States. *Journal of Marriage and the Family, 51,* 873–893.

Thornton, R., & Nardi, P. M. (1975). The dynamics of role acquisition. *American Journal of Sociology, 80,* 870–885.

Tilden, V. P. (1983a). Perceptions of single vs. partnered adult gravidas in the midtrimester. *Journal of Obstetric, Gynecologic, and Neonatal Nursing, 12,* 40–48.

Tilden, V. P. (1983b). The relation of life stress and social support to emotional disequilibrium during pregnancy. *Research in Nursing and Health, 6,* 167–174.

Tilden, V. P. (1984). The relation of selected psychosocial variables to single status of adult women during pregnancy. *Nursing Research, 33,* 102–107.

Tilden, V. P., & Lipson, J. G. (1981). Cesarean childbirth: Variables affecting psychological impact. *Western Journal of Nursing Research, 3,* 127–149.

Tocco, T. S., & Bridges, C. N. (1973). The relationship between the self-concepts of mothers and their children. *Child Study Journal, 3,* 161–179.

Tomlinson, P. S. (1990). Verbal behavior associated with indicators of maternal attachment with the neonate. *Journal of Obstetric, Gynecologic, and Neonatal Nursing, 19,* 76–77.

Trause, M. A., & Kramer, L. I. (1983). The effects of premature birth on parents and their relationship. *Developmental Medicine and Child Neurology, 25,* 459–465.

Trevathan, W. R. (1981). Maternal touch at 1st contact with the newborn infant. *Developmental Psychology, 14,* 549–558.

Trevathan, W. R. (1982). Maternal lateral preference at first contact with her newborn infant. *Birth, 9,* 85–89.

Trevathan, W. R. (1983). Maternal "en face" orientation during the first hour after birth. *American Journal of Orthopsychiatry, 53,* 92–99.

Trowell, J. (1982). Possible effects of emergency caesarian section on the mother–child relationship. *Early Human Development, 7,* 41–51.

Trowell, J. (1983). Emergency caesarian section: A research study of the mother/child relationship of a group of women admitted expecting a normal vaginal delivery. *Child Abuse and Neglect, 7,* 387–394.

True-Soderstrom, B. A., Buckwalter, K. C., & Kerfott, K. M. (1983). Postpartum depression. *Maternal–Child Nursing Journal, 12,* 109–118.

Tryphonopoulou, Y., & Doxiadis, S. (1972). The effect of elective caesarian section on the initial stage of mother–infant relationship. In N. Morris (Ed.), *Psychosomatic medicine in obstetrics and gynaecology* (pp. 314–317). Basel: S. Karger.

Tulman, L. J. (1985). Mothers' and unrelated persons' initial handling of newborn infants. *Nursing Research, 34,* 205–210.

Tulman, L. J. (1986). Initial handling of newborn infants by vaginally and cesarean-delivered mothers. *Nursing Research, 35,* 296–300.

Tulman, L., & Fawcett, J. (1988). Return of functional ability after childbirth. *Nursing Research, 37,* 77–81.

Tulman, L., & Fawcett, J. (1991). Recovery from childbirth: Looking back 6 months after delivery. *Health Care for Women International, 12,* 341–350.

Tulman, L., Fawcett, J., Groblewski, L., & Silverman, L. (1990). Changes in functional status after childbirth. *Nursing Research, 39,* 70–75.

Tulman, L., Higgins, K., Fawcett, J., Nunno, C., Vansickel, C., Haas, M. G., & Speca, M. M. (1991). The inventory of functional status: Antepartum period. *Journal of Nurse-Midwifery, 36,* 117–123.

Turner, R. H. (1970). *Family interactions.* New York: John Wiley.

Uddenberg, N. (1974). Reproductive adaptation in mother and daughter. *Acta Psychiatrica Scandinavica* (Suppl. 254, 5–115).

Uddenberg, N., & Fagerstrom, C. (1976). The deliveries of daughters of reproductively maladjusted mothers. *Journal of Psychosomatic Research, 20,* 223–229.

Uddenberg, N., & Nilsson, L. (1975). The longitudinal course of para-natal emotional disturbance. *Acta Psychiatrica Scandinavica, 52,* 160–169.

Ulrich, S. C. (1982). Psychosocial work of a secundigravida in relation to acceptance of her baby. *Maternal–Child Nursing Journal, 11,* 1–9.

Unger, D. G., & Wandersman, L. P. (1985). Social support and adolescent mothers: Action research contributions to theory and application. *Journal of Social Issues, 41,* 29–45.

Unger, D. G., & Wandersman, L. P. (1988). The relation of family and partner support to the adjustment of adolescent mothers. *Child Development, 59,* 1056–1060.

Van Cleve, L. (1989). Parental coping in response to their child's spina bifida. *Journal of Pediatric Nursing, 4,* 172–176.

Van Cleve, L. (1993). Alpha-fetoprotein testing: Opinions of parents of children with spina bifida. *Maternal–Child Nursing Journal, 21,* 20–26.

van Ijzendoorn, M. H., Goldberg, S., Kroonenberg, P. M., & Frenkel, O. J. (1992). The relative effects of maternal and child problems on the quality of attachment in clinical samples. *Child Development, 63,* 840–858.

Van Riper, M., Pridham, K., & Ryff, C. (1992). Symbolic interactionism: A perspective for understanding parent–nurse interactions following the birth of a child with Down syndrome. *Maternal–Child Nursing Journal, 20,* 21–39.

Van Riper, M., & Selder, F. E. (1989). Parental responses to the birth of a child with Down syndrome. *Loss, Grief, and Care, 3*(3/4), 59–76.

Vaughn, B. E., Bradley, C. F., Joffe, L. S., Seifer, R., & Barglow, P. (1987). Maternal characteristics measured prenatally are predictive of ratings of temperamental "difficulty" on the Carey Infant Temperament Questionnaire. *Developmental Psychology, 23,* 152–161.

Vaughn, B. E., Taraldson, B. J., Crichton, L., & Egeland, B. (1981). The assessment of infant temperament: A critique of the Carey Infant Temperament Questionnaire. *Infant Behavior and Development, 4,* 1–17.

Vega, B. R., Bayon, C., Franco, B., Canas, F., Graell, M., & Salvador, M. (1993). Parental rearing and intimate relations in women's depression. *Acta Psychiatrica Scandinavica, 88,* 193–197.

Ventura, J. N. (1982). Parent coping behaviors, parent functioning, and infant temperament characteristics. *Nursing Research, 31,* 269–273.

Ventura, J. N. (1986). Parent coping, A replication. *Nursing Research, 35,* 77–80.

Ventura, J. N. (1987). The stresses of parenthood reexamined. *Family Relations, 36,* 26–29.

Ventura, S. J., Martin, J. A., Taffel, S. M., Mathews, T. J., & Clarke, S. C. (1994). Advance report of final natality statistics, 1992. *Monthly Vital Statistics Report, 43* (5, Suppl.).

Virden, S. F. (1988). The relationship between infant feeding method and maternal role adjustment. *Journal of Nurse-Midwifery, 33,* 31–35.

Volling, B. L., & Belsky, J. (1993). Maternal employment: Parent, infant, and contextual characteristics related to maternal employment decisions in the first year of infancy. *Family Relations, 42,* 4–12.

Waldron, H., & Routh, D. K. (1981). The effect of the first child on the marital relationship. *Journal of Marriage and the Family, 43,* 785–788.

Waldron, J. A., & Asayama, V. H. (1985). Stress, adaptation and coping in a maternal–fetal intensive care unit. *Social Work in Health Care, 10*(3), 75–89.

Walker, A. J., Thompson, L., & Morgan, C. S. (1987). Two generations of mothers and daughters: Role position and interdependence. *Psychology of Women Quarterly, 11,* 195–208.

Walker, L. O. (1977). Investigating the semantic properties of two concepts. Unpublished manuscript, the University of Texas at Austin.

Walker, L. O. (1982). *Toward models of mother–infant dyadic development.* Final report, Division of Nursing PHS, U.S. Dept. HHS.

Walker, L. O. (1989a). A longitudinal analysis of stress process among mothers of infants. *Nursing Research, 38,* 339–343.

Walker, L. O. (1989b). Stress process among mothers of infants: Preliminary model testing. *Nursing Research, 38,* 10–16.

Walker, L. O. (1991, October). *Maternal empathy.* Paper presented at the Council of Nurse Researchers, 1991 International Nursing Research Conference, Los Angeles.

Walker, L. O. (1992). *Parent–infant nursing science: Paradigms, phenomena, methods.* Philadelphia: F. A. Davis.

Walker, L. O., & Best, M. A. (1991). Well-being of mothers with infant children: A preliminary comparison of employed women and homemakers. *Women and Health, 17,* 71–89.

Walker, L. O., Crain, H., & Thompson, E. (1986a). Maternal role attainment and identity in the postpartum period: Stability and change. *Nursing Research, 35,* 68–71.

Walker, L. O., Crain, H., & Thompson, E. (1986b). Mothering behavior and maternal role attainment during the postpartum period. *Nursing Research, 35,* 352–355.

Walker, L. O., & Montgomery, E. (1994). Maternal identity and role attainment: Long-term relations to children's development. *Nursing Research, 43,* 105–110.

Walker, M. K. (1992). Maternal reactions to fetal sex. *Health Care for Women International, 13,* 293–302.

Walker, M. K., & Conner, G. K. (1993). Fetal sex preference of second-trimester gravidas. *Journal of Nurse-Midwifery, 38,* 110–113.

Walz, B. L., & Rich, O. J. (1983). Maternal tasks of taking on a second child in the postpartum period. *Maternal–Child Nursing Journal, 12*(3), 185–216.

Wandersman, L., Wandersman, A., & Kahn, S. (1980). Social support in the transition to parenthood. *Journal of Community Psychology, 8,* 332–342.

Wapner, S., & Werner, H. (1965) *The body percept.* New York: Random House.

Wayland, J., & Tate, S. (1993). Maternal–fetal attachment and perceived relationships with important others in adolescents. *Birth, 20,* 198–203.

Wedell-Monnig, J., & Lumley, J. M. (1980). Child deafness and mother-child interaction. *Child Development, 51,* 766–774.

Weingarten, C. T., Baker, K., Manning, W., & Kutzner, S. K. (1990). Married mothers' perceptions of their premature or term infants and the quality of their relationships with their husbands. *Journal of Obstetric, Gynecologic, and Neonatal Nursing, 19,* 64–73.

Weinraub, M., & Wolf, B. M. (1983). Effects of stress and social supports on mother–child interactions in single- and two-parent families. *Child Development, 54,* 1297–1311.

Wenner, N. K., Cohen, M. B., Weigert, E. V., Kvarnes, R. G., Ohaneson, E. M., & Fearing, J. M. (1969). Emotional problems in pregnancy. *Psychiatry, 32,* 389–410.

Westbrook, M. T. (1978). The reactions to child-bearing and early maternal experience of women with differing marital relationships. *British Journal of Medical Psychology, 51,* 191–199.

Whiffen, V. E., & Gotlib, I. H. (1993). Comparison of postpartum and nonpostpartum depression: Clinical presentation, psychiatric history, and psychosocial functioning. *Journal of Consulting and Clinical Psychology, 61,* 485–494.

White, M., & Ritchie, J. (1984). Psychological stressors in antepartum hospitalization: Reports from pregnant women. *Maternal–Child Nursing, 13,* 47–56.

Wiggins, K. M. (1983). *The origins of attachment: An exploratory study of prenatal maternal attachment.* Unpublished doctoral dissertation, Syracuse University.

Wikler, L., Wasow, M., & Hatfield, E. (1981). Chronic sorrow revisited: Parent vs. professional depiction of parents of mentally retarded children. *American Journal of Orthopsychiatry, 51,* 63–70.

Wikman, M., Jacobsson, L. Joelsson, I., & von Schoultz, B. (1993). Ambivalence towards parenthood among pregnant women and their men. *Acta Obstetrica Scandinavica, 72,* 619–626.

Wilkie, C. F., & Ames, E. W. (1986). The relationship of infant crying to parental stress in the transition to parenthood. *Journal of Marriage and the Family, 48,* 545–550.

Wilkie, G., & Shapiro, C. M. (1992). Sleep deprivation and the postnatal blues. *Journal of Psychosomatic Research, 36,* 309–316.

Wille, D. E. (1992). Maternal employment: Impact on maternal behavior. *Family Relations, 41,* 273–277.

Williams, C. A. (1990). Biopsychosocial elements of empathy: A multidimensional model. *Issues in Mental Health Nursing, 11,* 155–174.

Williams, M. L. (1986). Long-term hospitalization of women with high-risk pregnancies. *Journal of Obstetric, Gynecologic, and Neonatal Nursing, 15,* 17–21.

Williams, T. B., Joy, L. S., Travis, L., Gotowiec, A., Blum-Steele, M., Aiken, L. S., Painter, S. L., & Davidson, S. M. (1987). Transition to motherhood: A longitudinal study. *Infant Mental Health Journal, 8,* 251–265.

Wilson, M. N. (1984). Mothers' and grandmothers' perceptions of parental behavior in three-generational black families. *Child Development, 55,* 1333–1339.

Winget, C., & Kapp, F. T. (1972). The relationship of the manifest content of dreams to duration of childbirth in primiparae. *Psychosomatic Medicine, 34,* 313–320.

Winkles, C. M. T. (1987). Maternal ambivalence toward impending motherhood. *Journal of Obstetric, Gynecologic, and Neonatal Nursing, 16,* 362.

Winnicott, D. W. (1958). Primary maternal preoccupation. In D. W. Winnicott (Ed.), *Collected papers: Through paediatrics to psychoanalysis* (pp. 300–305. London: Tavistock.

Winslow, W. (1987). First pregnancy after 35: What is the experience? *MCN, the American Journal of Maternal Child Nursing, 12,* 92–96.

Wise, S., & Grossman, F. K. (1980). Adolescent mothers and their infants: Psychological factors in early attachment and interaction. *American Journal of Orthopsychiatry, 50,* 454–468.

Wismont, J. M., & Reame, N. E. (1989). The lesbian childbearing experience: Assessing developmental tasks. *Image: Journal of Nursing Scholarship, 21*(3), 137–141.

Wolfenstein, M. (1953). Trends in infant care. *American Journal of Orthopsychiatry, 33,* 120–130.

Wolff, C. B., Portis, M., & Wolff, H. (1993). Birth weight and smoking practices during pregnancy among Mexican-American women. *Health Care for Women International, 14,* 271–279.

Wolman, W., Chalmers, B., Hofmeyr, G. J., & Nikodem, V. C. (1993). Postpartum depression and companionship in the clinical birth environment: A randomized, controlled study. *American Journal of Obstetrics and Gynecology, 168,* 1388–1393.

Wrasper, C. L. (1987). *Rubin's concept of puerperal change reexamined in normal healthy mothers during their postpartal period.* Unpublished master's thesis, University of Wyoming, Laramie.

Wylie, R. C. (1974). *The self-concept* (Rev. ed., Vol. 1.). Lincoln: University of Nebraska Press.

Young, R. K. (1986). Primiparas' attitudes toward mothering. *Issues in Comprehensive Pediatric Nursing, 9,* 259–272.

Youngblut, J. M., Loveland-Cherry, C. J., & Horan, M. (1990). Factors related to maternal employment status following the premature birth of an infant. *Nursing Research, 39,* 237–240.

Youngblut, J. M., Loveland-Cherry, C. J., & Horan, M. (1991). Maternal employment effects on family and preterm infants at three months. *Nursing Research, 40,* 272–275.

Zabielski, M. T. (1994). Recognition of maternal identity in preterm and fullterm mothers. *Maternal–Child Nursing Journal, 22,* 2–36.

Zachariah, R. C. (1994a). Maternal–fetal attachment: Influence of mother–daughter and husband–wife relationships. *Research in Nursing and Health, 17,* 37–44.

Zachariah, R. C. (1994b). Mother–daughter and husband–wife attachment as predictors of psychological well-being during pregnancy. *Clinical Nursing Research, 3,* 371–391.

Zahr, L. (1987). Lebanese mother and infant temperaments as determinants of mother–infant interaction. *Journal of Pediatric Nursing, 2,* 418–427.

Zahr, L. K. (1991). The relationship between maternal confidence and mother–infant behaviors in premature infants. *Research in Nursing and Health, 14,* 279–286.

Zahr, L. K. (1993). The confidence of Latina mothers in the care of their low birth weight infants. *Research in Nursing and Health, 16,* 335–342.

Zahr, L., & Cole, J. (1991). Assessing maternal competence and sensitivity to premature infants' cues. *Issues in Comprehensive Pediatric Nursing, 14,* 231–240.

Zambrana, R. E., Hurst, M., & Hite, R. L. (1979). The working mother in contemporary perspective: A review of the literature. *Pediatrics, 64,* 862–870.

Zeanah, C. H., & Anders, T. F. (1987). Subjectivity in parent–infant relationships: A discussion of internal working models. *Infant Mental Health Journal, 3,* 237–250.

Zeanah, C. H., Keener, M. A., & Anders, T. F. (1986). Adolescent mothers' prenatal fantasies and working models of their infants. *Psychiatry, 49,* 193–203.

Zeanah, C. H., Keener, M. A., Anders, T. F., & Vieira-Baker, C. C. (1987). Adolescent mothers' perceptions of their infants before and after birth. *American Journal of Orthopsychiatry, 57,* 351–360.

Zeanah, C. H., Keener, M. A., Stewart, L., & Anders, T. F. (1985). Prenatal perception of infant personality: A preliminary investigation. *Journal of American Academy of Child Psychiatry, 24,* 503–505.

Zeidenstein, L. (1990). Gynecological and childbearing needs of lesbians. *Journal of Nurse-Midwifery, 35,* 10–18.

Zilboorg, G. (1929). The dynamics of schizophrenic reactions related to parenthood. *American Journal of Psychiatry, 8,* 733–767.

Zuckerman, M., Lubin, B., Vogel, L., & Valerius, E. (1964). Measurement of experimentally induced affects. *Journal of Consulting Psychology, 28,* 418–425.

Zung, W. W. K. (1965). A self-rating depression scale. *Archives of General Psychiatry, 12,* 63.

Index

Social
skills and mothering, 188
sphere, expansion of, 178
Social support
attachment to fetus, 85–87, 266
attachment to infant, 249
during pregnancy, 74–76
emotional, 200, 201, 203
marital, 279–280
network, 199, 263, 273
perceived, 201, 263
social, 74–76, 199, 248, 249, 252, 262, 266
tangible, material, 203
Socioeconomic status (SES)
and feelings about type of birth, 103
and salience of classes, 107
and salience of maternal role, 205
and teenage mothers, 256, 264, 268
Stages
of grief process, 240–241
of maternal role identity, 17
Stillborn and self-concept, 33
Stress
during antepartal hospitalization, 66
employed mothers, 292, 294
life-events, 182–183
and maternal role identity, 184
during pregnancy, 44, 67
preterm birth, 226
related to norepinephrine, catecholamine levels, 75
single mothers, 277, 280
Synchrony, contingent behavior, 172, 180, 202
maternal behavior and infant state, cues, 159–163
mother–handicapped infant, 246–247
mother–infant and competence, 159, 172, 190, 207, 304
mother–infant, preterm birth, 227–231

Taking-in, taking-hold behaviors, 109–112
differences by parity, 111
cognitively, of child, 142–146

Tasks of pregnancy
Bibring's, 63
related to mothering, 65
Rubin's, 64
Teenage mother; *see also* Adolescent mother
characteristics and attitudes, 256–258
cognitive functioning, 258
cognitive preparation for parenting, 257
ego development, 258, 267
life space, 256
maternal competence development, 264
maternal role identity attainment, 258–268
maternal touch, 135, 259–261
partner relationship and maternal role, 200
perception of infant behavior, temperament, 193
self-concept, self-esteem, 118, 257, 258, 262
Temperament
defined, 155
infant's during pregnancy, 154
infant's related to maternal characteristics, 192–193
infant's related to maternal behavior, competence, 164, 195–196
infant's related to maternal attachment, 196
maternal related to maternal competence, 195
Temporal experience postpartum, 100–101
Theoretical constructs
defined, 3
Theoretical frameworks
ecological, 304
Mercer's, 12–16
parent–infant attachment, 151
Time
commitment to time in role and behavior, 273
difficulty recalling passage of postpartum, 100
orientation in, 109–110